About the author

Elana Muriels is an author, aromatherapist and creative arts facilitator running workshops for voice. She has provided a service as high priestess for both large ceremonies at events and within smaller circles and at other times has been a solitary practitioner. She approaches the subject of magic holistically looking at the interrelated parts in harmony with one another and with the focus always upon well-being and positive growth.

WHITE MAGIC: A HOLISTIC GUIDE TO SELF-INITIATION

Elana Muriels

WHITE MAGIC: A HOLISTIC GUIDE TO SELF-INITIATION

Vanguard Press

VANGUARD PAPERBACK

© Copyright 2017
Elana Muriels

The right of Elana Muriels to be identified as author of
this work has been asserted by her in accordance with the
Copyright, Designs and Patents Act 1988.

A CIP catalogue record for this title is
available from the British Library.

ISBN   978 1 784652 26 5

*Vanguard Press is an imprint of
Pegasus Elliot MacKenzie Publishers Ltd.*
www.pegasuspublishers.com

First Published in 2017

**Vanguard Press
Sheraton House Castle Park
Cambridge England**

Printed & Bound in Great Britain

Dedication

For Kev,
A dear friend and a shining star who brightened the lives of all those in
his orbit.
With love.

Acknowledgements

Thank you so much to my brilliant son who makes all my days sunnier, my kind and loyal Labrador who is always at my side, and to those close friends and family whose unwavering support, friendship and light make all the difference to my life. It is my greatest fortune and blessing to be sharing this journey with you.
All my love.

Preface

I have believed in magic all my life and knew with no uncertainty as a child, as most of us did, that there lay many magical things within and beyond this world that are just at our fingertips and within the sky we breathe. I spent hours fascinated by plants and spending time in the woods and over time my initial childhood loves grew and broadened. I was drawn to healing and then to massage and the healing properties of the plants I loved. I had a sense of intuition about which plants might do what by their look and smell and so I left a job at the bank and trained as an aromatherapist twenty years ago. My interest grew as I watched the energetic shifts of the people I treated in response to massage and the oils from the plants. It seemed logical to me that these properties extended beyond physicality and I began seeking the spiritual and researching the metaphysical. I have practised magic throughout my life, though I may not have named it as such initially, and what started with a quiet fascination with nature and plants led me to a spiritual path. I took my own initiation twelve years ago and have since increased my degree over time. I have been high priestess and have been honoured to provide ceremonies and service for both large gatherings and small circles. At other times I have chosen a solitary path.

Introduction

The choosing of the title white magic is simply to reflect a term that it is recognised, commonly used and easily understood with a clear emphasis on a practice of love and light. White is the brilliance of cumulative pure light. Yes there are many colours in the rainbow and we are all of them. Yes the sunshine and the full colour spectrum and darkness are all necessary parts of life, each perceivable and unperceivable shade and hue. Working with light we must still honour and recognise shadow for one cannot exist without the other.

This book is intended as a guide to the first steps or degree of spiritual self-initiation. It is holistic because it takes an overview and covers the basics of a number of interrelated subjects, each of which is worthy of a number of books in their own right. This offering may only hope to serve as their introduction and yet it is essential to look at them as a whole. To initiate something is to begin something and to take spiritual initiation is to mark the beginning of the path. The reading of this book in its entirety is initiatory in essence because all knowledge changes us and the known cannot be unknown. To any aligned with love and seeking, this book may open up a pathway and support the first footsteps upon the path. What this book does not do is to try to lay out all of the possible paths and religions in their entirety. Instead it offers a holistic overview drawing on commonly recurring truths and patterns across many faiths and belief systems and encourages the reader to develop their own path and identity. It is deliberately non-denominational and looks at the ways of aligning with good forces and higher vibrational energies across a broad selection of paths. Whilst examples are used throughout of many religions, cultures and spiritual practices, preference is given to the ones most commonly associated within a western esoteric context.

The subjects covered are intended to provide a framework from which the practitioner may build upon with direct experience and further learning leading to magical and spiritual initiation. When we are working magic, the art is in and of itself an affirmation of belief in those things that extend from and beyond the physical plane of matter in existence. Whilst magic has one foot in religion, myth and folklore, it has its other firmly planted in physics, biology, chemistry, astronomy, herbalism, anthropology, languages and perhaps cookery! The talented chef may well transfer the skills from saucepan to spell ingredient later on and show a natural aptitude for blending ingredients and instinctively knowing their qualities. By starting with a framework and developing an understanding of the interplay between relating subjects a grounded and reasoned foundation can be established and a reference point from which to differentiate information beyond that of the earthly sphere when it comes to it. The onus is always upon retaining the essential component of white magic, working with love.

Separation is the illusion for in truth we are all human beings, souls incarnated upon one Earth from one source, simply in different places on our respective journeys like waves in the ocean. By looking beyond the man made boundaries of separation at magic as a whole across different cultures and time we can see there are commonly held beliefs and magical practices, shared archetypes, recurring themes and universal truths that become apparent. Our focus then is not upon the ways in which we are different from one another but the ways in which we are the same. These pages seek out common beliefs, and recurring truths found throughout folklore, religion and myth whilst approaching them in a methodical way and seeking supportive practical, historical or scientific evidence. They could be seen as a collection of essays designed to guide and support the reader towards self-initiation or as a convenient reference book for the more experienced.

Written for all those who want to experience magic in their lives and do good with it regardless of background or path. What matters is not the path that went before but the path that lies ahead and the journey we envision and embark upon from here.

For all the healers who are already working white magic, the teachers, the students, for those who pray, for those who see the beauty of nature, for those who love. Open and welcoming of all religious and/or non-religious based spiritual paths of all persuasions, entirely non-denominational and inclusive of everyone. This book simultaneously acknowledges uniqueness and a multitude of individual practices whilst at the same time seeking out the threads of commonality and encouraging unity in diversity. By recognising and seeing the divinity in all these practices a wide world of mutually inclusive possibility is opened up in order that the reader might be encouraged to develop their own direction and path.

This book is written in three parts. The Foundation, the Theory and the

Practical Aspects of Magic.

Part One: The Foundation considers some underlying principles and establishes some basic ideas about what magic is and the nature of magic and of light and shadow. It examines and compares differences and similarities between cultural customs and looks at types of ceremony and prayer. It is designed to encourage self-inquiry through inward reflection in order to develop and define an individualised path and sense of direction. We can only ever meet another or the world around us as deeply as we have met ourselves and so this section encourages us to get to know ourselves and our inner workings. There are also suggestions for establishing a framework from which to work and some exercises to familiarise the reader with simple energy and breathing techniques, guided meditations and tools for future use.

Part Two looks at magical theory. It is less subjective and looks at the building blocks and components of life and at their workings. It is concerned with the greater defining principles of the world and universe around us and how and why they relate to one another specifically in a magical context. The governance of time, number, geometry, the cosmos and the constructs of the universe are the primary focus. The understanding of these subjects or at the least an introduction to them which is all one can hope to achieve within the pages of a book is essentially the tool kit of anyone who wishes to study magic. The deeper significance of even simple things is often revealed in line with the knowledge we attain to reach their deeper understanding.

Part Three: Practical Magic looks at the more involved action and doing aspects of magic. It also considers forms of physical, emotional and psychic self-protection, the different types of casting sacred space and ways of connecting with sacred spirit. There are development tools for writing and designing prayers, ceremonies, rituals and spells specific to the individual with examples given of some in various contexts and instructions as to how to construct complementary aspects into one whole using a number of cultural and spiritual pathways. Commonly used correspondences are given throughout the book where practical so that subject matters may be related to one another by the reader and logical patterns might be noted.

May our journey together through these pages be guided and illuminated by love.

White Magic, Initiation: A Holistic Guide to Self Initiation.

Part One – The Foundation

Part One: The Foundation considers the underlying principles of what white magic is, how it works and at the nature of light and shadow. It looks at ceremony and prayer and is written to encourage self-inquiry and inward reflection. There are suggestions for developing a personal framework from which to work and some exercises and meditations at the end of each chapter.

Chapter One
White Magic

As we step forwards, so the universe mirrors and answers us, advancing towards us.

White magic is a term most of us have heard and know and that we understand. It means working magic from a place of love to do good or in a higher service. It is the intention of this book to make white magic easily and readily accessible to the mainstream and to anyone with a will to do good and to act from a place of love. Everyone has magical ability, it is inherent. Magic itself is neither good nor bad and is defined by intention. The intention of white magic is aligned with love. The realms of white magic are bright and shining and plentiful and not to be relegated or confused with dusty corners of forgotten libraries or talked of as a thing of the past. Magic is everywhere, current, alive and well and positively beaming.

The word magic here is not just about the writing of spells or the concocting of potions although we will get to that in due course but is about belief. Magic is the belief in alchemy both within ourselves and reflected in our lives and within the universe that surrounds us. The belief that we may influence our experience of life and our immediate world around us by the use of our will and by the alignment of our will with good. It is the mixture of what some might refer to as belief, faith or religion depending on their viewpoint combined with the study of the natural sciences and the laws of nature. Faith and science are in truth two sides of the same coin and it is in the logical extension of the two where prayer and alchemy meet which we might refer to as magic.

The word magic comes from the Latin *magicus* "magic, magical" from the Greek word *magos* and from the Old Persian word *magush* "magician" a word for the "learned and priestly class" who were skilled astrologers and were able to influence or work with using unseen or natural forces. These were the Magi portrayed in the bible. Gradually the word magic has displaced the Old English word *wiccecræft,* wicca craft (the words witch or wicca mean wise) and *drycræft* from dry "magician", from the Irish word *drui* (druid) "priest, magician". The current workers of magic like the magi who went before are those who observe the stars, those who honour nature and are in communion with her and those who are studying natural sciences and a number of scholastic subjects. We could even say all subjects for magic runs through all of life.

The word alchemy derives from the Arabic *al-kymia* or more likely the name of Ancient Egypt *Kēme* which meant the black earth or lands as opposed to the desert that ran along the banks of the Nile. The word prayer derives from Old French *preiere*, based on the Latin *precarius* "obtained by entreaty". Each of these words has different cultural origins and shows the flow of spirit through millennia and across different parts of the Earth into our language and onto our pages.

The student of magic finds their ground work in the subjects of religion, mythology, history, psychology, archaeology, mathematics, folklore, philosophy, physiology, herbalism and most importantly the skills learnt through meditation and the ability hold clear and sustained thought. Knowledge of any kind whilst it may be categorised for logical study cannot be sectioned into boxes and there is a necessary and natural interplay between subjects combined with imagination that allows correspondences to be found, theories to be developed and naturally emerging patterns to be identified. There is generally far more studying than dancing around bonfires contrary to popular belief! Though definitely making time to be with friends dancing or singing around the fire can only be a good thing. Whilst there are many other worthy spiritual paths that do not require much studying generally the path of the magical practitioner seeking initiation (initiate) appeals to those with enquiring minds. To progress upon the magical path study of the aspects of nature and natural forces is necessary combined with personal development.

Magic is all around us here and now in our minds, our hearts, at our fingertips and spreads outwards with every connection we make and breath we take. Magic is what we know by so many other names, perhaps in this day and age by any other name less we be ridiculed for it. How quickly some forget that it was intrinsic fact and frame work to the context of life for almost every other society and culture on Earth before us. Most people have already worked some kind of simple magic at some point in their lives or do so regularly but perhaps do not recognise it as such. Certainly the word magic has faded from common use in everyday life. As it is reclaimed we can recognise the areas of our lives where magic holds us and weaves the threads.

Every person who ever felt wonder at creation, ever honoured tradition, ever sung in praise, or carried hope, or prayed, or believed in something greater than themselves has connected with spirit in some way and has therefore touched magic or glimpsed at its essence. Children know it, they are born knowing it, it is the adults who forget and question this certainty. Every healer, doctor, musician, creator, artist, maker, innovator, communicator, facilitator, carer and teacher have worked within the realms of spirit or had opportunity to do so. Anyone in service in some way to do good, either through their work or life is working in and with spirit at some level, whether that is in an earthly practical sense or as a result of higher guidance, inspiration, calling, purpose, or temporary alignment with such a path upon the journey. And working with spirit is somewhere touching the realms of magic.

Every person who has ever healed another, or known which plants may heal another is working magic. Every person who has ever lit a candle in prayer or with intention has worked magic. Every person who has acted upon superstition or folklore has worked magic. Every person who has watched and observed the astrological movements of the sky has some understanding or connection with the heavens and therefore also the realms of magic. Cultural customs, rites of passage, initiations, traditions, all can be thought of as relative to magic and ritual.

It is perhaps a symptom of our time that there has been a divide between the spiritual and scientific, a divide which is slowly healing as more and more people recognise that the two are of course two halves of one whole and that there is medicinal or scientific evidence to support many ancient spiritual practices and holistic therapies. Many people at this time seek to define their own spiritual paths and are returning to Mother Earth and gentler ways of being with nature.

When we pray we affirm some sort of belief in the Divine, or a source of goodness and high intelligence in nature. When we add essential oils to the bath we intuitively use our senses to cure and heal ourselves. When we pass knowledge and stories on to our children we are in the tradition of passing down through generations that which our parents and our grandparents, aunts and uncles taught us. When we see ourselves and our place in the line of our ancestors before us and our descendants to come we are in alignment with spirit and therefore magic. This recognition of the ancestral line and heritage is an integral part of all cultures and religions. The spoken knowledge or religious gnosis of the oral tradition is passed down, remembered and shared in stories, myths and legends throughout all of humanity. All cultures do this. These stories are part of our heritage: they flow through our bloodlines, our DNA and our soul connections.

Magic is found in the beauty of nature, in the rain on the leaves and the light through the trees. It is found in the love of others, animals and of all things and in the appreciation of the wild. It is found in history, culture, tradition, music, dance, creation. In every part of our lives, making up the tapestry. It is the tapestry. It is not some foreign concept to be found in books, though such may be useful for the imparting of information. Rather it is an integral part of life or the weave upon which life hangs, for magic is divine in nature and synonymous with nature, with spirit, with God/Goddess.

This book is written on the premise that all that is aligned with love is holy, divine and sacred by whatever name or form and to be respected and treated with reverence regardless of which way or path one chooses to honour or worship by. Love is the defining and guiding principle by which white magic may be identified. There are many religions and belief systems across the globe which have central teachings about living with love and compassion. There are also some that are not aligned with love and these operate against those things that are sacred i.e. they are sacrilegious. There are thirdly many paths that are neither, for example nature based paths that are impartial and in these instances the path may only be defined by intention. In truth the path of the individual may only ever be defined by intention and cumulative actions and regardless of which religion or faith one follows whether we are aligned with love or not is the direct choice of each person.

This book is intentionally written in a non-denominational way in order to be open to all. Although there are a large cross section of cultural references there are deliberately more examples throughout from the paths that are most relevant in Western esoteric tradition such as Wicca, Celtic and Germanic neo-paganism, Egyptian and Graeco-Romano traditions and the Kabbalah which is an esoteric school of thought originating in Jewish mysticism. Fuller explanations or information has been given wherever it is likely to be beneficial in further understanding of other esoteric texts and concepts. If the practitioner works through this book and all the exercises in its entirety by its completion they should have a groundwork from which to make sense of and understand most other esoteric books and literature.

Because this book is of a spiritual nature there are various different words for God or divinity used throughout it. Rather than allowing words for God to become a block the reader is invited to keep an open mind and to substitute any word for God or Goddess with any other that they feel more comfortable with. For example nature, love, Mother Earth, great creator, great spirit, source, universe, higher power, intelligent design, cosmic wisdom, creative flow, or good orderly direction. There is no need to use the word God unless it sits comfortably for you. Instead an open mind and the ability to wonder or to replace the word with one that feels appropriate for you is all that is needed. Whichever one you choose the principles contained within this book will still be effective.

Indeed all man made religions are by their very nature human attempts and expressions of spirituality. Most of the holy books of the world are made up of collections of manuscripts. These manuscripts have been written down and recorded by man very often hundreds of years after the events they describe. They have been interpreted by man, censored by man, coloured by cultural conditioning. Which manuscripts should be included and which should be left out has been decided by man. Human beings have political, emotional and cultural agendas. Even good people are so inclined. In other words our holy books are censored, interpreted and mostly incomplete works. This does not decrease their significance or their value but is an honest appraisal of their entirety and or accuracy. It leaves room for new interpretations, for growth, for expansion. The words of prophets from thousands of years ago may not be any more holy or sacred than the words of prophets now. The writings that are holy or sacred may be missing information or missing instructions as to how to interpret the information correctly.

All forms of the divine are recognised in the creation of nature. We see God expressed in creation of the world around us and as such nature is the commonality of all religions and belief systems. Nature is the divine creation, expression, essence or inherent spirit of all. We, mankind, are a part of nature and nature is a part of us. We are one with our earth, trees, sky and water. We are meant to be her guardians, her protectors, to live in peace and honour her and yet within the very religions and institutions so many of us profess to worship we seem to have forgotten this very basic truth. God/Goddess/Divinity is inherent in nature. How did we forget what seems so obvious? Somewhere the illusions of separation removed us from a truth that is inside every living thing. We belong to the earth, not the other way around. If we collectively spent as much time and money protecting the earth as we do arguing over which version of past events or which religion is correct we might all be significantly happier and healthier. We might remember our own divinity, recover our commonality and our humanity, find our place with earth. Many have forgotten but there are others who are remembering, there are others who are protecting her. There are people who are in communion with nature, who honour her, who walk gently upon the sacred ground. Gradually we are returning to her. We are sitting on the earth and finding gentler ways to live and ways to give back.

The only way to heal the world is to heal ourselves, one at a time. It starts with us. Those who are doing their work and living well are ultimately serving the whole. They are leading the way and guiding us and the good news is they can be found everywhere. They are the teachers of environmental issues, the finders of green alternatives and renewable energies, the inventors of new innovative ways of doing things. They are the holders of ceremonies where the people come to reconnect with each other and the land. They are the people who bring to the office a breath of a fresh air, a new way of behaving; a light where it's needed that brightens the day. They are the ones working in healthcare and emergency services, helping and healing others. They are the people who retain ethics and compassion in the boardroom or who put good social constructs in place or invest in things that will benefit society. They are the ones organising educational or social gatherings for a good cause. They are mothers and fathers raising their kids with love and compassion and teaching them about caring for the earth and for each other. They are the people quietly working on themselves and doing good. They are literally everywhere! When we change our focus from what's wrong with the world to what's right with the world and where can we do the most good something miraculous happens. We shift out of the fear that only adds to the problem and we shift into love and start finding solutions.

There are so many ways that people are bringing light and goodness into the world. They are not all necessarily leading alternative lives or working as healers or psychologists. They can be anywhere. There are many souls working and living in the mainstream who are bringing in massive amounts of light to environments where it is needed and where it can do the most good

24

and has the most impact. The actions of people working in mainstream environments, government and social projects have the ability to effect changes from the inside so to speak and to do something productive about implementing them in a good way. There are many others who are finding alternative lifestyles, choosing to be self-employed or to heal those who are not in healthy environments leading the way back to a simpler, cleaner and more natural way of life.

Being a spiritual being does definitely not mean that we need to live up a mountain for ten years, although that's fine if it's your path. The point is that we can be spiritual in any environment and when we follow our inner knowing or divine guidance we are instinctively and deeply drawn to where we are meant to be. What is the point of anything less than an all-encompassing spirituality that allows humanness and family and sex and life? Surely spirituality is a celebration of life! Isn't that the point? Being spiritual means showing up in the real world when it matters and bringing some good into the world. Light can be brought into any situation and any work place. Nor is it necessary to be of any particular religious or spiritual path. People working the most wonderful magic are of diverse and different faiths and hold entirely different beliefs from one another and that's a good thing because it is in diversity that we have the opportunity to heal division, to learn from one another and to come back to Mother Earth. Only diversity can reach the rest of the world. Gradually, one by one we come to remember, we're healing the world one heart at a time.

The words for God, Goddess, pantheons, deity, spirit and animism in nature have all been used throughout this book and sometimes interchangeably, not out of casualness or inaccuracy but out of a deliberate common recognition and a bringing together of faiths, bridging the separations in search of commonality. The focus is on drawing upon similarities and looking for recurring patterns and inherent archaic archetypes and stories that are deep within us and come from our humanity and ultimately from Mother Nature. When we connect with these stories that run through us and through earth and when we see God/Goddess in nature a healing occurs, a divide is gently brought back together and we become more whole, bringing us back to health and to oneness with the earth and with God/Goddess.

Why white magic? Why not rainbow magic, green magic or any other kind? Well because we all know and recognise the term. The expression "white witch" has been coined in modern day language to mean someone who works magic for good. It can be found throughout stories and folklore, fairy tales and speech. It is simply a way to define and classify what kind of magic it is that we practise. It denotes an aspiration to be and to do good and an inclination towards good. It should be noted too that white light makes up the totality of the rainbow and that shadow cannot exist without the presence of light. White light is the cumulative brilliance and highest frequency of all light.

There is an argument that the word white cannot be used to denote good because it somehow either omits shadow or in some way does a disservice to the word black. However language is complex and words often have more than one meaning or use. In this case they are words used to depict or imply a principle. They hold no further implication and they are not intended to denote actual colour. The same argument can be found with light and dark or any other similar analogy and may perhaps be better thought of as yin and yang principles which both have positive and negative aspects. This book could just as easily have been called positive, good, safe or ethical magic. However "white magic" is an easily recognised term.

Working white magic does not mean that we have to be by any means perfect, rather it perhaps just means we are trying our best and are able to see our imperfections with kind eyes. It's surprising how many paths leading towards health and healing seem to go through all sorts of trials and turmoil. Consciousness is often found in unconscious ways. Our job is not to berate and judge, it is to be compassionate, to have a sense of humour and to love ourselves. Simply to hold love and to accept the process. Trust the process. The soul knows the way. The soul always knows the way. When the intention is love we are guided and we are held and we are led back to health even if we have to go through some daunting territory. It's all right to have had a chequered path. It's all right to have imperfections. It's all right to get it wrong some days. It means we're human and we have shadow and parts we're working on. The point is that we are working. We are trying. We are doing our best. The definition of white then is that we are aligned and doing all this from a place of love. The realms of earth aren't easy; it's crazy down here in three-dimensional existence. Breathe, centre, start with love, stay with love. We owe nobody any explanation because some things are between us and God/Goddess.

There is within some modern pagan circles a prevalent idea that working within the shades of grey is balance and that allowing light and dark together is the balance. Well perhaps if we were talking about light and dark in terms of colour that could be seen as true but in terms of reference to magical intention this is not true. There are many people who are put off joining the types of moots, pagan groups and circles that are "open to all" as a result of this half dark half light principle. Feelings are always there for a very good reason and to tell us information. If something feels unsafe or not loving listen to that intuition and choose to stay in healthy love based environments. Of course lower energies feel toxic, it's logical. Understandably that's why many of these circles seem so unstable and fleeting. This is also one of the main reasons magic has continued to have some negative connotations in the mainstream even in the present day. People invariably fear what they do not know or feel is being hidden. By sharing information and bringing light and discussion to the subject fear can be removed and replaced with love and understanding.

Not so long ago, prior to some of later patriarchal views much of what we might now called magic was simply called life, or medicine, or common knowledge, or common sense even! Visit any healing convention, any mind body spirit weekend, any healing field of a festival or retreat and you will find white magic and practices of white magic. The holistic therapy industry is full of healers and modern day medicine men and women!

There are other lodges, covens or circles both private or open that operate from a place of light and love and that bring people together on the premise of a shared viewpoint, shared philosophy, shared values and a common way of practising. These groups or circles are generally open about the way in which they work and the person or people running it will likely encourage any new member or interested person to come and talk and ask questions before joining and may want to ask questions too. Taking the time to ask questions is always a good thing before attending any event. It can be helpful to remember that the best friendships are often formed over time too and that it is only as friendship deepens that we really get to really know the other. There's no rush. By stating clearly that a gathering is aligned with white magic it is much more likely to be attractive to those working in a light way and working with love. It also gives out a safe and secure vibe that is much more welcoming.

Until we find a circle that feels right for us what else can we do? We can work alone of course and do some very deep work in this way. We can connect with others on similar spiritual journeys online and join worldwide meditations and workings. We can sing to water or to the land either with choirs or alone. We can plant trees and spend time in nature. We can start a gathering of our own and advertise it locally even if it's as simple as a bonfire for the sabbat with friends. We can learn to live our lives with more intention, with more consciousness. Other options include seeking out friendships with those with similar interests and values by attending mind, body, spirit events and those aimed at healing or leading a healthful life, anywhere creative such as art classes or theatre groups, meditation groups, yoga classes, singing workshops, permaculture and forest gardening or whatever else floats your boat. There are lots of other like-minded souls out there. Anywhere we feel joyful and alive or inspired is probably somewhere we can meet one of our tribe.

Although light and dark is within all of us it is important to remember that we are in truth spiritual beings and that our shadow only exists because of our light. Therefore rather than fearing our shadow let's bring light to it, do our work within it and honour and recognise that it is here to teach and empower us whilst we learn to love ourselves even in the darker places. We love ourselves even though…(fill in the gap). We are trying our best and we see ourselves compassionately and patiently. We would never teach our children that they are half good half bad, simply that they are whole, complete, beautiful beings with many aspects that can take time to learn and understand. We would teach them that they can work on anything they wish to improve and we would seek to empower them to do that. Why would we speak differently to ourselves? Nor would we teach our children that it is balanced to behave in a way that is half dark half light in the very simplistic sense of being kind or nasty alternately, which is effectively the same premise as those who work black and white magic alongside one another in a misguided attempt at balance. Rather we would encourage them to be the best they can be and to understand any parts that are difficult or in need of attention or love.

When we work white magic we set the intention of wanting to do good and to use this magic for beneficial purposes. More than that we are aligning ourselves with all of the good and light cosmic and divine forces that will support our purpose. It makes our intentions clear. It also holds us to more accountability, to act more carefully and consider more carefully our own sets of ethics and our individual paths. It makes us examine ourselves and our lives more carefully, all the parts of ourselves and lives, including the shadows and the burning brightness capable of casting them.

Love is the Law.

Chapter Two
Beginning a Journey

All is One when Nought has Passed.

All journeys begin with setting a course.

Spirit, like water, eternally washes through the landscape springing up from the earth and rising into rivers that flow to the sea. Like water, coming up from the ground or falling from the sky, it forms one body and always returns to one source. And we, humanity, are part of this sea, this huge body of water and yet we are individuals like the crests of single waves in our experience of life.

Individual streams and rivers of spirit that come up from the earth may flow following the contours of the landscape through which their water must pass. They may branch off in several directions at different junctures to flow to each part of the earth. Each of these spirit rivers must follow the lay of the landscape or carve through the earth and the rocks making its way onward and each of these rivers will absorb different minerals and properties from the types of soil they travel through and will react to the climate and to the landscape in which they find themselves, whether that is rushing over rocks and into cascading falls or meandering through trees and jungles for miles upon miles and these properties may also alter over time.

Water brings life and attracts living creatures and peoples to it supporting them and so it is that around each of these rivers different people come and live. Each different community and culture of people will think of their water differently but they all acknowledge its divinity. They may have different names for their spirit rivers, different rituals or prayers for it, the water spirit itself may even be a little different in different areas, more acid, more alkaline, different colours from the soil, slower or faster flowing. These different cultures of people who live on these rivers are also part of the different ecosystems and biodiversity which has grown up around their river. The land of each place and the water of each place are in harmony with the people and the spirit of the water supports all life around it encompassing one another as they mutually evolve and co-create. It is in fact essential that these spirit rivers are different because the water in the west would not necessarily support the ecosystems that thrive in the East and vice versa. Each has acclimatised and adapted to support and nourish the people who live there, each is essential and each adds to the diversity and beauty of the whole of creation. So it is with religions and faiths and beliefs. Water never changes from being water any more than spirit would ever change from being spirit. It just looks a little different depending where we grow and upon the reflections of the sky.

There are as many paths as there are people and journeys and we may each only define our own. We can choose however whether to focus on our differences with others or whether to focus on our similarities and the things that bring us together and unite us. As babies we are all born with a natural predisposition towards happiness and to all things good. It takes social conditioning to forget this! God/Goddess, nature and goodness is inherent within us all of us. We are truly powerful because we are one with spirit and it flows through us. We are of course living in three-dimensional reality and earthly life can be full on! It's helpful to remember that the best we can do from here is to keep the doorway open in our hearts and in our minds. If we get lost or forget momentarily we can always find the door again. When we remember our divinity, even if that's whilst we're having a bad day we are held in our connection and truth with a warm heart centred feeling that can guide and support us.

When we begin any journey it's useful to have an idea of the lay of the land and to think about the direction we would like to take whether that is in terms of what sort of cultural or religious preference we have or the type of work we wish to do or our intention. When we are talking about white magic the word white represents a conscious choice that has been made. The practitioner has with full understanding and free will *chosen* that they wish to work with love and love works in an ascending way for good. What is meant by this choice of wording is not a lack of inclusion or acknowledgement of the rest of the rainbow spectrum contained within us but is inclusive of it. It is a recognition that we in our humanness, with our shades of grey, light and darkness, have made a conscious decision. All of creation comes from and goes back to source both within light and dark, black and white. The decision here is that of our own free will, even whilst embracing all the aspects of ourselves in our imperfect perfection, we are consciously choosing the ascending path towards deeper understanding, evolution and awakening. We

31

are trying and making an effort and this puts us firmly on a path. It is this deliberate choice of will to work in an ascending way towards and with the direction of spirit/nature that is the basis and the deciding factor of what constitutes white magic as opposed to any other kind. This conscious decision is ultimately a soul choice. It is primarily in nature that we see and experience spirit and it is in our communion with nature that we develop our relationship with spirit.

There are many practitioners of magic who work entirely and directly with nature and natural forces who are not necessarily believers of Divinity or God/Goddess per se but may believe in the inherent life force or spirit of the land. These people can still be said to be working white magic because they are in alignment with love and working with love. They are nurturing and protecting the planet and honouring the sovereignty of the land and planet directly. Love is love and good is good however it is expressed. We can apply the term white magic to those working for good even if our personal beliefs are quite different from one another's on the grounds that they are still doing good and working with love. In much the same way we often base friendships or relationships upon an appreciation of a person's good qualities, integrity and values even if we have some significant differences in other areas of life.

Some consider white magic to be solely defined as religious or faith based magic, working in alignment with God/Goddess in order to come into closer relationship with the divine. The onus is upon the personal transformation of the practitioner through healing and seeking inner change to higher awareness. The personal skills and abilities of an individual are still to be practised and honed but in alignment with this ideal in order that they may be effective and fit for purpose. In the same way studies of religion, ancient wisdom and natural sciences are undertaken to gain deeper understanding of the divine and not for earthly reward.

The counterpart to spiritual or faith-based magic could be said to be practical magic, which is the study of magic and the power of the mind based upon our abilities to change our worldly reality. Its focus is one of external change in the immediate environment and not one necessarily concerned with internal shifts in consciousness. This is the usual realm of herbal medicine, wealth, love, aspirations and all other earthly desires.

So there is religious and non-religious magic and magic used for higher service or magic used for other useful or good reasons. Whilst there are some who say that white magic may only be of the religious or faith based variety there is no reason why practical nature based magic cannot also be used for good or with love. Ultimately as a result of this service internal change often comes too because the inner and outer world will mirror one another. Beyond this there is no such division between the two inner and outer worlds, rather degrees of gradation. In addition when we take care of ourselves and we are well looked after and happy we are in turn capable of doing more for others. It is not selfish to take good care of ourselves, it is loving to take good care of ourselves. The definition then of white magic as it is intended here then is that we are working with love and therefore in alignment with a good purpose regardless of what type or whether it is religious or practical magic. Love is inclusive of both.

There are other types of magic chosen by some. Some choose to work in a descending way towards lower consciousness, aligned with negative spiritual forces to do harm or for selfish purposes. Working against nature and good orderly direction is generally what is known as black magic of which there are numerous forms. Others choose to work within the middle ground of the spectrum or within the shades of grey either deliberately or as a result of being undecided or uninformed until such as time as movement one way or the other takes place. The direction of this movement may be decided because it feels appropriate and a natural decision has been made, an awakening of some kind has occurred, or as a cumulative effect of actions in life tilting the balance one way or other so that movement is resumed. We may choose our direction, though it may prove to be over the course of life times. All life is in motion, all water flows! We choose a direction in each moment, or we meander and see where we end up whilst hoping for the best.

Whether one believes in divinity directly found in communion with nature (inclusive of humanity), animism, great spirit, one God-force, individual Gods and Goddesses, pantheon or any other kind of definition it is a recognition of some kind of divinity and spirit made manifest and that as such there is a point of creation, one source or first cause from which all came. And if all comes from one source then there cannot be anything else outside of this one source. All are one when nought, or the point of creation, has passed. It doesn't matter which course or path we choose if it is aligned with love it leads up. What matters is that we are swimming upstream together, sharing the waters towards the source or first cause from which all came. It is only in this journey back to the point of spirit, like salmon that swim upstream, that we reach oneness and transcend the illusory boundaries of separation. And yet there is a paradox here for even whilst we seek such union it is only within our individuated experiences of existence and in our diversity that we are able to learn from this reality. Furthermore separation is the necessity of birth into three-dimensional space and time existence and we cannot transcend in truth on the earthly plane except in spirit. We are all one. We are all individuals. Both statements are true. All of life is a paradox.

There are those who see spiritual evolution alongside physical evolution as mankind's ongoing journey over the course of time through generations of ancestors and learning to the technological age in which we now find ourselves. There are others who see man's physical evolution separately to his spiritual evolution and consider that spiritual evolution is a journey or development of the soul and an individual matter. Many people believe we reincarnate throughout lifetimes until such time as we learn the lessons needed to progress. Perhaps both schools of thoughts are true and bear some relationship to one another.

Reincarnation itself is a long held ancient belief of numerous religions and cultures and pre-dates Christianity and several other newer religions by thousands of years. Buddhism has its teachings on the subject as does Hinduism and the Kabbalah. Gnostic belief suggests various grades of initiation or existence between God and man and the process of the soul to return to source. The Egyptians believed in reincarnation or the transmigration of the soul from body to body between which incarnations the soul was weighed against the feather of Ma'at (truth) and found either wanting or to be of *maa kheru* meaning right speech i.e. honourable. The Celts too viewed death as entering the cauldron of rebirth and the womb of the Great Mother. Reincarnation then is not to be confused with or thought of as a "new age" idea, a label some seem to use when trying to dismiss the credibility of a thing. It is an ancient and widely held belief by many peoples and cultures across thousands of years. As with many other anthropological facts reincarnation as a concept developed in many places and different cultures independently of one another just as many other great truths. In the same way as you can find almost identical goddess figurines across the world from tens if not hundreds of ancient cultures that did not know each other, separated by time or location or both. So it is with reincarnation and other inherent beliefs that are somehow deep within us like the archetypes.

There are some fascinating books and texts on the subject both ancient and modern. I'd advise the reader to respect their own deeper intuition whatever it might say. By holding and examining these ideas alongside our personal experiences and beliefs we may consider each possibility with an open mind and then draw or form conclusions that resonate truthfully for us. In recurring patterns truth is found. Also in the open mind when we ponder such questions as these the universe is apt to answer by sending us whatever information we need by many means and synchronicities. We've all had that wonderful feeling when the information we were just wondering about falls into our lap, or a friend rings to tell us that exact thing in conversation as if by magic!

A lot of people at this time are changing and coming out of fear and moving away from conflict. We are privileged to live in an age and a place where this is possible. There is a shift in consciousness that's happening and has been happening gradually as the wheel turned over the last few hundred years. Deliberately focussing upon the good is not to deny there are things in the world that really need help, healing and change. However focussing upon things that frighten us only puts us into fear and immobilises us. When we concentrate on good we raise our vibration, we move into love and we usher in more love bringing about solutions and the change we wish for. Whilst we still need to do what we can to stop bad in practical terms, effecting positive change is one very real part of that and it is brought about by acknowledging all the good in the world and promoting what we can to help in order to develop and encourage it. Eventually then a tipping point may come. Weren't we as children taught to lead by example? Yes we've seen the industrial age and the age of enlightenment, revolutions and wars came and went, pollution and the effects of climate change were brought about along with the destruction of our rain forests and contamination of our seas and water sources. Sometimes it can feel too much. Sometimes it can be overwhelming. Our world is not at peace yet. It makes perfect sense that there are many people who would rather not take part in the discussion when it hurts so much. Awakening and changing can be daunting in places. It needs to happen slowly and gradually. It means looking at ourselves and our stuff and being responsible for ourselves. It means seeing what is happening around us, much of which can feel bigger than we are. Engaging in fighting tends to lock us in to conflict. Peaceful protest eventually wins through and leads by example. The way out of conflict then is to choose peace and may be to promote the good and focus our attention on the good. When each individual heals themselves and focuses only on the good we will have a generation of conscious healed adults bringing up happy empowered kids and in turn one day we will have a well adjusted society focussed entirely upon well-being and goodness. The journey then is first and foremost a personal one.

In truth we are eternal and nameless and all that passes through us and through our lives is like weather moving through us. Sometimes it is riveting, the story line grips us so much that we forget. We think that if we get too caught up we will somehow not be present or miss the moment. Of course that's not really true. The soul is constant, observing, able to be there and to hold the rest of us even in the moments we don't know it, even in the moments we feel lost, or tired, or defeated. Deep within us and through us our consciousness where God/Goddess is within us we are held and healed and experiencing life and the weather systems moving through us. We do not slip out of time. We do not lose the moment or ourselves with a careless thought. We are here, observing, feeling and learning where we have been all along.

Like the plants in the garden and like all things in nature we don't grow evenly and yet we have patterns. We thrive in different conditions and whilst we might be brilliant at one thing we may well be behind with others. Those yet to visibly begin their journey from one person's viewpoint might already be on it imperceptibly waiting, learning, watching. Not all journeys are visibly spiritual. We all have different life purposes to fulfil. Our business is our own personal path and choice. We all grow differently.

With each previous incarnation of ourselves we have grown and with each new life we at some point reclaim the knowledge and the ground we have previously covered very much as a student revises at the end of term. We then reach a point of new lessons and our incline becomes more gradual allowing us the time we need to absorb and process the new information. Whilst younger souls take the gentler slopes, old souls who have previously covered a lot of ground then often seem to climb a steep fast learning curve! It is often remarked upon that those following spiritual paths frequently seem to have had a lot to cope with throughout their lives either physically or in terms of emotional upheaval particularly in their early years. It is also often remarked upon that those walking spiritual paths have often led colourful and eventful lives. Both seem true and are perhaps because this is the only way in which enough ground could possibly be covered.

Shamans and elders from many cultures have described being tested by all sorts of forces and life events, and are often only able to become who and what they are as a result of having experienced the journey they have taken in order to gain the wisdom they have earned. They would not otherwise have been able to provide the guidance for the rest of their tribe or be able to hold the space for those who come to them.

Wherever we find ourselves we all have those ahead of us helping and teaching us, and those around us and following us. We are both perpetual student and teacher. We live in a time and climate where human existence in a patriarchal and monetary orientated society has left many thirsty for a new kind of spirituality in their lives. As a result more and more people are returning to nature, to esoteric or shamanistic practices and to the paths of magic.

The most common misconception about white magic is that it is somehow inferior in its complexity or aptitude to darker practices. This is not true. There is a common mistake that love and light is fluffy and not to be taken seriously. Anyone who has practised white magic or studied any loving philosophy or spiritual practice could tell you this is not the case. Love is the law and real love of the universal type requires us to step into truth, which is often far from easy. The word love may be seen synonymously with truth for when we are in truth all that is false is removed and there is only love.

The practice of white magic and its pathways comes with a responsibility not just for ourselves but for our actions and all those we are in relation with. It requires more of the practitioner because we are each accountable directly to divinity and spirit and no amount of earthly interference may tamper the scales. The reality of this is that when we make the decision that we wish to work in this way it is a decision not just about our magical practices but that of our whole lives which are in truth our ceremony. Every time we eat we are in ceremony, every time we pray we are in ceremony, every time we clean the house we are in ceremony, every time we laugh with friends or cry with friends... you've got it. Our lives are the ceremony and the celebration. Therefore physical life generally needs to be in harmony and in balance with magical ability and although one may be slightly further ahead than another for short periods of time, like the leaves on the plants, sooner or later the counterpart must catch up and do the work required to be in balance. In some cases this can mean a lot of catching up. Knowing something in theory and doing it in practice can be two different things! Bringing light and a sense of humour will help. It is a common worry that having a spiritual path can make one become too serious, however I would like to suggest that any spiritual path worth pursuing should increase our capacity for happiness and joy. These in turn further open our hearts and increase our connection with each other.

The terms neophyte, priest, priestess, follower, occultist, witch, wizard, sorceress, magus, shaman and light worker all have different meanings and connotations attached to them from various different paths. They are all however valid magical terms and names but the clearest terms that suit regardless of tradition or position are those of practitioner, i.e. the person practising, or initiate, i.e. the person who is initiated or studying to be initiated. Both words easily serve the purpose with no other connotations and one can practise or be an initiate of any level or path.

In the seeking of knowledge of the nature of magic and its workings it is worth taking into consideration that some things cannot be understood until they are experienced and with such things there is no telling how they will change us or our lives. Nor can knowledge be undone or easily forgotten. Once change has occurred we may continue to alter but cannot return to our original state. This is the nature of alchemy. In so much as it is possible it would seem wise to try to factor this into our decision about the course we choose to take and then knowingly enter into the unknown!

Paganism and the term "pagan" is a massive umbrella term to cover any and all religious and spiritual beliefs outside of the current main religions. The word pagan comes from the Latin *paganus* meaning "rustic" from the word *pagus,* "country district". *Paganus* also meant "civilian", its meaning later becoming "heathen" as one who is not enrolled in the army of Christ in the Roman Christian era.

Paganism is of course just the word we use for all of the previous religions prior to the current one. As a blanket term then it is as diverse as the cultures of the globe across all of time. Pick any religious belief system that is not a current one and it will fall into the category of paganism. Pick any reconstructed belief system based on a previous one that is not a current main religion and it will also fall into the category of paganism. Paganism then is not the studying of those beliefs without religion or faith then but a studying of all the spiritual pathways, religions and faiths of the world. Of course in one book this is not a possible thing, nor in one lifetime. We have to choose and set a course we wish to follow whether that is a course of one particular type of spiritual path or the eclectic study of many. Certainly by learning one belief system well we are more likely to develop a deeper spiritual relationship and have a thorough understanding. For this reason it is generally advised that the practitioner of magic initially chooses one particular spiritual path to follow or at least sets course with a general direction. This book though eclectic in nature and touching upon various world beliefs may serve as an introduction to the various pathways.

Most neo-pagan belief systems are reconstructed from old religions. Whilst reading the interpretations of others can of course be invaluable the clearest water is always to be found closest to the source. For that reason there is no substitute for reading the oldest available sources and studying the archaeological evidence of a society. Interpreting the facts directly rather than third or fourth hand will usually yield clearer results. There are of course cross-cultural common threads and connections between belief systems and it is in these threads of commonality that we find recurring patterns, archetypes and truths.

There are unique parallels to be drawn for example between the myths and imagery of ancient Egypt and of India. Walafrid Strabo a German scholar circa 809–849 AD writes: *"The lotus flower, sacred to Buddha and to Osiris, has five petals which symbolizes the four limbs and the head; the five senses; the five digits; and like the pyramid, the four parts of the compass and the zenith. Other esoteric meanings abound: for myths are seldom simple, and never irresponsible".*

At Alexandria, in Egypt, Indian scholars were a common sight. They are mentioned both by the Greek philosopher Dio Chrysostom circa 100 AD and by the Christian theologian Clement of Alexandria circa 200 AD. Indirect contact between ancient India and Egypt through Mesopotamia is generally accepted and there is evidence of shared elements of language and folk art as well as common spiritual practices such as worshipping the sun, worshipping the sacred cow, bull or aurochs, the snake, and the river. These themes also spread throughout the globe in later religions carrying their influence. Recently, archaeological evidence supports definitive contact between India and Egypt. A terracotta mummy from Lothal resembling an Egyptian mummy has been found and a similar terracotta mummy has also been found at Mohenjodaro. Egyptian mummies are also said to have been wrapped in Indian muslin. One who chooses to study Kemetic (Egyptian) religion then may also choose to study any shared Indian heritage. There is certainly research to support shared Egyptian and Indian heritage from the Vedic era.

Egyptian religious beliefs can be seen recurring in the Jewish Kabbalah. Indeed there are depictions of the flower of life design both in Egypt and in India pre-dating Judaism. Judaism in turn gave rise to both Christianity and to Islam and both then gave rise to the numerous denominations and variants of both belief systems all over the world, from Russian Orthodoxy to the whirling dervishes of Sufism. All over the world throughout history from the first migrations and the subsequent waves that followed there has been a sharing and blending of cultural and spiritual beliefs. Looking at the development of human language we can see the flow of knowledge and cultural influx over time and we will look at the origins of our own language in more detail later.

The historical tapestry of the British Isles is rich with multi-cultural influences. As a nation our story is one of invasion and settlement, of absorption and adaptation to new ideas. Pre-dating Christianity in the British Isles our heritage is one of the Neolithic Sun worship of prehistory, followed by the myths and the legends of the Celts and Brythonic peoples. Later this gave way to druidic beliefs and then later still to the adoption of Roman pagan deities and ideas and to both Latin and Greek influences in the written word and then to Christianity. The coming of the Anglo-Saxons brought new ideas, myths and sagas to the country, which temporarily reverted back to paganism in a blending of Celtic and Anglo-Saxon religion before merging with and influencing Christianity. The Vikings too brought with them further Norse Germanic religious ideas. All of these various influences make up our pagan past and neo-paganism tries to reconstruct these religions and adapt them to suit our modern world. In this way they remain current and evolve as all faiths always have done. The most common new age pagan paths are reconstructed Celtic Polytheism and Germanic Heathenism as above. Animism is a belief in the direct spirit of nature. Druidic beliefs and Wicca are the most usual types of witchcraft practised in the West. Both Druidism and Wicca have their own set of ethical beliefs and laws though these are of course open to interpretation as are their religious origins.

When we seek answers and ponder inwards the heavens are apt to answer

40

and will likely bring us the very information we seek.

Written Exercise

You will need a blank journal or a notebook suitable for the purpose, which can be kept for spiritual thoughts, reflections, recording dreams or moments of inspiration or vision. Some refer to this as a book of shadows or a book of illuminations. Sit somewhere comfortable where you can write easily. The following suggestions are given to encourage definition and clarity of your thoughts and ideas about your own journey so as to begin forming a personal foundation on which to build. Take your time and enjoy the expression of your ideas and writing about your own beliefs and thoughts. Write whatever feels right in response to the questions. There are no right or wrong answers.

1. Where is your spiritual water in life? What hobbies, pastimes, parts of life sustain, inspire, replenish and uplift you?

2. How would you describe or define your path? Can it be defined by a religion or a philosophy of some kind or is it organic and naturally evolving?

3. How do your spiritual beliefs influence and support you in life? Where do they help and do the most good?

4. Are you interested in the beliefs and customs of any culture in particular? Which places do you long to visit?

5. Are there any other thoughts that come to you that seem important for now, relevant or useful?

When you've finished have a read and keep it for later reference. One of the wonderful things over years is how our ideas and beliefs are constantly developing and it can be really helpful to be able to look back later on the ground we've covered. Here then on these pages are the beginnings of a personal foundation and connection with the sacred ground beneath our feet.

Chapter Three
The Rainbow and the Nature of Light

"If you want to find the secrets of the universe, think in terms of energy, frequency and vibration."

Nikola Tesla (1942).

Sunlight and water are the two main ingredients of life and the symbol of these in union is the rainbow. In fire and water alchemy can be found and so it is here in their fusion of the rainbow that our journey begins in earnest. When we understand the rainbow we begin to understand light and all things in creation under the sun.

The rainbow occurs often in mythology, religious writing and the arts and is an inherent part of human culture. In Norse mythology the rainbow bridge is said to connect Heaven (Asgard) and Earth (Midgard) and as such could be thought of as a part of Yggdrasil, the world tree which connects the realms. In the book of Genesis in the Old Testament the rainbow is a sign to Noah from God as a covenant that the Earth shall never be flooded again. In Aboriginal mythology the Rainbow Serpent is a creator God and is depicted as a common motif in aboriginal art work. It is seen as a giver of life because of its association with water and when a rainbow is seen in the sky it is considered to be the serpent moving from one watering hole to another. In Greek myth the Goddess Iris is the personification of the rainbow and a messenger of the Gods. She is known as a Goddess of the sea and sky and is said to pour water that she has collected from the sea from her pitcher into the skies and travel with the speed of the wind. In the tarot the Temperance card is often depicted as an angel who mixes fire and water into a vessel and pours forth a rainbow, symbolic of transformation and personal alchemy.

Rainbows have been used as a symbol of hope and as a political symbol of diversity and social change, as a symbol of peace and in more recent years as a symbol of gay rights and overcoming prejudice and as a symbol of racial tolerance, mutual support and union. In the alchemy of transformation and in the union of fire and water and the two supporting forces of life the arch of the rainbow brings hope, goodness and understanding.

The rainbow is a combination of airborne water and light that is reflected, refracted and dispersed in the water creating a light spectrum arched in the sky. Rainbows caused by sunlight always appear directly opposite the sun and they can be made not just from rain but also from any type of water in the air. If you've ever stood next to a waterfall or somewhere where there's a lot of spray on a sunny day you've probably noticed rainbows or whilst playing with the hosepipe in the garden.

The colour spectrum of the rainbow is continuous and any bands perceived by us are due to human colour vision. No coincidence then that the colour of the human eye the same part which also controls the pupil and therefore how much light we see is known as the iris, after the Greek rainbow Goddess. The word spectrum comes from the Latin meaning "apparition". The spectrum of the rainbow meaning the colours that "appear" or are visible to us within the rainbow. The most commonly used sequence of colours seen by the human eye in the rainbow are those described by Sir Isaac Newton, who numbered them seven which would have been logical to his day as science continued to use the ancient Greek Sophists classical system of natural history, the "Symbola", whereby all things under heaven are ascribed to sevenfold categories arranged by planetary correspondence.

In his optical experiment Newton shone a narrow beam of sunlight through a prism to produce a rainbow band of colours on the wall. It was his observation of these colours that then defined his colour spectrum. Originally in 1672 he divided the spectrum into five main colours: red, yellow, green, blue and violet. Later he included orange and indigo, giving seven main colours by analogy to the number of notes in a musical scale. He writes:

"The originall or primary colours are Red, yellow, Green, Blew, & a violet purple; together with Orang, Indico, & an indefinite varietie of intemediate gradations."

He then linked the colours to the seven notes of the western major scale with orange and indigo as semitones.

Whilst Newton's definition of the colour spectrum is red, orange, yellow, green, blue, indigo and violet it is common on more modern colour wheels that some choose not to include indigo as it is a tertiary colour whilst the others are primary or secondary as a result of their blending. It has also been suggested that the colour Newton has described as indigo is in fact deep blue and that the colour described as blue is the blue-green-turquoise colour called cyan. However you choose to divide the colours they all come first and foremost as a combination of all the colours from the "clear" or "white" light of their original source, sunlight.

Whenever we talk about the rainbow, or about white light, the light we are talking about is just one kind of electromagnetic energy which is made by up and down wave shaped patterns of electricity and magnetism racing along at the speed of light, which is four hundred times around the world in a minute. Making up this pattern is wavelength, which is the distance between successive crests of a wave, and frequency which can be understood as the number of waves in a given period of time or how compact the wave crests are. The visible light spectrum for humans goes from red, which is the lowest frequency and the longest wavelength our eyes can see, to violet which is the highest frequency and shortest wavelength our eyes can see, i.e. things that transmit a lot of light are high frequency, high pitch and high vibration and things that transmit very little or less light are low frequency, low pitch and low vibration. This principle can also be applied spiritually speaking when we talk about light beings, angels and even people who also have a frequency or vibration. In everyday speech we refer to someone's vibe.

Other types of electromagnetic energy which are not visible to us include infrared, radio waves, x-rays, gamma waves and microwaves. Light waves and these other types of energy that radiate make up the electromagnetic spectrum. We know that there are other living creatures that can see some of these other types of energy such pigeons, who can see magnetic fields and many insects that see ultraviolet colours. There are also different forms of this wave energy transfer which are not seen but are sensed by hearing or sensation. The other lower octave of energy waves well known to humans are sound waves and Sir Isaac Newton and others have attempted to correlate the two phenomena by ascribing pitch to colour. Newton's original correlations are Red – Do, Orange – Re, Yellow – Mi, Green – Fa, Blue – Sol, Indigo – La, Violet – Ti. This is interesting magically speaking as it suggests possible lower octaves of colours at frequencies we cannot hear and higher octaves of colours at frequencies we cannot hear producing duller or brighter tones. In the same way as black and white may have yin or yang positive or negative attributes so too it would seem can colours when they are representative of different types of energy.

These colours also correspond with the energetic systems of the body known as chakras which we will cover in greater detail later. Red being the root at the base of the spine dropping down into black beneath the feet, the primordial darkness corresponding to Earth and ascending through red and the rainbow of colours to violet at the crown rising into clear white light at source above the head. The light and the dark ultimately terminals and both the same source of creation where all originates.

The usual colours of the rainbow spectrum are a pure spectra meaning that they include all those that can be produced by the visible light of a single wavelength only and not variable ones. The table below shows the approximate frequencies in terahertz and wavelengths in nanometers for a pure colour spectrum. Colour spectra may vary across cultures and time periods, in the case of the chart below the colours are a little different to the Newtonian description, for example, Newton may well have described the deep blue colour as indigo because indigo dye was the most common and readily available pigment of his time which he would have seen regularly and he may have described the cyan as blue likening it to sky blue. In fact it would make sense because we all use things in our immediate environment as descriptive adjectives of a thing.

Colours	Wavelength Interval	Frequency Interval
Red	~ 700–635 nm	~ 430–480 THz
Orange	~ 635–590 nm	~ 480–510 THz
Yellow	~ 590–560 nm	~ 510–540 THz
Green	~ 560–520 nm	~ 540–580 THz
Cyan	~ 520–490 nm	~ 580–610 THz
Blue	~ 490–450 nm	~ 610–670 THz
Violet	~ 450–400 nm	~ 670–750 THz

The first, third and fifth colours of the rainbow are primary colours, red, yellow and blue and the first, third and fifth notes of a major scale form a major chord, the root, third and fifth. What this means is that when we combine physics, optics, light, sight, sound, hearing, art and music and ascribe colour to pitch if it were possible to hear the high frequencies of light waves we would experience the primary colours as a major chord.

Primary colours are major chords within the scale and one rainbow spectrum is an octave.

Red	Orange	Yellow	Green	Blue	Indigo	Violet
Root	Second	Third	Fourth	Fifth	Sixth	Seventh

These colours of light waves have a specific pattern of movement with particular characteristics and behaviours and light itself is "something" in that these waves of electromagnetic radiation behave by hitting things and reflecting, refracting and so on. Darkness then is the absence of the presence of that type of electromagnetic radiation or the contrast when out of reach of those light waves. Dark or light can also be used to describe the reflectivity of an object. Light-coloured objects reflect a lot of the light that hits them and dark coloured objects absorb a lot of the light that hits them, usually turning it into warmth. Between the extremities of light and dark are multiple other colours and shades of grey and these absorb some spectra of light and reflect others. We see the colour that is not absorbed and is therefore reflected back by the object, for an example an orange absorbs everything except orange. There are also fluorescents, which absorb certain spectra and transform them into others, which they then emit. Where the division of white light through the prism brings all the colours of the rainbow to the hands of the artist their re-blending through the use of paint in any combination of the same colours renders limitless combinations of colourful greys and darks and includes the return to apparent black.

The Sun itself is actually dark on the surface in the reflective sense, meaning that it would absorb the light that hits it but it appears light because it emits vast amounts of light waves. The Moon, however, is light in the reflective sense and we can only see it because it reflects the sun's light to us. It is dark in that it emits no light of its own. In a way it could be said that there is no such thing as total darkness in this universe because somewhere there is always light. It is a necessary fact of creation. My friend would regularly remind me that just because we couldn't see it here, it didn't mean the sun wasn't shining somewhere else! Ultimately light and dark are one from one source and one creation and any illusion we have of duality in black, white, grey scale or multi-colour is fantasy for whilst life in three-dimensional existence is of necessary poles it is still all the same creation. "All is one when nought has passed".

It could be argued that the primordial existence came from the dark and yet even then the word primordial comes from the latin *primordialis* meaning first of all or *primordius* meaning original. Both words signify a first, an origin i.e. creation. In short light may exist without darkness for it lacks nothing, it is not missing anything. Light may even create shadow. However darkness may only exist with light, for it is by its nature the absence of light. Darkness despite being a necessary part of all creation is not truly a thing on its own as such. For it can only ever exist in duality. There is not enough darkness in the world to put out the light of a single candle. Understanding this in a wider context, all is light and all is one from one source. All else is the absence of that one source.

There are many things that can transpire in the creation of a rainbow. For example the number of coloured bands in a rainbow may actually be different from the number of bands in a spectrum, especially if the droplets of water forming it are particularly large or small. Rainbows do not exist at one particular location; rather many rainbows exist simultaneously. However, only one can be seen depending on the viewpoint of the observer in relation to the droplets of light illuminated by the sun. Theoretically all rainbows are circular but from the ground usually only half a rainbow, an arch is seen. Sometimes light is refracted and reflected and reflected again within a drop of water and this double reflection creates a second rainbow above the first in reverse colour order. The secondary rainbow is fainter than the first one because more light is escaping from two reflections rather than one. Each rainbow reflects white light inside its coloured bands and has a dark area of unlit sky lying between the primary and secondary bows.

Twinned rainbows are different from double rainbows of concentric arches because they form from one single base and appear as two rainbow arcs split from one place. The colours of the second bow appear in the same order as the first. They are rare and their creation is caused by different sizes of water droplets from two different rain showers combined with some flattening from air pressure as the drops fall from the sky. When two rain showers with different-sized raindrops merge, they both produce slightly different rainbows and the two rainbows may combine and form a twinned rainbow that meets in the middle.

Reflected rainbows may appear on the surface of water below the horizon for example on a lake or in puddles. When this happens the raindrops deflect the sunshine and then reflect it off the body of water. In addition to common primary and secondary rainbows it is possible for rainbows of higher orders to form. The order of a rainbow is decided by the number of reflections of light inside the water drops that have created it and these internal reflections can create supernumerary rainbows, also sometimes called stacker rainbows. These are rare and consist of several faint rainbows on the inner side of the primary rainbow and sometimes also on the outer side of the secondary rainbow. They are slightly detached and have pastel-coloured bands that do not fit the usual pattern. More internal reflections can cast bows of infinitely higher orders. The rainbow sometimes seen around the Moon is called a moonbow and whilst many perceive them to be white or monochrome the full spectrum is there and some people can see all the colours. Long exposure photography can also capture this. It's also one of the times we get to see the whole circle and not just the arch.

The light of a rainbow is thought of as a blessing in many cultures and water that has been collected from, in or under a rainbow is considered as containing the magical potential of the rainbow. Even in modern western culture and films children are taught to make wishes upon a rainbow though the origins of this thinking is far more ancient. In beginning to understand the rainbow we see the forces of fire and water that sustain life and the colours made by their energy, frequency and vibration. By studying the rainbow we may begin to grasp the secrets of the universe in a visible way. By looking to the sky we see magic and alchemy in the rainbow, the place where heaven and earth seem to meet and by looking inside us to our inner rainbow of chakras which balance in the heart we see in our earthly reflection the point where heaven and earth meet in us and where we are open to alchemy.

Suggested Exercise

Spend some time painting or drawing the rainbow. It can be a great way to connect us with the heavens and open up our own magical qualities. It can also be really good for rebalancing the chakra system as well as being fun. If painting isn't for you try writing about the rainbow or better still making a rainbow with water spray on a sunny day.

Chapter Four
Relationship with Life Rituals

Finding Magic and Beauty in the Mundane.

The word "ritual" derives from the Latin *ritualis,* "that which pertains to rite" and is defined by the Oxford dictionary as a religious or solemn ceremony consisting of a series of actions performed according to a prescribed order.

Having begun our journey simply by becoming clearer about our personal beliefs and identifying areas of natural interest to us in developing a foundation we now look to the ceremony that is life. By looking at our life ceremony we will likely find that there is ritual in a myriad of the ways in which we live. By recognising these simple rituals for what they are we bring consciousness and awareness into daily aspects of living and we take our first footsteps towards initiation. Not that everything in life should be solemn at all or anything of the sort, in fact living lightly and with joy and gratitude for life is far more important.

By participating and creating ritual in our lives we develop a deeper relationship with nature and consequently with spirit. Everything we do takes on new meaning and greater significance. Giving thanks for food or thought to where it came from, the cleaning of our homes and meeting of our obligations, the laying of a fire and gathering of wood, these are all ritualistic and part of our ceremony. When we count the blessings and see the ceremony of setting aside allotments of time for a specific purpose such as bathing or the family meal where we come to talk and eat together with the people we love, this is part of our ceremony. Drinking tea with friends, playing music or singing or picking fruit to make jam can be part of the prayer when done with love! Finding the joy within simple things in daily life can also become ritual when we apply our minds to it. Many of these things are just normal and mundane but it is in the small things and the way in which we think of them, honour and observe them that can change them into what may be considered ritual.

Primarily by its nature this book's focus is the workings of magic, its components, framework and application. In order to access the full potential of this it is necessary that we first remind ourselves that our physical lives need be supportive to the purpose and that the two parts are one whole, which must be considered as such in a holistic view. We cannot work effective ritual magic and be out of touch with daily ritual and the magic already infused in life. That would be silly! Or incongruous at least. The river which is spirit runs across from one shore to the other and the rainbow bridge might only be ascended in arc when both are in balance.

The term ritual in the magical sense can cover many aspects. Both the simple and clearly held intention as we light a candle and ask for guidance or healing and the more elaborate workings of a ceremony can both be thought of as ritual. The workings of a ceremony for example may be far more intricate and involve the planning and co-ordinating of many correspondences and alignments to support our purpose. Yet this is still ritual. We will look in more depth over the coming chapters at a number of the individual components that make up ritual such as consideration of natural laws, archetypes, planetary aspects and natural rhythms and cycles.

Magic is all about influencing probabilities and situations so that they may manifest in a way favourable to our purpose, (our purpose aligned with love and spirit). Slight alterations of direction can have great consequences. These may be brought about because of divine intervention having aligned with good forces, angels or nature or as a result of asking or praying for help. They may be as a result of focussing our wills to alter the course of events. They may be the result of focussing our intentions clearly thereby bringing them about through visualisation and positive action towards a desired outcome. Or they may be the result of many contributing factors working together. These are all things to be considered when it comes to ritual.

Rituals can be informal fun filled events with a large number of people such as a Beltane ceremony with fifty flaming torches to light the Beltane fire where people can bring offerings, say prayers, dance the maypole and sing together. They can also be much more serious events where there is a more set approach, everyone wears the correct dress and has a copy of the running order or a written prayer or words to read. Others still are relaxed affairs with lots of singing in harmony and loving connection within the group all chanting for peace. Each is different and unique. There are never ending variations of uniqueness, as many as the melding of any given group of souls with a purpose in any given moment. No two are ever the same and each experience seems to teach something new.

Calendar ritual events, both solar and lunar, mark the passing of time and specific times of the year. In both our observation of the changing of the seasons and our participation in our according actions we enter into basic ritual. Throughout autumn we gather wood to see us through winter and in spring we plant new crops. For the Egyptians the observation and calculation of the heliacal rising of Sirius was one of the most important rituals as its visibility preceded the Nile bursting its banks and depositing black silt on the land which was essential for growing crops and also allowed preparation for the flooding and therefore the safety of the people. As such its rising set the Sothic calendar. Summer solstice is observed all over the world in celebration of the longest day and one glance at Stonehenge the preceding night will confirm modern pagan ritual in a multitude of varying forms with drumming, dancing, praying and many other forms of celebration. Interestingly, Stonehenge is aligned with the winter solstice, though you won't find it as busy in midwinter as it is in midsummer. Within the aspect of magical ritual these observances of the Sun, Moon and planets are essential as they allow us to choose favourable conditions to our purpose and to work with the tide rather than against it.

The drumming and dancing of those paying their respects or in communion with the Divine is definitely also ritualistic. Morris dancing is one of the best examples I can think of that is native to this country as consisting of traditions in the representation, dress and movements of the characters. In shamanic practices the impersonation or "taking on" of a totem animal is tantamount to transformation of the shaman in search of wisdom, guidance or healing and is ritualistic, often accompanied by drumming, chanting of specific songs or words and burning of specific incense or offerings. These are all ancient in origin, as old as humanity itself you might say in that they have developed with us over time from the first self-aware men and women, at whatever stage in time that consciousness was gained and an awareness of our environment and the natural world around us. When we connect through these ancient rituals we also connect with the most ancient parts of ourselves and our instinctive nature and knowingness and an older deeper primal connection with the elements that so many of us are removed from in modern life. Since when did we need a watch to know the time when we could glance at the sky and know it!

This deep knowingness runs through us as ancient as the stars and as new as the first light of the sun. It is inherent within us. Some call this the wild one. Before the layers of social conditioning, education and society beyond our immediate tribal and family groups there was only instinct and a direct communion with natural forces. When we acknowledge and thereby awaken this powerful connection within ourselves we empower ourselves by stepping into our fullness and bringing self-awareness to the sacred wild one.

The personification of one of these wild primal forces is the Archetypal Crone aspect of the Goddess who stirs her cauldron deep in the earth and sings things with resonance into being. Every one of us knows her buried somewhere deep inside us and connected to the core of our being. Sometimes we feel her stirring that cauldron when we look to the dark night sky; we feel her when we intuitively have knowing and follow a course of action from deep inside our being; we hear her song in our subconscious moments of wisdom.

An archetype is a psychic prototype or form within the collective unconscious which allows ordering of perceptions into meaningful patterns. All of us inherit the same archetypes, the same invisible patterns built into the structure of the human psyche and they manifest in personal and cultural experiences. Other examples include the Hero, the Divine Child, the Great Mother which might be seen as another name for the Crone aspect, Transformation, Death, and Rebirth. They manifest in myths, dreams, tribal lore, fairy tales, visions, scientific advances, numbers, religions and philosophies. Consciousness itself is organised by its archetypal forms and foundations.

In a religious context there are many indoctrinated forms of ritual. These rites are an outwards physical sign of a spiritual gift or grace, which may be bestowed upon those participating such as the Eucharist (Holy Communion) in the Catholic Church. The Eucharist is essentially a re-enactment of the Last Supper celebrated at daily Mass with the set words spoken in Latin to consecrated bread and wine, whereby through the power of Holy Spirit the bread and wine is said to *become* the body of Christ. This is otherwise known as Transubstantiation. In this context it is interesting to note the similarity here to an earlier Egyptian rite where the priests would consecrate bread said to be the body of Osiris in celebration of his resurrection.

Both feasting and fasting may be incorporated into ritual and these often have their foundations in tradition. The Jewish Passover, Pesach, is one of many of these examples and is steeped in both tradition and ritual from the observation of the date and time (sunset on the 14th of Nissan) for a set period of time of usually seven days. The day of the 14th is one of fasting called the fast of the first born which commemorates the salvation of the first-born. On this day any leaven bread is removed from the home as only unleavened bread may be eaten during this period. Lamb is often used as an offering symbolic of the sacrificial lamb in the temple. This is later eaten at the Seder feast at sunset which is a meal and gathering with detailed preparation of every aspect including the food, table setting, candles etc. and fifteen separate parts are observed with the correct blessings and prayers read from the Torah and spoken at each in turn in order. Seder means order. This is also a good example of the recitation of fixed texts to be spoken or sang in ritual combined with formal rules of behaviour for the participants and observations.

Rituals are often a way of expressing reverence for a deity or that which is perceived to be divine and are also a way of entering a state of grace with or from the divine. Certain words or gestures combined with images, objects and traditions form the components of ritual. Prayer is amongst these, as is the repeating of mantra. Through the repetitious uttering of prayer or mantra a meditative trance like concentration or elevated state can be achieved and when this is done either in an allotted or designated time or place, or in conjunction with set movements, it may be considered ritualistic especially for example if it is combined with the burning of incense which is deliberately chosen to enhance the experience. The choosing of which words, in either mantra or prayer, are themselves of great importance as the repetition of them by so many souls over sometimes hundreds or thousands of years sanctifies them further. Perhaps this is because of the will of each person who has ever uttered them and therefore the finite amount of belief that has been placed in them, or perhaps it is because of the devotion shown in a thousand-year-old prayer. It could be considered that with such belief over time the words become stronger and as such gather momentum or could be said to have the effect of amplification in their speaking or chanting. The Hindu Gayatri mantra comes to mind as an example.

Images too form such an important part of both magic and ritual. Images are seen both by the imagination, which could be perceived to be the ideas of the divine, expressed internally to us through our third or inner eye and by our physical eyes with which we see the outward world around us. Both these forms of images, internal and external, have the ability to express or represent magical information and experience to us by interacting with one another. Thus what we see outwardly may affect our internal reality and what we see internally may be reflected and reproduced into a physical or tangible representation of it, which we may then use in meditation to gain deeper understanding or within a ritual where we wish to convey these thoughts in another form suited to the purpose or to another person.

The use of specially prepared food such as the water, corn, fruit and meat within some types of Native American tobacco ceremonies is another aspect of ritual. Wine is usual in many different cultures globally and although less commonly, so are different types of plant medicines. These plants whilst they may be considered by some to be drugs in the Western sense of the word are thought of as sacred and central to shamanic healing and journeying in the societies from where they originate and are generally treated respectfully and not recreationally which is an illness of the West primarily. Examples are ayahuasca from the Amazon, various types of hallucinogenic mushrooms in many different cultures and mescaline cacti like san pedro and peyote. These plant medicines are used to experience altered states of consciousness and perspective within a shamanistic ritual setting and spiritual experience to gain wisdom, understanding, healing and or guidance. Traditionally they may only be given by the shaman or medicine woman/man in their tradition to those who come to them for healing or to hold ceremony. Regarding the use of these plant medicines in Western practices or in any way that is out of keeping with their tradition is not likely to yield the same experience because the plants have a connection with the landscape as well as the culture from which they originate. Removing them is like removing the context unless they are used in the correct tradition.

Interestingly a huge percentage of pharmaceuticals, which are far more common in the West originate in rainforest plants. The shamans of the Amazon believe that for every human ailment the rainforests hold a cure. So far approximately only one percent of all rainforest plants have been studied and sadly we are constantly losing valuable healing plants at a fast rate as the rain forests are cut down and destroyed by unethical and unscrupulous profiteers. Conservation of our earth really is the most important thing we can do for humanity and for all the species dependent upon us to protect them and stop harming their world too. Almost all medicine is in fact developed from or extracted from plants and those that are not are engineered to mimic them or specific parts of the plant in some way.

For anyone learning, to hold sacred space takes practice and sustained concentration, which could be unstable under the influence so to speak whether that influence is a strong painkiller or too much wine. Generally in Western traditions drinking alcohol is avoided until after the working has taken place except as an offering or in celebration of a sabbat ritual. Clarity of thought, stability and un-compromised ability is essential. We always joke that if you couldn't drive the car legally you have no right to be in charge of a wand!

The use of objects in ritual can play an important part or be the focal point in some cases as in the case of an idol or statuette of a God/Goddess. Examples are seen in the fertility Goddess figurines found in numerous cultures globally, which were often used in ritualistic behaviour in homes and in ceremony. These fertility Goddesses were used as a connection to the energetic forces or Goddess they personified and often the parts of the body associated with fertility such as the rounded stomach, full breasts, genitalia or generous hips are emphasised. It is commonly thought they were used in rites to call forth physical fertility for a woman or a couple or used in a community to call forth fertility of the land hence their association with bountiful crops and a successful harvest. One of the oldest and most famous examples of this is the Venus of Willendorf of the Upper Palaeolithic period dating to around 28,000–25,000 BCE currently on display in the Ashmolean Museum in Oxford. Interesting to note that in all cultures around the world for thousands of years the figure of woman and the Goddess has reverently been one of rounded curves and it is only since the two world wars and in recent times that Western culture has moved away from this image of desirable femininity.

Healing has many different places and forms in ritual. There were healing shrines in ancient Greece where a practice known as incubation took place, whereby a person would go to the shrine and perform a ritual before sleeping in the sacred place. This was done with the intention of receiving a dream from the divine which in turn may heal them.

Ritual has long been used alongside medicine in numerous cultures and the invocation of certain deities. To the Egyptians, Thoth was central to medicine because of his role as God of writing, wisdom and balance. The son of Apollo, Asclepius, represented the healing aspect of the medical arts to the Greeks and Romans.

The collecting and preparation of herbs may also be seen as ritualistic. In this country druidic custom was to collect St John's Wort at midsummer on the summer solstice. The reason for this was to gain the strength of the height of the Sun and for the plant to be imbued with the maximum amount of light possible to be stored for future use. Its astrological correspondence is logically also to the Sun and it was used to aid positive mental health brought by sunshine. With its bright yellow flowers and its uplifting properties St John's Wort was used to treat depression and it is still widely used today for the same purpose.

Purification rituals can vary massively and yet have similarities in principle from bathing before carrying out spell work or entering sacred space (with particular attention paid to the hair, head and feet as our physical terminals and those most likely to "hold" anything we might wish to remove), to baptisms performed in Christianity and submergence in blessed water, to making the sign of the cross with fingers dipped in holy water in the Catholic Church or to Buddhist ablutions prior to entering the temple. Certainly the UK is covered in holy springs and wells named after early Christian saints who often had roots stretching further back in antiquity into the pagan pre-Christian past. The Goddess Brigit, Brigid (exalted one) is one such example who in the medieval period was synchronised with the saint of the same name and said to share her attributes as the patroness of healing, poetry and smith craft. Both the Goddess and the saint are associated with sacred flames and with holy wells at Kildare in Ireland and in other places. Blessed water sources such as wells or springs are often associated with both healing and purification and pilgrimage may be made to these seeking either. In Native American traditions there are ceremonies of "going to water".

Purification rituals and recommended plants for the purposes of cleansing sometimes also mention exorcism in various listings of plant properties. Exorcism really just means to banish. Exorcism is the practice of banishing or evicting anything evil or lower frequency from a person or place and there are numerous examples of this practice from around the world although how such a thing is perceived or dealt with varies widely in approach. A plant listed as exorcistic may also be used in any clearing or cleaning of a place or thing and to remove negative or destructive forces or heavy residual energy. The revised Catholic rite of exorcism now says that priests who conduct exorcisms should deal with evil as a force lurking within all individuals, rather than one that threatens people from without. Shamanistic practices tend to see such things as external entities. However, they also consider that not all entities which cause possession are necessarily evil and that in contrast there are many who are benevolent and are here to teach or help or bring a message, healing or personal transformation to the person they inhabit. It should also be noted that not all shamanistic paths are aligned with love; some are and some are not. Many plants listed for this purpose are great for clearing energy generally and there is no need to feel fearful should you see exorcism written as a description of a plants properties. It just means it is a plant that is highly effective at cleansing and clearing a space.

As a side note regarding places that may be haunted, many of these places are not necessarily haunted by anything evil at all, these may just be spirits who happen to be there minding their own business and who want to be left in peace, or spirits who have something unresolved which needs resolution or loved ones they are watching over from the earth plane before they choose to leave. In these cases exorcism is not appropriate and there are much gentler ways to proceed. Indeed in many cases there is a perfectly good explanation physical or otherwise and the first part of our job is to look for one before eliminating it and considering other possibilities. Where possible leave spirits to "rest in peace". It is a sign of respect.

Protection both physically and psychologically from harm or intended harm are the focus of many rituals. The prayer said each night is a ritual. The rowan cross tied with red ribbon over doorways, or the horseshoe for luck, the dream catcher, planting rosemary which is the plant of Archangel Michael and the wearing of symbols or talisman in jewellery are all protective acts. House blessings are rituals designed specifically for this purpose and we will look both at protection and an example of a house blessing in more detail later. Housewarmings too are a kind of ritual, a welcoming of our friends and lives into our new home.

It is usual and customary in some rituals to make offerings to praise, please or placate in some cases. These offerings may be food or drink appropriate to the ritual, a physical item such as a crystal or piece of jewellery or gold, feathers or something of natural beauty, a poem or written prayer or incense made with care for the purpose.

Birth brings ritual in the form of baptism or naming ceremonies usually connected with entering a religion or spiritual path and concerned with the guidance and protection of the child both physically and spiritually by the appointing of additional guardians. Blessed water is the most common denominator across cultures for these practices in combination with recitation of words written for the responsibilities assumed by the parents, guardians and faith.

Marriages and hand-fastings too have ritual similarities and the origins of these are to be found in Ancient Egypt where wedding rings were first woven. Around 3,000 BCE the Egyptian phrase "without beginning, without end" came into common usage for describing the wedding ring. The ring placed on the finger is the circle with no beginning or end and the symbol of eternity and the hole in the centre might be seen as a gateway or door leading to events both known and unknown. There is similarity here in the ring with the magic circle cast or drawn in the earth around the couple in some pagan practices. The union of the couple is one not just with each other but with the Divine until such time as death returns them. Whist there may be an eternal natural connection and recognition between two souls who were once married in a life it might be unwise to deliberately ask for eternity! This may also include the making of soul pacts or karmic agreements knowingly with another in a magical context. It raises questions about the practicalities of future incarnations, shared karmic paths, individual progression of either soul and any further experiences needed by either soul independently of the other. Till death us do part is the usual way of things and the natural state of all life.

Coming of age in other cultures may once well have been the leaving of the village as a boy to hunt and to spend a fixed period of time alone, around or after puberty, before returning as a man to the tribe. Upon return a celebratory ritual or ceremony took place welcoming the boy into manhood. Puberty is often the defining time from childhood into adult in many cultures. Coming of age ceremonies in Japan have become a current custom on the second Monday of January and are celebrated to mark the age of majority, twenty. The ceremony may also act as a way of self-acknowledgement and effecting the change into adulthood. Most coming of age ceremonies in this country likely involve alcohol and celebration. A modern day example is the father who takes his son to the pub on his eighteenth birthday.

Whilst legally in this country coming of age is eighteen some consider that it is magically speaking twenty-one. These twenty-one years make up three stages each of seven years that need to come about before adulthood and basic personal responsibility are generally understood and the young adult is able to hold their own space and know their own mind. Some astrologers say there is a fourth set of seven years and that it is only at age twenty-eight or twenty-nine years old, upon experiencing our first Saturn return within our astrological birth chart that we truly develop into a new stage of adulthood. This occurs when Saturn returns to the point in the sky that it was at, at the time of our birth, and is said to bring with it a new maturity with each cycle. With the exception of low key celebrations such as sabbats it is not unusual to have a minimum age of twenty-one within magic circles in order that everyone present is emotionally and psychologically mature enough for the work to be undertaken. Celebrations are of course a different matter and likely to be open events without circle castings necessarily taking place. Up until this age a person may also be seen spiritually as a minor in some instances in karmic terms when it comes to matters of distinction between actions which have been consciously and intentionally carried out or those which have been done in the naivety of youth without full understanding. That being said this age threshold is a product of our time and culture and no doubt is variable in different places.

Death and burial each have their own ceremonies and customs in all cultures. The Tibetan Buddhists often choose sky burial which involves being laid out to rest after death with prayers and blessings at high altitude for carrion to eat the body thus returning to the earth. Viking burials involved bringing the things required with the spirit of the person into the other world and crossing water in a boat which was then set alight. Saxon burials were generally in the earth though similar in preparation with the adornments of station in earthly life and any offerings and tools perceived as necessary to continuation into the next world. The funerary pyre features prominently across the world as means of leaving this realm for the next. In the case of Ancient Egypt the preservation of the body and correct ritual of funerary text and offerings for the various nine parts and soul was observed before burial in catacombs, pyramid or earth. In all cases there are preparations made, a focus upon the elements and return to them and a concept of continuation of the spirit or soul into the other or another existence.

Commemoration ceremonies for the dead are also inherent across humanity. Festivals such as the Mexican Dia de Los Muertos on the 31st October celebrate, honour and remember the deceased. The 31st October is also the Gaelic festival of Samhein which marks the midway point between the autumn equinox and winter solstice and it is traditionally also considered a liminal time when the veil between the worlds is thin and we might connect with the dead and remember them. It is also in Samhein that we find the origins of dressing up in robes and disguising at this time of year in the modern day trick or treating. Correct dress, disguise or specific robes are something to be considered with all ritual and looking over the examples already given each will have its symbolic or associated choice of clothing. Initiation into spiritual groups or marking the path or development stages of an individual may also be cause for ritual and ceremony.

One foot in front of the other as we softly tread our way across the ground of the rituals in our lives and recognise their meanings we learn and find we have likely already wandered towards our first footsteps of initiation and we may now see that we are on a path of our creation.

Suggested Exercise – Finding the Rituals and Counting the Blessings

Sitting somewhere comfortable where you can write easily light a candle if you feel to.

Add to your journal or book of shadows/illuminations a list of at least ten rituals that are a significant part of your life and consider how they support you.

By recognising where they are, what things bring us comfort or are an essential part of our day we can develop them and become more aware of how and when we connect with spirit in our lives. We can also see all the ways that we are already being supported.

Write a further list of twenty blessings or good things in life.

Now draw a large circle and put your name in the middle. Around the outside of the circle write the names of all the people in your life to be thankful for.

We often feel richer and more supported and held when we take the time to notice all the things and people in our lives.

Ritual Check List

Some basic factors to take into consideration when preparing the ground work for a ceremony or ritual. These pointers are for clarifying the intention when it comes to writing or working a ritual later on in part three and are written with practical magic in mind. The clearer the intention the better!

1. What is the purpose of the ritual?

2. Which cultural background is it grounded in and who or what are you calling upon and why?

3. Is there a traditional date in this culture associated with this purpose that you could work on?

4. If not can you research auspicious and harmonious planetary correspondences and Moon phases to aid your working?

5. Is there a set text, prayer, mantra or song associated with your purpose and correct culture?

6. What about any movement, dance or music associated and of the correct culture or that feels suitable?

7. Do you need specific objects for this type of ritual and do they need preparation? What about clothing?

8. What about offerings? Are there traditional ones you can use? Or do you have something appropriate that seems perfect?

9. Do you have a place you want to visit somewhere? Or an uninterrupted space at home or outdoors?

10. Is there anything associated with self-protection from this culture or associated with this purpose that it would be wise to obtain or study first?

Chapter Five
Types of Initiation

God/Goddess is omnipresent, when we are in our hearts we remember that *Omni* includes us and all living things.

Whatever pathway we choose to follow or to learn upon, whether it is one of our own creation or one laid out before us where others have led the way, there are various degrees and stages of initiation and these are to be found throughout our life learning, rituals and personal growth. It is then not the path itself that initiates us though it may guide us into the natural phases of initiation, rather it is in our learning and study of our chosen path and our corresponding lessons in life which allow us to develop gradually with the incline or speed best suited to us.

The ultimate initiation is sometimes referred to as reaching enlightenment. In death some say that such a soul may have a choice as to whether they wish to incarnate again or not as they have learned what they needed within this arc. They may also have a choice of incarnation within further arcs of higher rainbows of existence unknown to us. For most of us we look to our first footsteps of initiation. These might be found more often than not at the point in time or evolution where the first awareness of being a soul in a body takes place. There is a shift in consciousness, an awakening, sometimes gradual and sometimes more abrupt depending upon the person and their capabilities. There is a sense of purpose or of being more somehow and we reach out to the heavens for answers. When this time comes the universe answers the call and guides us to the places, people or information needed. This is often a gentle and gradual realisation brought about by spending time in a sacred place or in nature or around someone who will discuss topics that we have previously been unaware of. It's all in the timing.

Some consider that the highest form of initiation possible is the person who is able to be his/her higher self at all times and that this can happen when the soul overrides the personality and the wants, needs or desires. It is similar to the view that we must constantly try to remain present. My own thought is that our personality is an important part of who we are and that it seems kinder and more compassionate to want to be authentic. In fact there's a ridiculousness about denying parts of ourselves and an impossibility. Aren't we trying to get more in to ourselves and not further removed from ourselves? Closer to love not further from love? It makes no sense to start by denying our humanness or by aiming for being less of ourselves. What makes more sense is loving more of ourselves, accepting more of ourselves and seeing what happens. It makes more sense that the highest form of initiation is being most deeply in ourselves. Our consciousness never leaves us. We are here where we left ourselves experiencing ourselves and life.

If divinity is inherent within us then that includes our personality and our feelings. Let our consciousness and quest for presence be answered with love and with earthy practicality that allows us to take good care of ourselves and deal with life compassionately and with good humour. When our needs are met we are happier and able to give more to others as well as allowing us the time and peace of mind to be mindful in the other aspects of our lives.

The act of taking a spiritual initiation in and of itself brings us into alignment with the path we seek because we have at a soul level affirmed our intention. This is not like being indoctrinated into a religion as a child because as an adult in full understanding this is a *choice*. Over the course of time strength of spirit and soul presence will naturally increase in the initiate. Reaching a state where we could be said to be most "in ourselves", is a gradual process because an adjustment period is needed as we tip from one side towards the other. There may otherwise be a certain amount of "turbulence" for want of a better word where the physical self and psyche are not prepared or aligned for the incoming of such force of spirit contained within the soul and so to begin with we are given a low "volume" which is increased over time, probably years or even lifetimes. This gradual and natural process cannot be rushed or even sought particularly. It is organic and probably so out of necessity. Those who have followed their path for a long time have a certain presence about them and this is something often felt by those around them and as their abilities increase so too does the volume of spirit, for the two are relational.

For most of us as we learn and aspire to this ideal on our journeys we ebb and flow and have moments or hours perhaps where our highest self is driving and we are most in ourselves, interspersed with combinations of more earthly natures or out of ourselves. A seemingly peaceful and mindful morning can for most of us be broken by something as simple as burning the toast or dropping a glass resulting in a smash and shouting, albeit momentarily. This is human nature. This may well be a good thing as it allows us to remain grounded as we increase our capacity. We need down time and resting periods that break up the process. A friend of mine sometimes likened this to driving lessons! Over the gradual course of time under the instruction of spirit or a physical teacher or the guidance of an established path laid out before us we may be taught how to drive our own car and the need for dual controls may be lessened as the volume is increased until we are in command of said vehicle.

It is quite possible for a person one moment to be reflecting on something serious and the next moment to do something silly and be roaring with laughter and messing about. Have you ever had a fit of the giggles in church or a serious setting? In fact there's something important about that which is that it is in our humanness, our perfect imperfection, our laughter, tears and celebration that we find ourselves. We were not designed to live in a stoic or joyless way of being. We were designed to feel and see and express all in a million different ways. For most men and women it is in the un-cloistered occupations and preoccupations of daily life that we find ourselves and therefore our spirituality needs to be in tune with how we live.

Our lives can only be our ceremony when we can see the worthiness in all that we do, even when that means sitting in the laundrette and even when that means sharing a drink in the pub with our friends, even when we are covered in mud from the garden, or have paint in our hair, or we are aching and tired after a long day's work, or revelling in our sex and sexuality and finding comfort in our lover's arms. In all our humanity there is spirit. In a way these life celebrations that were always a part of the older pagan cultures got lost in patriarchal religious cultures of the time and it is only now in a more liberal and reasonable age that they may be reclaimed. Most of us live in the real world and it is in real life where we need to show up. It's in the cities and workplaces and homes that ceremony and celebration of life is needed. This is where the love is needed and where more joy and love might be found. Perhaps it is easier to be "spiritual" whilst meditating in an olive grove or on a mountain but it's not how life is. We need this ceremony to be interwoven, encompassing, accepting of our earthliness, families, lives, loves and jobs.

The other thing about the pursuit of spiritual attainment is that we are all here for different life purposes. We have different missions! It might be that Bob is here to seek enlightenment through a Buddhist path. It might be that Fred is here to invent wonderful technology but has little spiritual interest in this life. It might be that Jane is here to learn languages and study communication in many cultures and goes to a church but only at Christmas or for friends' weddings. George doesn't go at all but finds great meaning in writing poetry. The point is that we don't know what anyone else's purpose in being here is. We don't know what they're here to learn or what their experience is. The atheist and the preacher are both here learning from different viewpoints and experiencing different realities. It's subjective. In truth it just doesn't matter what anyone else is doing. When we see others with understanding and compassion then it's likely that we will see the worth in what they are here to do and it will be obvious that Fred's technology is going to help thousands of people and that's what he's busy doing; that Jane will translate operas bringing joy and artistic beauty to many and that Mike is in apparent turmoil because it's a path to healing and this is just his process even if it's not immediately visible. Love and kindness changes how the world looks. Everything is about context and when we see our lives in the context of evolution through lifetimes or even as a species it becomes clear that diversity is a deliberate and necessary part of the weave.

When we stop comparing ourselves to others and love ourselves enough to be free of that mindset, we blossom. Comparison and competition are unhelpful and unhealthy because they undermine us. When we let go of them we remember that we are each already beautiful and fine just how we are, divine in origin and able to shine. Empowered, happy, loving people empower and encourage others around them. We are all unique and have a soul purpose and life plan and a message or something we are bringing to the world. When we step into our purpose we can see this. No one else on planet Earth can complete our life purpose except us. We are all needed. It's all hands on deck!

Within our lives so far we have already learned many life lessons and developed valuable skills which might be considered as individual initiations of a kind. It may be that life has brought us the opportunity to learn unconditional love with our child, or patience listening to a colleague, or understanding and compassion for animals, and these have been a part of our development. Difficulties and sadness in life, which we have overcome or grown from, may too have been a necessary part of our learning. In terms of

65

practical aspects of magic perhaps we have developed our tarot reading abilities, studied cultures and religions or learned about the healing properties of plants. These are initiations of sorts too, lessons and skills of another kind.

Magical initiation is the threshold and the doorway inward, for the only way out is in! It is the beginning of understanding and the beginning of a new phase of the journey. It marks a stepping up into oneself and into light whist simultaneously dropping down deeper into oneself to shine that light upon the shadows. It brings consciousness to the unconscious and awareness to the unaware and it does this by degrees. The point of initiation marks a point in time and as a stage of learning reached by an individual on their chosen path. Initiation in a magical sense is a formal recognition and an agreement reached between the individual and spirit. In itself it could be thought of as a promise, dedication or agreement with divinity to a chosen path through study, personal development and further commitment. It is above all else a soul choice to evolve. It could also perhaps be thought of as the universe becoming conscious of itself through the incarnated soul of an individual.

Everyone is different but it is usual to have a learning or study period of around three years before taking this step. In truth it takes three years generally to gain an understanding of a path, to consider what initiation means personally and to study the subjects needed in order to reach a stage of development where we are ready. If three years seems a long time please consider that many degrees are longer and this is of much greater significance. When that point in time comes that the student initiate is ready and secure on their path there is what can often best be described as a natural convergence of the internal trinity i.e. the physical, psychological and spiritual aspects of the individual are in alignment with each other and with spirit. This convergence, this balancing and meeting point of all then is the point of initiation and is usually accompanied by a real sense of knowing and recognition. This moment may also be marked with an initiation ritual or ceremony of some kind.

Initiation marks the *beginning* of the path and is not an aim in itself really. Any title attached to the degree of study achieved as an initiate is an honour that is a side effect so to speak and not the thing that is to be worked towards. Of course it's a nice thing to acknowledge where we are and one another's achievements but ultimately this is between us and God/Goddess regardless of what may or may not be sewn upon our robes. Whatever was sewn there was after all only put there in honour of service. Likewise the obtaining of any physical rank is not in itself always accurate as to correspondence of initiation at soul or spirit level. With this in mind it can definitely be said that self-initiation or dedication is as significant and worthwhile as any performed by a coven or lodge, in that ultimately it is only the soul of the individual which has the free will to make such a promise or commitment and that there is in any case no cheating of the Divine. Ultimately the ascending path will be achievable by our own efforts and the will to do so. Whilst this book is written as a guide it may be that some who read this have already studied for years and are ready now and have chosen this book for that reason. It may be that this really is the first introduction and that more time is needed to develop a path. The heart knows and the individual soul knows the way.

There are as many right paths of initiation as there are individuals seeking spiritual advancement in as much as each person's journey may vary in experience even for two souls sharing the same route. As in life the well-trodden pathways by those who have gone before through one religion or system often seem the kinder and more likely to lead to the desired destination whereas the less trodden pathway may meander, come to a halt or eventually lead to a better-trodden path. That is for each of us to find in our own ways as we will. It is said amongst many that the God or Goddess chooses us in any case and not the other way around. We each find our way.

The Initiations and the Inner Reflections of the God/Goddess

Magically the internal trinity can be likened to the trinity of Jungian psychology where there is frequent reference to the idea of the aspects of the self. Three of these aspects that we can all identify with are those of the highest self in alignment with spirit, the mother or father self who runs our day to day affairs and the inner child who feels and experiences with innocence. All these aspects have lessons for us and all are sacred and worthy of consideration and respect. Only when all of the parts of us are loved and listened to is it likely that we will find balance and that they will all function well together. Devoting ourselves to our psychic well-being, emotional health and balance is the foundation and the key to all else that may follow. Opening up our internal dialogue and working with all the aspects of ourselves will likely over time bring into alignment any lower parts with our highest selves. We can learn to love the wonky or confused parts of ourselves that might not have had the time they needed before. Eventually then over time it may be that our higher consciousness through our inner connections will be in the driving seat. Note here that when the mother or father or the inner child parts of the psyche are referred to as the lower parts their importance is not to be diminished for each part is an essential part of the whole. In the macrocosm these three parts could be seen as reflections of the maiden, mother and crone or the son, father/God force and elder/spirit and it is in these three parts that we may look for natural initiations of each.

The Maiden Goddess and the Son God

The reflections of the archetypal maiden and son are to be seen in the inner child. This part of ourselves is youthful, boundless, unspoiled, innocent and wide eyed to the beauty of all around us. He/She meets the world with wonder and joy, with natural fascination and enthusiasm. Here is the playful, loving essence untainted, unrefined and unrestricted by the confines of society who feels without censorship, sometimes talks without censorship, has a natural sense of fairness and can be both the most loving and perhaps the most unreasonable aspect on occasion. Here too is often the seat of any deep and old emotional healing connected to safety, security, family relationships and how we sit in relation to others within groups with which we identify, personal identity, owning ourselves and our personal power and anything related to instinct. These things can surface within us in all manner of ways usually as unchecked emotions or unquestioned thought processes driving our actions at least until the point where we question and rebalance them. The correspondence in the body is with the base and sacral chakras (red and orange).

The initiations of the inner child reflect the lessons of the Maiden Goddess and the youthful Son God and are to be found in self-discovery and discovery of the world, creative aspects, matters of illusion, lack of worries, gaining independence and self-responsibility. The maiden/son archetypes are both about emergence and the first stirrings of awakening, new life, renewal and growth and the process from the darkness into spring both seasonally and in life in their respective ways. Only when we address them and secure our foundations and do the necessary work in these corresponding lower chakras of the body and centred around our emergence and awakening to personal responsibility and the eventual removing of that which is illusory do we obtain a steady platform. Speaking in terms of the practical aspects of magic there is a focus upon being accountable for one's actions and any consequences thereof, holding space and appropriate boundaries and the fundamental deepest connections to nature.

Interestingly these three phases of the self do not necessarily develop in order or proportionally. Each path is different and tailor made to the psyche and soul development of the individual. This deep maiden/son work is often the hardest to do and for some may only be brought about when the higher aspects have progressed enough to "hold" the space needed to gain entry deep enough into the self to achieve what needs to be done. We may work the internal rainbow from the top down or from the bottom up but either way in the end the total sum needs to balance in the heart.

The Mother Goddess and Father God

The aspects of the archetypal Mother Goddess and Father God run our daily lives and the practicalities of adult existence and are to be seen in the reflections of the internal mother/father. Responsibility now extends beyond the self to encompass any children or others we have a duty to in any way. Both are sacred principles, masculine and feminine and regardless of our sex we have the facets of each. Where the mother nurtures and guides the father protects and guards. Both have gained maturity enough to recognise that nurturing, guidance, protection and guardianship of the self is key and that whilst some sacrifices may be made for others on occasion this is done in a considered and balanced way without undue detriment to the well-being of the self. The natural inclination to preserve and protect our children may be the only exception but even then it is necessary for them that we are balanced and healthy first for how else can we take care of them? It is interesting to witness in ourselves and in others how much emotional growth and change come to those who are parents. Some of the same qualities are often found in those who are aunts or uncles, who have professions in teaching or medical roles or other familial relationships and any in which responsibility or care for others is highlighted.

Romantic relationships and how we are in relation to our partners are also present here, bringing with them issues of communication, boundaries, expectations and understanding. Clear communication skills generally, forward planning, meeting obligations, taking care of practicalities, action and assertiveness are also in this domain and in these is the ability to follow one's passions in life and therefore find fulfilment. Where do we shine? That's why we're here! Whilst the understanding and knowledge of what this is may come from higher up i.e. the higher self (spirit), the skills and abilities to obtain it and to live a fulfilling life lies here.

The initiations of the mother/father are found in abundance, fertility and growth, the gaining of knowledge, the pursuit of life goals and contentment when these are in balance. Sexual, psychological and emotional fulfilment and maturity is reached. They are the internal God/Goddess archetypes awakened and conscious bringing also conscientiousness and all that that implies. In terms of the wheel of the year this period covers the stirrings of summer to the ripened harvest and we like the fruit ripen our dreams made manifest, our knowledge expanded into wisdom through experience. The initiatory themes in life echo these many aspects and they can of course all be applied magically speaking too from a practical stance. Immediate thoughts of the responsibilities of working with others and any duty of care we may have to anyone to whom we may provide a service through our work comes to mind. Harmony found within ourselves and with others, healing, self-confidence and freedom are here. So too are clarity of mind and the ability to act upon it. Groundwork, preparation, practical things that need to be done and attentiveness are in this sphere. The most important of all initiatory paths are those of love and truth, both giving and receiving and the recognition of love and truth, how they may actually look and manifest when they are healthy and in balance in our lives. These are essential to magical workings for without them our workings would be hollow. The domains and associated life lessons of the mother/father God/Goddess are those of the solar plexus chakra (yellow) the heart chakra (green/pink) and the throat chakra or Akasha (blue) which is a two directionally flowing pathway of expression between the heart and the higher self.

The Crone Goddess and the Elder God

The reflections of the archetypal crone and elder are seen in the internal higher self or wise one, the calm observer and the capable practised hands of guidance and competence to navigate life's ups and downs. Great life experience has brought wisdom and insight and clarity to situations that may otherwise seem confusing or daunting. There seems to be an understanding and knowing that all things come to pass and as such the natural rise and fall of things are now integrated somehow in the way of being. There is a kind of inner grace, strength and wisdom here brought about through life lessons learned. For women that have reached the age of menopause particularly, it is here that a woman truly comes into her power as she is no longer governed by her cycle.

In all indigenous societies the crones/elders are honoured and treasured as the guardians of knowledge and the seers and their wisdom is sought out and valued. The lack of honour of the crone/elder in the West is symptomatic of our broken connection with spirit and all that is deep within being below the surface levels of existence. This crone/elder spirit whilst it may only be physically lived in those years of our life is inherent within all of us and we can tap into the deepest and highest parts of our being into the all-knowing wisdom he/she embodies. Deepest and highest is not a mistype but intentional for it is in the depths of ourselves, in the connection with the ancient wild one that we find our highest alignment with spirit and full strength of soul in the realm of the crone/elder. She/He cannot be anything less than our best and getting there will take the whole journey of our lives in becoming.

We find the corresponding aspects of the crone/elder in our highest self and inner wisdom where spirit comes down through us in the Crown chakra (violet) and the Third Eye chakra (indigo) and manifests in our mind. The pathway then from mind travels through our Throat chakra (akasha) to meet our soul sitting in the heart. This open channel of the throat is also our open channel to connect the upper and lower aspects and to express or channel spirit. It is here that opens up and pours forth sound when we chant or reverberate sound from spirit. These Third Eye and Crown chakras directly correlate to both higher self and to the crone/elder archetypes of the God/Goddess.

The crone/elder are the seat of our ancestral connections and our heritage stretching back in antiquity to the point of creation. They are the carriers of wisdom and have the gift of sight, past, present and future. They are in the song of creation itself, they are in the depths of the earth. They are time and timeless. They have knowing now beyond speculation or question and as such they are our intuition, psychic awareness and foresight. They are beyond the point of self or ego and are interconnected at a high level to all of existence. Despite the fact that this highest self is working at spirit level it is here that we travel the deepest drop inwards to our being. The inversion of the rainbow within the iris of the eye comes to mind in that when we are within the realms of indigo and violet we drop to the depths of what is ancient, universal and timeless. From the top to the bottom or the bottom to the top, still it is in the heart where we meet.

The initiations of the crone and elder are found in all of this ground and in the more practical aspects of magic that surround psychic ability, sight, observance and understanding of the natural rhythms and patterns of things, inner peace, consideration for matters of global or universal importance and all associated workings done for higher good or causes beyond the personal sphere and anything within the spheres of deep intuition and collective consciousness.

The corresponding chakras of the body have been given here for the purposes of healing work and alignment when working with some of these concepts. Please note that for each of these chakras there is more detailed and inclusive information in the chapter The Body and the Inner Rainbow.

Meditation to connect with the Crone/Elder

If you are experienced by all means meditate alone or if you are new to meditation ask a friend to read to guide you by reading the journey slowly out loud. Alternatively record yourself reading it and then play it back. Read slowly and allow yourself time to breathe.

Sitting somewhere with both feet flat on the floor and hands resting palms down on legs so as to create a closed and grounded circuit of the body get comfortable and close your eyes.

Take some deep relaxing breaths and allow yourself to drop all the surface thoughts by letting them drift from you.

Pay attention to your breath, the natural rhythm, the rise and fall of your body, the sound of it.

Feel the air on your skin, your clothing soft against you.

Notice any noises, birdsong, or anything in the background drift in and out of your awareness. Notice that you are in a safe, secure and held space.

You might want to visualise gold light around the perimeter of your home and around yourself.

Then when you feel ready to do so naturally drop deeper within.

Allow any thoughts or feelings that want to be noticed to surface and acknowledge their presence whilst letting them pass through.

Imagine you are walking through a woodland.

The air is soft and fresh, there are twigs underfoot and soft peaty earth. The light falls through the trees and you feel relaxed.

You are drawn towards a large oak tree somewhere deep in the woods.

It is as if you know the way already somehow and your feet find the way one after the other.

The beautiful dappled green leaves filter sunlight and you can smell moss and fresh earth.

As you approach your tree you see in the trunk a doorway and walk towards it.

Your hands touch the familiar bark and the wood and the branches feel welcoming.

You open the doorway and find a wooden tunnel that leads you down into the earth.

You follow the gently winding wooden tunnel and come out into soft blue daylight and an entirely new landscape. New and yet ancient and familiar to you.

Look around you...

What does the sky look like?

What sort of weather is there?

What is growing there?

How does it smell?

Are there any animals?

Any sounds?

As you walk along the pathway you come to a dwelling and as you enter you see the Elder/Crone welcoming you.

You enter the dwelling with them and take a seat.

Listen to them and wait to see what he or she has to tell you.

Is there anything you feel you need to say too?

If there are any questions that seem important? If it feels right to then now is the time to ask them.

After a few minutes, whenever it feels safe and appropriate to your internal clock...

Say thank you to her or him and then make your way back along the pathway towards the tree.

Enter the tree and walk back through the tunnel to emerge safely back in the woodlands and walk gently back up the path you came on.

When you feel ready to, come back to yourself slowly and open your eyes gently.

Give yourself some time to just sit and breathe and look around you at the room you are in. This can be quite a deep process and it is really important to feel grounded and secure afterwards. Maybe spend some time with your feet on the earth or drinking some sweet tea. Don't worry if conversation didn't naturally occur, even taking the journey has significance. Don't forget to write down the experience and anything that will help you later. If you are with a friend and read to each other you might want to share your experiences.

Chapter Six
Ethical Practice

The first foundation of justice is not to harm others."
(Fundamentum iustitiae primum est ne cui noceatur).
Cicero 44 BC, De Officiis Book 1

Just as any number of other professions have codes of conduct and ethics by which they are governed so too the practitioner of white magic considers the principles by which to work. Magic itself is a tool that we can use to bring about changes and as with any tool it is the intention of the person using it that is key to the outcome. We are responsible for how we use our abilities and the stronger those abilities are the more accountability we have. This chapter is partly to consider what might be considered as ethical magic and good practice and partly to consider how other lower types of magic work, in particularly some of the stickier types of magic that come up commonly in various spell books and magical writings. Casting light upon these things is the way to make them visible. We can then look at alternatives and where possible shift from any negative position or way of working to a positive one. At the end of the chapter there is a short exercise offered to help with constructing a personal code of working ethics or guidelines.

Love and truth are the balancers of all things. The Egyptians called this principle living in, with or by Ma'at who was the Goddess of Truth and Justice and who was responsible for the weighing of the heart of the individual in the afterlife. Ma'at was also seen as law and the founding principle in civilisation of good living and honourable action. On the Kabbalistic Tree of Life judgement is found in the balance of the pillars of severity and mercy and in direct alignment with the central pillar which aligns the light of the Sun, the heart (Tiphareth) and the light of the Divine Kingdom, crown (Kether). This is written about in greater depth in the chapter on The Tree of Life.

In modern day Wicca the Law is "do what thou will and it harm none".

The word none being inclusive of self-harm and any violation of another, which some also interpret as live freely and do only good.

All of creation is formed from the mind, from consciousness and within the mind of the Creator. This divine consciousness or God consciousness is omnipresent, that is to say it is within all of creation and all living things. We simply have to choose to be in alignment and open to it. We too as co-creators manifest our own reality and existence and shape the world we live in. We are not hollow vessels but incarnate souls in the image of the divine with sentience, aptitude and ability, opinion, expression and freedom of will.

We need look no further than the nearest bookshop for validation in the form of hundreds if not thousands of books on psychology and the powers of positive thinking, manifestation, abundance and NLP (neuro linguistic programming). That our thoughts directly have an impact upon our lives and shape our worlds is known to be true. There is also scientific reason to suggest that reality itself is subjective and a direct result of consciousness. The research seeking to reconcile quantum mechanics and the theory of general relativity are ongoing. The studies and theories of black holes and the fact that a tiny piece of matter like a photon or electron can exist in multiple possible states simultaneously as a "wave of potentials" expressing itself as multiple possibilities and creating an interference pattern even though it is one single particle is evidence. The fact that furthermore its behaviour and reality change dependent upon whether it is observed or not prove that our physical world might be guided by non-physical properties such as consciousness. (Double slit experiment.)

All of life is interwoven, all of life is connected. We are not separate from one another or from the rest of existence and for the most part separation is an illusion created by imbalance often as a result of cultural, religious or political conditioning. No healthy, loving being of balanced and well mind deliberately chooses to damage or hurt others, self-defence excepted, nor harm the earth we live on. In actuality when we harm another human being or living thing we harm life which is sacred and connected to all of us. The seemingly eternal paradox of earthly life is separation from source in order to experience three-dimensional existence. When we consider that all manifestations start within the mind it becomes obvious that working with our own minds, thought patterns and mindfulness are fundamental to co-creation of our reality.

Love is Law

Love is the law and the whole of the law. Everything else is illusion. Love is truth and all else is illusion. Love is clear upon the scales of Ma'at. We are required to step into our truth, lovingly and in balance by being authentic. When we work from a place of love we are in balance with all of life and with God/Goddess and we will manifest balanced and loving results. We are also afforded a certain amount of protection by working in this way because we are working at the frequency of love and are therefore not on the same bandwidth as those things outside of it. We will discuss this in greater detail in the chapter on psychic protection.

It is also good practice to work when we are feeling most in balance in ourselves and feeling calm and centred as worried, nervous or distressed emotional states muddy our waters internally and the outer expression or experiences gained will likely be their reflections. If we are not sitting in the heart it is not the right time to work. At any time of distress try lighting one simple white candle and asking for support, peace and assistance with the situation.

Intention

In establishing clear intentions before we undertake any work we are already aligning ourselves with our purpose. Our clear intention is the single most important part of the manifestation process and it is this held intention that sets the course and direction of events. Unclear intentions or indecision will likely produce erratic results or unsatisfying outcomes. The clearer we can be in defining our purpose and holding the intention in a positive way the easier manifestation will be. Writing it down can help with the process of getting it clear.

Motivation

Each intention held is of course as a result of a decision we make in life and only we know the truth of our motivations for taking that decision or course of action and whether or not they are honourable and done from a place of love or not. If we do a good thing but do it with muddled motivations or mixed feelings we again stand to risk muddying the waters of manifestation and diverting the course of our desired outcome. This means we have to be really honest with ourselves about what we want and most importantly why. It's worth taking our time to get really clear with ourselves. Honest motivations give the best results.

Wording

Sometimes we get exactly what we ask for. I once attended a full moon ritual many years ago where the lady running it cast a circle widdershins mixing several magical systems together and then proceeded to call "all the fairies and all the witches"! Thankfully her intention was so muddled it was ineffectual. She was actually a nice lady but she hadn't considered her wording and perhaps may not have been very experienced. What would have been the outcome had she got exactly what she had asked for! It was badly worded and I learned a lot that day. Firstly it is definitely worth always finding out the purpose and intention of the ceremony if somebody else is running it before attending, asking questions and wherever possible meeting the person or at the least checking out their credibility with others. Secondly this was a lesson about being careful and appropriate with wording. There are ways of using wording safety nets where appropriate such as "in a way that is beneficial for all" for example. Thirdly this was a lesson that we never know when we will need to be able to hold our own space or the space of an entire circle or group if it is necessary and we are able, even when we think someone else is responsible for the ceremony. No matter how nice they are or how good their intentions, they might make a mistake because that's what people do sometimes.

Clarity of Mind

In order for us to hold clear sustained intention and have sufficient focus to work well we need clarity of mind. Anything that promotes clear mental states and that we find useful can help here. Mint tea is fantastic for a quick answer to clearing mental fog and meditation or yoga can offer more significant results. Something as simple as walking the dog in the woods can blow away the cobwebs and improve our mood and concentration.

Conversely anything which impairs our judgement or clutters our mind is likely to be unhelpful especially alcohol or drugs prescribed or otherwise. If we are over the limit to drive our car or take a breath test, or if a strong medicine packet warns against operating machinery or excessive side effects, then we are over the limit to work with magical forces. Our grip on the forces we may connect with may well be unreliable and our judgement impaired. We are also not in full command of our faculties of self-protection which may leave us vulnerable to external interference.

Good practice would suggest not drinking or taking anything that has an effect on our capabilities except perhaps a small amount of wine offered in a ritual for example until after all work is safely completed and any working space formally closed down and we have had some grounding time. Any magical system that suggests working whilst "under the influence" is not one focussed upon the well-being of the practitioner or those they are working with or duly concerned with the effects of any workings undertaken. The only obvious exception being shamanic practices in their correct tradition where the space is held by the shaman.

Children and/or during Pregnancy

Whilst it's lovely to include our children and to celebrate life with them we must always take care to protect them. As a suggested rule of thumb children can be included if they have asked to come and take part, have their parents or guardian with them and it's for something safe and appropriate like a baby naming ceremony, a hand-fasting or other celebration. It can also be appropriate to work to help or raise healing energy for a child when the parent has come to ask directly on their behalf. Under the age of twenty-one they have not yet come of age magically speaking. Children are not yet fully developed physically let alone psychically, emotionally or spiritually. Nor are they old enough to fully understand all the implications of anything they might take part in or necessarily be able to hold their own space and as such are far more vulnerable than adults. As an initiate we have a duty of care to all who we work with and this is never more highlighted than when children are concerned. Pregnant mothers should also be aware that their unborn baby is vulnerable in the same way and should be considered as a child being carried into sacred space. Extra protection could be worn by the mother, a blessed cord or prayer tie of some kind perhaps. Any working undertaken during pregnancy should if possible be only when necessary and of a gentle nature. Workings beyond those already covered or where there is any greater risk are not suitable for children until such time as they come of age and can make an informed choice for themselves.

In Judaism the Kabbalah and mysticism were not taught until the age of forty! Thankfully we don't have to wait that long but it does put it in context that it was only considered suitable after time had been taken to fully learn the other aspects of the faith before such sacred and powerful knowledge was considered. Some attribute the works and miracles of Jesus to this form of spiritual magic and he is referred to in some instances as a magician.

Using a Clear system of Magic

Whilst this book is written using many examples from many cultures this is to present and find commonly recurring themes and most definitely not a suggestion that they should be mixed up. Mixing up different magical systems is likely to produce unclear and unreliable workings as there is no steady foundation or frame of reference to work within. Whilst there may be a little overlap and cultural blending from natural development of culture it would be completely nonsensical to have a conversation in Greek in a Celtic stone circle using Egyptian hieroglyphs! It would be bound to produce chaotic and unstable outcomes or none at all. Even in the more plausible case of two archetypes that represent the same aspects of divinity, for example the Goddess Diana (Roman) and the Goddess Artemis (Greek), the two may react and feel completely different to work with internally through our point of contact with them. In the same way Saint Brighid may feel entirely different to the Goddess Brighid from whom she takes some of her attributes. Likewise each culture has its own system and it makes sense to study the culture we are interested in and learn about the spiritual beliefs and practices associated with it.

In Egyptian the presence of each of the four sons of Horus may be requested at each of the pillars of the four directions in turn when we cast the temple space. This is because they represent the four pillars of the sky. In a modern angelic circle we light candles at the four quarterly directions and request the presence of the correct Archangels. In other examples the four Greek winds are called, or the Druidic elements of Land, Sea and Sky (and Sun), or the four directions with their correct corresponding colours in the North American Lakota tradition. It would make no sense to mix these things up with other systems or the incorrect cultural deities. Each system has its own entirety and structure and each is worked differently and feels different and produces outwardly effects uniquely.

The only exception to this is where a complete magical system such as the Kabbalah may allow for and encompass other cultures, through the correct use of its teachings and applicable rules, by following the natural correspondences to the emanations of God (Sephiroth). For example Ceres a corn Goddess may be ascribed to, encountered or called upon in the sphere of Earth (Malkuth). Even then to use the system correctly care is taken to call forces that are harmonious to one another and compatible to the purpose. By developing ways of working clearly and studying our chosen path and its customs and rituals we are increasingly likely to produce good and stable results. Even more so as the effort we put in to our preparation is proportional to our attainment.

On a separate note daily prayers to divinity in more than one guise, God, angels, Goddess, pantheon etc. are fine and that this is not the same thing because we are not trying to construct a ceremony when we are just praying. It is no more than a recognition that the Divine expresses itself in many ways and that God/Goddess has many names and forms. However when we include a prayer in a ceremony we have probably thought about who we are praying to and why in advance and our prayers would be supportive and harmonious to our purpose and the system we are choosing to work with whether that be praying to Cernunnos in the trees or to Archangel Michael whilst we're lighting incense.

Astral Travel and Consciousness Projection

There are one or two books that suggest trying astral travel to beginners but putting that time and effort into meditation instead and building up sustained clarity of thought is more likely to yield helpful results. With practice when our inner clock knows when it is time to come back and we can do so instantly and at will, then that might be the time to consider progressing with meditations of a different nature in that they are predetermined with a guided path and purpose or destination. The travelling aspect will then naturally occur when it does. Initially it should only be for short periods of time and distance. Some people find it helpful to have a candle burning next to them to come back to as a focal point as well as a second person preferably of more experience around if possible. Time should then be spent grounding feet on the floor with the candle burning until normal functioning is resumed. If you feel a wobbly vibration or a shaky feeling then getting outside with both feet on the earth and hands on the earth too can help. So can hot tea and chocolate or anything sweet and resting. Television and other external stimuli may have the opposite effect and prevent closing down properly so it can be good to wait a little while. Candlelight or natural light and a peaceful space can help.

Some people astrally travel anyway especially when they sleep and may or may not be aware of it. If this is the case for you and you're aware of it keeping a dream journal can help so you can look more clearly at where you are going and why. Keep a pen and paper near your bed so that you can jot things down before they "disappear" on waking. Also the building up of meditation and clear concentration skills will likely prove helpful and provide the tools needed to travel only at will and in alignment with purpose. Astral travel feels different from normal dreaming; there is a very real sense of being there. It is common to wake with a head that feels like a "bowl full of water" as someone recently described it to me or with a sensation of having travelled a long way very fast. Beyond this mention here, this is a more advanced subject matter for another time.

Free Will

All beings have free will. Some things may be predestined or fated, others are within our influence and how we choose to act or react, influence or not is within our choosing. Free will is our right. No one has the right to interfere with our will and we do not have the right to influence another. The trouble with that is that an assumption has been made that behaviour is always conscious! A lot of human behaviour is not conscious. The more conscious we become the more we can become aware of our behaviour and our choices and actions. Regarding the working of magic however magic is planned generally and considered. Therefore we have opportunity to make sure we are acting in a way that respects the free will of all. More so we also interfere with another's free will in full knowledge should we choose to do so regardless.

Influencing the free will of another is something frequently discussed about spell work and its sometimes haphazard results. Many love spells are directed for instance at a specific individual and are designed to directly influence them. Spells that may seem harmless like a charm involving taking a lock of a desired partner's hair, or suggesting we put our hair or nail in their tea causing them to dream of us at night, work effectively by binding or invading the other person. If we steal a strand of their hair we steal their DNA, either that or we may have given them ours! Such cases violate the person's right to choice and free will and then quite possibly psychically invade their thoughts and sleep! When we look at how it works it's not so harmless. We have to consider not only what it does to the other person but what such a hold over them may be doing to us energetically too. No one has the right to possess or bind another. They are not a handbag! They can choose what they want to do. We can only choose what we want to do. Any spell that projects a desired outcome or behaviour onto another person without their consent is definitely questionable.

By shifting our attention from the "other" back to ourselves and our reality we reclaim our power and allow ourselves to be open to receiving divinely planned solutions. When we let go to attachments of how we think a thing should manifest and concentrate purely on asking for favourable circumstances for ourselves and for beneficial outcomes we welcome all sorts of alternative solutions. Positive affirmations can really help the manifestation process especially when we wobble! Very often if magic is needed at all or even considered to influence another it is a sign they are not moving that way naturally. Anything forced is against good orderly direction. Sometimes there's a perfect answer that we just couldn't see yet and it's probably something better! That's when good magic can be employed to nudge it along.

Magic invariably does hurry things along and tends to achieve in a much shorter period of time that which would take much longer solely through meditation. In general any type of magic that is aimed at one specific person should be considered carefully.

Free Will and Control

Free will extends clearly into the area of control. Being in our free will brings balanced control. Being out of our free will brings the unbalanced kind. When we have balanced and healthy control and make good choices for ourselves and act assertively or decisively within our own lives everything flows and is easy and synchronicity or serendipity occurs. This kind of control operates from a place of love. When we have unbalanced and unhealthy control, the kind where we feel the need to control various situations or people in our lives it does the opposite. This kind of control operates from a place of fear. Fear is the usual cause of an imbalance in control. Love is the usual remedy to come back into balance.

If it feels as if we have some kind of blockage and everything seems to be working against us or going wrong, it is worth considering whether these very clear signals indicate we are going the wrong way and working against the natural order and flow. If this is the case seriously question all the whys and wherefores before working magic. Are these obstacles to overcome or clear signals shouting wrong way? Is there a lesson here, is there a need for rest, is it just the timing? Do we have all the information, are there unknown factors? Using magic to force something is likely to be unpredictable at best. By all means we can give healthy encouragement to a situation but be aware that if we are working to force something which feels awkward and ignore that inner sense of knowing we are likely working in direct opposition to the natural course of events. Could we as a consequence deny ourselves an opportunity we didn't know existed or something better than we had imagined?

Another time when the issue of free will and control comes up is when the magic is to help somebody else or influence something affecting them. Even when we're offering help there are things to consider. Can we be sure that we know what is best for them? What if we're wrong? This is where it might be mindful to take some time to think about it or ask them if they would like the help. If after contemplation we still think they could really use a helping hand then there are ways of doing this cleanly without trying to control the outcome beyond asking for assistance for them and the importance is all in the wording for example we could say, "if it is in their highest good" or "if it is in alignment with their will". Saying "if Sharon would like the help please send her support and make this as easy as possible for her" is different to saying "please heal Sharon" who may or may not have wanted our help or who may or may not have valuable things she is learning from this experience that we know nothing about. This leaves the choice with her at a soul level and with heaven. We could then combine this with burning herbs or candles conducive to the area of help asked for, for example a blue candle for healing and lavender traditionally known as cure all.

Free Will and Respecting Personal Boundaries

Free will also extends into respecting personal boundaries both for ourselves and others. It is a two-directional thing as with all relationships. Being mindful of our boundaries and paying attention to those of others means respecting ourselves and them by honouring free will.

The first side of this is about respecting other people's personal space and boundaries. If we deliberately "read" someone who does not want the intrusion it can be really invasive and we are acting against their will or choice. This might be the deliberate detailed reading of a person either psychically or energetically without their knowledge or consent or the reading of cards about another person's business in a way that does not bear any relation to our own role and relationship to them. For example asking the cards, "How do I relate to L and what can I do to help this situation?" is a very different thing to asking about their personal circumstances and what they should be doing to help themselves, which is none of our business. I'm sure we've all experienced frustration at some time or other when a friend or family member has pried into our business or been nosey and insensitive of our needs. It can feel like a violation of personal space and will and it can feel disrespectful.

There are of course times when we see something unavoidably or that is very visible to us or where we read someone unintentionally and this could be thought of differently as it is not deliberate and may well have be presented to us for a good reason. Perhaps we needed to see that smoky dark grey aura so that we knew to stay away from someone dangerous to us and this is information that will help us to stay safe or make a good judgement call. Or we picked up on that person's discomfort not to be intrusive but because we could help them in some way.

The second side of this is that it is equally important if not more so to respect our own boundaries because we need our personal space to feel happy and secure and to have an environment in which growth can occur. Healthy boundaries also protect us psychically from any mud-slinging or negativity around us. Our boundaries can help to shield us from draining experiences or interactions with anyone seeking more from us than we want to give and just as importantly as shielding from those who are energetic takers is shielding from those seeking to offload, life's energetic dumpers. Sometimes boundaries can be about damage limitation too such as keeping to a tight schedule and not being there too long when we know that we need to spend time somewhere that isn't good for us. My dear friend says, "When it's raining it's raining!" When our boundaries are being strained or pushed they can warn us through our thoughts and feelings that something isn't good for us and also warn us when we are engaging in anything which is toxic for us. Like everything else we have to make judgement calls. Pack that umbrella! It is here that anger may play a useful part in alerting us to where our boundaries lie and where our truth is. Anger if harnessed and balanced can also be the fuel that enables us to act and to assert ourselves.

We can recharge our boundaries by spending time in nature or sleeping and we can respect our own needs and boundaries and practise saying no to people when we need to. For many people this takes learning and practice.

Free Will and Hexes and Cursing

Hexes and Cursing are the infliction of cruelty, harm or punishment on another and are in direct opposition to free will. A hex generally means working a spell specifically to do harm or punish someone. A curse usually means to hold ill thoughts towards a person or situation and to wish them harm or punishment but not necessarily to work any kind of spell. In neither case has the other person consented to this. It is an act against their will.

When someone has deeply hurt us, and especially when we feel that we are the innocent party, there can often be a desire to lash out and it's okay to feel that way sometimes. Our feelings are like the weather and when someone has acted unfairly it is a normal and healthy reaction to feel anger or sadness and to communicate this to them or set appropriate boundaries. However there is a difference between what we think momentarily or feel and what we actually choose to act upon.

Hexes and cursing are a very low frequency toxic form of magic and will almost always burn the user as well as the person they are intended for. To sustain such a thing means carrying hatred and anger and pain within us and focussing our attention on it, which in turn locks us into a low frequency and will likely attract further corresponding unpleasant life experiences and company. Projecting these types of magic towards another soul may possibly also have karmic consequences, as above so below, as well as any other repercussions as a result of psychic mud-slinging.

In circumstances where someone has seriously wronged us or someone we love the alternative to resorting to such a thing as a hex is to call forth justice. Generally it is also worth waiting three moons where possible to see if the situation has resolved itself. Things may have altered in that length of time or more light may have been shed upon the circumstances. More often than not we may find a way to work through it in other ways and let it go or we gain the compassion to see that the other party is already suffering and working through their own karma. It might be that we need three moons to calm down and detach a little from the situation too.

If after that time has passed the wrong has not been righted or it still feels appropriate and we have done anything useful that we can in the practical sense on the earthly plane, then we could consider requesting Divine Justice. Before we do this we must be sure our actions have been scrupulously clean and we have kept our integrity in the matter. Justice is multi-directional and will fall on both sides so should not be undertaken lightly. Like-wise this is not an exact science. Who is to say justice will fall just for this one thing and not for this lifetime. If after factoring all this in it still seems the best course of action available, then there are simple ways of requesting justice and in most cultures whether we are appealing to a spiritual court, to the scales of

Ma'at, to the archangels, or to the Gods, most pathways have some archetypal form of divine universal justice we can call upon. Be aware justice doesn't always look how we think it should look but then we don't know what that other person is thinking, feeling or carrying or what will play out in their lifetime and in truth that part's not our business. Our business is giving it to heaven in good faith and loving ourselves enough not to carry it for a lifetime. There is a divine law and order and both are found within love.

Free Will and Respectful Calling of Spirit

Just as we speak to anyone we love and respect politely so too we talk to spirit in the same way. There are many types of magic that suggest summoning Gods, Goddesses, gatekeepers or spirits. Note the word summoning: it is not generally speaking a polite word or a gentle invitation but a way of making a demand of their presence. This violates their free will because it removes their choice entirely. Even a friendly spirit might be more than a little annoyed at being disrupted in this way. Whilst there are many who mean no disrespect when working in this way, a large part is again down to intention, it makes sense to be respectful in how we invite or call upon spirit. If any book suggests wording that doesn't sit quite right or feel right for you change it and adapt it to something that does. It is always more mindful to invite than to demand.

Discernment of Who and What we Work With

All beings have an energetic signature or harmonic resonance that is unique. The fine tuning of the virtual radio dial and differentiating between spirits through what can only be described as their pitch of frequency is something which is learned over a prolonged period of time and not something which can be imparted in a book though there are things to look for. The basic and obvious things however are the use of self-protection, a further held sacred space opened for the duration and later closed and most importantly that these things and any communication made should be done with respect and love. These same things are key when it comes to spell work also.

As people, our individual frequency can be thought of as being made up of two relative parts. The first of these is generally consistent and is based upon the long term and average overall progression of the soul. It can be thought of as our base line, established over lifetimes. The second of these is variable moment to moment depending upon our emotions and thoughts and what's happening in any given moment. These daily experiences and emotions then show up as fluctuations and adjustments of a subtler nature on our base line energy. This is why a good person having a bad day does not feel energetically the same as someone nasty or dangerous on a bad day. The frequencies of the two base lines are still miles apart and would be even if the exact same events of the bad day had happened to each of them simultaneously. Magically speaking this is good news for the practitioner aligned with love!

Suggested Exercises

Research three different professions that appeal to you where there is a clear code of ethical conduct perhaps through a duty of care or client confidentiality.

Write a list of the ten things that seem most important to you about them. For example making an initial assessment, or client confidentiality may be ethical guidelines.

How could those be applied magically or spiritually speaking?

Now write your own ethical guidelines. This can be as long or as short as you feel. It's between you and God/Goddess.

Although there might be similarities in places for each person who does this it will be unique because the onus is upon what is right and true for the individual. This ethical code may well evolve and change over time as new experiences arise but having some clear guidelines about what works is a good place to work from.

Chapter Seven
The Body and The Inner Rainbow

In the forecourt of the Temple of Apollo at Delphi there is a plaque that reads in Greek γνῶθι σεαυτόν, which transliterated is *gnōthi seauton* and translated into in Latin *nosce te ipsum,* meaning "Know Thyself".

"Know Thyself". Herein lies the true key to the entrance to the temple, the inward journey of self-discovery. If divinity is omnipresent and to be found within us, then it is inward that we may seek knowledge.

It is said throughout numerous systems around the world that archetypal man has three parts. In the modern era we refer to them as body, mind and soul or body, mind and spirit. Plato names them as reason, spirit and appetite. The Hermetica sees them as a threefold intelligence within us made up of; rationality or sensory intelligence, intuition or emotional intelligence, and spirituality or spiritual intelligence. The Kabbalistic system recognises them as *Nefesh* which is the lower part of the soul linked to instinct and desire, *Ruach* which is the middle soul or spirit where morality and distinguishing between good and bad can be learnt and *Neshamah* which is the higher soul and through the intellect allows man to have awareness of God/Divinity. The Egyptians too recognised the threefold connection between man and the Gods. In each of these belief systems there is an acknowledgement of our earthly physicality and humanness, our individual souls and our more direct connection with spirit in the heart-mind. It is a recurring theme, an inherent truth known across cultures independently of one another.

It is in this threefold self-knowledge that we may seek insight into our larger universal reflection. We begin then with inquiry of the mind and body through the study of anatomy and physiology and the physical and spiritual energetic systems.

Regarding the more practical aspects of magic it is certainly true that before we can connect safely with external forces it is necessary to be able to work effectively at a personal level and to develop a good understanding of our own energetic systems so that we know what is normal for us in any given circumstance and how to direct, hold and harness all that we contain. There are many different types of practices we can adopt and learn from that can help us get in touch with our bodies and energy systems. For some people this might mean yoga or qigong and for others meditation. There's no right or wrong place to start and it's often best to follow our natural inclinations because they're there for a reason. As with anything we can't specialise in any one area until after we have covered all the basics in some depth. The study of magic is no different. Understanding our own body and energy systems is fundamental. Perhaps we have high energy and need to learn to ground ourselves really well. Perhaps we have days with low energy and we need to learn to listen to our bodies well, rest, recharge and respect the ebbs and flows. These things make a big difference when working magic safely.

The physical body is a wonderful and complex organism. Yes we are flesh and blood but we are also consciousness and soul with predispositions, strengths, weaknesses and natural rhythms to observe and understand. Each part of us, physically and mentally has its correspondence within the cosmos and we can seek to align ourselves with these and deepen our point of our internal connection. Whilst all these points should align, it is the heart and the mind in combination where these connections are most important. This combination is sometimes referred to as the heart-mind. The heart chakra when open and fully functioning allows deep love, compassion and acceptance on both a personal and universal level. The crown chakra when open allows us to align with divinity through mind, to be in the mind of creation and for the mind of creation to be within us. It is essential these two points of heart and mind be in harmony and cooperation with one another. This first point of contact within ourselves is also the initiator of further points of contact with spirit. Without this open heart and harnessed mind the rest is semantics for this is the primary key of all higher work. Love opens the doorways and lifts the frequencies.

The Aura

The human body is made up of physical, etheric, emotional and mental bodies containing the chakra points, meridians and numerous pressure points. The combined energetic bodies make up what we call the aura or the auric field. Over time and with practice we can teach ourselves to see these auric fields and at the end of the chapter there is a simple exercise to help with this ability.

Auras generally look like light or energy surrounding a person. They may be predominantly one colour or a combination of colours and the brightness, intensity or tone of those colours may alter depending upon a person's overall well-being and their current state of mind. This is because our overall frequency may increase or decrease depending upon different variables. For example if we feel sad our aura may be a little duller or fainter than usual. If we feel happy it may be brighter and shinier than usual. People who have auras that are predominantly one colour may be feeling something relevant to the colour. Certain shades of blue may signify tranquillity or good communication. Alternatively a person who has an aura that is generally always the same colour may also have a specific life purpose signified by the colour. For example a person who studies ecology may have a green aura and spend a lot of time in the countryside. It may be that their soul's purpose in this life is to work with nature.

The etheric body is the spirit breath or life force immediately surrounding our physical body and is the first layer within the aura and lies closest to the physical skin. Known by different names in different cultures, Madame Blavatsky named it the etheric body and the term was later accepted by her peers to replace Hindu terminology within Western culture. In Vedantic thought it is called the prana-maya-kosha. It is also just as commonly known to us as Prana in Sanskrit or Chi in Chinese. The Egyptians called it Ka, of which the most probable translation is life-creating force.

The emotional body is the second layer of the aura and is closely linked to our feelings both in the present moment and potentially to past emotional experiences. Anything weighing us down, i.e. sadness, insecurity, anger etc. is felt here. This is the field in which memories and past wounds are also often held until cleared or healed. This is the part of the energetic field that can be worked on through the use of tapping techniques like EFT or similar treatments for release of energetic blocks.

The mental body is the third layer of the aura and is closely linked to the emotional body as you would expect because it is of course our thoughts which create and generate our emotional responses. It is here we find the causes of many of our feelings. Thoughts such as "I should" or "I shouldn't" invariably lie here within the mental energetic field. This layer of the aura can be worked on in combination with the emotional body and the whole energy system when releasing or healing stored memories or past pain. It can also be worked on with various counselling techniques such as cognitive behavioural therapy or neuro-linguistic programming. These terms for psychological techniques are included purely for interest as related subjects and for the benefit of those who may already use or study these or similar techniques. However, the advice of a trained councillor or health care professional should be sought if looking for therapy of any kind.

Our physical experience of earthly life tells us that reality is made up of material things and that the world around us is an objective one but whilst Newtonian physics supported this theory, that the universe is made of physical parts, the later research of Albert Einstein and others suggests that it is made up of immaterial energy waves. If that is correct it is in studying these waves, which are made of light, sound and vibration that we may look to understand how the material world is created. Within waves such as audio signals, radio waves or light, the rate of vibration (contraction) and oscillation (expansion) when measured are expressed as frequency. When counted cyclically per unit of time, the unit for frequency is hertz (Hz) per second. (See the Chapter on the Rainbow and the Nature of Light.) Frequency and vibration play very important roles in creating the structures of matter because they help organize matter, giving it appearances and uniqueness. Regarding the energetic waves and frequencies of the body we may best look to the internal rainbow of the chakra system.

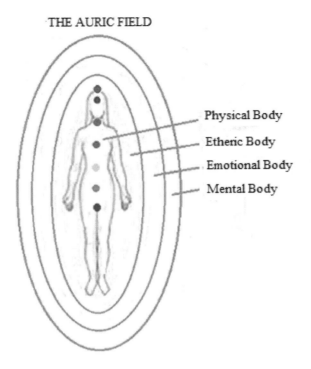

THE AURIC FIELD

Physical Body

Etheric Body

Emotional Body

Mental Body

The Chakra System

The word chakra comes from the Sanskrit Hindu word meaning, "spinning wheel of energy". Chakras are said to be the power houses of the body and receive and transmit life force energy. These vortices of energies relate to our individual and collective connection to each other and to the earth and greater universe. They spin and rotate like spinning stars or quazars connecting through the centre of a torus in a two-directional flow absorbing life force energy through the yin/ida channels and emitting it through the yang/pingala channels. Yin/ida are the feminine forces representing earth and yang/pingala are the masculine forces representing sky. (Quazars are celestial objects that emit an immense amount of energy in the form of light and radiation from a compact source thought to be a black hole located in a galactic centre.)

The sacred masculine and feminine within us act as the two poles of our personal energetic systems like the terminus of a battery. In their polar opposites they allow the flow of energy to support and carry our life force, chi or prana flowing through our meridian lines or nadis which are the energetic rivers of the body powering the chakra system. This flow of energy is sometimes referred to as kundalini and rises through the spiritual channels activating each chakra, which emits its own frequency and connects to the body's auric field.

Each chakra is located within the central channel of the body and aligned from the base of the spine to the top of the head forming part of the body with the breath channels. Each is also at a major endocrine gland and nerve plexus. Whilst there are variable systems and interpretations from place to place, the chakra system has seven main power houses that are commonly agreed upon in both the Chinese and Ayurvedic systems, which we will briefly touch upon here along with their most frequent depictions and some basic information as to which things they affect or govern.

Whilst the main seven chakras and their colours and attributes are agreed upon the frequencies they operate at are not. Whilst some sources give these they have not been included here. Intensity of colour, speed or strength of energetic flow changes from person to person and moment to moment. It is likely that the chakra frequencies are variable in any case and the best ways of working with them is through corresponding sounds or colours. The physical energetic frequency does also not take into account the spiritual frequency or pitch an individual soul is operating at either and it is only these two factors in relation to one another that gives an accurate overview. Harmonic resonance is multidimensional not linear.

The lower three chakras correspond to earth and the upper three to heaven, the balancing point is found in the heart. When our chakras are blocked or unbalanced it usually means that we are not absorbing enough cosmic energy through the elements, or diet or exercise. Perhaps we need to get out in that sky! Similarly if we are overcharged, blocked in some way or unbalanced we can look to the same probable causes and spend some time with our feet on the earth or learning to quieten the mind in order to process that which needs clearing. The seven chakras correspond to the colours of the rainbow as denoted by Isaac Newton and also to the seven notes of the harmonic scale. In other words each chakra has a colour/light emission and a sound/pitch. Newton recognised the classical Symbola system used by the ancient Greeks and divided the visible light spectrum of the rainbow into seven colours accordingly. The Symbola system ascribes each of the seven colours to corresponding musical notes, days in the week and objects in the solar system. This ancient referencing system of the correspondences of natural phenomena is still held in high regard by many and is commonly used in esoteric writings both past and present.

The Muladhara, Root or Base Chakra

The root chakra is located at the base of the spine and is the negative pole of the body orientated to Earth. It is depicted by a red lotus with four petals. This is the chakra that connects our life force, our etheric body, to our physical body. It relates to the earth, matter, solid, dense, the base of the spine, the gonads and adrenal medulla, controlling the fight or flight response. The primary interest here is survival and connection to the tribe or family. It represents vitality, survival instincts, feeling supported and the emotions of desire, anger, jealousy and greed. Any fears of attack or injury either physical or emotional, abandonment, destruction or illness, are held here. It is the seat of all conditioning, learned behaviour, messages and core beliefs from those learned in childhood from family onwards. It is effectively the foundation that we build upon. An imbalance of the root chakra may manifest as disconnection or a lack of interest in the world, obsession, addictions, volatile emotions, selfishness or low energy. Health issues that can be healed here are any emotional or psychological damage pertaining to the sphere, deep fears, sexuality, stability, security, lower back pain and sciatica.

Truth – We are all one and connected to all of life. We are never alone.
Colour – red
Stone – red carnelian
Earth at Feet – rhodonite
Keynote – C
Element – Earth
Energy – grounding

The Svadisthana or Sacral Chakra

The sacral chakra is just below the navel in the lower stomach and abdomen. It is depicted as a white lotus with a crescent Moon and six orange petals and is related to the testes or ovaries and to reproduction. This is the conductor of the body's communications and is associated with water and emotions. It represents creativity, sexuality, pleasures and frustrations and it is the seat of our core beliefs. The home of the male and the female waters it is fluid and formless. The things addressed here are species and relationships with ourselves and others, sociability, basic emotional needs, pleasure, satisfaction, control, sexuality and sensuality and any tendency towards either promiscuity or frigidity, intimacy issues, addictions, over or under eating, body image, guilt and core beliefs. Physically it governs reproduction, mentally creativity and emotionally joy and enthusiasm.

The lessons learnt here are those of honouring one another and that difficult and hurtful people and relationships are here to teach us something.

Truth – What am I meant to learn from this? What would love do?

Colour – orange

Stone – jasper

Keynote – D

Element – water

Energy – life force

The Manipura or Solar Plexus

The solar plexus chakra is depicted by a yellow flower of ten petals with a downward triangle and is between the belly button and the diaphragm and connected to the lumbar part of the spine. It is associated with the pancreas and with the metabolism, digestive system and adrenal glands. This is the last of the lower three earthly chakras of the body and is also where we emanate physical and sexual energy. Here is the Sun of fire radiating outwards and bringing about transformation by turning both food and prana into energy. This is the seat of our personal power where matter meets movement; the solar plexus is the domain of our identity, ego, assertion, self-esteem, self-expression, wellness, vitality, vigour, accomplishment, values and decision-making processes. This chakra also regulates and balances energy so that we

97

have reserves at times when we need them. This chakra is both about creation and destruction as well as fear versus courage and is the first manifestation of will.

Health issues that can be addressed in this area are physically those of digestion, acid or adrenal burn out and mentally those of personal power. Any imbalance or blocks here may show as dis-empowerment, over sensitivity, feelings of rejection, distrust, anger, volatile temperament or control issues.

The lessons of the solar plexus are to do with equality and recognising all beings not as superior or inferior but as perfect beings in their own right.

Truth – I see the God in you. I see the God in me.

Colour – yellow

Stone – citrine

Keynote – E major

Element – fire

Energy – power

The Anahata or Heart Chakra

The heart chakra anahata or padma-sundara is located in the heart and is depicted by a circular green flower with twelve petals containing a hexagram that functions as a balance between the sacred masculine and the sacred feminine and as the bridge between earth and heaven. The heart chakra is the central melting pot capable of holding, directing and driving the entire flow of the meridians and the energetic system. The heart chakra connects with the auric field and is our bridge to the astral plane, the point where light radiates out of us and we connect to the whole universe. Love is Divine power. Here within the chest is soft spacious lightness, an opening where breath rises and we connect to all things.

The heart centre relates to the thymus a part of the immune system which fights illness and also to cardiac muscles. Healing work done in the heart can alleviate stress and heal emotional wounds and any feelings which do not serve us. The feelings of the lower three chakras can also affect the heart and the energy rising can be diminished where there are blocks from things that remain unhealed. The lessons of the heart are those of compassion, empathy, peace, kindness, care, generosity, forgiveness, empathy, giving, hope, nurturing, emotions, acceptance, learning to make honourable choices for ourselves, love in the external world and love as a state of Divine being or unconditional love. Seeking things, people and places that make us happy and keep us balanced is good heart medicine as is laughter!

Imbalances in the heart and blockages may present as an internal experience of alienation, shame, feeling broken or inferior or unlovable, a loss of self-discipline or difficult relationships.

Truth – Love is truth and Love is all.

Colour – green (sometimes pink)

Stone – malachite or rose quartz

Keynote – F

Element – air

Energy – love

The Vishuddha, Akasha or Throat Chakra

The throat chakra or akasha is depicted as a silver crescent within a white circle with sixteen light blue petals located in the throat at the thyroid gland. The throat chakra creates sound and rhythmic pulsation. It is the vessel through which all the energy of the other chakras flows as it moves up and down throughout the body vibrating. In this void of the throat chakra we connect to the void of the aether or akasha through spiritual channels, to the akashic records and to collective consciousness. Our throat chakra is the point of expression of our sum total. It helps us to transmit our higher-minded thinking and purpose; it can also align us with them.

This is the centre of communication and personal development or growth through expression. When this centre is healthy we are able to express and communicate clearly with others and, most importantly, with ourselves not just in our actions but through our thoughts and feelings and their expression. In this void, this empty space there is opportunity for realignment, patience, confidence, independence, clear thought, memory, sound, spontaneity, resonance and synchronicity. The lessons here are about speaking truth, faith, will power, spirit, karma, honesty and union with divine will. Are we expressing and creating harmonic or discordant vibration? Are we receiving harmonic or discordant vibration? We emit and receive transmission in frequencies in interaction with others.

This is where any health issues around sore throats and stiffness in the neck can be addressed but also where any stresses and tensions held in our body through lack of communication caused by fear of saying the wrong thing or creating frustrations in our lives can also be worked upon. An imbalance or block in the throat chakra can manifest as difficult self-expression, lying and doubt. Honesty and forgiveness frees us from the past.

Truth – I honour myself and others with clear communication and healthy self-expression.

Colour – sky blue, cyan

Stone – howlite, lapis, turquoise

Keynote – G

Element – air (aether)

Energy – communication

The Ajna or The Third Eye/Brow Chakra

The third eye chakra is depicted with ninety-six petals, as a two-petalled lotus with forty-eight petals on each side. It corresponds to the colour indigo and is located at the centre of the forehead. The third eye is the point of intuition and soul consciousness, deeper vision beyond matter, knowledge, wisdom, inner perceptions, clairvoyance, and introspection. Here is where we can seek clarity of vision to free ourselves from the illusory and abstract, fantasy, clutter and noise by learning to balance the higher and lower aspects of ourselves and to listen to our inner guidance. All our beliefs both positive and negative are held here and we can change them at the core. This chakra concerns spiritual direction, growth, wisdom, dreams, understanding, open mindedness, detachment, intuition, and development of psychic ability. Existence outside of space time as consciousness.

Associated with the pineal gland which is light sensitive and produces melatonin the third eye addresses any health issues related to sleep imbalance either through insomnia, disturbance or oversleeping and migraines.

Imbalance or blocks in this chakra may manifest as abstractions, constructs, coordination problems, fantasies, clutter and noise both psychic and or physical. The lessons of this centre are about learning to discriminate truth from illusion and the seeking only of truth.

Truth – When we listen to intuition all that is outside of that truth falls away.

Colour – indigo
Stone – amethyst
Keynote – A
Element – all
Energy – insight, wisdom

The Sahasrara or Crown Chakra

The crown chakra is called the Sahasrara, which means the thousand-petalled lotus. It is the source of pure consciousness and is the positively charged pole of the body located at the top of the head emitting white or violet light at the highest frequency of the internal rainbow and connecting us to our outer auric field. This chakra is the point of transcendence and connects us to the divine, breaking down the illusion of separation and self. The crown is the point of cosmic awakening and connection to all things. This chakra correlates to spirit and to thought and from here the cycles and patterns of life can be observed with newfound understanding. It is here we receive divine guidance, wisdom and purpose. The crown represents intuition, spirituality, integration of the self, inspiration, trust, ethics and selflessness.

The health implications of this chakra affect the nervous system and the skin and any imbalance here may be experienced as lack of purpose, a loss of meaning or mental confusion. The lessons here are about releasing anything we need to let go of, living in the present moment, clarity, peace, divine acceptance of order and moving our consciousness into ourselves. This point is the pure state of being. Moving beyond the limitations of manmade beliefs. We are limitless and one with the limitless light. The highest connection of the heart chakra and alignment to love.

Truth – We are One.
Colour – amethyst/white
Stone – amethyst or clear quartz
Keynote – B
Element – all

Energy – transcendence

Breath

Learning to breathe. It's amazing how many of us don't breathe properly. It might seem an odd thing to say but there are so many people who breathe shallowly from the top of the chest area without ever realising that their breath is rarely deep enough to fill their whole chest cavity and stomach. The simple act of taking full deep breaths increases our oxygen and energy flow throughout the body bringing in spirit breath or prana which sustains and replenishes us. It also helps reduce stress and grounds us to the earth. We are so much more able to be in tune with ourselves and our whole being when we breathe well and in deepening our breath we enhance our natural state of being and connect more fully to our present consciousness.

Simple Breathing Techniques

Standing feet shoulder width apart in a relaxed state lift your arms up to the sides reaching above your head on the in breath and then release the breath slowly and bring them back down to your sides on the out breath. Do this for a few minutes or until it is a natural time to close.

This simple movement opens up the diaphragm, gets the oxygen circulating and can really connect us and get us more into our bodies in a very simple effective way.

For anxiety the seven eleven breathing technique can be useful when we need a way to focus or steady the breath using the mind. This is a really simple to help to regulate the flow of air and restore balance until we get the hang of deep natural breathing. Doing this for a few minutes a day will soon bring about natural deep rhythmic breathing as a state that occurs without effort.

Counting slowly from one to seven on the in breath, allow the breath to travel into the stomach first, gradually rising slowly and filling the chest cavity. Then counting slowly to eleven on the out breath, releasing the breath first from the chest and then gradually from the stomach.

Take up singing! Singing is breathing for the soul, encourages deep rhythmic breathing, heart connection and healthy expression.

Moon Cycle/ Menstruation

For women this is a really important natural cycle and is a deep source of connection to Mother Earth. Regardless of whether we are regularly bleeding with our cycle, the cycle is always still there. It is an inherent part of us. There are many women who may not bleed regularly and who still maintain a rhythm with their bodies and the moon regardless of any hormonal birth control methods. Like-wise there are women of menopausal age who do not bleed but are deeply connected with their cycle and able to stand in their full power constantly as a result of this phase in their life. Knowing our pattern is also the most simple and ancient method of birth control known by all women. We are at our most powerful at this time and in many cultures this is widely acknowledged. In Native American traditions there is often a moon lodge which is a female only comfortable space where the women can go during their moon time to retreat quietly to observe the body cycles, go deep within and renew life coming back with wisdom and visions for the tribe.

Getting to know our own pattern, both physically and emotionally is valuable and empowering. This moon work is important as it increases self-love, awareness and empowerment. It is an essential rite of passage into womanhood. As women it is precisely our feeling nature which is our strength and this is through the womb connection to life. This is a subject much overlooked in the West and which we need to rediscover and receive teachings on. When we honour our moon time and understand our rhythms we truly step into our power and reclaim our divine knowing and femininity. This knowing whether instinct or intuition is something we must learn to develop by tuning in and paying attention. When we listen to it we know what to do in each moment and that we are doing the right thing in order to meet our needs and requirements. Some may also perceive this to be divine guidance of the sort that we are able to receive through the intuitive senses. We are a reflection of the Goddess and when we honour her sacred cycle in ourselves we come into alignment with her and with our power.

The male power cycle is primarily solar but it is relation to the feminine and vice versa. Both are inherent within all living things.

The Mind and Mindfulness

We may only touch upon the subject briefly here and only in the context of working magic within the confines of these pages. In truth the working of magic is mostly in mind. Mindfulness is the defining difference between mind or intellect and the conscious aware use of the mind or intellect. If we put our energy into becoming mindful we bring awareness to intellect and we align with love and with the God mind or higher consciousness.

In the Western world we live in it is often difficult to remember to make time to clear and to nurture our minds. How often do we think of something of greater importance and as we seek deeper understanding become distracted by our own thoughts interrupting us. Further to that how can we hope to send out a clean conscious magical intention if we are unable to sustain any clarity of mind and that intention is broken by mental noise? Add to that the hustle and bustle of daily life and our other obligations and it is easy to become distracted. However, we must learn to still and quieten the mind if we wish to be able to control and direct our thoughts positively into manifestation. Ever noticed how exhausting it can be to spend time with someone with a lot of mental noise and turmoil?

Our state of mind and balance is also of vital importance when considering undertaking any kind of magical work. For those who suffer from depression or any other imbalance, which is very common in our society, (figures suggest one in ten people or more are affected at some point in their lives), it may at times be advisable to abstain from working magic. Health comes first and this definitely includes health of mind. Instead focus upon self-healing and those practices which promote good emotional health until such time as stability has been re-established or the upset has passed and there has been time to rest and recharge fully and clarity of thought has returned to normal. Then usual work can be resumed. Sometimes this means a day, sometimes this means a year. Trust the inner process because the soul knows the way to healing.

At these times when we are not feeling our best the efforts put into affecting something else might be better used directing that energy for ourselves. Also we are our very own microcosm and whatever we project outwards can and usually will make manifest in the macrocosm around us. It is therefore important to work when we feel most balanced and calm. Those who work magic whilst unbalanced in some way are likely to later have results which reflect that and unstable outcomes. Sometimes in order to be kind to ourselves we need to make a judgement call about if we're really up to this now or whether a period of rest would be wiser and our working to be resumed later. In a group or circle this means being really honest with one another either by letting the others know if and when we're not up to working or by gently saying to someone else that they look like they need a rest if we are concerned.

This principle extends not just to those with depression or anxieties but to all of us within our daily lives. If we're tired, feeling sensitive, over emotional, in physical pain or having a bad day for any other reason which has caused us to be out of balance it would be wise to work when we feel back to normal and in balance. The weight or the lightness of what we carry with us into our work can and will affect the frequency we are working at and directly effect of our undertakings.

All of that being said we're all human and we all have stuff! We have to make a good judgement call. There is a lot to be said for acceptance of ourselves in all our imperfections and there is a certain wisdom and strength to be found in learning how to live with certain difficulties or limitations and balancing them in our daily lives. Everyone has something they struggle with. Is this not also a kind of spiritual alchemy of a gentler sort? Some things perhaps we learn to live with or manage or adapt to.

Meditation is the most obvious thing to help with achieving balance and clarity of thought within the mind. The eastern style of practice suits many but not all. Lots of people prefer to meditate sitting or lying comfortably. It can be useful to light a candle somewhere safely near-by and perhaps some incense. Some people find music a distraction. For others it helps. In general it's a good idea to choose something calming and without lyrics. There are many good books or, even better, classes out there. Sometimes it might mean trying a few different ones until we find one that works but it is such a valuable gift to have that it's well worth the looking. There are also many people who do not subscribe to any conventional meditation but achieve a meditative state through exercise or time spent in nature with the trees or near water.

The two exercises that follow are designed to help familiarise us with our energetic systems and to get used to working with them in a simple way that is easy to learn. There is also a short-guided meditation at the end to recharge the energetic system.

Auric Exercise
Designed to increase sight and awareness of the aura.

Sitting or standing somewhere you feel at ease, relax and breathe deeply with both feet on the floor or earth beneath you.

Take a few slow breaths to drop in and centre yourself.

Put your two hands together palm to palm and take a few more breaths becoming aware of the energetic circuit of your body.

A few more breaths and shifting your attention to the connection of your palms.

Slowly move them apart just by a fraction, about half a centimetre. Hold this position and take a few more breaths.

Allow your eyes to focus in on the small space between them and you should be able to see light around your fingers.

You will also almost certainly be able to feel it, there's a warmth there (even if you have cold hands) which has a similar feel to two magnets for want of a better way of describing an indefinable quality.

Take a few more breaths and move them a little further apart, by about an inch.

The light between your hands should still be visible. You should still be able to feel the energy between them.

If you do this daily you will soon be able to increase the gap until you reach a stage where you can play with and manipulate a ball of light between your hands. Later this ability to direct energy will be an essential skill.

Each time you finish put your hands over your heart chakra and return to yourself any life force i.e. prana.

If this doesn't work for you don't worry for some it comes easily and for others it may be that other areas are stronger and this comes later but keep practising.

When you feel ready to and are proficient with this simple exercise you can move onto the next stage. For some people this may be a few days for others weeks or hours.

Expansion Exercise
Projecting a Shield of Light

As before relax and breathe deeply. Both feet should either be on the floor or earth if standing or sitting upright so as to remain grounded, or touching one another if you are lying down. Your arms should be either by your side with your palms resting against you in sitting or standing positions or hands touching one another or placed over your heart chakra if lying down. By holding your body in this way you create a "closed circuit" from any outside interference patterns.

Continue breathing and follow the breath and rise and fall of your body.

When it feels appropriate allow yourself to become aware of the energetic field surrounding you and as you do so pay attention to your heart and the warm sensation of the heart chakra, which is our point of connection with creation.

With each breath allow that connection to open and visualise white light above you and below you, rising up you from your feet and flowing down you from your head and centralising in your heart.

As the two streams of light fill up your body they may make you feel warm and meet in the heart.

To begin with it might look like a small white ball of light like the one you held in your hands before and feel warm and gentle.

Take three more slow deep breaths and allow it to expand to around a one foot sphere across your chest, becoming warmer.

Take three more breaths before letting it expand further projecting a full sized sphere all the way around you as far as your fingertips could almost reach.

You will almost certainly feel lighter and brighter and warmer.

This sphere or bubble of light you now stand within is a light shield, the first and most basic form of self protection and is the precursor to casting a circle later.

Spend a few minutes or as long as you want whilst your concentration is able within your bubble feeling the warmth and getting used to it and then when you are ready take one deep breath and as you exhale allow it to disappear and the energy surrounding you to go into the heart as in the last exercise. It might be helpful to put both hands on the heart chakra when you finish, regardless of what position you started in to make sure you have closed the circuit so to speak. Sit or stand upon the earth and breathe for a minute or two to make sure you feel grounded. If you feel any tingling sensation also place your hands on the earth palms down to discharge anything you do not need until the sensation goes.

Guided meditation to Recharge and Realign the Energetic System

This is a two part guided meditation. The first part is designed to recharge the energetic system with new renewed life force or prana and to clear out any old energy. The second part is to realign and balance the chakra system.

You may find it useful to get a friend you feel relaxed with to read you through this or even better record yourself reading, giving yourself time to breathe and space to drop in deeply and then play it back to yourself when you're ready.

Sitting or lying comfortably, relax and breathe deeply.

Both feet should either be on the floor or earth if standing or sitting upright so as to remain grounded, or they should be touching one another if you are lying down. Your arms should be either by your side with your palms resting against you in sitting or standing positions or hands touching one another or placed over your heart chakra if lying down. In this way you create a "closed circuit" from any outside interference.

Close your eyes and put your focus purely into your breathing. Notice the easy flow of air in and out and think about filling up your tummy and chest with breath and then releasing it from the chest and tummy. Do this for as long as you feel like you need to and really relax into it. Allow the breath to flow rhythmically, deeply and easily.

When you are ready to, focus upon your feet and visualise them filled with golden light, feel the warmth radiating inside you and relax. Take three breaths.

Then let the light spread upwards to your knees and feel the warm golden light. Take three breaths.

Let the light travel upwards, three breaths at a time, over your thighs,

three breaths at a time over your hips,

over your stomach,

light spreading up to your chest,

three breaths at a time light through your arms,

spreading up through your throat

and then your neck,

your face and head until your whole body is full of golden light and you can visualise it and feel the emanation all around you.

You are filled with light and radiating a golden glow.

Notice how deeply peaceful, safe and warm you feel.

Allow the light to remove and release from you anything you feel you no longer need in this moment and feel it become brighter and intensify slightly, becoming almost white.

You are warm, peaceful and recharged with golden white light.

One at a time we will focus on each chakra in the body.

Starting from the root chakra at the base of the spine place your attention there and visualise the colour red. Take a few deep breaths until it feels right for example a warmth or sense of security, and the colour brightens a little.

Working upwards in turn, we put our attention on to:

The sacral chakra and abdomen, visualising the colour orange. Then take a few deep breaths until it feels right and the colour brightens again.

The solar plexus glowing a warm yellow. Each time taking time to breath.

The heart chakra shining in a beautiful green or soft pink. Breathing.

The throat chakra, a crystal clear blue. Free and relaxed breath.

The third eye, a deep indigo. Breathing each time as the colour brightens.

And the crown chakra, amethyst, violet, turning into white light. Peaceful breathing.

The soft white light pours down filling you with peace and happiness and love.

Resting into the safe relaxed feeling notice the earth underneath you supporting and holding you and with each breath feel your deep connection to Mother Earth deepen.

After a few moments, when you feel ready to say thank you to the light.

Take your time and when you are ready to come back and very gently open your eyes.

Take your time to adjust and look around the room around you.

There is no rush, no need to move in a hurry, just a day to enjoy and a moment to be peaceful in.

Place your hands over your heart chakra for a few moments.

Part Two – The Theory

The chapters on magical theory look at the building blocks and components of life and at their workings. They are concerned with the greater defining principles of the world and universe around us and how and why they relate to one another specifically in a magical context. The governance of time, number, geometry, the cosmos and the constructs of the universe are the primary focus.

Chapter Eight
Seven Universal Principles
The Kyballion

Good order is birthed from disorder and this is the natural progression divinely inherent within all of creation. These are the keys to seeing this good order, the Great Creator at work.

The Kyballion, is a set of Hermetic teachings upon seven universal principles concerning the laws of existence. They are said to have been passed down by word of mouth for centuries and were only put to paper in 1912 published under a pseudonym of "Three Initiates". The teachings are said to be based upon seven principles which were taught by Hermes Trismegistus who was known as the great priest and God Thoth to the Egyptians and as the God Hermes to the Greeks. It is said that Hermes lived in Egypt and that he taught many others including Abraham. Whether this is accurate or not cannot be proven any more than other knowledge said to come from the Gods. It is possible that a high priest was later deified or that a high priest of Thoth channelled this information. Certainly priests, prophets, sages and numerous others people from all walks of life have been given messages from spirit or the Gods in every religion on Earth.

Although the source of the Kyballion, Corpus Hermeticam, cannot be confirmed there is no doubt that the Hermetic teachings have become well known and are widely studied. For the student of religion, philosophy and science, they act as the key to tying all the different schools of thought into one cohesive body of knowledge. Regardless of path the principles retain their integrity and are relevant.

The vastness of the universe is too big for most of us to begin to comprehend its make-up but these principles break up some of its workings into understandable constructs which we can grasp. As such regardless of its origin, it is a valuable tool as it enables us to look at these concepts. If you wish to read the book it is called *The Kyballion by Three Initiates*. The following is offered as a simplified explanation and account of each principle and how we may harness that knowledge. Any previous study grounded in philosophy, psychology, physics, biology and mathematics is helpful because it will expand upon them and allow deeper understanding. For now a basic idea of the concepts is enough. At this stage of learning these principles are here as ideas to think about and their practical application will develop slowly over time. As we become aware of the concepts so they become noticeable and present themselves in life and we recognise them in practice.

"The Principles of Truth are Seven; he who knows these, understandingly, possesses the Magic Key before whose touch all the Doors of the Temple fly open." — The Kyballion.

Principle of Mentalism – "The All is Mind; The Universe is Mental".

The ALL is mind. This is the idea that reality, the material universe, all of existence and life is spirit which can be thought of as a universal infinite living mind. All of everything. All is the whole of creation and God/Goddess. In other words God/Goddess are consciousness (mind) and there can be nothing else. Just as the thoughts we create find a way to express themselves as words and deeds shaping and co-creating our reality around us, so too the whole of creation is an expression of a universal and infinite living mind or consciousness. This omnipresent consciousness (God) is within us and we are within it. The All, omnipresent God consciousness is indefinable and unchangeable and yet all things contained within it are in constant becoming, change and cycle forever manifesting and creating.

All things are created by mind and all things are a manifestation of mind. This applies both universally and personally within our lives which means that by adjusting our mind set we can transmute one thing into another and create the world around us. This transmutation of mind from one state to another is mental alchemy. We have the capacity to change our minds, to change our thoughts and to manifest them. By aligning with love we can change our thoughts and therefore our experience of the world. By aligning with love we can manifest loving and healthy results aligned with the Divine mind. In many ways some modern psychotherapies are working with this principle. Cognitive behavioural therapies, positive affirmations and clinical hypnosis are all examples. During the manifestation process as we change our minds or shift our consciousness to one that is beneficial to us and focus our attentions and intentions upon a desired outcome we are more likely to bring them about as a direct result. For example the person who regularly says "where there's a will there's a way" is much more likely to find solutions than the person who repeats negative beliefs such as "if it can go wrong it will go wrong". We manifest our beliefs and expectations. This is why optimists genuinely appear to have better luck and even when circumstances are not easy they seem able to look for the blessings in a situation and turn it around!

There is a paradox at the heart of this principle which is that although we may understand that "the All is mind" we can never know the absolute truth because our relative truth is that we are within that mind and part of "all". We are governed by the laws of existence and though we may grasp that some aspects of reality are not as they appear to be neither are they illusory in that they are real in our experience of them. What we may learn to do however is to live well in the earthly sphere and to understand and use the natural laws to change our experience by raising ourselves up overcoming lower forces by raising our vibration.

When working with magic Mentalism is our foundation. We shift our mindset into a loving healed and balanced one and focus our energy towards a desired outcome.

The Principle of Correspondence – "As above, so below; as below so above".

We've all heard the expression "as above, so below" and there are instances where this idea can be applied in the other direction through use of consciousness, "as below, so above". There is harmony, agreement and correspondence between the planes of existence, physical, mental and spiritual. The principle of correspondence explains the relationship between the macrocosm and the microcosm and draws similarities between these two worlds. Each plane works on the same principles so understanding them on one level is the key to being able to use them as a bridge to higher levels of existence. If we reflect God/Goddess we may align ourselves and transcend the planes into higher consciousness or God consciousness. On a physical scale just as we reflect the whole of universal creation within our bodies so an atom reflects us. One way to see this is by comparing the way our solar system, our cells and our atoms are organised. The solar system has a clearly defined centre, the sun, around which things are arranged. Within our body each cell also has a centre called a nucleus as do atoms which also have a centre called a nucleus where protons and neutrons are found. This principle helps to understand the things that are either too small or too large for us to see in plain sight through observation of how they work. The colours of the rainbow too are mirrored within our bodies in the chakras.

Our actions or realities on a personal and individual level may also reflect those on a cultural or global level. Examples can be found in many different facets of daily life. How mankind treats the planet at present is reflected in our personal microcosm of our individual carbon footprints and our ethical choices when we shop and recycle etc. How we see the sacred feminine at this time is reflected in different cultures as the global movement of restoring women's rights makes progress largely thanks to the hard work and bravery of the women who have pushed for it and also in the improving standard of education. Our ancestors respected the sacred feminine and worshipped the Goddess in equality with the God and in ancient Egypt women had equal rights. How we are changing our beliefs and becoming more open-minded both personally and as societies is reflected in the worldwide advent of new technology such as the internet and freedom of information which can overcome cultural barriers and take us into a new era. As these social barriers dissolve on a global scale so too they dissolve within individuals whose experience and thinking have been broadened in a way that it would not otherwise have been.

In magical work this principle is primarily about our mindset when we work. As we enter our sacred space and work our magic our mindset is everything i.e. it is of no use working for peace whilst we feel anxious and concerned, we must first find the point of inner peace and then work. If we want to work for abundance we first need to prepare our mind by counting our blessings and feeling the abundance we desire so that it may increase. We align ourselves on this plane of existence by finding the right frame of mind i.e. abundant thoughts create abundant feelings, which in turn manifest abundance.

The Principle of Vibration – "Nothing rests, everything moves, everything vibrates".

Scientific research has proven this principle of vibration to be true and that all things do indeed move and vibrate at their own pitch or frequency. This principle is not just applicable to the physicality of matter although it includes it but applies to matter, energy, mind and spirit. Matter is the slowest moving of these and has lower pitched frequencies of density and we interact at this level in our physical form. Energy moves a little faster as a result of physical movement and expenditure such as release from fuel. The mind is faster again and here we engage with our consciousness. Spirit is the fastest and moves at such intensity and speed that it seems to us to be peaceful and still. Have you ever watched a spinning top as a child? The quicker it spins the more centred and still it appears and yet as it slows we see the wobble and the movement.

The higher we move into the realms of spirit as we work, the deeper it is necessary to drop deep within the self and into the heart because you cannot connect with spirit in its purest form with only the mind and it is in the quietening of the mind and opening of the heart that we can connect with the higher realms. It is this deep, dropping inwards that allows the appearance of slowing down and peace where we can reach our highest potential. Dropping inwards to peace is also the only way to hold or contain a large amount of fast moving spirit; otherwise like the spinning top we may become unstable.

Just as before when we prepare ourselves to work, sitting in our sacred space or circle we shift our focus inwards. The higher the plane we wish to connect with the deeper we drop inwards so that the coupled function of the mind (mentalism) and the highest frequency of spirit (vibration) available to us with our open heart can occur. It is here with our open heart and mind that we raise our vibrational frequency to align with the work we are to undertake. We do this whilst at the same time remaining grounded and acknowledging our foundation and roots. These roots and foundation chakras are actually our balance and what we are anchored in and it is therefore important too that we have done our personal work here and have a sure footing. We speed up to raise heavy situations towards spirit for solution and we slow things down to manifest spirit into grounded earthly results perhaps by taking manageable steps that we are guided to take.

We align our frequency and speed.

The Principle of Polarity – "Everything is Dual; everything has poles; everything has its pair of opposites; like and unlike are the same; opposites are identical in nature, but different in degree; extremes meet; all truths are but half-truths; all paradoxes may be reconciled".

Everything in three-dimensional existence is dual and has poles of opposites. It is the nature of cosmic birth. To be part of time and space involves birth and therefore separation from the source. Up and down are both identical in their nature but different degrees of the same thing. So too with hot and cold, it is the degree that changes not the essence of the thing. Like and dislike, love and hate, positive and negative are not so very different in their respective natures but vary by degree. It is therefore possible that we are able to change one thing into its opposite by changing its degree or vibration within us and therefore within our manifestations by the alchemy of the mind. We cannot always choose the circumstances we find ourselves in but we can choose what we do in them and our long term if not immediate reactions to them.

In magical working an example of how this can happen is that we start with one feeling i.e. negativity towards a situation that we wish to improve. We focus our attention onto that feeling and we gradually shift its degree using our mind (mentalism) and its frequency (vibration) from one pole to another. We move internally from negative to positive feelings about the situation in order that we work in a positive way and attract a positive outcome. It doesn't even matter if the first feelings of positivity have been synthesised by the mind because it still changes the mindset and we find ourselves able to see a bigger picture and see more clearly the positive aspects of the situation or even potential positive things that we can call into being as a result. We can entirely alter a situation from bad to good internally by thinking in loving ways in order to change our feelings towards it. This may bring hope, solutions, a more positive mindset, promote actions towards improving the outcome and alter the course of events or the unfolding of a situation. The result is twofold: firstly that we feel better already and are better able to come up with new ideas and solutions or secondly that the situation may have entirely changed for the better. When we apply this principle within a magical working through setting intention and or prayer it can speed up the process and bring things about much more quickly. We shift towards the opposite pole through use of loving thoughts.

The Principle of Rhythm – "Everything flows, out and in; everything has its tides; all things rise and fall; the pendulum-swing manifests in everything; the measure of the swing to the right is the measure of the swing to the left; rhythm compensates".

The patterns of creation are all around us in the cycles of all life. Everything has a motion, an ebb and a flow between its poles. The sun rises and sets each day and the length of the day varies depending where it is in the larger solar year cycle, the precession of the equinoxes every twenty-six thousand years (approximately) follow the ecliptic path. The planets each have their own path and cycle. The tides of the sea move with the gravitational pull of the moon and the moon itself has her twenty-nine day cycle too. We too have patterns within our physical bodies as we move with the time of year and within our lives as we sleep when it's dark and wake when it's light (disregarding electricity).

By becoming keen observers of the patterns around us in nature and creation and within our own beings we can learn to be in harmony with them and understand them thereby freeing ourselves from being governed by them. It is an entirely different experience to consciously work with planetary movements for example and to understand the deep-seated responses of the soul in relation to the current astronomy than to be deeply affected without the same understanding. The initiate understands the natural patterns and lives with them. The uninitiated may feel the natural patterns deeply but not realise why certain phases in life have presented themselves. The natural patterns are the governance of time and all things within time.

The personal patterns we learn to identify within ourselves can be incredibly valuable to us whether they are behavioural or physical as they allow us to become more conscious of ourselves and understand better which ones are healthy for us or not and which ones to take notice of. We can use this knowledge in our daily lives to our benefit just as we would observe the seasons and weather for the patterns to best plant seeds in springtime. Some of those patterns can be obvious physical ones too, like if we know we are likely to be tired on a Friday night after working hard all week it would be wise to either give ourselves time to sleep first or choose another day to work magic such as Sunday when we're feeling good and well rested.

When we are planning to work magic one of the first things we can do is to look at the moon phases, astrology and planetary alignments, times of day etc. and see when would be the most favourable time to do the work we are planning. Understanding the natural rhythms, patterns and cycles of nature allows us to harness them by working with them. We are far more likely to be successful when all the natural forces are supporting the direction we wish to take. For example cleansing or clearing may best be undertaken approaching dark moon. For a woman too it may well be that dark moon coincides with menstruation and that this can be a good time to connect with the powerful crone energy within. Our own emotional cycles and energy levels or patterns should also always be taken into consideration before working wherever possible. We observe and work in harmony with the natural rhythms.

The Principle of Cause and Effect – "Every Cause has its Effect; every Effect has its Cause; everything happens according to Law; Chance is but a name for Law not recognized; there are many planes of causation, but nothing escapes the Law".

For every cause there is an effect and for every effect a cause. This one happens to coincide with Newton's third law of motion: "To every action there is an equal and opposite reaction". It could also perhaps be thought of as the principle of there is no such thing as coincidence! This principle states that everything in creation is governed by natural order and universal law and that if all is mind (mentalism) i.e. consciousness itself, then it would be impossible for anything to exist independently outside of it. The implication here is that nothing is undetermined. Yet that is really only a half-truth because freewill is the other half of the same truth. Whilst these two thoughts may appear to be in opposition to one another they are but two sides of the same coin and the two polarities of degree of the same thing. There is a further paradox of cause and effect in that some effects are caused externally to us and we feel their effect (some may call this fate or destiny) and others are of our own making or influence and we have a part in the causation. Yet somewhere in all examples there is still a cause and nothing is outside of this law. The principle goes on to explain that everything obeys the causation of the higher planes but has the ability to create an effect by causation to the lower planes. This means that we have the ability to be cause rather than effect within the material realm at least. At a physical level this principle may mean that we consciously choose our own course of action and decide our direction rather than being swept along by other people or by life or without direction.

One way to reflect upon this principle is to look at one stitch in the weave or a brush stroke in the bigger picture. Like a tapestry each stitch has its significance. Like each painting each stroke changes the picture. If an ancient ancestor had met a different girl first instead of the wife he married all the future generations of the family he would have had may well never have existed. He may have had a different family. His descendants may have been of historical importance and the world now may look different as a result. This principle acknowledges the connections between all things past, present and future and our parts of the whole. It acknowledges the chains of events that affect decisions, outcomes and actions years in advance of their occurrence. It accounts for seemingly random things that years later prove to have been the catalyst to events of great significance. Nothing just "happens". Everything is exactly as it is supposed to be. It takes us beyond the point of should bes and into the acceptance of IS. This understanding of the interconnectedness of all becomes increasingly visible over time through magic. In our understanding of this principle and our place within the all we can become effect rather than cause within the physical realm. Surely here is one of the reasons we undertake the work of the initiate to begin with, the knowing that we have influence and are capable of effecting change directly in our lives, surroundings and circumstances. We visualise our direction and then take positive action to effect change or align ourselves with our desired course. The act of working magic could itself be seen as this principle exactly as an example of considering and working in a loving way with all that we can to be the cause of a desired effect.

The Principle of Gender – "Gender is in everything; everything has its

Masculine and Feminine Principles Gender; manifests on all planes".

The principle of gender is that the masculine and feminine principles are manifested in everything. Note here that the word gender is from the Latin root meaning to beget, pro-create, generate, create or produce. This is not about sex in the way we think of the word, although it may be included in the whole, it is about creation. It is an acknowledgement that it takes both masculine and feminine principles to create and that this is what makes up the universe. The masculine principle, yang, is the raw energy, the output and the impetus or drive. The feminine principle, yin, is the containing, directing and harnessing of that energy into form through the creative process. Only when both work together can creation occur. Psychologically, regardless of whether we were born male or female we need to embody both of these attributes and ideally we need both to be in balance with one another in order to manifest our energy and thoughts into creation through our actions and harnessing of them.

In the workings of magic we particularly need these two sides of ourselves to be in balance in order that we work in a balanced way. Vast amounts of energy can be wasted if we are unable to direct them effectively and likewise all the directing in the world won't manifest much if there is no impetus there. We all know someone who has fantastic plans but is somehow unable to see them through or commit to the actions necessary to bring them to fruition. Likely also that we all know someone who despite their best efforts and a lot of doing never seems to achieve their desired outcome because the initial impetus was never there. Just as in daily life, so too in magic. We work with balanced masculine and feminine principles to bring into creation.

Practical Exercise

Look for and write down three examples of each of the seven universal hermetic principles at work. It's only when we work with them that we see exactly how prevalent they are in every area of life. Once you've started looking patterns become apparent and new significance may be found in the previously mundane.

Initiating a relationship with Trees and Plants Exercise

There is an innate wisdom and knowledge inherent within each of us and a collective consciousness with which we can interact at any time we choose. Some call this divine guidance, others intuition. This gift may be visibly seen and tested with plants. This exercise is a simple and effective way of increasing that ability and learning useful things in the process. It is also an excellent way to become accustomed to tuning in to frequencies and to building a working herbal knowledge.

Whenever you have the opportunity, take a pen and paper out with you when you are going to walk somewhere or be in nature or if you don't have one with you take a picture on your phone to look up later. Using technology isn't cheating when it's a learning tool. Often this can surprisingly include a trip to the shops. Even town centres and car parks have trees and common plants. Common weeds, leaves from trees or wild flowers are all useful here.

Spend time with the tree or plant you have chosen. How does it feel? What are its leaves like? What does it look like? What does it smell like? The smell is really important.

The smell and feel of any plant can and will tell you its purpose. Stop when you come to something that draws you and is plentiful. Hold the plant and feel it, smell it observe how you react to it. Write down what you intuitively feel this plant may do and how it smells and feels to you. Consider what it might do or be useful for physically for medicinal or practical use and magically any potential properties. These magical uses are often logical extensions of the plant's physical uses but on a higher arc. Then come home and look them up.

The more you do this the more often you will get it right and build up your own knowingness and connection not to mention you may well be surprised at how many you get correct just on intuition!

There are similarities between certain plants in smell and energetics once you begin to recognise them. At the very least if not you will build your knowledge through their study upon return. This is really valuable later when it comes to spell work as plants and their properties are our most valuable ingredients. A good friend of mine would also add here that our food is our medicine and that we should all know our herbs.

N.B. It is better not to pick plants unless they are really plentiful and of course do not eat plants without knowing what they are, what they do and if you have any allergies. If in doubt seek the advice of a herbalist.

Chapter Nine
Sacred Geometry and Number

The harmonic resonance of all things has geometric form and all geometric forms have harmonic resonance. To see sacred geometry is to see the great architect at work.

Sacred geometry is such a vast topic that it is often left out in these sorts of books and it doesn't always get covered with basics and yet it is fundamental. Geometry was a subject which did not inspire most of us at school if truth be told but then our mathematics teacher never took us outside and showed us flowers or nature or how it applied to life! If she had it would likely have had us all captivated and its worth would have been known to us even as children. In geometry and number we can find the divine order of the universe and of creation and see reality as it is actually made. Geometry is rare in that it engages both the logical and objective left side of the brain and the intuitive subjective right side of the brain. It truly is both art of science and science of art and it connects the universe. It is sometimes referred to as Universal Architecture or the fingerprint of God.

This like all the other chapters of this book is intended only as an approach, the initial leading in, to the subject in the hope that it offers a glimpse of the possibilities and infinite value of its secrets that might later be built upon. In relation to magic this subject opens up sacred ground quite literally. In understanding shape and number in the creation of life around us all other known attributes and correlations take on new meaning and significance. When we draw a pentacle or a circle let us know its meaning and do so with intent and with knowledge of its significance otherwise these are hollow gestures. When we see or notice a recurring number or a pattern in daily life let us be made aware of its meaning.

It has been said that the older the source the purer is the water. Nothing is more ancient or purer than geometry. Our ancient temples, monuments and historical cities hold secrets for us to see if we but look for they have been built using geometric proportions of significance. Even the shapes found in the crystalline structure of human DNA and beyond that of our physical bodies to the world around us are entirely made of the same geometric shapes found in the rest of creation and echoed in the sacred sites and temples of Earth. To enter the physical temple of the body we "know ourselves" and recognise our shared sacred geometry with the rest of creation.

The word geometry comes from Gaia-metry and literally means earth measuring. It is the measure not just of land but of all. Our ancestors worshipped the Earth and recognised nature as the manifestation of divinity. Temples from many cultures are built according to the geometric proportions found on Earth. Copying these proportions into their construction may have been seen as a way of imbuing them with this divinity. By studying the orbits of the planets each mean orbit can be related to one another in ordered geometric relationships. The planets themselves are considered in many belief systems to be Gods.

The Law of Causation states that all things have a cause and this includes the First Cause of creation by or from Source. The First Cause in creation then is no mere coincidence or some accidental big bang resulting in a staggering set of coincidences beyond belief but is the conscious decision of divinity with intention and intelligent design. There may have been a bang but if there was it was no accident. Perhaps the divine splitting or reflecting of itself in expression? An explanation of the creation process is given in the Bible in Genesis. However, it was never intended to be taken literally but as an analogy. At the time it was written it was a usual practice to preserve and pass on information vocally in stories in a way that it might be remembered for future generations. This is common in all cultures and a way of teaching and remembering vital information in a time when it was seldom written and few people had books. It is widely speculated that this creation story is based upon the older teachings of the Egyptian mystery schools.

The traditional tools of geometry are the ruler and the compass and it is generally agreed that straight lines represent the male principles and that curved lines represent the female principles.

Divinity or Source cannot be depicted beyond the void of our reality in timeless form . However the compass must pivot upon the paper and this tiny pinprick or hole might be considered as the point of creation or the eye of God.

For reference, here too is the significance of the eye of Horus, the pupil being the dot upon the paper.

.

Dot

At this point we can only depict with lines the Divine consciousness, which reaches out with a beam of thought or light in three lines. One from above to below, one from front to back and one from side to side. i.e. the four directions above and below, three axes.

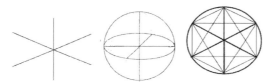

These three lines may then be connected at the end points. Using the curved female lines of the compass a sphere is formed. Then using the straight male lines of a ruler an octahedron is formed.

Within the octahedron also lies the hidden shape of the hexagram through the connection of the points of rotation where the octahedron meets the sphere.

In a two-dimensional form here lies the first circle (sphere) and the first square (cube) in creation.

Universal Numbers

The universe was made spherical because it is the only shape that can be completely self-sufficient that is also capable of containing all other shapes. It is represented by the number one. However in geometry it may sometimes also take a second number which is purely representative of what it is being used to depict. In the usual geometers diagram of the universal sphere this number is twelve because it contains the twelve houses of the Sun, astrological signs, or the twelve Gods made manifest in the cosmos. No coincidence that our watch has a face with twelve hours of the day and night

As a two-dimensional depiction of the universe as a sphere, a flat circle it may then be divided further to represent light and dark, or matter and ether, symbolic of duality in existence and necessary to creation. This can be shown on paper by drawing a square within the first circle and then drawing a second circle within the square which thereby halves the area.

Using more advanced mathematics, (factorials and square roots) the geometer's diagram of the universal sphere often takes the number 1746 which is known as the "number of fusion." It is briefly mentioned here because it combines and fuses together the positive and negative of both masculine and feminine principles found in the numbers 666, which is considered the number of the Sun (masculine) + 1080, which is considered the number of the Moon (feminine). This is significant alone but even more so later as the beginnings of Gematria may be found here. Gematria is the study of sacred meanings found through words and their associated numbers within the Greek, Arabic and Hebrew alphabets.

As an aside regarding the number 666, its truth is that of the Sun and it is not in and of itself bad, evil or harmful in any way. Quite the opposite for the Sun correlates to perpetual light, the heart and eyes of the Divine and to truth and balance. That being said it is worth considering as with all things any thought forms of the collective human consciousness to which we belong, quantities of finite belief and any or all associations of a thing before using it. This number has sadly been misused by many through its effective inversion. If you should choose to use it in magic do so with complete clarity of thought and love and be-aware that there are no discordant thoughts or doubts internally before proceeding. In terms of number sequences and being aware of patterns just as 222 can reassure that all things are in balance 666 can be an indicator to pay attention to balance or that something may be amiss.

The circle represents eternity and timelessness, oneness and the source of all potential. The circle is also a square in that one is always contained within the other. In truth they are one. Positive and negative, male and female. In creation the points of the square attract inwards collapsing towards the centre and the perimeter of the circle pushes outwards expanding. This creates the push pull unity of opposing principles or duality in balance.

We have already seen a square and a second circle inside the first. Within this second inner circle may be added a six-pointed star called a hexagram which is two interlocking Pythagorean triangles. (We saw this hidden shape, the hexagram, within the rotation of the octahedron above.) Hexagrams are also known as the Star of David and or the Seal of Solomon.

Finally within the six-pointed star a third circle may be added, which halves the area again and is one sixth of the area of the first largest circle on the outside. This smaller central circle represents the earthly sphere including the orbiting moon.

The number 5040 is significant because it is the combination of 1080 the number of the Moon and 3960 the number of the Earth.

Proportionally these three concentric circles are in a ratio of 1:2:3. This image then depicts the geometers universe.

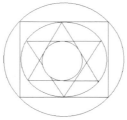

Whilst twelve is the cosmological number for the male in creation and represents the houses of the sun, its female counterpart is seven and represents spirit and the planets. Both must be recognised for only in their union is there order and balance. Although twelve is the number of the cosmos, within the earthly sphere all things are numbered decimally from one to ten. Within this decimal system seven is sacred as it is the axis or pivotal point of the numbers one to ten. This can be seen simply here:

$(1 \times 2 \times 3 \times 4 \times 5 \times 6 \times 7 \times) = 5040$ or $(8 \times 9 \times 10) = 5040$

There are seven planets or recognised wandering stars in esoteric teaching (and a further three in higher octave), seven rays of light and colour in the visible light spectrum and seven related notes in the diatonic scale.

There are twelve houses of the sun, twelve months in the solar calendar, twelve notes in the chromatic scale and twelve hours upon the face of the clock marking time. This governance of time may also be seen in the cycles of the houses of the sun, whose great months are each 2160 years and the sum total of which is 25920 years also known as the great year, corresponding to one complete cycle of the procession of the equinoxes.

These exact ratios may be seen in the architecture of The Great Pyramid at Giza and at Stonehenge and many other sacred sites aligned with the heavens, hidden within plain sight. Within the ancient circles and temples of the world there are geometric blueprints echoing multiple sacred geometries.

The Earth's geometry is made up of the trinity shining light through the zodiac and manifesting on Earth.

One source reaches out upon three axes, like the three lines depicted above, i.e. trinity...

3   The Trinity – Maiden, Mother Crone and/or Father, Son and Holy Spirit

x 12   The Cosmos – Expressing through the Twelve signs of the Zodiac

x 10   The Earth – Manifesting in the earthly number of creation 10 which also corresponds to the spheres of the Sephiroth upon the Tree of Life.

= 360

It makes logical sense that circles and all things encompassed within three-dimensional earthly existence can be made within 360 degrees.

And further-more that their outward expressions whether in terms of colour, ray, note, or day of the week are found in the number seven, that of the Goddess.

The diameter of the Sun is 864,000 miles, which is 400 x the diameter of the moon, and the Moon's distance from Sun is 400 x its distance from Earth, which is how and why they line up so perfectly when there is an eclipse. This is no accident or chain reaction of coincidences but intelligent design in all its beauty.

In trying to understand a little more of that beauty let us return to a sheet of paper with our compass and start by making that little pinprick sized point of creation and drawing one sphere which two dimensionally is a circle...

Vesica Piscis

This first sphere is just a compass point and a circumference. Then follows a second sphere of equal size which overlaps so that each passes through the centre of the other. In creation this is perhaps the self-expression, duplication or self-reflection of divinity. This cross section of both spheres is called Vesica Piscis and is said to be the eye image from which light is projected. In human beings this shape is found both in the outer shape of the eye and within the lens of the eye which adjusts the focus of light and perceives light in the visible spectrum. This shape is sometimes referred to as the image of birth. Also as the image of light and consciousness in creation.

Whilst the Flower of Life pattern and its counterparts, the seed of life and the tree of life, are ancient in design and examples are to be found both in ancient Indian temples and sacred Egyptian carvings, most of the written material we have with the inclusion of the egg of life and fruit of life is modern and theoretical. That being said the unmistakeable reappearance of the same design in holy places across the world is the testimony of its significance and sanctity. Leonardo DaVinci studied the pattern now known as the flower of life and it's mathematical properties. His sketches show the geometrical structures of both the flower and its components in *Codex Atlanticus, fol.459r* (1478-1519).

The Flower of Life Pattern

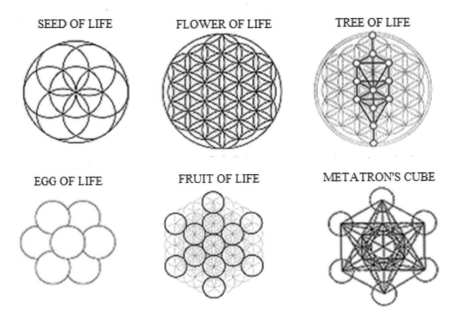

SEED OF LIFE   FLOWER OF LIFE   TREE OF LIFE

EGG OF LIFE   FRUIT OF LIFE   METATRON'S CUBE

The Seed of Life

From the innermost point of the sphere the next sphere is projected. At this point these spheres are still theoretical and are representative of Divine consciousness or thought. Each time a sphere is completed another is projected until the pattern resembles a six-petalled flower around a centre. With completion of the seventh sphere this pattern is known as the Seed of Life. It is found in matter universally in all life forms, atoms, cosmic bodies and stars.

This Seed of Life design is sometimes shown as a basic one-dimensional depiction of the "Tube Torus" shape, which is formed by ratcheting the Seed of Life and duplicating the lines of the Tube Torus in its design. The Tube Torus is the only pattern in creation which can fold in upon itself.

The Flower of Life

The highest expression of light in creation containing the entirety of all the patterns.

From this seed of life can be added an additional six spheres (referred to as second vortex motion) and then another six spheres (third vortex motion). This creates the Flower of Life pattern sometimes also called the language of light. This represents the way in which consciousness creates. The oldest known image of the Flower of Life pattern is carved into the granite at the Temple of Osiris in Abydos. Each of the vesica piscis found within this pattern has perfect golden mean proportions and the significance of this will shortly become apparent. Two further vortex motions create the Fruit of Life pattern. In this way the pattern itself is said to represent the cycle of a fruit tree. The fruit contains seed – tree flower seed, tree flower seed, etc.

The Tree of Life

The Kemetic Tree of Life pattern has existed for thousands of years originating it is thought within the Egyptian mystery schools and later taught as the Jewish Kabbalah independently of the Flower of Life pattern. It may be found within the pattern by drawing lines from the points of contact of the seven spheres of the Seed of Life. Superimposed the interconnected circle points can be seen aligning with the Tree of Life. This image is engraved into two sets of three pillars both in Karnak and Luxor in Egypt five thousand years ago.

The Egg of Life

The egg of life pattern is taken from the Flower of Life pattern by removing six of the spheres and it has eight spheres (one is hidden from view behind central one when shown in 2d representation flat). This structure is the same as that found in the embryonic creation of all organisms on the planet.

The Fruit of Life

The Fruit of Life pattern is taken directly from the flower of life pattern and has thirteen circles representing sixteen spheres (some of these are also hidden in 2d). When lines are drawn from the connecting points of these spheres, 78 in total, the form of Metatron's Cube is revealed.

Metatron's Cube

Within Metatron's cube is hidden a second hyper cube called a tesseract. If you draw lines from each point of these cubes to one another all the parameters of the first three two-dimensional shapes of the platonic solids are revealed.

The Platonic Solids

There are five regular figures in solid three-dimensional geometry which are associated with the five elements, three of which are made with equilateral triangles. It is thought that the late Neolithic people in the Scotland had platonic solid ornaments of carved stone one thousand years before Plato as well as others that were not symmetrical. This is quite possible given that we know that prehistoric Britons knew the dimensions of the Earth and land prior to 3000 BC as all the major time periods of the Sun and Moon are congruent with the design of their sacred sites and monuments.

Each of these five platonic solids can be contained and are congruent with the shape of the sphere and this is the only shape that is capable of containing them all.

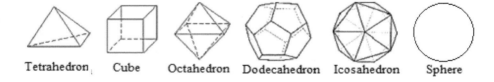

Tetrahedron   Cube   Octahedron   Dodecahedron   Icosahedron   Sphere

These platonic solid shapes are arranged into dual pairs with the exception of the tetrahedron which has the potential for its dual hidden within it.

The tetrahedron corresponds with the element of fire and has four triangular sides.

The cube with six sides corresponds to Earth and it pairs with the octahedron with eight sides which corresponds to air.

The last pair are the icosahedron with twenty sides corresponding to water and the dodecahedron with twelve pentagonal sides corresponding to ether or spirit.

There are in addition to these building blocks a further thirteen shapes called the Archimedean solids which are sometimes referred to as semi regular polyhedra with highly symmetrical shapes.

The Golden Ratio, Spirals and Fibonacci

The golden mean or golden ratio is the number approximately equal to 1.618033989...

If you divide a line into two parts so that: the longer part divided by the smaller part is also equal to the whole length divided by the longer part, you will have the golden ratio.

The golden mean or ratio is a pattern that is integral to the whole understanding of nature and it is found in everything from human anatomy (see Da Vinci's Canon of Man) and the cochlea of the inner ear, to nautilus shells, ammonites, butterflies, insects, plants and flowers. Architects used it in the design of the Parthenon and the Pyramids and it has also been used in numerous famous works of art.

The golden ratio sometimes called Divine Proportion, when plotted numerically creates a sequence that emerges. We can see this as a fractal pattern. In recent years scientists have been suggesting that the study of fractal patterns can lead us to a greater understanding of the universe and that they may make up a unified field essential to universal structure.

Following the analysing of data scientists report that fractal patterns and possibly the golden ratio have been discovered in outer space for the very first time. They have been studying a specific kind of stars called RR Lyrae variables using the Kepler Space Telescope. Unlike normal stars these RR Lyrae variables expand and contract, causing their brightness to adjust dramatically, and in so doing create pulsations. These golden stars are at their youngest over ten billion years old and their brightness can vary by two hundred percent over half a day. These pulsations aren't random or arbitrary but are in fact pulsating in an orderly fractal pattern. It is possible that this pattern is in accordance with the golden mean and more research is warranted. Although we have seen the golden ratio in nature all the time this is the first time it has ever been identified in space. Whilst some of these stars pulsate with a single frequency, observations confirm that others pulsate with multiple frequencies.

Fibonacci

The golden mean when it is in the form of the spiral is almost impossible to draw by hand though we may do it using technology. There is however another way of drawing this golden perfect spiral which is by use of the Fibonacci sequence.

Fibonacci was an Italian mathematician who studied older sources of Indian mathematics and introduced the system to the West in 1202 in his book *Liber Abaci*. The system effectively mimics the golden mean spiral through observation of the growth sequences of plants such as the number and order of leaves growing from a stem or the uncurling fern. Lilies and irises have three petals, buttercups and wild roses have five, delphiniums have eight petals and so on.

The numbers of the sequence start 1, 1, 2, 3, 5, 8, 13, 21, 34, 55, 89, 144 ad infinitum. Each number can be calculated by the addition of the last two in the sequence. Using this Fibonacci sequence it is possible to plot a graph which will approximate the golden mean spiral by using them as ratios for squares and then connecting the corners by curved lines or arcs.

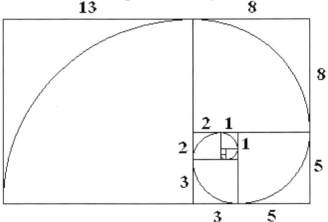

Music, Harmonics and Sound in Geometry

Plato had theorized that the Universe as a whole is simply a resonance of the "Music or Harmony of the Spheres".

In the Chromatic Greek scale used in the West, there are twelve notes to an octave and each scale step represents a semitone interval. This chromatic scale also has twelve major overtones and many minor overtones and these may be heard sung in the prayers and chanting of the East outside the mosques. In a Diatonic Greek scale there are seven notes to an octave. The term diatonic is usually taken to mean the "white note scale" i.e. without the black-keyed semitones of the piano but it may also be applied to all heptatonic scales both major and minor. They are often used as a pair. Notice the union of twelve and seven. The perfect fifth is the golden mean of musical sound just as it is to be found in the number five.

Each musical note corresponds to a colour in the visual light (and electromagnetic) spectrum. It therefore also corresponds to a chakra in the human body. Each sound has its own vibration and frequency and this can be observed in sine waves on graphs that represent sound waves. Sound waves are disturbances in air which are made up of atoms. Sound can be visualised then both as a wave and as a vibration. As note pitch gets higher the wavelength gets shorter, as note pitch gets lower the wavelength gets longer. This is true of all wavelengths in ascending and descending scales in the audio, electromagnetic, light spectrum of the rainbow. Music then can greatly affect our own resonance and pitch depending what we choose to listen to or, more importantly, that which we choose to align ourselves either for cathartic release or for inducing good and positive feelings. There is sympathetic resonance between number, shape, music and colour and the initiate can align with this.

Cymatics is the study of visible sound. Sound literally has geometry to it and visible geometrical vibrations of any given sound can be seen using sand or coated particles on a metal plate and then playing a sound into the plate. The vibrations of the sound make the particles arrange themselves on the plate, sometimes into beautiful geometric patterns or mandalas. "Om" when chanted for example creates elliptical patterns like the paths of planets orbiting the sun. Our thoughts and our words are supremely powerful. In the beginning there was sound. Sound is the start of manifestation. Most of the mandalas, yantras and sacred patterns and symbols of the East are based upon sacred geometry and Divine expression found through meditation. Some of these symbols organically arise in cymatics.

A good example of a sacred geometric yantra can be seen in the sri yantra meaning "holy instrument" or "holy wheel" which is said to be the mother of yantras and from which all other yantras are said to derive. The sri yantra shows nine triangles that can be interlaced in such a way as to form forty-three smaller triangles symbolic of the cosmos. Singing and other ways of creating harmonics can be one of the fastest and most powerful components of magical workings.

Nought and Infinity

Divinity cannot itself be expressed as anything upon paper for it is without dimension and in geometry it is shown only as the self-sufficient pin prick of a dot which the compass makes upon the paper. The dot in the centre also then represents a cross section of the two poles or axis and the point of Divine law and order. The dot might also be considered as the point of nought and as the point of infinity which are in truth both its polarities and union. All ise one when nought has passed.

One

This Divine dot then may expand with consciousness to encompass itself and the only possible shape this may be is a circle. This circle then may rotate in many directions and become a sphere. All other life in the uni-verse is contained within it and part of it. The circle symbolises eternity, without beginning or end and as such has heavenly and spiritual associations.

Two

The Divine consciousness projects in re-creation or reflection of the first in self-expression thus creating two circles which overlap one another as a vesica piscis. Here then are the two parts and duality in nature which are also in balance and in harmony with one another.

Three

In three we see the first real number because one and two are essentially abstract. Its shape is the triangle and the triangle may be found in the icosahedron's hidden hexagram, the rhombus, which is a pair of equilateral triangles bases to base, the interlocking triangles of the hexagon and in some rectangles. When the third circle is added to the two of vesica piscis here too we find the trinity in the form of the triquetra. Three of the five solid elements are also composed of triangles.

The trinity is Divine in nature and is found in all things of heaven and earth. Within mankind there is body-mind-soul, father-mother-child and the three generations of youth, middle age and old age. In time there is past, present and future. In the aspects of the Goddess, Maiden-Mother-Crone. In the aspects of the God Son-Father-Holy Spirit. In matter there are protons-electrons-neutrons. There are three primary colours and human vision is trichromatic.

Pyramids are representative of the trinity of spirit and are built on earth (square).

Four

The shape of four is square and four is also the first square number, 2x2=4. Its association is with Earth as the platonic solid cube and it is the preferred building block of man and found within the architecture of Earth. Four symbolises reason, stability and order. It is found in the four quarters and their associated elements. There are four directions north, east, south and west and four winds or pillars. There are four seasons of winter, spring, summer and autumn. In the Kabbalah there are four worlds Atziluth, Briah, Yetzirah and Assiah.

Five

Five is the number of humanity, life, spirit incarnated and the pursuit of knowledge. "In cannon of number man is the measure of all things". Humankind is made as a five-sided figure with golden ratio proportions with four limbs and one head. The famous depiction of Leonardo da Vinci's archetypal man, said to have been learned from Vetruvius before him, shows this in perfect form. Five is also the number of life and of living spirit. On all trees with edible fruit there are five-petalled flowers. There are also some flowers with pentagonal stamens and geometrical patterns around the centre. The apple, which is said to be the fruit of knowledge, contains the five-pointed star in its centre. Pentagons also have golden section within them and are governed by the phi ratio. The Fibonacci ratio, three eighths, representing the perfect fifth leads to the golden mean in music.

Note the connection to twelve also as pentagons occur as the sides of dodecahedrons. More importantly still perhaps is the connection to ten for fives must seek another of the same kind to procreate.

Six

Six is the number of union and marriage and relates to matter. It is found within the first square and circle, (sphere and icosahedron) with hidden hexagram, in union at the point of theoretical creation which was discussed at the beginning of the chapter. The hexagram is also known as the Star of David or Seal of Solomon. The union of any two equilateral triangles may make a hexagram. Six is also found in the hexagon. It is said to be the perfect number as 1+2+3=6 and 1x2x3=6

Hexagons are found in crystals, honeycomb and orderly structure.

Continuing with six seems to be the perfect place to include a brief few words about the Mer ka Ba. The name comes from the Egyptian meaning, Light Spirit Body. In Hebrew this translates as Throne-Chariot of God. The merkaba is often depicted two dimensionally by the two interlocking triangles of a hexagram which represent three sided pyramids. It may depict the union of the male and female trinities of the God and Goddess as one Divine source. Some consider it to be a vehicle of consciousness or a living field of light to align with God/Goddess. Certainly it is worth meditating upon. In the book of Ezekiel it is described as a chariot of heavenly beings. In the book of Enoch it is described where Ishmael ascends to heaven to behold the vision of the merkaba and enters the six halls to God. This is in keeping with various beliefs about the seven levels of heavens in some cultures, the seventh hall being the final one we may not surpass even in spirit whilst in earthly form.

Seven

Seven is sacred as a symbol of the Goddess and Divine feminine principles. Its shape is the heptagon, which unlike other geometric shapes cannot bisect a circle to a whole number or be made with a compass and ruler. It is associated with sound, light, the un-knowable and the seeking of wisdom, matriarchal ways of life and the great mystery. It is often associated with dreams, prophecy, oracles and art. In the earthly sphere seven is the axis or pivot point around which all revolves. Seven is also the number of the planets (not including those in higher octave) and therefore the key number in the planetary magic. Sevens are found in the holy day of the Sabbath, in the notes of the heptatonic scale, the colours of the rainbow, the chakras and the heavens.

Eight

Eight is the first cubic number 2x2x2 and it can be halved and halved again without changing its proportions. Its associations are balance, justice, friendship, stability, practicality, counsel and upholding natural law which supposes all mankind to be equal.

Nine

Nine contains within it three trinities and represents the principles of the sacred triad at their fullest potential. In the earthly domain of tens, nine is the final number and as such is a boundary. The Greeks called nine the horizon to the void or Ennead. It is also the number associated with human pregnancy and gestation. Nines represent fulfilment, completion, reaching a zenith and endings and births.

The repetitive multiples of nine all reduce back to nine in the addition of their two digits. 9 18 27 36 45 54 63 72 81 90

Ten

Ten relates to all earthly existence and to marriage in humanity and life. The key to ten is in the union of pentacles, ten of which make a perfect circle. Two interlocking pentacles will combine to form the ten-pointed star. Two pentacles or things of earthly origin are needed to procreate and ten is therefore the number of manifestation on Earth. No coincidence that there are ten spheres upon the Kabbalistic Tree of Life.

Eleven

Like seven and nine-sided polygons, eleven-sided geometrical shapes cannot be drawn with a compass and a ruler and the number is as such an outsider associated with soul mysteries. It bridges the gap between the earthly ten and universal twelve.

Mathematically it produces a number sequence in multiplication beginning in

$11 \times 11 = 121$

$111 \times 111 = 12321$

and culminating in

$111111111 \times 111111111 = 12345678987654321$.

Twelve

Twelve corresponds to the zodiac and the twelve signs of the ecliptic. Twelve may be found in three squares, four triangles or two hexagons. Twelve is the masculine principle and pertains to the body and to all the masculine principles and attributes of rational order, settlement, civilisation and patriarchal society. Its shape is the dodecahedron, which also contains the twelve pentagons, the symbol of humanity.

Suggested Exercises

Take a walk and look for examples of sacred geometry in nature.
Get out the paint and paint a mandala.

Chapter Ten
The Tree of Life

Trees protect our humanity by connecting us with Mother Earth in shared breath. We must in turn protect and respect the trees. From acorns grow oaks.

The Tree of Life or sacred tree is universally recognised as the source of life across almost every culture throughout history and it's not surprising because human beings and trees breathe each other! Human beings are infinitely connected on the deepest possible level of symbiosis in shared cylindrical breath with the trees. Our lives are entirely dependent upon them and on the other vegetation that supports us and all life on Earth. Trees and all other plant life that grow as a result of photosynthesis also quite literally contain the alchemical rainbow as a direct result of the absorption of sunlight and water, in a way that is unique to them.

The photosynthesis process begins with the stomata in the tree's leaves sucking in carbon dioxide from the atmosphere and then, powered by sunlight, combining this carbon dioxide with water and turning it into sugars which the tree feeds on. As they photosynthesise the stomata in the leaves then pump out oxygen.

For humans breathing is an essential process that sustains life. It delivers oxygen, via the lungs and respiratory system, to where it is needed in the body for cellular respiration and renewal whilst simultaneously removing carbon dioxide. The atmospheric gases inhaled are diffused in the pulmonary alveoli and once dissolved they are circulated around the body by the movement of blood in the circulatory system which is pumped by the heart. On exhalation the gases we breathe out are four or five percent higher in carbon dioxide and four or five percent lower in oxygen than that which we breathe in.

The breath has always been connected to the concept of the life force and many of the words for spirit are associated with words for breath for example *chi* in Chinese, *prana* in Sanskrit and *ruach* In Hebrew. Conscious breath control is common in many spiritual practices and forms of meditation as well as less consciously developed for speech control and any form of voice training such as singing. From breath comes our capacity to express and create with sound. Perhaps this is one reason why some of Earth's creation stories begin synonymously with the breath or sound. In some stories the spirit breath of God moves either over the face of the water or the Earth and in others God speaks, "In the beginning there was sound". The breath is acknowledged universally and so is the tree in one form or another.

When we connect and commune with the trees we also connect most deeply with the Earth and with the God/Goddess. This basic understanding is at the heart of most religious iconographies and is represented by the Tree of Life. Any disconnection or removal from this truth and from nature is also likely to cause a symptomatic disconnection from divinity and we see this prevalent in the cultures of the West in our current times reflected in our society and our treatment of the planet. Perhaps as with the rise and fall of other empires and as with the extinction of other creatures, we may disappear with the next turn of the wheel as a consequence of our treatment of Earth. Alternatively in these times as we witness a mass awakening and shifting in consciousness humanity will find new ways of being resourceful and taking better care of the planet. The recent surge of re-education and interest in green living gives cause for optimism.

When we identify ourselves with the sacred tree and with nature we take our rightful place in this symbiosis and in acknowledgement that we belong to one another. We and the tree: many patterns begin to emerge and deeper insight can be gained. Among the Sng'oi indigenous people of Malaysia a person and a tree are considered to belong together and the person is thought to have a connection not just with the tree but with any descendants that grow from its seeds.

Trees are considered to carry prayers to the creator and act as guardians of the land on which they stand. As the carriers of prayers, trees are sometimes tied with clooties an ancient practice continued until this day. Clooties are cuts of cloth tied to the tree by people offering thanks or praying for assistance in some way. The pair of guardian yew trees at the entrance to the ancient Knowlton henge site, dating from around four and a half thousand years ago circa 2500BC and the later added twelfth century church, are often to be found adorned in this way. So are trees at the bottom of Glastonbury tor and at many sacred sites all over the British Isles. Certain types of trees like yews especially are revered for their longevity and are often to be found on sacred sites both pagan and Christian.

Forests cover one third of the Earth's land mass and provide a home to eighty percent or more of land based plants, animals and insects. The concept of the family tree is certainly a common one in biology and we can think of the trees as an analogy for us too. Individually if each of us were to be represented as a tree, the connections in our lives, of our families and friendships might also be trees connected through the forest by the shared network of roots and they in turn each have their own connections. Keeping healthy relationships and connections, whilst pruning harmful ones, keeps us healthy as a whole allowing us maximum sunlight, conducive to growth. Our roots are in the ground drinking the water that supports our life force and our branches are stretching into the Sun taking in the sunlight, also supporting our life force. Each ring on the trunk represents our incarnations. As life force enters us and flows through us it renews and replenishes the internal rainbow of the chakra system and fills and opens the heart space which is our point of balance, beauty, love and truth and our point of connection with all living things and with the whole of creation. From here all things are possible.

In Norse cosmology the world tree is called Yggdrasil and is described as the biggest and best ash tree, which connects the nine worlds. The branches reach far into the sky and heavens and three roots reach far into other realms, one to the holy well Urdarbrunnr in the heavens, one to the spring Hvergelmir and another to the well Mimisbrunnr. It is unclear where all the worlds are in relation to the tree and branches but the Gods are pictured as being in the sky in Asgard, which is their heavenly realm and is connected to the tree Yggdrasil by a rainbow bridge called the Bifrost. Living within Yggdrasil are a dragon at the bottom and a wise eagle at the top.

Wacah Chan, is the name given to the Mayan world tree. Wacah Chan is associated with the Ceiba, a tall tropical tree with a mostly branchless trunk and a huge spreading canopy. World trees are a prevalent motif in creation accounts, cosmologies, mythology and iconography of Mesoamerica and examples can be seen not just from the Maya but also the Izapan, Mixtec, Olmec and others. In Mesoamerican context world trees embody the four directions and also serve as an axis connecting the planes of the underworld and of the planes of the sky with the Earth.

The Buddha is said to have found enlightenment (bodhi) beneath the Bodhi tree, which was a large and very old sacred fig tree in Bodh Gaya in India. In religious iconography the Bodhi tree is depicted with heart-shaped leaves. The term "Bodhi Tree" is also widely applied to currently existing trees, particularly the Sacred Fig growing at the Mahabodhi Temple in Bodh Gaya, which is a direct descendant planted in 288 BC from the original specimen. This tree is a frequent destination for Buddhist pilgrims. Two others are also believed to have been propagated from the original tree. Sacred fig trees are planted in close proximity to every Buddhist monastery.

Genesis, the first book of both Judaic and Christian scriptures, describes both a tree of knowledge and a Tree of Life within the Garden of Eden. The Tree of Knowledge is commonly depicted as an apple tree, the apples themselves signifying earthly wisdom and containing within them the five-pointed star. Interestingly the Christian symbol of peace is the dove with the olive branch and the rainbow, a sign of the covenant between God and man. Throughout the scriptures there are references to prophets and messengers receiving the word of God either on mountains or with trees.

The Teutonic words for temple, _horgr_ in old Norse meaning "altar or sanctuary" and _hearg_ in Old English meaning "holy grove or temple" suggests the oldest sanctuaries of worship were originally in the woods in sacred groves of trees. Worship in sacred groves is a recurring theme throughout the world. The Celtic Tree of Life _Crann Bethadh_ was believed to represent the cycle of life and intrinsic connection of nature as well as to connect heaven and earth. It was a central part of early Celtic spirituality. The Ogham alphabet in almost entirely based upon Sacred Trees and tree lore. Of these trees amongst the most sacred are the oak, the ash and the hawthorn. Wherever these three trees were found growing together was considered a holy place of worship, prayer and vows and it is from these three trees that the word "oath" comes.

In Egypt the acacia and sycamore were both seen as holy trees and perhaps as symbolic of the mystery school teachings. These mystery school teachings included those of the Kemetic Tree of Life which was later taught in the Judaiac mystery schools as the Kabbalistic Tree of Life as a result of the teachings being passed down from initiate to initiate. The Egyptians held that certain objects and qualities in life were sacred and they ascribed them to certain Gods. They also ascribed certain hours of the day and night to different Gods. In other words different Gods governed different times of the day. There are depictions of the journey of the solar barque or Sun boat, which is the boat of the Gods that sailed the sky bringing light to the world, travelling through regions of space and time. These regions of space and time were dedicated to each God in turn. In what is commonly known as the Egyptian "Book of the Dead", or the "Book of Going Forth by Day", there are relevant prayers for travelling through stars, space and time dedicated to the Gods and as protection from lesser entities.

The Dendera zodiac is the first to depict the zodiac as we have come to know it with a mixture of familiar symbols such as the bull and Hapi, the God of the Nile, in the place of the nowadays more familiar Aquarius. The Greeks later adopted this system and incorporated these practices into the ones we still use today. The Greek hermetic "Symbola" system covered all kinds of planetary correspondences and covered every area of life and interest. Animals, body parts, minerals, medicine, colours, numbers, perfumes, all were allocated in accordance with its nature or effect. The attributes of the Gods and planets were logically and systematically aligned. Arab and Jewish practitioners alike could see the value of the whole and expanded upon its structure. Subsequently the zodiacal, elemental and planetary correspondences, colours and even foods were ascribed to an ordered matrix. It can be argued that just as the Egyptian and Greek teachings were learned, shared, inherited, amalgamated and incorporated into the Jewish Kabbalistic teachings so too by extension the Kabbalah is relevant to all paths with a shared common origin such as Islam and Christianity. It is also relevant to all studying esoteric material.

It is primarily in the teachings of the Kabbalistic Tree of Life that the modern day practitioner may gain understanding as to how all things under heaven are ascribed to their corresponding planetary sphere. It is also in this context and upon this system that most Western esoteric material is founded and without this knowledge much of its meaning is obscured and illogical. To use correspondences with no knowledge as to their how and why would make them almost meaningless and unfounded on anything substantial or reliable. The Kabbalah then is essential to unlocking much of the hidden significance of other writings, for these correspondences are given in the vast majority of esoteric literature, certain scholarly, medicinal or scientific findings of their time and herbals. Therefore any student of magic needs to have a functioning understanding of how the system works even if their chosen path is another because without this understanding the vast majority of available literature and any deeper understanding of its significance remain hidden.

The Kabbalistic Tree of Life

The following is intended as an introduction only and as an invitation of further study in order that the practitioner has a basic understanding of the logical workings of the system.

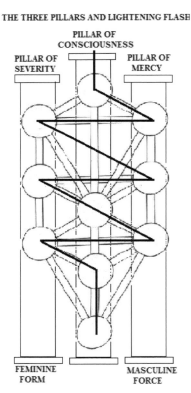

THE TREE OF LIFE AND 32 PATHS   THE THREE PILLARS AND LIGHTENING FLASH

Kabbalah means "to receive" and refers to the tradition of receiving sacred teachings through the oral tradition. The Kabbalah of the West primarily uses the symbol of The Tree of Life as an illustration of the organising principles found in the structure of creation and the dynamics of the relationship between God/Divinity and creation. In studying this symbolic illustration we may gain direct understanding and a working knowledge of the structure of the universe around us and within us, for it depicts the macrocosm and the microcosm and everything in between showing first the emanations of divinity and the creation process including the zodiac and planets of our solar system, the qualities of spirit we may seek to attain and effectively a map for the journeying soul. Some consider this map is guidance leading back to the heavens from which we came, others consider it a means of progressing through the twenty-two initiatory paths of existence known as The Fool's Journey and symbolised in the major arcana cards of the tarot. These twenty-two pathways further correspond to the letters of the Hebrew alphabet and therefore to sound in creation.

Although the Kabbalah originates in the Jewish faith and tradition as a complete and comprehensive magical system it is open to being sympathetic and inclusive of other faiths and cultures. This is because other cultural concepts or guises of God or Goddess are seen in the context of aspects of the one Divine source and limitless light of creation. Therefore it is possible to work with any number of religious or cultural belief systems within one inclusive whole. For anyone wishing to gain a better working experience of this system in more depth seek out a copy of *The Mystical Qabbalah* by Dion Fortune. She writes, *"The Qabalistic cosmology is the Christian Gnosis. Without it we have an incomplete system in our religion, and it is this incomplete system which has been the weakness of Christianity"*.

The Kabbalah, similarly to many other belief systems, acknowledges different planes of existence within creation and that creation is multi-layered and in a constant state of flow. The tree itself is the point where all planes of existence reside and the ebbing and flowing cycles of life, death and rebirth are visible. Here too the accumulation of the elements, earth, air, fire, water and spirit, which are the essential components of existence. To understand them is to begin to understand the workings of magic.

The Tree of Life is made up of four worlds (the planes of existence) and ten Sephiroth (spheres) that combined are an interconnected chain of emanations descending into existence from the Divine. Each of these ten Sephiroth is a different expression of God and each of these four worlds is different in nature and function. Out of the *Ohr Ein Soph* which translates as "the limitless light", the cosmos manifests itself through thirty-two paths of wisdom. Ten of these thirty-two paths correlate to the ten spheres of the Sephiroth and the other twenty-two correlate to the initiatory paths connecting the spheres to one another. The tree is symbolic of the flow of creation from the Divine to the lower world and back and can be seen two directionally not just as a map of the way upward to the heavens but also as a depiction of divinity evolving in self-expression and manifesting outwards into positive existence. Each Sephirothic sphere functions as a vessel, which may contain, harness and pour forth light and life-force into the next and manifestation. This downward flow is often likened to the lightning flash. (Please see diagram).

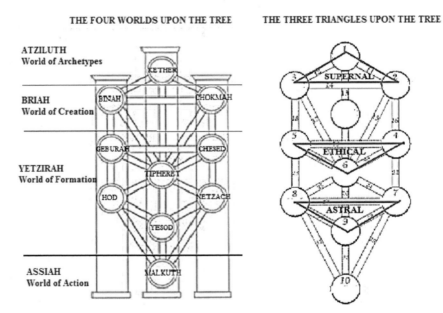

The Tree of Life can be divided into four horizontal sections that represent the Four Worlds (see diagram). Simultaneously the whole tree can be considered in each of the four worlds as four layers of reality, four spiritual realms or planes of existence. They could be considered and experienced as spirit, mind, heart, and body. These four worlds are also symbolised in the tarot by the four different suits of cards according to the four elements.

Atziluth, The World of Emanation

Atziluth the world of emanation is related to the three Sephiroth at the top of the tree, Kether (Crown), Chokmah (Wisdom) and Binah (Understanding). These three are referred to as the supernal triangle and they are entirely spiritual in nature and are separated from the rest of the tree by the Abyss which is a veil between the unperceivable and perceivable worlds. For this reason Atziluth is also known as the concealed world though some consider this veil may be transcended through Da'ath (spiritual knowledge), depicted on the first diagram. Within Atziluth the three Sephiroth are in union with God and there is no separation from source. The world of Atziluth is best described as the world of the direct emanation of deity flowing outwards from the limitless light beyond Kether the Crown and into the ten spheres of the Sephiroth in procession. Atziluth is a world of deity transcendent, imageless and formless, without separation. It is associated with spiritual ideals, with the Shekinah (the female aspects of God/Goddess) and with the tarot suit of Wands and the element of Fire.

Briah, The World of Creation (the throne of God)

The world of Briah corresponds to the Sephiroth of Binah, the sphere that births the emanations of the supernal triangle into existence to the spheres beyond the Abyss. Briah is therefore the world of creation and the ten Sephiroth of this world are more accessible to human contact through the archetypal mind of the deep psyche. This is also the realm of the archangels and each of the ten Sephiroth are associated with different archangels. Briah is associated with the tarot suit of Cups and the element of Water.

Yetzirah, the World of Formation

The world of Yetzirah is the world of becoming and comprises the next six Sephiroth which make two further triangles upon the diagram of tree. Emanations are channelled from one Sephiroth to the next in the process of formation or becoming. Yetzirah is the world of the Astral Light, the picture consciousness of perception and imagination where ideas take shape. This is the realm of the ten choirs of angels ruled over by Archangel Metatron and of many holy creatures and elementals. In this realm there are also imaginary visions. To learn discernment as to which are genuine requires mental discipline. Yetzirah is associated with the tarot suit of Swords and the element of Air.

Assiah, the World of Action

The world of Assiah is the world of manifestation and corresponds to the Sephiroth of Malkuth, the Kingdom i.e. Earth. Here in the Kingdom is the cumulated expression of the manifestation process as channelled down through the Sephiroth and their many influences into physical existence. This is the material world of matter and energy primarily as solid, liquid, gaseous, electric or etheric. Within this realm are the Ofanim, the celestial beings who guard the throne of God and the Angels that combat evil who are governed by Archangel Sandalphon. Assiah is associated with the tarot suit of Pentacles and the element of Earth.

There are additionally different names for God pertaining to each of the Four Worlds. The different names represent and recognise the actions and underlying principle of the various Sephiroth or aspects of the Divine. These names are included with the details of the Ten Sephiroth.

The Three Triangles

Upon the tree there are three triangles, three trinities of Sephiroth each of which is made up of a pair of opposites upon the pillars with a central union in the pillar of equilibrium and consciousness. These three trinities form the total of the manifestation process from Divine source of Kether to the Kingdom of Earth (333).

The Supernal triangle comprises Kether the point of source, Chokmah the father and Binah the mother at the top of the tree and this is effectively the trinity of God/Goddess unfolding above the point of the Abyss.

The next six Sephiroth are sometimes referred to as the six the Lesser Countenance and they make up two further triangles.

The Ethical Triangle is made up of Chesed (Mercy), Geburah (Justice) and Tiphareth (Beauty). It is in the balance of Tiphareth that we see Justice tempered with Mercy. Justice without Mercy is tyranny and Mercy without Justice is anarchy.

The Astral Triangle of Hod, Netzach and Yesod consist of the Mental, Astral and Vital. These higher planes can be bridged through uniting our vital force, intention and clear intention upward to the Wisdom and Love of the Divine. It is from here that the act of Ritual vibrates upwards into the higher worlds.

Malkuth, the Kingdom is at the foot of the Tree of Life and is the physical Earth at the bottom of the three triangles, the realm of their manifestation. Some consider this to make the last triangle a quaternity in truth and either view is valid. In this case it is symbolic of the triangle in union with the square meaning heavenly trinity in union with physical Earth i.e. manifestation.

Below the Tree of Life are the realms of darkness that are known as Hell. Whilst these are not the focus of our attention it is necessary to be aware of their existence.

The Ten Sephiroth

Whilst there are many ways in which to consider the Sephiroth of the Tree of Life they do show uniquely well the manifestation process through the emanations of the elements and planets from the source to the earthly plane. Our priority for the purposes of this book is to understand them as an operational system which allows connections between spiritual qualities, skills and planetary functions to be made. The spheres of the Sephiroth in turn each correspond to different names and emanations and experiences of divinity. Whilst some names appear more masculine than feminine to our Western ear it is worth remembering that the entire tree is built upon the equal and essential balance of both male and female energies and that God is both.

Amongst cosmologists and physicists there is a theory of inflation which hypothesises the initial causation or spark of the "big bang". This theory describes the propelling and expansion of creation as something like a cosmic growth spurt, doubling in size every trillionth of a second at the closest moment to creation. The theory then goes on to say that this creates uniform geometry on an enormous scale and universal waveforms resulting from gravitational waves. The energy released from the initial "bang" or creation alongside the radioactive gravitationally self-propulsive waves then slows down and reduces the expansion process much like jelly does as it is cooling and solidifying.

In quantum mechanics everything fluctuates and there is always uncertainty. In a way it is part of the pattern that not everything fits neatly into place, there are jiggles and all is not precisely smooth. Particle physicists and astronomers now have their telescopes trained upon deep space looking for these ripples that they have theorised about by studying the fabric of space and time in the afterglow from the initial bang of creation. Effectively they are looking for the oldest light in the universe and they hope to find it against the background of microwaves as visible directional patterns made from polarisation stretching the space signature of the beginning of time. It is as yet an unproven hypothesis but fascinatingly alike to the descriptions of the supernal triangle of creation through the polarisation of Chokmah and Binah.

The ten Divine emanational Spheres of the Tree of Life correspond to the point of creation and physically speaking to space and the cosmos and to seven of the ten planets and Earth. The other three planets are assigned as the higher octave of the first i.e. Pluto is the higher Octave of Mars and therefore belongs to the same sphere. The first and highest of the Spheres is dedicated to their initial impulse into being and creation and this is called Kether, the Crown.

1. Kether, Crown

From the supernal infinite light (Aur Ain Soph) the source of divinity pours forth the stream of consciousness and the point where this consciousness emanates outwards is the Crown, Kether. As with the three lines at the beginning of creation in sacred geometry, it is three pillars which define the Tree of Life. It is from here the point of Kether, at the top of the pillar of consciousness that these three pillars begin and in turn all of creation. Kether is the sphere that contains all that was, is, or ever will be. It is the point of absolute unity and a point is often depicted on the tree to illustrate this.

Here are the first whirlings of existence, the first emanations of God, the dot of the compass, the concealed of the concealed, the holy of holies. Un-

154

knowable and beyond understanding, without a beginning or an end, Kether is the sphere of outpouring life spiralling into creation. In this creation process, the four elements are born, Earth, Air, Fire and Water. These are represented by the Seraphim (the angels of Kether) called Chaioth ha Qadesh meaning the Holy Living Creatures. These holy living creatures are the Bull (Taurus), the Lion (Leo), the Eagle (Scorpio) and Man (Aquarius) i.e. the orientation of space via the use of the fixed signs of the zodiac. From here the four elements flow into the next sphere of Chokmah. The Divine name of Kether is Eheieh meaning I Am or I will be what I will be. The Archangel of Kether is Metatron meaning the Angel of Presence, head of the Order of the Seraphim.

Kether Correspondences:
Corresponds to universe and astrological whole.

Functions – the point of creation, union with God. spirit, life force.

Archetypes – nothing, everything, love, light, source, Great Spirit, creator, architect.

Image – an ancient bearded king seen in profile from the right.

Symbols – the flame, the Sah, the point in the circle, the crown, the swastica (in its pure form the four arms represent the primordial elements swirling around a point), the infinity symbol (lemniscate), Ones 111.

The root of the powers of air. (The roots of space, breath and sound.)

Tarot – the four Aces.

Plants – The sacred lotus, almond blossom.

Incense – ambergris or whatever is most precious to you.

Colour – brilliance, pure brilliant white, pure white brilliance, white-flecked gold. (Where four colours are given these are to correlate with the four worlds.)

Metal – gold, meteorite.

Stones – diamonds, clear quartz.

Chakra – sahasrara or crown, above the head.

Body – the cranium. The crown chakra regulates the pituitary gland that connects the central nervous system and the entire system of hormone producing glands.

Animals – swan, hawk.

Godforms (Creator Gods) – Ptah, Osiris, Zeus, Brahma, Shiva, Christian

Trinity 3 in 1, Great Spirit.

2. Chokmah, Wisdom

Chockmah is the Godhead where active potent masculine life force expands and is sometimes referred to as *Abba* the Supernal Father. This Yang kinetic impetus is the inspired mind of God, Wisdom, taking form. At the head of the pillar of mercy Chokmah represents the stage where the entire energy of the universe is made manifest through polarity in pairs of opposites or fluid energy exchange between the poles of the male and female pillars. The male and female pillars of Mercy (male) and Severity (female) quite literally are Force (male) and Form (female). Where the head of the male pillar (Chokmah) is the Father and Life, the head of the female pillar (Binah) is the Mother and Death. Death which is implied as a result of birth, for all things once born must eventually die.

Chokmah is the sphere that contains and channels this limitless, disorganised, unrestrained, surging vital energy entering the world and is considered as the primordial maleness of the universe. This is the Sephiroth and first creation of which we are capable of any awareness and comprises the sphere of the fixed starts and the twelve signs of the Zodiac. The Divine name of Chokmah is Yah meaning God, strength or vastness. The Archangel is Raphiel meaning secret of God, part of the Angelic Choir of Ophanim (meaning the Wheels).

Chokmah Correspondences:
Space – the stars and zodiac.
Functions – kinetic force and expansion in creation.
Archetypes – bearded male figure.
Symbols – the phallus, the cross, the standing stone, the tower, the straight line, the cloak (spirit incarnated in human form), inner robe inner light, twos 222.
Element – the root of fire.
Zodiacal Correspondence – the zodiac.
Tarot – the four twos and the four Kings.
Plants – mistletoe, rosemary or any others associated with archangels.

Incense – musk, frankincense, sacred blends, blends appropriate for the zodiac.

Colours – pure soft blue, grey, pearlescent grey or iridescent, white flecked with red blue yellow.

Metal – tin.

Stones – star ruby, turquoise.

Chakra – ajna (third eye, pineal gland).

Body – the left side of the face and head and left brain.

Primeval man.

Animals – owl.

Godforms (Father Gods and Stellar Deities) – Amoun, Thoth, Nuit, Isis, Odin, Athena, Vishnu, Hermes, God the Father.

3. Binah, Understanding

At the head of the pillar of Severity Binah, sometimes called either Ama meaning the Mother or Aima the Primordial Mother, receives the emanated influx of cosmic energy from Chokmah (the zodiacal signs). The sacred womb of the Divine, she contains and then births creation. In birth, the vast limitless cosmic light of chaos must pass through her and be restricted and concentrated into form. Such is the nature of three-dimensional existence. Binah, like a "palace of mirrors" reflects the light of Chokmah (wisdom) and by so doing increases it in myriad ways. She is the Divine feminine wisdom, *Sophia* and it is through the governance of natural law and restriction that we come to find understanding in the microcosm. Her qualities include rational deductive thought, contemplation, deep intuition and knowing and the ability for repentance. She represents cosmologically the planet Saturn. The Divine name for Binah is Elohim meaning "Gods male and female". Elohim is sometimes referred to as Divine breath, intuition or spiritual intelligence. The Archangel is Tzaphqiel meaning Contemplation of God. The Angelic choir is the Aralim meaning the Thrones or Mighty Ones.

Binah Correspondences:
Time.
Planet – Saturn.

Functions – forming through restriction. Constriction and crystallisation. Law.

Archetypes – the Celestial Queen, Father Time, The Ancient.

Symbols – cauldron, scythe, keys, hourglass, compasses.

Element – the root of water.

Threes 333, the triangle and the three pointed star. The first number from one and two taking form. The north pole of the planet Saturn has a hexagonal cloud i.e. two triangles.

Tarot – the four threes and the four Queens.

Plants – all sedatives and belladonna.

Lotus, lily, opium poppy, aconite, barley, beech, elm, gladiolus, hellebore, hemlock, hemp, ivy, nightshade, patchouli, slow, yew, woad.

Incense – myrrh, storax.

Colours – crimson, black, dark brown, grey-flecked pink.

Day – Saturday.

Metal – lead, (silver, iron).

Stones – sapphire, pearls.

Body – the right side of the face, right brain. Skin, bone structure, teeth, cartilage, spleen, knees, glands, circulation.

Chakra – ajna (third eye, pineal gland).

Primeval woman.

Animals – crocodile, goat, bee.

Godforms (Mother Goddesses and those governing Time) – Isis, Nephthys, Bhavani, Frigga, Demeter, Kronos, Juno, Hecate, The Virgin Mary, Danu, Ceridwen, Shakti, Bhavani.

Daath, Knowledge

Daath, meaning knowledge is not always depicted on the Tree of Life because it is invisible and not in truth a Sephira. It sits below Chokmah and Binah where there is an Abyss, which is the name given to the veil of separation between the perceivable and unperceivable worlds. The Abyss which divides us from heaven cannot be crossed physically in life however at the point where Chokmah (Wisdom), Binah (Understanding) and Tiphareth (Beauty) combine, comes Daath (Knowledge). Found through inward reflection is Gimel the thirteenth path, that of the High Priestess. This path energises the entire central pillar connecting the principles of Kether and Tiphareth in consciousness. Here lies the gate to inner knowing and the doorway to the temple.

4. Chesed, Mercy

Benevolent Chesed (meaning Mercy) is sometimes referred to as Gedulah (Greatness). Chesed is considered the first Sephira of the manifested universe and contains all of the holy powers received from the cumulative outpouring of the Source, Wisdom and Understanding. In truth he is the first reflection of the supernal trinity and so it is no wonder he reflects Love and Mercy, a state of Grace. The greatness and magnificence of the Goodly King presides as organised force actively constructing and expanding in the business of creation. From him flows forth abundance to all the other spheres. He is the loving Father, protector, preserver and his is a domain of organisation, up-building, peace and law. The Divine name associated with Chesed is El meaning God or Power. The Archangel is Tzadqiel meaning Justice of God. The Angelic Choir is Chasmalim meaning Brilliant Ones.

Chesed Correspondences:
Planet – Jupiter.
Functions – expansion and majestic leadership.
Archetypes – the mighty old king upon his throne, the good ruler, the priest.
Symbols – tetrahedron, pyramid, the royal sceptre, the staff, oak crown, cup of abundance, cornucopia.
Element – water.
Fours 444, four pointed star, squares, building blocks.
Tarot – The four 4s.
Colours – deep violet, blue, deep purple, deep azure flecked yellow.
Plants – all analgesics, oak, pine, cedar, juniper, maple, sycamore, olive, shamrock, opium poppy, borage, green tea, agrimony, sage.
Incense – cedar, nutmeg, pine resin, hyssop.
Metal – tin.
Stones – amethyst, sapphire, lapis lazuli.

Body – left arm, left shoulder, left adrenal, adrenalin flight response. Cellular development, preservation of soft tissues of the body, intestines, liver, digestion, hips and thighs, arteries, feet.

Chakra – Visuddhi (throat).

Animals – unicorn, centaur, eagle.

Godforms – Amoun, Isis, Hathor, Jupiter, Poseidon, Zeus, God the Rainmaker, Indra, Brahma, the Dagda, Thor.

5. Geburah, Strength

Geburah, Strength or severity is also known as Din meaning Justice and Pachad meaning Fear. Geburah is a female passive restrictive strength, not dissimilar in essence to Binah, and it is through that directed strength that motion is brought to matter. Before this point matter may be calm, expansive Chesed building his empire certainly seemed joyful and all seemed in balance and order but when direction and movement is introduced it causes great stress and strain and a certain amount of turbulence i.e. stormy weather! Severity... All of existence in this three-dimensional reality is created in duality and there cannot be calm without strife nor love without fear. As spiritual beings in physical bodies we learn through this polarised reality. Here is the sphere of strength, the sphere of the protector, of justice, of destruction as a necessary disinfectant that cleans all things that pass through it. Geburah is fiercely honest, sincere and protective. The Divine name associated with Geburah is Elohim Gebor, God of Strength. The Archangel is Khamael meaning Severity of God and the Angelic Choir are the Seraphim meaning Powers.

Geburah Correspondences:

Planet – Mars.

Functions – directed movement through will.

Archetypes – the warrior, the protector, the champion.

Symbols – swords, lance, shield, scourge, helmet.

Element – fire.

Fives 555 – the pentacle, pentagram, five-pointed star (elements + spirit and movement).

Tarot card – the four 5s.

Plants all irritants and caustics, oak, strychnine, holly, atropine (naturally occurring in belladonna and mandrake), coca, thistles, nettles, cacti, ginger, peppermint, mustard, hawthorn, wormwood.

Incense – tobacco, opopanax, asafoetida, galangal root.

Colour – orange, red, bright scarlet, red flecked with black.

Day – Tuesday.

Metal – iron, sulphur.

Stones – rubies, garnet, red agate, bloodstone.

Body – right arm, right shoulder, right adrenal, adrenalin fight response, limbs, nose, ears, sexual organs, excretory systems, gall bladder, red blood cells.

Chakra – Vsuddhi (throat).

Animals – basilisk, horse, bear, wolf.

Godforms – Ma'at, Horus, Nepthyts, Ares, Hades, Mars, Tiw, Thor, Christ in Judgement of the World, Vishnu.

6. Tiphereth, Beauty

Tiphereth, also sometimes called Melekh (King) or Ben (the Son) is in the centre of the whole system of the Tree of Life both physically and spiritually. Here in this beating centre the emanations of all the other spheres combine flowing in from above and in turn flowing downward to fill those below. A bit like the circular breathing of a highly trained musician, here is the breath of light, the spirit breath (Ruach) extending outward and inward in perpetuity, the mediator gathering, directing and redistributing all.

Here is where the overlocking triangles of heaven and earth, male and female meet, overcoming differentiation, separation and polarisation, finding Union in perfect love and perfect trust. Here is consciousness and the soul in balance in the equilibrium of tree. Tiphereth is the lower arc of Kether capable of aligning us with God consciousness and akashic records through the opening of the heart combined with mind. Tiphereth is the higher arc of Yesod showing us the highest truth of our emotions before their reflection. This is the place of transmutation between the planes of force and form in the central pillar where our consciousness rises.

Tiphereth is the giver of life and corresponds with the sun. In the mirror of the human body whilst the physical centre may be that of the solar plexus the heart is just above in Da'ath and the pair work in union. Whilst Tiphareth is our clear cut individualised consciousness, this is also the seat of our higher self and first initiator. The Divine name of Tiphareth is Jehovah Eloah va-Daath meaning God of Knowledge. The Archangel is Raphael meaning God's Healing. Sometimes Archangels Michael and or Metatron are also ascribed to this sphere. The Angelic choir is the Melekim meaning Kings.

Tiphereth Correspondences:

The Sun – orbital centre of the solar system.

Functions – connects with Divine source and gives balance, fusion and power to the entire system.

Archetypes – the Solar King, The Eternal Child.

Element – air.

Symbols – the Rose Cross, Solar cross, Breastplate, Solar diadem, Depictions of the Sun Shining, Solar Cup symbolic of Ruach (the Spirit Breath of God), The Grail.

Sixes 666 in their pure form of light, six-pointed stars, interlocking triangles in balance, the hexagon, hexagram and Merkaba.

Tarot – the four 6s and the four Knights.

Plants – predominantly healthful plants with a beneficial or warming effect. Also those associated with relevant solar deities. St John's Wort, acacia, witch hazel, bay, laurel, oak, ash, vines, and by extension some alcohols, camomile, marigold.

Incense – frankincense, amber, cinnamon, kyphi, copal.

Colours – clear rose pink, yellow, salmon pink, golden amber.

Day – Sunday.

Metal – gold.

Stones – topaz, yellow diamonds, sun stone, amber.

Body -solar plexus, breast and heart. The heart, the immune system, thymus, the eyes, the upper back, blood circulation, distribution of vital fluids and energy.

Manipura – solar plexus.

Animals – phoenix, lion.

Godforms (solar deities) – Osiris, Ra, Horus, Khepera, Sekhmet, Buddha, Apollo, Adonis, Dionysus, Bacchus, Aurora, Christ, the Son of God, Krishna,

Lugh, Bel.

7. Netzach, Victory

Netzach is the lowest of the Sephiroth on the right hand pillar of Mercy. It is in Netzach the seventh stage where the light of Tiphereth is broken up in to many-rayed manifestations but is not yet individualised into one thing or another, as such they take the collective forms of nature or of culture. This energy can be expressed at a human level through music and the arts. Netzach reflects the fiery energy of Geburah but it is tempered by the balance of Tiphareth and becomes desire and emotion. Netzach is therefore the sphere of earthly love and love of nature, love that may take many different forms and be expressed in many different ways!

Through the polarity of the sphere we get to experience the "other" through relationships with friends, lovers and family. We identify with people and we learn and imagine new ways of being that are different to our own. We tap in to collective instincts and natural forces and all of the Archetypes inherent within us and our cultures. Love must be balanced with Mind and the position of Netzach on the tree reminds us to look to Hod for stability and balance. Netzach alone may confuse and unbalance the unprepared and inexperienced practitioner with illusions and delusions. This is the sphere often referred to as the Green Ray because of the association with nature and it is here that instinct, emotions and ideas begin to take imagined forms that may later manifest. This is also the sphere of elemental energy closely connected with sex and therefore life. The Divine name of Netzach is Jehova Tzabaoth meaning Lord of Hosts. The Archangel is Haniel meaning Grace of God and the Angelic choir Elohim meaning male and female Gods, also called the Order of Principalities.

Netzach Correspondences:
Planet – Venus.
Functions – love of nature.
Archetypes – nature, flame of the sea.
Element – fire.
Symbols – the lamp, the girdle, rose, candlestick, mirror, necklace,

163

seashells, pearls, the sistrum, flaming torch, garland of flowers, cup, chalice.

Sevens 777, the seven-pointed star, the heptagon, the heptagram, interlocking triangle and square i.e. (heaven and earth).

N.B. The planet Venus also has an association with the five-pointed star due to the pattern made by the ecliptic course of the planet.

Tarot – the four 7s (Empress)

Plants – predominantly aphrodisiacs and those plants which alter states of mind to those receptive to love. Additionally any plants associated with any deity of love. Damiana, cannabis, pachouli, verbena, roses, cherry, dittany, myrtle, cyclamen, tulip, hibiscus, catnip, geranium, ladies mantle, mugwort, peach, pear, strawberry, plantain, primrose, vervain, yarrow.

Incense – rose, benzoin, sandalwood.

Colours – amber, emerald, bright yellowish green, olive flecked with gold.

Day – Friday.

Metal – copper.

Stones – emeralds, malachite, jade, rose quartz.

Body – the loins, hips, sexual organs, left arm and hand, kidneys, veins, mouth, throat, sinuses, neck, lower back, lymphatic system and skin functions including the scalp and hair. Also nerves, muscles tone and relaxation.

Chakra – manipura, solar plexus.

Animals – lynx, cat, raven, dove, all carrion birds.

Archangel – Haniel.

Godforms (deities of love) – Inanna, Hathor, Bast, Aphrodite, Astarte, Asherah, Nike, Venus, Ishtar, Freya, Brigit, Lakshmi, The Messiah, Bhavani.

8. Hod, Splendour

Hod (Splendour or sometimes translated as Glory) is at the foot of the pillar of severity opposite to Netzach with which it is paired. Hod is a reflection and continuation of the principle of form on the astral plane just as Netzach is a continuation of the principle of force. Hod is especially the sphere of magic because it is here that forms may be formulated to represent or personify natural forces that may be aligned with. The word Glory in the context of this sphere has been likened to the reflections that enable us to see the breathtaking beauty of the sky in that it is only through reflection taking forms that we can see divinity. This far down the tree reflections may also trick the mind and it is only when the pair work together that the love necessary to access the sphere of Netzach at all makes genuine connection and can distinguish the difference when in balance with the mind as to which forms are to be trusted. The quality sought in this sphere is therefore Truth. The Yetziratic text says the eighth path is the absolute, perfect intelligence, instrument of the primordial. The Divine name in Hod is Elohim Tzabaoth meaning God of Hosts. The Archangel is Michael meaning he who is like God and the Angelic choir is Beni Elohim meaning Sons of Gods (male and female implied) but is more usually referred to as the Archangels.

Hod Correspondences:

Planet – Mercury.

Functions – the transmission of Divine intelligence.

Archetypes – the Divine Messenger, the hermit, a hermaphrodite.

Element – air.

Symbols – quill, book, Scrolls, names (words of power), versicles (mantras), Apron (craftsman, maker).

Eights 888 – the eight-pointed star, octagon, octagram, interlocking squares and double cubes.

Tarot – the four 8s.

Plants – predominantly plants with a cerebrally stimulating or enhancing effect. Also those associated with relevant deities. Peyote, moly (which is thought likely to be snowdrop), cannabis, sage, rosemary, peppermint, mushrooms, oats, anise, fennel.

Incense – storax, mastic, white sandalwood.

Colours – violet purple, orange, russet red, yellowish black flecked with white.

Day – Wednesday.

Metal – quicksilver (mercury).

Stones – opal, fire opal, agate.

Body – loins and legs, right arm and hand, right kidney.

Chakra – manipura (solar plexus).

Animals – jackal, fox, swallow, ibis, apes and baboons.

God name – Elohim Tzabaoth, Lord of Hosts.

Archangel – Michael.

Godforms – Anubis, Thoth, Hermes, Mercury, Ganesh, Odin, Loki, Christian God as inspirer of scripture and healer.

9. Yesod, Foundation

Yesod means Foundation and is also sometimes referred to as Tzadiq-Yesod-Olam meaning the Righteous is the Foundation of the World. This Sephira is directly below Tiphereth on the central pillar and contains the culminated forces of Hod and Netzach i.e. the formulation of form combined with the forces of nature. In this sense Yesod is womb like holding safe which is birthed into Malkuth the Kingdom of Earth below. This womb like Sephirah of Yesod corresponds to the Moon and it is important to notice that Tiphereth above it corresponds to the sun. Their relationship upon the central pillar is key because in Tiphereth (the Sun) we see the Divine light of Kether reflected and amalgamated in a point of balance and then in turn that light is reflected again into Yesod (the Moon). The Moon is also connected to the Earth (Malkuth) in the sense that its composition is made up of the same material and it orbits around our planet. This same material and common formation can be considered as an etheric double and the Earth and Moon therefore as two poles in constant flux governed by cycles of the Sun both as day and night and the Moon phases which are a result of the amount of sunlight reflected on the Moon surface depending upon the changing angles of the Moon in relation to the Earth and sun. Within these Moon phases we find the governance of all the tides of Earth's oceans and bodies of water. It is the etheric double or blueprint of Yesod that is ultimately manifested into Malkuth (Earth). It is therefore in Yesod that magic is worked as it is from here that the astral forms may be engaged with and result in effect in the physical world.

The Yetziratic text reads:

"The ninth path is the pure intelligence, so called because it purifies the Numerations, it proves and corrects the designing of their representation and disposes their unity with which they are combined without diminution or division."

Wescott, tr W.W. *Sepher Yetzirah Or The Book Of Creation* (1887)

Yesod then is a filter that distils the combined influx of the spheres above before their manifestation into the kingdom of Earth.

Magically it is of vital importance to understand that this reflective sphere may also have shadow. Its currents carry the images of the combined human unconscious in dreams, visualisation, imaginings and all emotions. The images of the astral are far from trustworthy alone and to distinguish truth depends both upon capability and the extent to which the work is guided by the Divine or in higher service of some kind. The Divine name of Yesod is Shaddai El Chai meaning Almighty living God and the Archangel is Gabriel meaning God is my Strength. The Angelic choir is Kerubim meaning Angels.

Correspondences:
The Moon.

Functions – purification of the astral prior to manifestation.

Archetypes – a beautiful naked man, very strong. Lady of the night.

Element – water.

Symbols – sandals symbolic of walking the circle, treading holy ground, perfumes, changing focus of consciousness.

Tarot – the four 9s and the Moon.

Nines 999 – the nine-pointed star, nonagon, enneagram, three triangles.

Plants – all abortifacients or those with appropriate lunar properties – mandrake, ginseng, orchid, lavender, violet, willow.

Day – Monday.

Incense – primarily roots and those that affect the emotions: jasmine, ginseng, costus, all fragrant roots.

Colours – indigo, violet, very dark purple, citrine flecked azure.

Metal – silver.

Stones – quartz.

Chakra – Muladhara.

Body – sexual organs, vital current (chi or prana), meridian lines, the central nervous system, kundalini. The Moon also governs the vegetative life energy of plants.

Animals – cat, Elephant, tortoise, toad, frog, dolphin, animals related to water and serpents which move by undulations corresponding to the Moon phases.

Godforms of the moon, fertility or virginity – Shu, Zeus, Diana, Artemis, Selene, Luna, Hecate, Isis, Ma'at, Atlas, Ganesh, Vishnu, The Holy Spirit (Virgin Mary), Ourobouros (the serpent with its tail in its mouth).

10. Malkuth, Kingdom

The last Sephiroth on the Tree of Life is Malkuth, the Kingdom. Some of the additional names of Malkuth are Malak meaning the Queen, Kalah meaning the Bride and Betulah meaning the Virgin. This sphere is sometimes also called Shekhinah, the female presence of God and the polarity of the outpouring of Kether. It is said that after the initial separation of source into light, Shekinah descended to Earth and to humanity in order to be a vessel for the Divine.

It is in Malkuth that the combined flow of the Divine through the Sephiroth is manifested into the physical world for the Kingdom is the final receptacle. This is the last point of evolution before returning to source. Where the previous spheres were active Malkuth is not and provides stability and grounding both physically as it is linked to Earth and in the Divine creative process. Malkuth upon the tree is often depicted as a Sephira of four coloured quarters representing the four elements made manifest.

Malkuth in its earthly connection represents the grounded nature of humanity. This is the sphere of mundane practical life where we may live however we can best. It is how we live on Earth and aligned with Spirit that truly makes a difference in our world and is the legacy we leave behind us, in the work we have accomplished, the relationships we have nurtured, the people we have loved, the good we have done and the way we have raised our children. Our true work is here. Without our actions upon Earth i.e. in the sphere of Malkuth being in alignment with Divine will the rest is semantics and whatever magic we may work in other spheres may at best provide haphazard results or none at all. Note too that if magic is to be effective in any way it is highly important to ground and manifest the energies in some kind of physical form or action and this is one function of Ritual. It is in Malkuth that karma is generally worked out and it is in Malkuth that more than anything else the key is to answer our true calling and to learn to use our natural gifts.

When we do that we open ourselves up for all manner of good manifestations!

Malkuth is the gate through which Spirit manifests into physical form and in Malkuth life is subject to disintegration over time and ultimately death. Malkuth is sometimes called the Inferior Mother in reference to Binah the Superior Mother, for both birth life and therefore bring death.

The Yetziratic text reads:

"The Tenth Path is the Resplendent Intelligence, because it is exalted above every head, and sits on the throne of Binah, (the Intelligence spoken of in the Third Path). It illuminates the splendour of all the lights, and causes a supply of influence to emanate from the Prince of countenances."
Wescott, tr W.W. *Sepher Yetzirah Or The Book Of Creation* (1887)

The Divine name of Malkuth is Adonai ha-Aretz meaning Lord of the Earth. The Archangel is Sandalphon meaning Co-Brother, for he is the brother of Metatron the Archangel of Kether. The Angelic Choir is the Eshim meaning Flames.

Correspondences:

Earth

Functions – illuminates the splendour of all the lights i.e. manifests all the Sephiroth in the Divine Creation.

Archetypes – a young woman crowned and veiled representing Isis of nature, Nephthys, spiritual forces hidden from outer form.

Element – Earth.

Symbols – tens 101010, the ten-pointed star, two interlocking pentagrams or two pentacles forming a ten pointed star, i.e. two life forms joining together to manifest in the physical world, the circle without beginning or end, the Sphinx, the Altar (as above so below), the equal armed cross (four elements balanced).

Tarot – the four 10s and the four Pages.

Plants – corn, cereals, willow, lily, ivy, pomegranate, clover, meadowsweet, oak, ash.

Incense – sandalwood, any other wood based incense with a low earthy note.

Colours – yellow, citrine, olive, russet and black, olive, russet and black flecked with gold, black rayed with yellow.

Stones – rock salt.

Chakra – base/root (between the anus and sexual organs).

Body – the feet, the anus, base of the spine, the body as a whole, death, suprarenal gland regulates adrenalines (right side, survival) and endorphins (left side, patience).

God name – Adonai Malekh, the lord who is king or Adonai ha Aretz, lord of Earth.

Archangels – Metatron (also of Kether), Sandalphon (guardian of Earth), Uriel (for the physical element of Earth as represented in a magic circle or as guardian of the North).

Animals – horse, hare, frog.

Godforms of the Earth, Corn Goddesses, Gods of the underworld – Geb, Isis and Nephthys (Sphinx as synthesis of the elements), Osiris, Persephone, Demeter, Adonis, Psyche, Ceres, Lakshmi, Christ incarnated, The Virgin Mary, Anubis, Morrigan.

In Separation

Often described as below the Tree of Life there are further realms assigned to the qlipoth. Dion Fortune describes the qlipoth as evil and averse and says that *"these are awful forms, dangerous even to think upon"*. *The Mystical Qabalah p. 227* (1935). Within these realms the cosmic excreta cannot return to the planes of organised form until they find balance and equilibrium. The first of these is what is commonly referred to as Purgatory. It is said that there are various levels and degrees of these realms. Any kind of magic performed here is of an evil kind and any instruction to work in this way is not concerned with the well being of the practitioner or anything else. Here is Chaos on a lower arc and this sort of magic unsurprisingly attracts chaotic results. In the first realm of Purgatory once the necessary, healing, cleansing and work has been done and balance restored it is possible some of these things may pass back through Malkuth which acts as a cosmic filter. (Salt of the earth.) Once purified they may filter back through Earth into the normal channels of evolution.

It is necessary to be aware when working with positive aspects of the tree that all things have shadow and that any imbalance of forces may and will come up and be dealt with. For example an imbalance of force in Geburah could be Justice lacking Mercy. This must then be tempered and the balance redressed. In the Shadow of the tree is its reflection and the emanation of unbalanced destructive forces of each corresponding sphere.

Some things that appear dark are shadow and are cast as a result or in reaction to light. Some things that appear dark are darkness and the absence or denial of all light. This may also be considered as the difference between positive and negative evil.

Negative evil is found where there is an imbalance perhaps caused through hurt or confusion which can be corrected and most importantly where there is an underlying want/will at some level to return to balance. Eventually the inertia will be overcome and momentum towards evolution resumed. Here lies the tipping point of the scales of justice balancing contending forces. We cannot deal with evil by cutting it off only by absorbing and harmonising it much like rehabilitation.

There are however also those things and spheres of further separation and these are the realms of Positive evil. Positive evil is a force moving against the good orderly direction, against the current of evolution through choice or will. These are things which it is not safe to deal with and these things should be left to the love of the Divine to absorb and harmonise with directly and is not our concern or business beyond self-protection and awareness.

Our business is with the good orderly direction and with Love.

We focus our attention on Love.

Love is the Law.

Exercises

1. Plant a tree. If you can plant ten. Make sure they are native.

2. Write a list of ten different deities from any culture or religion and research them.

Then use the Tree of Life to understand which Sephiroth they correspond with and their planetary correspondence.

Choose one of them, whichever feels right and look for corresponding plants, herbs, flowers, colours and so on. You will need a herbal reference or the internet.

Chapter Eleven
The Four Quarters and the Solar Wheel of the Year

The solar horse pulls the sun chariot through the sky and the wheels have eight spokes made of four quarters and four cross quarters that mark the holy days or sabbats of the turning seasons.

The Sacred Tree sits within the earth, roots sinking deep into the soil. At the foot of the Tree are the four quarters that represent the four directions of the Earth (East, South, West and North) as aligned with the magnetic poles, the stars and the sky. These same four quarters represent the four elements of Air, Fire, Water and Earth made manifest in the physical world. Sunlight shines upon the leaves, the air gives them breath and movement and the vast root systems of branching latticed roots draw water up from the earth into the tree extracting nutrients and storing life energy as well as keeping the tree standing and stable in all weathers.

The Four Quarters

In magical, spiritual or religious practice it is usual for the four elements of the quarters to be associated with, represented by or guarded by, four guardians, four winds, four pillars, four archangels, four Gods or four directions. These vary depending upon the culture and the belief system and yet share common ground. The four elements are the essential components of life in their direct forms as physical reality and as such make up the rest of the world around us and within us, in our breath, body, blood and spirit. Scientifically they are also expressed as four states of energy: liquid, solid, gaseous and electrical. When combined with a fifth element, Spirit, they are ascribed to the platonic solids. (See the depiction in the chapter on sacred geometry.) The four directions or quarters make up the four parts of the world. This is why the symbol for Earth is often depicted as a circle with a cross.

The four elements may also in a more philosophical light be thought of as spiritual essences and natural forces or powers reaching from the physical world back up the Tree to the point of source. It is in this context that they are widely called upon, revered and worshipped, either directly in nature for example at sacred groves of trees, or as Archangels, Elemental Gods, rulers and guardians of Earth and many other elemental beings from many cultures. Direct communion with the elements is also the primary basis for circle or temple casting or for holding sacred space in many forms. One of the Hebraic names for God is YHVH (Yod He Vau Heh) and the four lettered name is commonly attributed to the four part symbols of the elements, the four directions and/or the four worlds of emanation, creation, formation and action.

Four is embedded into the ancient philosophies and creation stories from around the world. The Mayan creation story, the Popol Vuh, is about four Gods and the first four men. The Native American Hopi, Navajo and Zuni peoples as well as many others have customs and stories interwoven with the four directions as represented by the four quartered cross of black, red, yellow and white as well as similar designs and this motif is a recurring theme. The Hopi story of creation says this is the fourth age of Earth, the first being endless space, then dark midnight and then the age of animals before the present completion.

There are four Vedas, (Sanskrit for knowledge) a large body of texts originating in ancient India. They comprise the Rigveda, the Yajurveda, the Samaveda and the Atharvaveda and they are the oldest scriptures of Hinduism. Each Veda has been categorised into four major text types: the Aranyakas (rituals and ceremonies), the Brahmanas (commentaries), the Upanishads (meditation, philosophy and spiritual knowledge) and the Samhitas (mantras and benedictions). In turn, the Samhitas for example are grouped into four further categories. Fours are the foundation, the substantial base that holds all else.

There are four pillars of the world in Egyptian mythology as represented by the four sons of Horus. There are four arms of the Solar Cross, which is a physical representation of the actual Solar Cross of the sky's annual cycle and the yearly death and later rebirth of the Sun God which was used by the Celts pre-dating Christianity. The swastika symbol, also a four armed cross, in its purest form was used throughout the world for thousands of years before its misuse. The Kuna people of Panama believe the swastika shape represents the octopus that created the world in all four directions. The ancient Greeks used it to represent movement in art as early as the eighth century BC. The Hindus used it for thousands of years. Considered to be the swirling point of creation around source, the stars around the pole or the four elements creating, it is still a revered and holy symbol among Hindus, in Buddhism and Jainism. The Sanskrit word swastika means auspicious object and it is often displayed with four dots at the four angled arms. Like all crosses it is representative of the design of Four which symbolises wholeness, stability, balance and secure foundations.

In magical practice the four elements and/or the four directions are always called together in their totality. For example Fire and Water are not called without Earth and Air, North and South are not called without East and West, for it is only in their unity and equal measure that they provide a stable and solid base in which to ground the us and the working and in which to later manifest results. Likewise in affording protection to the working it would be a pointless exercise to call upon three representative guardians whilst leaving one quarter unprotected. Care is taken then that all the elements and directions are called and over time the practitioner learns to balance the forces internally.

In this context of mediating forces, it is of note that one of the main principles in Chinese medicine is a balancing of the internal forces and any imbalance is often considered to be the cause of illness or disease. The forces are then mediated through the acupuncture points and the rebalancing of chi perhaps alongside dietary advice or herbal medicine. Note that the word "element" is different in the context of Chinese medicine. The elements (the Wu Xing) are referred to as wood, fire, earth metal, water and correspond to the five planets Jupiter, Mars, Saturn, Venus and Mercury. This sequence is called the mutual regeneration sequence and form a philosophy that describes and relates interactions between all things in the universe. Each phase or element is strongly related to the next as they flow into one another. This is often depicted upon the five points of the pentacle. An apt use of the five-fold nature of man shown within the sacred geometry of the fives.

It is worth noting too that the majority of religious, anthropological and magical books both modern and antique touch upon principles of the quarters or elements or their spiritual representatives. They are the essential foundation of Life and the roots of our tree. Whether Wiccan, Druidic, Asatru or Angelic, the orientation of the altar and the essence of all ceremony start with the four quarters. As such a working knowledge of the elements and the wheel that they sustain is necessary to understanding the larger proportion of literature on the subject.

The Earth element is usually described as female, hence the downward facing triangles of the diagram. In truth the physical Earth and land we walk upon is always the first of altars. She is the Mother and gives birth to all life, she nourishes life, she sustains us, she supports and grounds and holds us. Her recesses and caves and soil are her womb and her cornucopia our sustenance. She holds all and in her layers of rocks and salts she purifies all. Our physical bodies, our flesh, our blood, our bones are from her and a part of her in birth and when we die we return to her. From her we have our practical earthly abilities, skills and functions.

The Air is described as male primarily and the sky as father. He brings breath to all life and he carries the sound of creation and indeed he scatters the seeds of creation. He fills our lungs and gives us voice and communication. He blows away the cobwebs of our mind as he blows the leaves. He caresses all and watches over all.

The Fire element is usually seen as male and as the physical embodiment of the sun. The male elements are depicted by the upward facing triangles of the diagram. This male embodiment of the Sun gives warmth and light bringing life through photosynthesis. The alchemy of fire itself purifies and burns and changes wood for example into heat. Within us the Sun physically brings melatonin (which aids good sleep) and serotonin (which makes us happy). Macrocosmicly Fire is our Spirit breath, inner fire, passion, creativity and drive.

Water is attributed to the female. She is the sea and the rivers, streams, lakes and rain. She is the primordial source of creation from which the mound of earth rises in various creation stories. She is Life source and she cleanses and washes away and replenishes us. Within our physical bodies we contain a large percentage of water and she is us. We drink from her and she renews us continuously. She rules the emotions and it is within the deep wells of our water that we express tears of sadness or joy. A significant proportion of the water on Earth has been proven to originate in the solar nebula which means that it is nearly a million years older than our solar system and pre-dates the formation of our sun. Yet it is only in the union of water and sunlight that life occurs.

In the central point of balance where the four elements meet is the tree and the point of spirit where all connect to one another and to the rest of creation.

The diagram shown of the Elements upon the cross gives the elements in their most common designations of direction in Western philosophies. It should however be noted that the directions and elements correspond differently in other cultures and Earth is not always necessarily assigned to the north. Fire may be east in one culture because this is the direction of sunrise and Fire may be south in another because the heat of the Sun is in the south and below the equator and because this is the path of the sun. What matters in such a case is not the direction but an understanding of the logical reason for its designation and respect for the correct cultural system from which we are working at the time and from where it originates. This allows a clear intention, a logical way to work and is based upon reason.

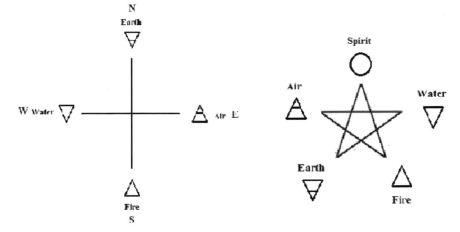

The Pentacle, a five-pointed star is considered by many to be the four elements in action and in combination with Spirit, five being the number of mankind and of creation in union of pairs. The assignations of which elements correspond to which point of the pentacle are not as clear and the depiction given is simply the most commonly found.

The Wheel of the Year

The position of the Earth within the solar system creates all of the seasonal cycles of the world. The calendar and seasons are based upon three astronomical phenomena, the rotation of the Earth about its axis, a day, the revolution of the Moon around the Earth, a month, and the revolution of the Earth about the sun, a year. Within the celestial sphere which contains all the stars and planets, the Earth rotates around an axis of North and South Poles. At right angles to the Earth's axis is the plane of the equator, east to west, which divides the Northern and Southern hemispheres of the globe. By extension of the earthly N, W pole and E, W equator we have celestial poles and a celestial equator also. The Sun is the only star we revolve around and as the Earth rotates the Sun rises in the east and sets in west. At night some of the stars also rise in the east and set in the west, though others do not and simply rotate around the pole. Over the course of one year the Earth moves around the Sun and the Sun appears apparently to have moved in a complete circle amongst the stars. This apparent path of the Sun is called the ecliptic.

The plane of the ecliptic path makes an angle with the plane of the equator and these correspond to the tilt of the Earth's axis. The two points where these planes intersect are the two equinoxes of the solar year, the vernal equinox which is spring in the Northern hemisphere and falls around the 20 March and the autumnal equinox which falls around the 22 or 23 September. The word equinox comes from the Latin *aequus* (equal) and *nox* (night). At these two times of year the tilt of the Earth's North and South Poles are perpendicular to the Sun neither inclining towards or away from it and the centre of the Sun is exactly over the Earth's equator meaning the duration of daylight is theoretically the same at all points on Earth's surface. On the day of an equinox, the Sun rises everywhere on Earth (except at the Poles) at about six a.m. and sets at about six p.m. approximately.

Whilst the Sun goes around this ecliptic path once a year, the Moon goes around it just over twelve times and every time it does so we have a lunar month. When the Earth, Moon and Sun are in alignment, that is to say approximately in a straight line, we have a lunar conjunction also known as dark or new moon. The length of times between these conjunctions is an average of 29.53059 days, twenty-seven and a third days for the Moon to rotate to the point from which it started plus two more days to catch up with

Sun's movement. This is known as the Synodic month and is the basis of all lunar calendars, which we shall discuss further in the next chapter. The Earth revolves around the Sun in about 365¼ days, that is, about 12.4 lunar months.

Twice a year the Sun reaches its highest or lowest points relative to the celestial equator and these two points are known as the solstices. At these two points the seasonal movement of the sun's path, as seen from Earth, appears to us to stop and be still before changing direction. The word solstice comes from the Latin *sol* meaning Sun and *sistere* to stand still. The sun's westerly motion never stops because the Earth is always in rotation but the sun's motion in declination comes to a stop at the moment of solstice. As seen from the North Pole, the Sun reaches the highest position in the sky once a year in June. As seen from the South Pole, the Sun reaches the highest position once a year in December. When it is the summer solstice at one Pole, it is the winter solstice on the other. The day of the solstice is either the longest day of the year, midsummer, or the shortest day of the year, midwinter. Together with the equinoxes, the solstices are intimately connected to the seasons and these four points are the quarters of the year.

The four quarters of the solar year have been observed and celebrated across time since antiquity and in numerous cultures around the world and any celebration, ritual or tradition honouring the natural seasons that they govern has its roots based in the Solar wheel of the year and theses four points of observation. Beyond these four points, which are around 21 December, 20 March, 21 June and 22 September a further four, marking the cross quarters of the year are also celebrated. Most commonly these are around 1 February, 1 May, 21 August and 31 October. These fourfold and eightfold divisions of quarters and cross quarters make up the Wheel of the Year and have earthly association with the square and the cube, the building blocks of man, stability and order. They also have direct correlation to the four directions and their elemental correspondences.

The four seasons of Earth are therefore Solar festivals marking a seasonal change caused by the Sun. The cross quarter days are often marked by fire festivals and those of agricultural significance. These festivals also have deep connections with the intrinsic nature of man's psyche through millennia of earthly incarnations and their turning can be seen and felt within a myriad of patterns within our lives and all life around us. All things in nature are cyclical, a perpetual ebb and flow of growth and retreat tied to the Sun's annual death and rebirth.

The Four Quarters are assigned:

East	South	West	North
Air	Fire	Water	Earth
Dawn	Noon	Dusk	Midnight
Spring	Summer	Autumn	Winter

The diagram below shows the solar cycle, the four elements, the names of the commonly accepted modern day pagan and Wiccan sabbats (which are holidays assigned to the quarters and cross quarters), the zodiacal correspondences of the calendar and the season in which they fall.

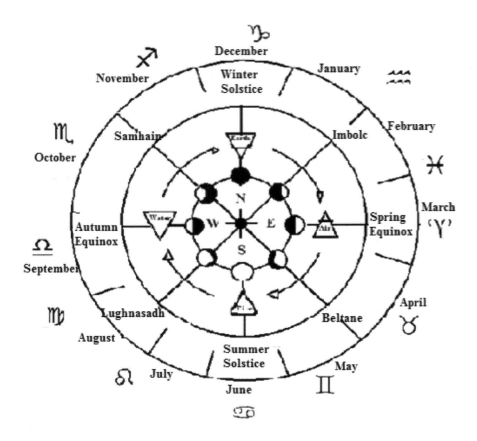

The Wheel of the Year, Quarters and Cross Quarters

The solar wheel governs all things in earthly existence, the seasons and the natural rhythms. In most cultures around the world the turning of the wheel is marked and celebrated at the eight natural quarters and cross quarters of the cycle in some way or another. These celebrations are either in direct recognition of the Sun or a holy day of some kind marking a changing of season.

Some of the first forms of calendar we have or evidence of ways of keeping time are Neolithic stone circles aligned with sun and stars. Throughout the British Isles and Europe there are thousands of these circles and indeed throughout the world. In ancient Egypt in the Nabta Playa west of Aswan communities needing to predict the weather built one of these stone circles dating back to 5000 BC. This circle is the earliest evidence of weather forecasters becoming astrologers and tracking time. The central stones of the circle are aligned with the circumpolar stars which are visible all year. When the sun shone overhead no shadow meant that it was midsummer and that the rains were approaching bringing with them the promise of life for the coming year. Other stone circles are aligned to summer or winter solstice, the journey of the Sun through the sky and to the cardinal points connecting stars, land and the turning seasons.

The most commonly used English names for the Sabbats of the Wheel of the Year tend to be Celtic and Germanic and this is because they have been adopted by Wiccan culture. There are eight traditional Celtic Sabbaths and eight traditional Asatru Blots or Seasonal Festivals. Each of the festival days was generally ruled by a governing deity, a God or Goddess, variably dependent upon the regional area.

From the hunter gatherers of the Stone Age to the settled farmers and fishermen, the turning of the year and the seasons were of huge importance to our ancestors, their lives utterly dependent upon good harvests or successful hunting, mild winters and enough rainfall. In truth this is still the case, though many of us are removed from the planting and harvesting process and from hunting, our food is still grown and farmed and harvested and it is still nature who provides everything that supports our existence. Although we have the luxury of being able to buy items that someone else has grown for us, or meat that has been reared on a farm somewhere else we are still utterly dependent upon Mother Earth.

The Eight Solar Holy Days	Corresponding Dates	Christian Holidays
1. Imbolc	2nd February	Candlemas and Lent
2. Vernal Equinox/Ostara	20th - 21st March	Easter
3. Beltane	1st May	May Day (secular)
4. Summer Solstice/Lithia	20th - 22nd June	Day of Saint John
5. Lammas/ Lughnasadh	1st August	First harvest (secular)
6. The Autumn Equinox/Mabon	22nd – 24th September	Michaelmas, harvest festival
7. Samhain	31st October	All Hallows Eve
8. The Winter Solstice/Yule	20th-23rd December	Christmas

N.B. May Day and the first harvest are secular not Christian but are recognised in our country and modern calendar alongside the Christian dates.

The Solar Holy Days

2 February – Imbolc, Imbolg, Oimelc, Brighid's Day, Candlemas, Gŵyl Fair y Canhwyllau.

From the dark cold earth of the midwinter stir the first whirlings of movement and life. The snows give way to rains and winds and the light begins to increase slowly. It is a time of stirring, the beginnings of awakening from sleep and the time for rebirth. For our ancestors before the age of electricity and in indigenous communities the dark days and the cold determined the priorities for our well-being and security. Responsibility and self-love and care are highlighted now and this is a time where these basic obligations need to be met. Food at this time of year would most likely have been scarce and consisted of what was left of whatever had been stored and preserved. Very little is yet growing in the soil in February but snowdrops and the first crocuses of the year begin to peep through the surface and the trees promise new leaves soon with tiny sprouts of green. The constant effort to keep warm and dry means lots of wood chopping, hopefully seasoned from preparation in autumn. Keeping things clean from the mud can also be time consuming in cold wet weather.

The preparation time of the earth whilst seeds germinate beneath the surface is our preparation time for making plans for spring. When a day comes which is not raining vegetable plots need preparing and turning over with the now mulched leaves of last autumn and the winter wood fire ashes ready for planting time.

Now is the time of new beginnings, illumination, inspiration and initiations of all kinds. Resolutions have been made and goals are aspired to. It's a time of growth for all of life both under and peaking through the earth's surface and internally for us emotionally and psychologically. The first signs of spring and the returning sunlight mark the passing from winter into spring and the beginning of the agricultural year. In many of the Northern and Western pagan traditions this time also marks the changing of the Goddess from Crone to Maiden as the increasing light awakens the Her and the rebirth of the Sun is celebrated as the young God. Despite his youth his life force is felt as the days become longer and his warmth fertilizes the earth causing seeds to germinate and encouraging new life.

The Gaelic name of this festival was Imbolc and it was celebrated in Ireland, Scotland and the Isle of Man as a fire festival marking fertility and light and across much of Europe, the North and West, candles, torches and fires were lit in its honour. The word Imbolc comes from the Old Irish *imbolg* "in the belly" referring to the pregnancy of ewes. Medieval etymology uses the term *oimelc* "ewe's milk" marking the increased flow of milk that signified the soon coming spring. Megalithic monuments such as the mount on the hill at Tara in Ireland, which are aligned with the Imbolc and Samhain sunrise, bear testimony to the festival's observance since Neolithic times.

Traditionally the Imbolc festival was associated with the Goddess Brigid the light bringer, who emerges from the earth bringing the spring. It is the first of the four fire festivals. There are similarities which may be drawn between Brigid and the story of Persephone of the Greek Elysian mysteries who comes out of the underworld before spring returns. Brigid is the patroness of poetry,

183

smith craft, medicine, arts and crafts, cattle and other livestock, sacred wells and serpents. She originates as the daughter of the Dagda and is one of the Tuath Dé Dannan in the text of the *Lebor Gabála*. The feast of Saint Brighid, her later Christianised personification, is also celebrated on this day. The Celts called this festival Imbolc or Oimelc, meaning ewes' milk referring to the increased flow of milk returning to the animals that signalled the soon coming spring.

Later the Church replaced the celebration of Bride (Brigid, Brighid, Brigit) with Candlemas, which is the feast day of Mary of the Candles. Candlemas was celebrated in Ireland and Wales and the Welsh equivalent is called Gŵyl Fair y Canhwyllau, Mary's Festival of the Candles. Christians acknowledge Candlemas as a celebration of three things: the presentation of the child Jesus, Jesus' first entry into the temple and the Virgin Mary's purification. Now is often a time of purification for us too after the long winter, welcoming in the sun. We intuitively clean our houses top to bottom, let the light in, clear out anything no longer useful and burn any rubbish. So too with our lives at this time! Release, remove, clean, clear and welcome in the new with consideration and celebration.

20 – 21 March – The Vernal Equinox, Alban Eilir, Ostara, Eostre, Easter

The land is reborn with colour and movement. There is a great awakening, a softening in the air, countless animals are emerging and new life is everywhere. Daffodils trumpet their sunny petals heralding the returning sun and life's a little brighter. Green shoots are coming out of the earth and poking up through the soil of their bed. The animals that were in hibernation wake up hungry and looking for food; lambs are born; the summer birds return from their migration in the South and the amphibians come out of the depths seeking the light. For us, this is the planting time. Time to double dig the soil and put in the hardier plants and seeds and to germinate the more fragile ones carefully nestled into propagators, window boxes and greenhouses to be nurtured until the weather is warmer. Instinctively we clean out the shed and the greenhouse, air our homes and do the deep spring cleaning welcoming the light in!

The word Ostara or Eostre comes from the Germanic Goddess of the Dawn by the same name. Many of the stories about Ostara are about light overcoming darkness and this is the point where the young Sun God (or the Oak King), steps into his power uniting with the Goddess and winning victory over the old God of Winter (or the Holly King).

Giving brightly decorated eggs, a potent fertility symbol at this time is a common pagan tradition that has continued into the present. In England and Northern Europe eggs were often used in folk magic by women who wanted children. The Goddess moves from the Virgin Maiden aspect of Imbolc into her Mother aspect and conceives the new Sun God now to be born nine months later at the winter solstice. In the Christian story Easter is celebrated as the time of Christ's resurrection from the dead. There are similarities between the Christian Easter and Pesach, the Jewish Passover.

The spring equinox is a point of balance, where day and night are equal and effectively we pass a threshold for this is the doorway allowing us to step from the dark half of the year into the light half of the year. Our lives echo the cycle and we recognise the importance of nurturing new projects and ideas. We seek to redress the balance in our lives, throwing out that which no longer serves and welcoming in new things that will. Traditionally this is a time to sew new seeds for the coming harvest and the same can be said of our lives. This is the time for setting intentions, laying foundations, preparation and planning. We reorganise our systems and become more industrious with our time, energised and renewed with the Sun. This is a good time for exploration, creativity, change, prosperity, balance, truth, honesty, clarity, sincerity, gaining confidence, opportunity, emotions and productivity.

1 May – Beltane, Calan Mai, May Day

The warmer days at the beginning of the summer season is marked with Beltane, the second of the four fire festivals, more commonly known as May Day in recent times. People dance the maypole, an ancient tradition to represent the male and female uniting, the energy of the dance around the phallic pole connecting with ribbons and awakening the earth beneath it and channelling through the people around it. Traditionally this is the time for weddings, hand-fastings, new relationships, courting and "maying" (flirtatious and or sexual encounters in the woods). Beltane is a time to bring increased abundance and fertility to all aspects of our lives and to give thanks for the areas where they exist.

Beltane is the last of the three spring fertility festivals, the other two being Imbolc and Ostara, and celebrates the return of fertility to the land as well as bringing fertility to the people. The festival marks the changing of season into summer and where Samhain, its opposite in October, is about honouring death, Beltane honours Life mirroring the unification of the Goddess and the God. The name Beltane is an anglicised version of the Irish *Bealtine* or the Scottish *Bealtuinn*. Tene means "fire" and Bel after the name of the pastoral God Belenus, the shining one who is usually depicted as the Sun God. Bel also means "brilliant".

The Celts celebrated Beltane eve with dancing and two large Bel fires lit from the nine sacred woods in honour of Bel. The fires are sacred and considered to have given blessings, healing and purification to all who walk between them. Traditionally cattle were driven between them to bless them with health and fertility for the coming year and of course people would walk and dance between them too to receive blessing. This is still done for those participating in modern day rituals. In Ireland, the fires of Tara were the first ones lit every year at Beltane and all the other fires were lit from Tara's flame. Elsewhere household fires would be extinguished and re-lit with fresh fire from the Bel Fires and the ashes from the Bel fires were scattered on the land to encourage fertility and fruitfulness. On *Nos Galan Mai* or May eve, Welsh villagers gathered white thorn branches and flowers which they used to decorate the outside of their houses to celebrate and encourage new growth and fertility.

Although there is no Christian equivalent May Day is still recognised in present day culture alongside the Christian Calendar and is steeped in community traditions such as village fairs and morris dancing, which itself dates back to pagan times. Beltane is a good time for increasing our creativity, listening to intuition, working with the faery and elementals, connecting with trees and plants and psychic or spirit work as it is a liminal time when the veil between the worlds is thin.

20 to 22 June – Summer Solstice, Alban Hefin, Midsummer or Lithia, the day of Saint John

The June summer solstice brings intense sunlight and is the peak time for photosynthesis for plants. The long light days and evenings of summer bring a time of plenty and ease and at summer solstice we enjoy the bounty and celebrate the light and the sun. This is a good time to gather herbs as this is the zenith of the sun's power and in picking them now the essence can be effectively stored. Traditionally this was always the day to collect St John's Wort, a bright yellow flower said to lift the spirits, which is still used to treat depression by modern herbalists. Amongst the attributes of the plant are not just its medicinal properties but also it is thought the height of the sun's power and light and consequently the good feelings associated with it. Coincidentally, as with Goddess names that were changed to Christian Saints' names, the 24 June has become Saint John's day and it is after his name that we know the plant! Fires and festivities are held on the evening of the 23 June, the night before. The summer solstice was traditionally celebrated with fires, feasting and festivities.

Some say that summer solstice is also the correct time for collecting wands from trees however it is better to take them at the winter solstice. Or ideally just after winter solstice as light and power is increasing. In the summer it is damaging to the tree to cut branches from it, whilst in winter when the tree is dormant it may actually be beneficial and encourage new growth for spring. A wand taken respectfully to the needs of the tree will always be more effective than one that has caused harm. In any case the wand may be blessed at the summer solstice by placing it in the sun. It is also worth remembering that all established trees see many seasons and contain them all within their rings of growth unalike from herbs that may only flower and be collected at certain times of the year. The potency or fire is within the wood.

Whilst the summer solstice marks the longest day and the shortest night it is in reality also the turning point. It is a time of fullness, movement and blossoming life and is marked throughout the whole world. In the Sun God story He now ascends to His height of power before beginning the descent brought by this pivotal point in time to death and rebirth. This story is mirrored in some Wiccan traditions as the time of the Oak King, the Lord of Summer, being killed by the Holly King or becoming the Holly King, the Lord of Winter. In the Mother Goddess story the Goddess is now pregnant with the Sun God who will be born at winter solstice, which is directly opposite on the Wheel of the Year.

Midsummer is the time for favourable workings with the sun's strength, warmth and light. It's a good time to bring those qualities to any areas of our lives in need of them. Sun energy illuminates all things whether it's a way forward with new plans or bringing light to our shadows, re-energising us and charging up or cleansing any sacred items, showing us how to relax and enjoy life, how to step into our personal power, asking for strength, rebalancing, justice, healthy control, success, making plans and goals and spiritual work are highlighted. High summer throughout June and July is also the traditional time for pilgrimage to sacred sites such as holy wells and standing stones.

1 August – Lughnasadh, Lammas, Calan Awst, First Harvest

Lughnasadh is the third of the four great Celtic fire festivals, and its emphasis is on the first harvest. The name Lughnasadh comes from the Irish God Lugh one of the chief Gods of the Tuatha de Danann. It is Lughnasadh in Ireland, Lunasdál in Scotland, and Laa Luanys in the Isle of Man. In Wales it is known as *Calan Awst*. It was later Christianised as Lammas from the Anglo-Saxon, *hlafmaesse,* meaning "Loaf-Mass". Its ancient origins as the first harvest festival are continued even now in the tradition of eating bread from the first grain milled into flour for the year. In some rural areas it is also called Bilberry Sunday, marking the day to climb the nearest "Lughnasadh Hill" and gather the black berries for jam.

The days of late summer are still long, light and warm. Fruit is beginning to ripen and swell. This is a time of waiting and relaxing, enjoying the warmth as flowers blossom, bees make honey and everything grows. The Goddess is waiting too for the new Sun Child to be born and changes aspects from Mother to Crone as She oversees the harvest of the Earth.

In terms of physical practical jobs we begin to harvest and to gather the earlier crops, fruits and berries and we watch over and tend to the things still growing whilst we wait. This is a gestation period of sorts. Now is a good time for counting the blessings and appreciating what we have, giving thanks and showing gratitude both to the Earth and to one another, recognising abundance in all its forms in our lives whether as wealth, health or friendships. Where possible, resting is good too and enjoying the playtime of summer whilst it lasts.

22 – 24 September, The Autumn Equinox, Mabon, Michaelmas, Harvest Festival

At the point of the equinox the night hours are again equal to those of the day and this is the mark of autumn. Coincidently the sign of Libra begins at this time. The scales symbolizing Libra are a direct link to the harvest, as this is the time where the farmers brought in their goods to be weighed and sold. The autumnal equinox is commonly called Mabon after the God Mabon ap Modron of Welsh literature and mythology. His name is related to the Roman-British God Maponos, meaning "Great Son". Modron probably comes from Dea Matrona, the Divine Mother Goddess of the Gauls. The Welsh name and also druidic name for this festival is *Alban Elfed* meaning the light of the water. *Meán Fómhair* is the Gaelic name meaning middle harvest because this is the second of the three harvest festivals and the time for completing the grain harvest that was begun at the first one.

The Christianised version of Mabon is as Michaelmas, the feast day of Archangel Michael. It has been suggested that the church may have considered assigning the other quarter days to Archangels too based upon evidence of the spring equinox briefly being described as Gabrielmas commemorating Gabriel's announcement to Mary on Lady Day.

Mythically, this is the day of the year when the Lord of Light or the Oak King is defeated by his twin or other self the Lord of Winter or the Holly King. It is the time of year when night conquers day and the only day when he can be defeated. In other renditions of the story we see the Sun God beginning to grow old. Traditionally the second harvest of Mabon marks the completion of the grain harvest begun during Lughnasadh. Celebrations revolve around the gathering of crops and thanksgiving for the abundances of the harvest. This is a day of reckoning and taking stock in many ways both physically giving thanks and reflectively in life weighing up our current positions and prioritising before moving forwards.

189

31 October, Samhain, All Hallows' Eve

Samhain is the time we prepare for winter. The fields are fallow, the leaves are falling and the forests animals prepare for hibernation and are busily gathering their stores. We do the same and it is customary to bring cattle and sheep down from hills and pastures to shelter for the winter months and to slaughter those necessary for food supplies. Meat may now be smoked or salted for preservation. Everything else that can be gathered from fields, trees and bushes is now harvested and stored or preserved in any way possible. This is an industrious time of drying herbs, making medicines, jamming fruit, canning and pickling vegetables, brewing alcohol and stocking up supplies of candles and wood for winter fires.

Samhain is the third and last of the harvest festivals and its name means "summer's end" from the Scottish Gaelic *Samhuinn*. In Scotland and Ireland, Halloween is known as *Oíche Shamna*. In Wales it is called *Calan Gaeaf*, the winter's calend or beginning on the 1 November and Samhain. The night before is known as *Ysbrydnos* or "spirit night". In early Ireland tribes of people gathered at sacred sites such as Tara for the main feast day of the year and fires were lit. The Druids at Tlachtga lit the first fire of the night and brought it to Tara and the seat of the High King which was thought of as the heart of the land. Throughout the country old fires were put out and new ones lit from the torches carried from Tara. Many offerings, gifts and prayers were offered into the fires for the harvest festival and the coming winter. In Christianity All Hallows' Eve or Hallowmas precedes All Hallows' Day also known as the Day of the Saints or Feast of All Saints celebrated in honour of all saints known and unknown. The word saints here may in some contexts refer to all Christians and therefore the day remembers and honours any deceased members of a congregation.

In the story of the Goddess and the Sun God, the Goddess is now in her Crone aspect as the ruler of the Otherworld and she bids farewell to the Sun God as He passes over into death to face His rebirth at the upcoming Yule. As the Sun God journeys to the Underworld, He gathers unto Himself all those who have passed over to death since the previous Samhain, to guide them on their way to the afterlife. In the Wild Hunt stories as the doorway to winter opens, the spirits of the hunt move through the skies collecting lost or wandering souls to take them home to the other side. Leading them is the huntsman of mythology who in Wales is Gwynn ap Nudd, the King of the Faeries and in England, the God Herne the Hunter. In the story of the Oak King and Holly King it is now the Holly King who sits on the throne as the Lord of Winter with the Crone aspect of the Goddess beside him. Traditionally this spirit night is the time for connecting with spirit and for honouring the ancestors and loved ones on the other side. It is also the best time for divination as the veils between the worlds are thinnest allowing us better vision. Workings of divination, contacting spirit, death and by extension sex and rebirth, harvesting, reaping, releasing anything not needed for winter, preservation, transformation, preparation, inner work and personal development.

20 ⁻ 23 December, Winter Solstice, Yule, Christmas

The dark days and long nights bring the cold; there are frosts most mornings and evenings and the first snows fall. Fields and trees are barren and food is scarce. Animals sleep deep in their hibernation awaiting warmer days. This is the indoor time for keeping warm and well, busy with winter pass times like spinning and knitting and the making of artistic or practical things to give as gifts to loved ones. It's a good time to repair anything that needs fixing ready for spring and keep on top of managing the wood and food supplies. Mostly it's about staying warm, conserving energy and resources and resting. We rest and wait.

The winter solstice is the darkest time of the year. The word solstice means stand still and refers to the three days around 21 December when the sun appears to "stand still", or rise and set in the same place. This midwinter point is like the in breath, going into darkness and stillness, before the out breath that follows as the light slowly returns. It is the turning point of the wheel from which the days shall grow longer and the hours of sunlight will return. The name Yule comes from the Norse word for wheel and Yule is therefore the doorway the Wheel of the Year. The later Roman year with which we are accustomed these days began with January, named after the two-faced

God Janus, who faced both backwards and forwards also acting as a doorway to the year on the 1 January, the month bearing his name which falls just ten days after Yule. In Welsh the solstice is called *Alban Arthan* meaning light of winter. In Christianity the birth of the baby Jesus Christ, the Son of God is celebrated on 25 December. Rituals for welcoming back the Sun date from the dawn of civilization, as communities came together to celebrate life with feasting, music, dance, light and fire. This is still the same and many Christmas customs including the making and giving of gifts for our loved ones, decorating and celebrating of the evergreen fir tree, the making of Christmas pudding using the dried harvest fruit and the lighting of the Yule log are steeped in our Celtic past. In ancient Rome, the winter Solstice was welcomed with a feast known as Saturnalia celebrating the God Saturn who governs all of time.

The Goddess again in her Mother form now gives birth to the new Sun God and after giving birth she returns to her maiden form in preparation for the new cycle. The birth of the young Sun God is also celebrated by others as the victory of the Lord of Summer or the Oak King once more over the Lord of Winter or the Holly King.

Traditionally this is a time to rest, reflect and enjoy each time with our family and friends. Workings of personal issues, death and releasing of the old, family, friendships and relationships.

Suggested Exercise

Getting to know the culture and researching the correct calendar for the work we are undertaking is always important. Choose two cultures you are interested in and research them.

What season is it and where are you in the solar cycle?

Is there a holy day associated with the season?

Prepare a small celebration or low-key ritual such as a bonfire with some prayers or incense offerings to mark the next holy day.

Chapter Twelve
The Moon and Lunar Calendar

Even when we see darkness there is light somewhere on the other side of the moon, hidden from our eyes, invisible from Earth.

The Moon has no luminescence of her own and in fact her light is the reflection of the Sun. This reflective quality is also at the truth of her nature and she governs all things that reflect, the first of which is water. Her phases govern all the tides of the oceans and bodies of water on earth. The element of water is deeply connected with our emotional water element psychologically and so it is the Moon which bears the most relation to our emotions. Where the Sun represents our higher self and perpetual light so the Moon represents our earthly reflections through our personality, phases of being and perceptions. With all manner of inner development work and practical magic our observance and understanding of the Moon and our connection to her is as important as our connection and observance of the Sun. By learning and deepening our understanding with her we are able to work to our advantage with her phases and tides and not against the current. Quite often the literal current! Adaptability, resourcefulness and innovation can be used creatively in such a way that we can either time our work for the perfect moment or harness the natural flow by adapting our mindset. For example a working to remove disease or unrest from a situation could be altered to a working to call forth good health or peace if required.

The moon phases have their own wheel and cycle and we are all familiar with her changing appearance in the sky. There are approximately 12.4 lunar months to each solar year. Thus some solar years have twelve and some years have thirteen moons. Each of these individual cycles of the moon last an average of 29.53059 days which is known as the Synodic month (29 days, 12 hours, 44 minutes, 2.8 seconds) and is the basis of all lunar calendars. The Moon is waxing (growing) from dark Moon to full Moon and the Moon is waning (shrinking) from full Moon to dark Moon.

Within this cycle the moon reflects the fourfold and eightfold phases of the solar year with her four quarters and eight phases including the cross quarters. These eight phases are each approximately 3.6875 days long and we will look at these in closer detail shortly. Just as the Sun embodies the masculine trinity she embodies the female trinity of the triple Goddess and most commonly is associated with the female principle.

Although the Moon is usually portrayed as female in Wicca and most western pagan paths this varies and around the world there are also many examples of lunar Gods such as the Egyptian Gods Khonsu or Thoth. In the case of Thoth he also represents the planet Mercury who rules over Gemini. This is interesting because of the dual aspects here. Gemini is always represented as twins, the image of two faces could be associated with the second being reflective of the first i.e. the Sun and Moon or as two eyes, one of Horus, (the Sun) and one of Thoth, (the moon). The Moon card of the tarot also brings our attention to the possibilities of duality and reflections and bringing awareness to those things that may be proportionally hidden or unclear.

The Roman Moon Goddess is Luna and it is from her that the word lunar comes. Luna is sometimes seen as one aspect of Hecate or is sometimes seen as an epithet denoting a Goddess generally. Roman Goddesses such as Diana are also associated with the moon.

Whilst it is more common for the Moon to be ascribed to the female principle it is of course equally relevant to both men and women in our embodiment of this cosmic force within our personality and emotions just as the sun is life force and higher perpetual light of being to us all.

The word month comes from the Anglo-Saxon word *monath* which means moon. Historically the month names are lunations (cycles of the moon). Depending upon the culture the first day for each month may be counted from the dark moon, from the new crescent in the sky, or in some cases the full moon's zenith (conjunction). In Rome the priests observed the sky and announced the new moon and month.

Most calendars pre-dating the current Gregorian system were luni-solar and combined the solar year with lunation by means of intercalary months. These intercalary months occur seven times in a nineteen-year period or more simply put on average every 2.7 years, the exception being the Islamic calendar which is solely lunar. This nineteen-year-period known as the metonic cycle is remarkable because it is almost an exact common multiple of the solar year and the lunar month. The purpose of the intercalary month which was inserted between lunar months was to make the calendar year correspond to the solar year. We see a remnant of this on the 29 February every four years as a leap year. The luni-solar calendar is still observed in many religious calendars and the dates for Passover and Easter are both calculated in this way. Easter is the first Sunday after the full moon that follows the vernal equinox.

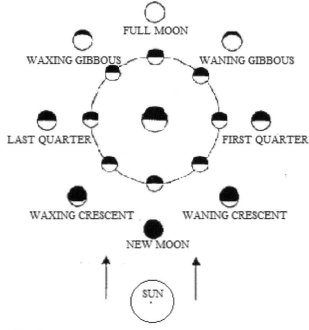

Moon Cycle

Please note I have rounded up to 3.7 to the nearest digit from 3.6875 days for practicality. These phases are often counted as 3.5 days in modern books but this is not correct and the best way to calculate it is to buy a good moon diary.

Dark New Moon

Nought to 3.7 days. Moon rises at dawn and sets at sunset. Dark Moon is also called the new moon depending upon culture. (In other cultures such as Judaism the new moon is the first crescent appearing in the sky which follows shortly afterwards and this is worth bearing in mind when reading material referring to it.) Note the dual energies listed in the appropriate actions below are deliberate. This is because we release the old as we move into the darkest point of the moon and then re-emerge and go forwards welcoming the new as the 3.67 days are divided equally over the period of time where this zero point is reached.

Dark moon means that the sun is shining on the other side of the moon and that the moon is between the sun and the earth in alignment which is why we can't see it and there are no reflections! To us it appears as darkness. The high and low tides of Earth are accentuated at this time. This is the Crone phase of the Lunar Goddess.

For many women this is also their moon time or menstrual time and the strong connection with the moon allows us as women to go into our own Crone aspects with her. In some Native American traditions the women may choose to spend this time in the Moon Lodge connecting with this inner Crone and part of the psyche to emerge later with vision and guide the way forwards for the community.

This dark time of the Crone is in its nature transitional. She is both death and the transition to the point of rebirth. Our intuition is heightened as is psychic ability and insight.

Travelling into the darkest point (1.8 days approximately) her initiations and pathways are those of change, transition, releasing, removing, clearing, cleansing, casting out, quitting addictions, divorce, dealing with enemies (appropriately), asking for justice, removing obstacles, sorrows and hurts, resolving quarrels, issues of separation including theft or emotional separation.

Travelling out of the darkest point (1.8 days approximately) her initiations and pathways are those of transformation, rest, new beginnings, planning, attracting positive energy, new growth, planting, calming, divination, renewing, regeneration, health, self-improvement, drawing in love or other qualities, improving situations and protection.

The crone aspect of the Goddess understands and has the wisdom of universal love both of self and others and she teaches this to us when we are open to her invitation. Wisdom is only ever earned through experience and intellectual understanding is no substitute for this and so it is only when the timing is right or we open ourselves to her lessons that we may see them in our lives and learn them. Examples of the crone Goddess can be seen in the Celtic Goddesses Cerridwen and Morrigan.

Corresponding Time of Year – 21 December, Winter Solstice. Direction – North.

The colours of the dark moon are black, dark purples and blues.

Suggested crystals are those of the right colour such as obsidian, rainbow obsidian, apache tears or any other you find with properties suitable to the dark moon's aspect. This principle can be applied either by colour or by property to all moon phases. So long as there is a logical basis for the choice of a stone it will usually serve the purpose.

Waxing Crescent

The Waxing Crescent Moon begins to make the first slither of the D shape heralding the daughter aspect of the Maiden Goddess in the sky at 3.7 to 7.1 days of the cycle. She rises mid-morning and sets in the evening. At this point the moon is one eighth behind the sun, which is the part we see forming the crescent.

Her initiations and pathways at this time are those of making plans, information gathering, laying foundations, new beginnings, improving health, attraction, calling forth, welcoming in, emotions, finding stability, animal welfare, luck, friendships, jobs, employment, useful purpose, courage and optimism. This is still a time of regeneration after the transformation from the dark phase. Resting and taking good care of ourselves is important as the moon gains strength. Like young seeds that have not long germinated new projects need nurture and care as they develop and gain strength. Examples of the Maiden Goddess are Diana (Roman) or Artemis (in Greek) both youthful huntresses associated with women, childbirth, birth, the hunt, wild animals, wilderness, virginity, protection and fertility.

Corresponding Time of Year, 1 February (Imbolc). Direction, North-East.

The colours of the waxing crescent are green, white, orange and red.

First Quarter

The First Quarter Moon, waxing forms around 7.1 to 10.8 days in the cycle. She rises at noon and sets at midnight. At this point the moon is at a right angle to the sun as she moves around the earth in her cycle and we see her first D shaped half. Light and dark are in equal balance and the tides of earth are minimised. This is the pivotal point between the Maiden and Mother aspects and the threshold of womanhood. Maiden Goddesses are often found in the roles of the artist, the guardian or the lover across time and various cultures and it is in this phase of the moon where more of the sun is reflected and the point of light and dark balance shifts in favour of the light of the sun that we see the young Goddess consorting with the God as his lover.

The recurring themes of the crescent moon apply in beginnings, making improvements, attraction, calling forth, welcoming, emerging, movement, finding, making, creating, friends, money, opportunities and manifestations. The instinctual nature of the maiden and her intuition and courage are highlighted now. A time of motivation, decisions and careful action symbolised by the weighing up of half light and half dark. This time of half and half may also be seen as a doorway to other places in much the same way as between times of the year and light.

Corresponding Time of Year, Vernal Equinox (Ostara). Direction, East.

The colours of the waxing first quarter moon are white, pastel colours, red and silver.

Waxing Gibbous

The Waxing Gibbous Moon occurs between 10.8 to 14.5 days into the cycle. She rises mid-afternoon and sets around three a.m. in the dark hours of the next morning. At this point the moon is three eights behind the earth and five eights are visible to us reflecting sunlight. Here is the beginning of the Mother aspects of the Goddess and her secrets of initiation and the pathways offered to us now are those of growth and growing both in our personal development and in our external realities and magical practices. One of the key lessons at this stage is patience and recognising that time allows fullness of development. This is a time of gestation and waiting, meditation and centring. Projects are now under way and need nurturing; protection of ourselves and our interests as they grow is wise as is tying up loose ends. It's a time to boost and store energy, to rest and watch attentively, increase communications, regenerate and prepare for the coming full moon.

Corresponding Time of Year, 1 May (Beltane). Direction South-East.

The colours of the waxing gibbous moon are white, pastel colours, red and silver.

Full Moon

The Full Moon reaches her most powerful height of full light, on the opposite side of the earth, fully reflecting the sun between 14.5 to 18.2 days of her cycle with her mid point peaking with one day either side, showing full in the sky. She rises at sunset and sets at dawn. The sun shines on her fully and there are earthly tidal extremes again. Remember at this mid point that in actual fact the correct phase length of each is 3.6875 days not 3.5. It's really useful to have a good moon diary!

The full moon is the Mother aspect of the Goddess embodied in Goddesses such as the Celtic Goddess Danu and the Egyptian Goddess Isis. It is a time of high energy which can be used to align our will and as such is of magically great importance.

Pay attention to dreams and creative processes, divination, surfacing feelings, love and relationships with family, friends and lovers. This is a time of great potency and fertility and often coincides with ovulation for many women. The original contraception or pregnancy aid was watching the sky! That being said it is not a fail-safe method.

Goals, transformation, psychic abilities, strength, love, empowerment, fertility and power are all found in this initiatory phase. Cleanse, purify, charge, recharge and strengthen resolves, protection of the home and any aspect of life where these forces are needed. Power boosts and matters of courage, healing, money, communication, justice and ambition are all favourable at this time. It is also an intuitive and productive time where fertility, magic, meditation, domestic matters, beauty, money, creativity and psychic abilities are highlighted. Be aware of heightened emotions in this phase and that this is not a good time for making decisions.

Visit the sea, go to water, recognise the fire in the water as the sun reflected in the height of the full moon and as the highest aspect of ourselves coming through in our personal journey. Take this opportunity to imbue any personal jewellery and crystals or magical working tools with the height of both male and female principles and put things out in the height of the moon or wash them in water reflecting the light. Now is a good time for any major workings at the obvious climax of the moon's power.

Corresponding Time of Year Summer Solstice (Midsummer). Direction, South.

The colours of the full moon are blue, white, silver, cream, yellow and orange.

Waning Gibbous

The Waning Gibbous Moon is disseminating from approximately 18.2 to 21.9 days of her cycle. She rises in the evening and sets mid-morning. Although this is still the Mother aspect of the Goddess and feminine principle this is also the beginning of the journey inwards. Her tides have turned as she leaves the height of the sun's light and moves into the beginnings of shadow. She has rotated further around the earth and five eighths of her face are visible to us. The Mother Goddesses associated with harvest and autumn are most appropriate to her phase and these include the Egyptian Goddess Bast and the Roman Goddess Ceres.

As she reflects the sun, we in turn reflect her turning inwards. Her initiations are those of introspection, sincerity and assessment. Now is the time to take stock, review our endeavours, correct mistakes, settle disputes and make amends. Healing, calming and inner attunement are highlighted often through the practice of gratitude, giving thanks, sharing, building knowledge, vocal expression and clear communication and meditation. Now is also a good time to banish any negative influences such as stress, addiction, negative relationships or anything that is harmful in any way. By extension any areas of protection relating to this and protecting from negative influences or harm can be worked now. Emotions are still likely to be running high but in this more level headed phase decisions can be made safely.

Corresponding Time of year, 1 August, The First Harvest (Lughnasadd).

Direction South-West.

The colours of the waning gibbous moon are dusky white, pale grey, golds, creams, pinks.

Last Quarter

The Last Quarter Moon waning comes from 21.9 to 25.6 days of the cycle. The moon rises at midnight and sets at noon. She moves to the second right angle between the sun and earth, making the Crone C shape in the sky as she moves through the pivotal point between the Mother and Crone aspects. There is low tide variation again as the balance of light and dark return.

The initiations and pathways of this moon phase are both those of the wiser older mother coming into autumn and the beginnings of the Crone or elder female principle are those of deep intuition, introspection, clear vision, divination, wisdom, knowledge, decision making, sharing, vocal expression and communication. Associated Goddesses may be found in those with triple aspects and both in Mother and Crone aspects. Two examples are the Irish Goddesses Morrigan who embodies Badb, Macha and Anand, and the Welsh Goddess Arianrhod who is the mother aspect with Blodeuwedd the maiden and Cerridwen the crone.

Now is the time for overcoming obstacles and energetic blocks, removing, releasing, banishing, cleaning, clearing, casting out all that does not serve our highest good. Remember to be mindful of what fills the gap as vacuums have a tendency to fill quickly. Use this time for self-analysis, resting, recuperation and meditation.

Corresponding Time of year Autumn Equinox 21 September, the Second harvest (Mabon). Direction, West.

The colours of the waning moon are blues, light greys, purples and pinks.

Waning Crescent

The Waning Crescent Moon is now fully in her Crone aspect at 25.6 to 29.3 days into the cycle. She rises in the dark hours at three or four a.m. and sets in the afternoon. She has moved further around the earth and closer to the sun blocking our view of all but an eighth of her face in reflection.

Her lessons and initiations are found in the recurring themes of removal, throwing out rubbish, cleaning, clearing, removing, banishing, letting go and endings. As she journeys deeper inwards so do we, moving further into introspection, analysis and reflection. She ensures we are meeting our needs and our obligations and brings responsibility. Now is the time for alone time, meditating, trusting our insight, scrying and other forms of divination. The inwards motion can be likened to the retreat into the cave or cauldron and into death which will bring rebirth in the next phase. All crone Goddesses are associated here and those crone aspects of triple Goddesses also. Key words are death, banishing, releasing, clearing, divorce, addictions and health through removal of disease. This is the preparation time for the new dark moon before she moves back into the darkness. (See New Dark Moon.)

The colours of the waning crescent moon are blues, greys, purples and pinks in their deeper shades.

Corresponding Time of year 31 October (Samhain). Direction, North-West.

Moonstone is suitable for all phases of the moon as is silver.

A **Blue Moon** is considered to be either the third full moon between either solstice and the following equinox or the fourth full moon between equinox and solstice, according to *The Farmer's Almanac* published in 1818. Modern thought subscribes to it being the second of any two full moons in any 29.5 day cycle.

A **Black Moon** is the observance of the third dark moon between solstice and equinox, or fourth between equinox and following solstice or as the second dark moon in a 29.5 day cycle.

Regardless of which system is correct they occur with the average frequency of intercalary months, seven times in nineteen years and both are thought to be particularly potent.

Suggested themes of the months and moons for working magic and for personal development.

January – new beginnings, protection, personal issues, setting goals, reversing or releasing.

February – purification, healing, growth, responsibility, self love.

March – new beginnings, exploration, prosperity, balance, truth, honesty, clarity, sincerity.

April – balance, creativity, change, confidence, opportunity, emotions, productivity.

May – creativity, intuition, faery, trees and plants, psychic work, spirit connections.

June – protection, strength, decisions, responsibility, personal issues, owning power, power, control.

July – relaxation, preparation, success, dreams, divination, plans, goals, spiritual work.

August – harvesting, reaping, appreciation, gratitude, abundance, wealth, health, prosperity, friendships.

September – balance, organisation, cleansing, clearing, peace.

October – divination, contacting spirit, death, rebirth, justice, balance, harmony, release.

November – transformation, preparation, strength, communication, inner work, personal development.

December – death, rebirth, family, friendships, relationships, personal issues.

See how the suggested themes of the months echo the astrological themes of the corresponding times of year in the chapter on Astrological Timing. Also notice how there are correspondences to the wheel of the year i.e. the equinox points are all about balance, the dark months are an inward journey and the light months are the outward journey of exploration.

Astrological Moon Phases

The moon orbits the earth and makes aspects in alignment with the astrological signs of the zodiac. This cycle takes just under twenty-eight days, an average of just over two days in each sign. There are always thirteen of these cycles in a solar year. Working with the aligning planetary aspects enhances and strengthens workings as the response varies under these influences and allows favourable timing and conditions to suit our purpose. For example when the moon is in Libra justice is likely to be more forthcoming than in any other sign.

Be aware of both good and bad traits that may arise depending upon balance i.e. Gemini in balance is good communication and multitasking but out of balance may spin into the chaos of over communicating and overdoing in an unhealthy way.

These are keywords only for easy reference and further information on each house or sign may be found in the chapter Astrological Timing.

Moon in Aries – action, independence, leadership, authority, risks, energy, enthusiasm, expression, spontaneity, rebirth, willpower, healing. Head.

Moon in Taurus – practical matters, security, permanence, endurance, money, prosperity, possessions, confidence to speak, growth, affection, sex, devotion, harmony, love. Throat, neck, ears healing.

Moon in Gemini – communication, intellect, ideas, learning, multi-tasking, networking, deals, transactions, sorting disputes, moving house, writing, travel. Hands, shoulders, lungs.

Moon in Cancer – home and domestic life, family, motherhood, pregnancy, scrying, divination, emotions, psychic work, protection, sympathy. Chest and stomach.

Moon in Leo – vitality, power, courage, authority, leadership, opportunity, confidence, courage, strength, kindness, fertility, childbirth. Back, spine, heart.

Moon in Virgo – organisation, attention to detail, reaping rewards, employment, intellect, health, fitness, diet, acquiring and improving skills, analysis, logical choices, precision, solutions, purification. Intestines and nervous system.

Moon in Libra – justice, court, law, partnerships, unions, marriage, contracts, agreement, increasing and attracting, love and friendships, beauty, cooperation, courtesy, charm, eloquence, friendships, balance, harmony, artistic work, mental stimulation, karmic resolutions, spiritual and emotional balance. Lower back and kidneys.

Moon in Scorpio – loyalty, transformations, power, psychic growth, insight, scrying, secrets, ownership, sexuality, libido, passionate love, single mindedness, concentration, rebirth, wisdom, karma, instinct, healing the mind and emotions. Sexual organs.

Moon in Sagittarius – Philosophy, religion, faith, generosity, adventure, journeys, study, learning, honesty, understanding, hope, optimism, imagination, legal matters, writing, publications, travel, truth. Liver, thighs and hips.

Moon in Capricorn – organisation, ambition, building, rules, discipline, determination, spiritual matters, structure, sincerity, recognition, career, political. Knees, bones, teeth and skin.

Moon in Aquarius – science, freedom, creative, problem solving, invention, technology, science, extra sensory abilities, friendships, social life, establishing and maintaining of social groups, freedom, intuition, independence, heightened perception, resourcefulness, transcending emotional rule, breaking bad habits. Calves ankles blood.

Pisces – spiritual and psychic, creativity, dream work, clairvoyance, telepathy, music, arts, care, compassion, peace, devotion, inspiration, empathy. Feet and lymph glands.

If you have a moon calendar or diary it should inform you of the astrological sign the moon is in. However another useful tool is an ephemeris which will also show you when the moon or other planets are in a certain sign.

Regarding astrological and moon planting guides and almanacs it can be useful to have a book or two on the subject. As a general rule of thumb plant above ground and also pick fruit for eating when the moon is waxing. This is also the time for potting and re-potting. Plant below the ground when the moon is waning. This is also the time for pruning, weeding, harvesting for storing and composting. At the new crescent plant leafy veg., herbs and seeds. At full moon plant anything watery like tomatoes, peppers and onions and collect seeds. This is also a good time for fertilising.

Just after full moon plant root veg., biennials and perennials and at dark moon cut wood and spray fruit trees.

Whenever possible plant in productive or fruitful astrological moon phases and harvest in barren ones.

Productive – Taurus, Capricorn.

Fruitful – Cancer, Scorpio, Pisces.

Libra is semi fruitful.

Barren – Aries, Gemini, Leo, Virgo, Sagittarius, Aquarius.

Moon stones and crystals should where possible select the phase of the moon in colour and in the properties you seek in your working. The more correspondences the stronger the connection and the better such a stone will serve its purpose. The same may be said of choosing plants, herbs and incense. Some of the more commonly used stones associated with the moon are clear quartz, opals, moonstone, pearl, mother of pearl, selenite, calcite and amethyst.

Amongst the insular Celts just as the day was seen to begin after the Sun had set, so too the Sun's year was seen as beginning with darkness. The year was divided into a light half and a dark half and began at Samhain. The Celtic year was primarily counted in lunar months whilst also recognising the solar cycle. The early English Anglo-Saxons too, prior to converting to Christianity and adopting the Roman calendar, used a luni-solar calendar based on the cycles of both Sun and moon.

The Anglo-Saxon Months

Much of the recorded information we have about the Anglo-Saxon months and calendar comes from a treatise written in Latin by a Northumbrian monk called Bede in his *De Temporum Ratione (On the Reckoning of Time)*, written in 725 AD. This treatise tells us a huge amount about the knowledge of his day including information about the cosmos, the spherical shape of the Earth and an advanced understanding of the seasonal cycles of the Sun and the Moon and their relation to tides. Bede describes not only the Anglo-Saxon heathen calendar and how it was calculated prior to Christianity but also the later Julian calendar and instructions for calculating the correct Christian dates for Easter and other religious observances based upon the Hebrew Bible. From his work we know the Anglo-Saxon origins of the names of the months in English as well as observances about Heathen festivals and the worship of Anglo-Saxon Gods and Goddesses.

The solar-lunar calendar year was divided into two halves, light and dark, which were governed by the spring and autumn equinoxes with marked importance given to the summer solstice (midsummer) and the winter solstice (midwinter). The months were counted by moons, each beginning at the full moon. There are 12.4 lunar months in a year and therefore the months moved around and an intercalary month was added at midsummer, when needed, in order to realign the months with the seasons.

December to January – Ærra Geola and Æfterra Geola

The year began at the New Year which was on 24 December three nights after the winter solstice. This time period lasted for twelve days and was called *Geola*, the old English word for Yule which means Wheel and is the origin of the word "Yuletide." Yule, *Geola* fell between two months and these were therefore called *Ærra* (before) *Geola* and *Æfterra* (after) *Geola* signifying the first and last months of the year, the entry and exit points of the wheel before the midnight of the winter solstice. The evening of 24 December was called *Mōdraniht*, which translates as Mothers' Night and was traditionally when the Goddesses were worshipped with votive offerings.

For reference the Old Norse equivalent months are *Mǫrsugur or Jól (Yule)* in the first half of the month and *Þorri (Thor),* the latter half of the month.

February – Solmanoth

The word *monath* is the old English word for month and means moon and most of the Anglo-Saxon month names end in "monath". Following the month Æfterra Geola (after Yule) is Solmonath which is thought to mean Soil or Earth month from the Old English word *Sol* meaning soil or mud or possibly Sun month also spelt *Sol* marking February as the time that the light of the Sun begins to return to the land. Bede also says that Solmonath can be called the "month of cakes" which they offered to their gods in that month.

March – Hrethmonath

According to Bede this month is named after the Goddess Hreða or Rheda "to whom they sacrificed at this time". It is likely that any rituals may have related to the beginning of Spring and new growth because of the time of year however there is no existing lore about her. Her name eventually became Lide in some Southern dialects of English.

April – Eostremonath

Bede writes that this month was named after the Goddess Eostre and that feats were held in her honour. He also adds that now "they designate that Paschal season by her name, calling the joys of the new rite by the time-honoured name of the old observance". Paschal is an old word for Easter taken from the Hebrew *pesach*, meaning "Passover". Most European languages still use a form of this word to mean Easter: in French it is *Pâques*, in Danish *Paaske* and in Scottish Gaelic *Cáisg*.

May – Thrimilce

May was the month of *Đrimilcemonað*, when livestock were so well fed on Spring grass that they could be milked three times a day.

June – (Ærra) Litha and July – (Æfterra) Litha

The month of June was called *Ærra* (meaning before) *Liða* and July was called *Æfterra* (after) *Liða*. Of these summer months Bede explains that Litha means "gentle" or "navigable", because in both these months the calm breezes are gentle and they were wont to sail upon the smooth sea.

Though some have suggested that Litha refers directly to the solstice there is no etymology of the word to support this. However, in a culture that divides the year into light and dark and marks the midwinter as the dark doorway to the solar year it is logical to suggest that midsummer at the height of the sun wheel would be similarly marked especially as it was in other pagan cultures across both Europe and around the world.

August – Weodmonath

August was called *Weodmonað* meaning weed month although *weod* could in this context mean plants, crops, vegetables, herbs or wode.

September – Haligmonath

Haligmonað means holy month and Bede says that the name refers to a "month of sacred rites". These are most probably celebrations and religious festivals giving thanks for the harvest and the summer's crops.

October – Winterfylleth

Like the insular Celts before them the old calendar predating the later Anglo-Saxon one divided the year into a light half and a dark half.

Of October *Winterfilleð*, Bede writes: "*Originally they [the heathen English] divided the year into two seasons, summer and winter, assigning the six months in which the days are longer than the nights to summer, and the other six to winter. Hence, they called the month in which the winter season began "Winterfilleth", a name made up of "winter" and "full Moon", because winter began on the first full Moon of that month.*"

In medieval Scandinavia there was a similar two season system with winter beginning in mid-October and summer beginning in mid-April and in heathen Iceland, the period of two days when winter began was called *Veturnætur* (Winter Nights) and was a holy time for sacrifice and feasting.

November – Blotmonath

Traditionally the month to slaughter any livestock for winter *Blotmonað* means blood month. Animals to be kept over winter had to be kept warm and fed with hay and so the practicalities meant slaughtering those destined for the pot or for preserving for the winter months. Bede writes it is a "*month of immolations, for then the cattle which were to be slaughtered were consecrated to the Gods*".

December – Ærra Geola

December returns the Wheel to the Yuletide.

The Anglo-Saxon Days Of The Week

English	Anglo Saxon	Meaning	Norse	Norse Translation
Sunday	Sunnandaeg	Sun's day	Sunnudagr	Sunna's Day
Monday	Monnandaeg	Moon's day	Mánadagr	Manis Day
Tuesday	Tiwesdaeg	Tiw's day	Týsdag	Tyrs Day
Wednesday	Wodnesdaeg	Woden's day	Óðinsdagr	Odins Day
Thursday	Thunresdaeg	Thunor's day	Þórsdagr	Thors Day
Friday	Frigesdaeg	Freya-Frigga Day	Frige's day	Frjádagr
Saturday	Sæterdaeg	Saturn's day	Laugardagr	Pool or Washing Day

Norse has been included so that similarities may be drawn between the God and Goddess names.

N.B. Saturn is a Roman deity that has been integrated.

The Roman Calendar

Bede also writes about the Roman calendar and about how the Christian holy days are calculated. The English word calendar derives from the Latin word *kalends* a diminutive of *kalendae* meaning "the called". *Kalends* were the first of these "called" days that were assigned to the first day of the month and signified the first visible crescent of the new moon, the months being lunar. (NB the Romans counted from the first visible crescent and not from dark moon.) The days in the Roman system were called and counted forwards towards the next new moon by the number of days left, for example *II. Kal. Maius* meaning that two days are to be counted until the first day of May would make the date 28 April. The Welsh word *calennig* meaning New Year Celebration also comes from the Latin root as does the German *kalender* and the French *calendrier.*

The first Roman calendar was lunar and perhaps based upon a similar Greek one and it had ten Lunar months and a period of time in the depths of winter that was unassigned. Whilst these *kalends (*new moons) were originally called, as were the half moons *Nonae* (the Nones) and the full moons, *Idus* (the Ides)*,* this eventually gave way to regular set days that were no longer called. In 713 BC the King Numa Pompilius reformed the calendar adding the two months we now know as January and February to make a total of twelve and re-designating the number of days in various months. This made a year of twelve months totalling 355 days. There was then a further intercalary month added when necessary to February, the month of purification which marked the end of the religious year, in order to stay approximately in sync with the solar cycle.

The calendar was further reformed by Julius Caesar in 46 BC who reassigned the lengths of the months. The month previously called *Quintilis* became named *Iunius* (June) after him. There were still twelve months and an intercalary month where necessary. These reforms were finalised in 8 BC under the reign of Augustus and the month of *Sextilis* became *Augustus*.

The Gregorian Calendar instituted by Pope Gregory XIII later established January as the first month of the year. This is the familiar calendar which we still use today. The accumulation of quarter days that make up the extra day in February every leap year is for the same purpose as the intercalary months of the Romans before us, in order to keep in alignment with the solar cycle by allowing for the quarter day discrepancy. Dates used by Roman scholars vary but were usually based upon the year that Rome was founded, the most widely accepted of which is that given by Varro of 753 BC. Should you wish to research ancient Roman texts this could prove helpful. Thankfully most of us spend little time with the complexities of dating pre-Julian dates and we now use Anno Domini or Before Christ.

The Roman Months are familiar to us!

The origins of their names are given with their translations where appropriate:

Latin	English	Origin/Translation
Ianurius	January	Janus the God of Doors with two faces, looking forwards and back
Februarius	February	Named after *februare* the Latin meaning to purify.
Martius	March	Mars, the Roman God of War.
Aprilis	April	Probably derived from *aperire*, meaning to open in reference to flowers or possibly from the Goddess Aphrodite.
Maius	May	Probably from the Goddess Maia associated with Earth (*Terra*), who was the eldest of the seven Pleiades and the embodiment of growth. Her name comes from *maius, maior* meaning greater. Alternatively from the word *maoires* meaning ancestors also from the word *maior.*
Iunius	June	Juno, the protective Patron Goddess of Rome.
Iulius	July	Named after Iulius Caesar during the calendar's reform (previously *Quintilis).*
Augustus	August	Named after Augustus when the reforms were concluded previously *Sextilis*).
September	September	Meaning the Seventh month which it was originally as January and February did not exist until 713 BC. It is now the Ninth month.
October	October	Meaning the eighth month. It is now the tenth.
November	November	Meaning the ninth month. It is now the eleventh.
December	December	Meaning the tenth month. It is now the twelfth.

Julius Caesar wrote in his *Gallic Wars: "(the Gaulish Celts) keep birthdays and the beginnings of months and years in such order that the day follows the night".* Meaning that they counted the days from sunset rather than sunrise. The civil calendar used by most of the world has not correlated the moon cycles with the month since the month lengths were standardised to twenty-eight, thirty or thirty-one days. Despite this intellectual separation we are intrinsically connected at the deepest level with the natural cycles.

We are part of the whole and although life, death and rebirth can be taken literally within our lifetimes so too they play out in our lives effecting profound change within us.

The Anglo-Saxon calendar as well as many other lunisolar calendars have twelve not thirteen moons/months and sacred days that make up any shortfall or when necessary a thirteenth moon may be added to a year as an intercalary month such as with the Gaulish Coligny Celtic calendar to reconcile the lunar and solar differentiation.

The Gaulish Coligny Calendar

The Gaulish Coligny Calendar is a fragmented bronze plaque that was found in 1897 in the remains of a Roman Temple of Apollo in Coligny, Ain, France dating from the second century. It shows twelve repeating units i.e. months, made up of twenty-nine and thirty smaller units i.e. days and appears to correspond to the lunar months of the solar year. The solar year was approximated with the use of an intercalary month every two and a half years. The additional months were intercalated the first before *Samonios* the summer month and the second before *Giamonios* the winter month. The names of which seem to be cognate with the Irish terms for Samradh (Summer) and Geimredh (Winter). In total this calendar would come to 354 or 355 days per year. Because the text is fragmented and the calendar has had to be reconstructed the name of the first intercalary month is not known for definite but is thought to be *Quimonios*. The name of the second intercalary month is reconstructed as *Rantaranos* or *Bantaranos*.

The months were divided into two halves made up of two "weeks" the first of which is fourteen days and the second of which is either fourteen or fifteen days long dependent on the month and marked with the term *atenoux* or "renewal" from the Old Irish word *athnugud*. The basic unit of time is likely to have been the fortnight or half-month and this is also suggested in Celtic folklore. Julius Caesar had observed that periods of time were counted from sunset rather than sunrise and that therefore measurements of time were measured in nights. This can still be seen in the term fort'night and the now unused se'nnight. It has been suggested that since the Celts always began their months at the new moon, that this meant that the major festivals would be held under the full moon.

The following month names are probably accurate. However the equivalent times of year are much speculated and based upon a dark and light half of the year approximating what we know of the Celtic calendar that was observed and recorded by the Romans. The translations for the months are given very tentatively and more as suggestions because the calendar is written in Gaulish and although the words have proto Celtic roots they are not easily comparable to the other Celtic languages with one or two exceptions and the records of Gaulish language are limited. The words that have been given appear to show some semblance to Irish, Welsh or other proto Celtic similar words but are entirely unconfirmed.

Gaulish Months	Possible Translation	Days	Probable Equivalent
Samonius	Summer's End	30	Samhein i.e. October – November
Dumannios	Dark or Sheltered	29	November – December
Riuros	Fat or Frost	30	December – January
Anagantio	Indoors or Not Travelling	30	January – February
Ogronnios	Frost or Cold's End	30	February – March
Cutios	Wind	30	March – April
Giamonios	Winter's End	29	April – May
Semiuisonns	Midsummer	30	May – June
Equos	Horse	29	June – July
Elembiuios	Deer Hunt?	29	July - August
Aedrinios	Fire, Heat	30	August - September
Cantlos	Song	29	September - October
Cialo Bis	Extra Moon	30	Intercalary, every two and a half years

The Egyptian, Babylonian and Hebrew calendars are a little more complicated than the month names already given but this is a brief description of their outlines. These calendars are relevant to understanding any and all magical workings and religious celebrations of the cultures from which they originate.

The Egyptian Calendar

In Egypt the Moon was ascribed to the God Thoth. The Egyptian lunar cycle was counted from the first day of the dark moon like the Masais and the Wadschaggas East African tribes. He supports this with text from the temple of Khonsu in Karnak that writes, *"Conceived in the darkness of invisibility on the first day of the month, that He is born as the new crescent on the second day, and that he wanes after the day of full moon, the fifteenth day"*. He also quotes an earlier text from the middle kingdom about Thoth who is small on the second day and great on the fifteenth day.

The Egyptian lunar cycle was twenty-five years in length and was divided into sixteen years of twelve moons and a further nine years of thirteen moons which were referred to as great years. The lunar calendar ran alongside the civil calendar which was based on the observation of Sirius which was appeared in the sky around 21 July each year and heralded the inundation of the Nile. The rising of Sirius *wp rnpt*, the "Opener of the year" marked the beginning of the Sothic year and Civil Calendar.

During and prior to the Old Kingdom, the months were thought not to have been referred to by individual names. Instead they were numbered within the three seasons which were *akhet* (inundation), *peret* (growth) and *shemu* (harvest).

By the middle Kingdom each month had its own name which evolved into the new kingdom month names. These individual months were named after important feasts or religious celebrations that fell within them. The lunar year normally accounted for 354 days and whenever the month began within eleven days of certain feast dates it was intercalary so that the feast didn't fall in the incorrect month. This intercalary month happened every two or three years, as the length between the shortfalls was 2.4 years, and was dedicated to the God Thoth, *(Dhwty)*. Some of the Egyptian names for Lunar months are the same as the names for the Civil months of the Sothic year suggesting the year may once have aligned when the calendar was first made.

Note that vowels are not written in Egyptian hieroglyphic texts but are supposed when written in transliteration for pronunciation. For those who want to learn the basics of the Egyptian language there are a number of good books on the subject. Thanks to the modern age there are many texts transliterated and translated in full available to us now.

The Civil Egyptian Calendar – Names of the Months.

Old Kingdom	Middle Kingdom	New Kingdom	Latin Script
Seasonal/Lunar			
Akhet I	Tekh	Dhwt	Thoth
Akhet II	Menhet	Pa-n-ip.t	Phaophi
Akhet III (Hathor)	Ḥwt-ḥwr	Hwt-hwr	Athyr
Akhet IIII	Ka-ḥr-ka	Ka-hr-ka	Choiak
Peret I	Sf-bdt	Ta-'b	Tybi
Peret II	Rekh wer	Mḫyr	Mechir
Peret III	Rekh neds	Pa-n-amn-htp.w	Phamenoth
Peret IIII	Renwet	Pa-n-rnn.t	Pharmouthi
Shemw I	Hnsw	Pa-n-ḫns.w	Pachon
Shemw II	Hnt-htj	Pa-n-in.t	Payni
Shemw III	Ipt-hmt	Ipip	Epiphi
Shemw IIII	Wep-renpet	Msw-r'	Mesore

In 238 BCE the Ptolemaic rulers reformed the calendar to make every fourth year 366 days long. This was initially unsuccessful until the year 25 BCE when the Alexandrian calendar came into effect. The reformed Egyptian calendar continues to be used in Egypt as the Coptic calendar of the Egyptian Church and by many of the people. For the purposes of aligning the Egyptian dates with the modern calendar it is possible to use an online calculator where the rising of Sirius is calculated exactly and the equivalent dates of the current year are given for the Coptic months. For timing other workings the current Coptic Church calendar could be used.

The Babylonian Calendar

The Babylonian calendar also counts three seasons of four months, each with an individual month name, however they counted the new moon from the first visible crescent and not from dark moon. The Babylonian year started in the spring and the dates of the months align to their Zodiac, each beginning with the new crescent moon of the first day of the month, which started at sunset. The calendar was observational until 499 BC when the months were regulated by meteonic cycle. In the cycle of nineteen years, an additional month called Adarru 2 was inserted as an intercalary month, except in the year that was number seventeen in the cycle, when the month Ululu 2 was inserted.

Season	Month Name	Deities	Zodiac Sign	Gregorian Date
Res Satti 1	Araḫ Nisānu	Anu and Bel	KU (Aries)	March/April
Res satti 2	Araḫ Āru	Ea	Taurus	April/May
Res satti 3	Araḫ Simanu	Sin	Gemini	May/June
Res Satti 4	Araḫ Dumuzu	Tammuz	Cancer	June/July
Mišil Šatti 5	Araḫ Abu		Leo	July/August
Mišil Šatti 6	Araḫ Ulūlu	Ishtar	Virgo	August/September
Mišil Šatti 7	Araḫ Tišritum	Shamash	Libra	Sept'/October
Mišil Šatti 8	Araḫ Samna	Marduk	Scorpio	Oct/November
Kīt Šatti 9	Araḫ Kislimu	Nergal	Sagittarius	Nov'/December
Kīt Šatti 10	Araḫ Ṭebētum	Pap-Sukkal	sah ibex (Capricorn?)	December/January
Kīt Šatti 11	Araḫ Šabaṭu		qā (Aquarius?)	January/February
Kīt Šatti 12	Araḫ ddaru/Adār	Erra	Pisces	February/March
Intercalary	Araḫ Makaruša	Ashur		
	Addari ~			
	Araḫ Ve-Adār			

The Jewish/Hebrew Months

217

The Hebrew moon/month names originate from the Babylonian moon/months given above and their equivalents are listed below. The lunar month of the Jewish calendar begins when the first glimpse of the crescent moon becomes visible after the dark of the moon. This is called rosh chodesh, the first of the month. The Hebrew lunar year is about eleven days shorter than the solar cycle and like the other similar calendars uses the nineteen year Meteonic cycle to align it to the solar cycle by means of an intercalary month every two or three years.

Season	Month Name Gregorian Date	Deities	Zodiac Sign
Res Satti 1	Araḫ Nisānu March/April	Anu and Bel	KU (Aries)
Res satti 2	Araḫ Āru April/May	Ea	Taurus
Res satti 3	Araḫ Simanu May/June	Sin	Gemini
Res Satti 4	Araḫ Dumuzu June/July	Tammuz	Cancer
Mišil Šatti 5	Araḫ Abu July/August		Leo
Mišil Šatti 6	Araḫ Ulūlu August/September	Ishtar	Virgo
Mišil Šatti 7	Araḫ Tišritum Sept'/October	Shamash	Libra
Mišil Šatti 8	Araḫ Samna Oct/November	Marduk	Scorpio
Kīt Šatti 9	Araḫ Kislimu Nov'/December	Nergal	Sagittarius
Kīt Šatti 10	Araḫ Ṭebētum December/January	Pap-Sukkal	sah ibex (Capricorn?)
Kīt Šatti 11	Araḫ Šabaṭu January/February		qā(Aquarius?)
Kīt Šatti 12	Araḫ Addaru/Adār February/March	Erra	Pisces
Intercalary	Araḫ Makaruša	Ashur	
	Addari ~		
	Araḫ Ve-Adār		

Although it is not possible to give the moons or months of all the different cultures, there are examples of each kind of calendar here whether purely lunar, lunar-solar or sothic and these principles can be applied in understanding to any other comparable system. Each culture has its own calendar, moon names and relevant celebrations and it is of great importance that we learn and understand the culture we choose to work with and respect the customs we are communing with.

Lunar Exercises

Choose three specific purposes for which you could work magic, for example a house blessing, looking for a new job and healing a relationship and then work out the best moon phase for each.

Also consider the most favourable planetary influences for the examples you have chosen i.e. waning moon in cancer would be good for inner emotional work.

Then seek out appropriate stones, crystals, herbs or incense ingredients.

This correspondence seeking will be valuable later.

Try keeping a moon diary for at least nine consecutive months observing your own emotions, thoughts and dreams and becoming aware of any patterns over the lunations. You might want to include this in a book of shadows.

Chapter Thirteen
Astrological Timing

"Sometimes I have a terrible need of, shall I say the word, religion. Then I
go out at night and paint the stars."
Vincent Van Gogh 1888 CE

Timing is everything! Or at the very least, certainly a significant consideration in life and in magic. To quote a friend of mine, "each event will have its time". All things have their natural flow and rhythm and knowing how to wait when necessary for the opportune moment is a useful skill. So too are the abilities, skills and knowledge to fare as well as possible in any given circumstances and current climate and make the most of what is in the moment when one doesn't have the luxury of being able to wait. We look to the planets and to the zodiac for guidance and illumination, for clues and probability yielded by the positions of the heavens.

In our galaxy alone there are a couple of hundred billion stars and scientists think it is probable that many of these could have planetary systems. Whilst they may be currently invisible to us there is already technology being developed that can detect the gravitational wobble caused by the gravity between a star and its planets which supports this theory. Our galaxy is 100,000 light years across and beyond our galaxy there are a hundred billion others in the vastness of space. We are part of the interconnected whole picture, children of the starry skies, and Earth has its place moving through space.

The sky is sacred in all early religions. It is a given. How often do we find ourselves watching the sun breaking through the clouds and feeling that same sense of wonder at the overwhelming beauty of it that has been felt throughout the history of our kind for as long as we have been looking at the sky? Our ancestors knew it and we know it as surely as we know we are all under the same sky, the same starry map, the same heavens with the same breath in our lungs sustaining us. It goes beyond theories, mythologies and uncertainties to the surety of a deeper primal origin we recognise as Nature inherent within our beings and the elemental fabric we are woven from. It is logical, unquestionable then that we would of course seek deeper understanding and initiation through connection with celestial forces both externally, looking out at the heavens and the stars, and internally through the points of spiritual contact mirrored within us which relate to the planets and universe around us.

Our galaxy is called the Milky Way and appears as a dim glowing band arching across the night sky in which the naked eye cannot distinguish stars. It is one of billions of galaxies and within it our Sun lies close to the inner rim in Orion's Arm (named after the constellation Orion) which is thought to be twenty-seven thousand light years from the Galactic Centre. The Sun's orbit around the Milky Way is expected to be roughly elliptical and it takes our solar system about 225-250 million years to complete one orbit about the centre, an intense radio source which is likely to be a massive black hole *(Sagittarius A)*, at a speed of approximately 156 miles per second. In time relatable to our experience that is the equivalent of just over 94,000,000 miles in seven days or 1,190 years to one light year.

Astrology and astronomy differ in that whilst astronomy is the science of observing the stars, astrology interprets the meaning of their position relevant to us and our position from Earth. The emphasis then is on the seer and the relationship between seer and cosmos. The two studies are in truth a pair and the observation of the former of the stars and planets in astronomy reflects the latter's informational astrological forecast and predictions. Our ancestors knew this and studied the night skies and interpreted their meaning. It is only the arrogance of recent years that has divorced the two parts neither of which is complete without the other. There is little point in having knowledge if it is not to be used or if deeper understanding is not to be sought.

There are two main types of astrology practised today. The predominant one in Western culture is that of the Tropical Zodiac and its premise is based upon all things revolving around the Sun at the centre. Whilst this may be true, on Earth we see an optical illusion, for whilst the Sun is stationary it appears to move as we travel through orbit and making its way through constellations in order of progression and is visible to us by varying relation of the Sun to the background of the stars. These stars and constellations are what we refer to as the ecliptic path and makes up the zodiac. This ecliptic path creates an endless, eternal circle divided by seasons dependent upon the ebb and flow of breathing light as Earth travels its trajectory around the Sun. Whilst this is of course correct, the system itself does not allow for the wobble of the Earth and the procession of the equinoxes, therefore a day is lost every seventy-two years and consequently over time the system has drifted in relation to the true position of the stars. The names of the twelve signs of the tropical zodiac may initially be confusing or misleading as they were named after the constellations of stars that they were in at the time the system was implemented and since then they have moved. **The twelve signs of the Tropical Zodiac are therefore to be considered just as conventional names for the thirty-degree segments of the celestial sphere they currently fall within. These no longer correspond to the constellation they were originally named after.**

As soon as we grasp that the rest makes sense. It is sadly a bone of contention that divides astrologers and astronomers where it need not.

The other type of astrology is the Sidereal system, that is to say stellar, such as described in the Vedas and is called "Jyotish" in Indian which means "science of light", meaning the science of observing celestial bodies which reflect their energy and light upon the Earth. Both systems divide the ecliptic into a number of signs named after constellations but the Sidereal system defines these based upon the fixed stars and is therefore astronomically literal whereas the Tropical system defines these based upon the position of the vernal equinox. There is currently a discrepancy of approximately twenty-five days between the dates of the signs between the two systems which has gradually drifted apart over the period of time since the Tropical zodiac originated at a rate of approximately 1.4 arc degrees per century or one day in seventy-two years, suggesting they aligned approximately one thousand eight hundred years ago.

The Egyptians used a Sidereal system of observation and time measurement by constellation and the thirty-six decans, or small groups of stars that rose in succession upon the horizon, formed its basis. Because a new decan also appears heliacally every ten days the Greeks named them *dekanoi* or "tenths". These thirty-six decans of ten days made up 360 days of the year and there were then an additional five epagomenal days added to compose the solar year. The solar year is six hours longer than the Sothic year and the two realign every 1460 years, a problem that these days we account for by adding an extra day in leap years! These decans were first depicted on coffin lids and tombs and started with Sothis (Sirius), significant as the first day of the Sothic calendar, with the following groups of stars and their corresponding deities. The depiction on the astronomical ceiling of Senemut's tomb is particularly beautiful and shows the personification of stars and constellations with decans. Whilst the names of the thirty-six decans are known their relationship to modern star names and constellations are not. The Egyptians also ascribed certain planetary hours to individual Gods which in time evolved into the tables of planetary hours commonly used today. These are included in the chapter on Planets.

After the Alexandrian conquest there was a merging of Babylonian astrology with the Egyptian decan astrology resulting in what we recognise today as horoscope astrology. The Hellenistic blending of Graeco-Romano language and influence comprise the formation of current Western Tropical astrology and with it the planetary associations of the Greek system. Both sidereal and tropical systems work and do so accurately but work in different ways. Because of the differences in the way the two systems work it may at times be necessary to adapt or translate information from one system to another, much as one might transpose a musical part from standard tuning for a Bb clarinet. For instance a visible alignment in the sky or something one has read about in an astronomy magazine (as opposed to an astrology magazine) is in real time and is astronomically literal. It must therefore be researched either in the sidereal system or translated to the tropical one in order that the name is correct for the sign and constellation it falls within. As the tropical system is most usually found both in Western magical writings and pages that may be of interest on the internet, it is the logical choice and what we will consider in more detail here.

Diagram of the Sidereal and Tropical Zodiacs and their positions to one another and to the physical constellations of the stars in the sky.

THE ALIGNMENT OF THE THREE ZODIACS

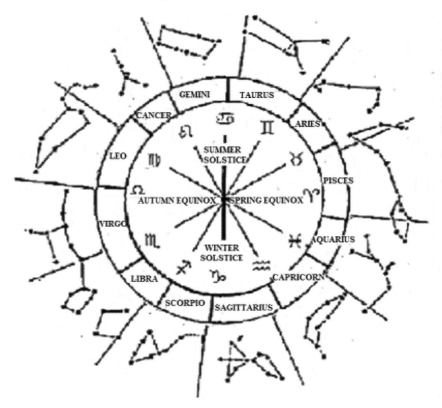

Inner Wheel - Tropical Zodiac Symbols aligned to the tropical points i.e. the equinoxes and solstices.

Middle Wheel - Astronomically Aligned

Outer Wheel - Sidereal Zodiac aligned over the constellations and divided into twelve equal parts.

The Atrological Symbols of the Tropical Zodiac

♈	Aries	♉	Taurus	♊	Gemini
♋	Cancer	♌	Leo	♍	Virgo
♎	Libra	♏	Scorpio	♐	Sagittarius
♑	Capricorn	♒	Aquarius	♓	Pisces

There is of course never any substitute for spending time outside under the stars and for having a living, breathing relationship with them. The man who only reads about them in books will never connect and commune with them as closely as the one who sits beside the fire for hundreds of nights and watches the skies. Also the most powerful timing astrologically for working magically may well be when our experience is observational and or in real time. If you can look up at the sky and see Venus before working with her it will give a further depth and meaning to the work. Likewise if Fred next door tells you that next week there is a meteor shower and says you can look through his telescope you might like to look up any significance of the phenomenon. Or if there is an alignment causing a partial eclipse it's worth a bit of study and research to work in real time with physical events and direct connections. Here lies the marriage bed of observational astronomy and astrology with meaning and interpretation.

Most books about magic give a standard chart of planetary hours to work from, however without understanding how these are calculated these are of little value. These planetary hours are also never any substitute for accurate timing through the use of the astronomy. It is always preferable to work when you can see a visible planetary transit or know of one occurring with which you can work. The planetary tables are however referred to and included in numerous magical writings and therefore they are included in the next chapter. Planets and hours and moments and cycles do not happen independently of one another. They are one whole, one intrinsic ecosystem operating in context and entirety with one another and their counterparts are reflected in this way in us. We contain aspects of all the planets travelling through all the signs in all the houses and we are more than the sum total of our parts. Life is holistic.

There are of course many transits not observable to the human eye, certainly without the aid of advanced telescopes and yet we still know and can predict through science and the certainty of the ecliptic path the journey of the planets through the sections of the sky. These days this is very much simpler than it used to be, with the advent of computers there are many sites offering natal charts and what was once done with an ephemeris and books of charts and tables may now be done with a few clicks. I suspect that most people with an interest these days, like me, use the internet to research planetary timing, alignments and staying abreast of current news and upcoming transits. Of course that is very useful but beyond that if we want to check for the strengths and weaknesses of a particular date then chart reading is an essential skill. For instance one of the strengths of the summer solstice of 2015 is that it could be a particularly potent time for shining the brightest light and bringing illumination into the unconscious and emotional inner world, as the Sun will be coming into the sign of Cancer. It is also necessary to have some understanding of some basic astrological terms in order to understand even the most user-friendly information. By learning basic astrology and chart reading we may see the planets holistically in context within our lives and psyches and the cosmos. This is a subject for another book in order to do justice to the subject even at a preliminary level. Here we must content ourselves with the briefest introduction to the astrological signs of the tropical zodiac and in the next chapter to the planets.

Regardless of which sign we may be born in we are all some combination of all twelve and our learnings varied. Magically we seek to align ourselves with the element, planet and sign and to harness natural abilities and seek out preferred properties for example the willpower found in Aries or Mars rather than aggression. Whilst it may be of great benefit to learn and study our individual chart and to be encouraged primarily it is at a cosmological level that we are concerned. Our focus here is with the interplay and dynamics of planets regarding impact either on a soul level which is applicable personally or generally and also impact on evolutionary consciousness or to aid, promote and assist workings. Also to have awareness of any timings or factors that might be a hindrance or challenge to workings.

The twelve signs of the zodiac have been referred to often as the twelve mystery schools, comprising three modalities (cardinal, fixed and mutable) and four elements (Earth, air, fire, water).

	Fire	Earth	Air	Water
Cardinal	Aries	Capricorn	Libra	Cancer
Fixed	Leo	Taurus	Aquarius	Scorpio
Mutable	Sagittarius	Virgo	Gemini	Pisces

1. The astrological signs of the zodiac move slowly through their natural progressions in date order. Most of us know approximately when they are and know if our friend is a Gemini and born in May for example.

2. The planets travel through the signs along the ecliptic path.

The twelve houses are the regions of space through which the planets pass every twenty-four hours in perpetual motion east to west. They move quickly changing in hours.

When interpreting the movements of the heavens the planets represent the What, the psychological function or identity, for example Mercury in Aries might look a little self-interested and communicate very directly and Mercury in Aquarius suggests visionary thinking and intellectual communications.

The astrological zodiac signs themselves represent the Why and How, the purpose or the reason whether it is for growth or experience for example. They show us motivation, agendas and direction.

The houses of the Sun represent the Where, the circumstances, or area of life. They could be thought of as set designs or stages. For instance Mercury in Capricorn in the first house, might suggest someone who appears to be capable, quick witted, logical and responsible.

Regarding their magical uses, the houses move very quickly in hours and vary massively depending upon location, even a few miles can make a difference, so in terms of working with them, unless we seek something very specific it is most likely that we are considering them in order to understand them in our own birth chart or in the chart of someone we know and less likely that we are factoring them into our magical workings. Our primary focus then is upon the twelve astrological signs of the zodiac and upon the planets and the archetypes of both. Each sign of the zodiac has a planetary ruler assigned to it, as do the houses. There are also recurring and parallel themes and traits often found between a sign and its ruler. These planetary assignations are the basis for these correspondences.

The Twelve Astrological Signs of The Tropical Zodiac

The tropical zodiac signs are large regions of stars measured by the equinoxes. Technically they do not align with their namesakes and constellations but are gradually moving and progressing through the sky along the ecliptic path until such time as they complete the great year and realign. The diagram given shows their approximate current position. In terms of earthly time each sign lasts approximately a month and their conventional dates are included below.

When we're looking at the astrological signs of the zodiac we are looking at the why and the how, the context in which a planet may be working either in us or cosmically. They show psychological processes, needs, attitudes and modalities of being that are likely or to which we are predisposed and they highlight areas of potential growth or difficulty.

The first three signs are very new and unaware learning about separation into defining the self and understanding the immediate environment, the second three are about becoming aware, the third three move into awareness of the other and the last three move outwards beyond the self, seeking Source and unity. The pattern of quarters then repeats.

N.B. The planetary ruler and corresponding house are given so that their similarities can be noted and drawn upon and the connections made between them.

Emerging out of the infinite, the soul desires to separate from source so that it may experience and return. In order to do this it must first define itself:

Aries – The Hunter
Establishing and defining the self through separation.
21 March – 19 April
Cardinal Fire – creative fire that starts begins and changes.
Archetypes – hunter, warrior, pioneer, daredevil, survivor.
Symbol – The Ram, charging, fierce and unyielding towards either

victory or self-destruction.

Planetary ruler – Mars

Corresponds to 1st House.

I, me, my, identity, who I am, I exist. This is life force, freedom, the will to exist and to be. Starting with separation in a desire to experience the self.

Primal, instinctual, unconscious, impulsive, intense, direct, honest and combative. Sex, hunger, desire, wants, needs, courage, daring, will.

Aries must learn to choose wisely, for desire is often about choice and he must learn to live in the presence of fear but still act clearly and decisively. All actions have consequences. When desire and action are in balance the best results are yielded.

The shadow aspects of this sign are egoism, selfishness, narcissism and extreme pushiness. We all have a first house somewhere! Part of the lessons in this house are not to suppress or deny or avoid these parts of ourselves in whatever area they present but to accept them and instead use and harness Aries' presence to do good. In his most noble role Aries is the protector and the guardian of the Gate.

Examples of the logical magical extension of Aries are works and endeavours requiring power, strength, will power, staying power and empowerment. When that strength is harnessed for good it can move mountains! Fortuitous timing may be found when a planet transits Aries and by so doing becomes stronger in its purpose and natural attributes.

Taurus – The Bull

Exploring the self and earthly senses.

20 April – 20 May

Fixed Earth – patient, secure, stable and fertile, developing senses.

Archetypes – Earth Spirit, musician, silent one.

Symbol – The Bull, the horns symbolic of fertility and cornucopia.

Planetary ruler – Venus

Corresponds to 2nd House.

Taurus applies the impulse of Aries and grounds it, turning it into reality. Despite the male implication of the word bull Taurus is intrinsically feminine in nature and the horns here, other than the constellation of stars which the sign was once named after, are a reminder of fertility and cornucopia. Taurus is the most physical and earthly of the signs. She is peaceful, solid, instinctual, reverent, grounded and serene and finds contentment observing the earth and sun. Her delights are found through the earthly senses of touch, smell, taste, sight and sound. She is sensual, self-sufficient, dependable, calm and content in just being. She enjoys and acquires wealth and physical security and seeks simplicity and serenity. This may manifest as a stable job, a well-ordered or beautiful home and reliable relationships.

Her task is finding serenity and keeping it. Her lessons may be found in maintaining a peaceful environment and in learning to soothe and quieten the mind. This may often be found in music or in earthly pursuits and hobbies such as gardening, massage, pottery or cooking.

In her shadow aspects the serenity and silence of Taurus can be taciturn and aloof. Her liking for security and wealth can make her possessive and uncompromising. Never moving out of her comfort zone can stop growth and cause blockages which may lead to stagnation over time.

Magically, works associated with Taurus are those of creative visualisation and earthly manifestation, all workings associated with the earth, ecology or landscape, works of love and earthly attraction, creative artistic expression, fertility rites and one might consider this timing for works where victory or success may need encouragement to blossom favourably.

Gemini – The Twins

Discovering and learning the environment and surroundings.

21 May – 21 June

Mutable Air – changeable mind and perceptions, duality.

Archetypes – teacher, storyteller, witness, journalist, trickster, student.

Symbol – The Twins, they are One and they are Two, duality.

Planetary Ruler – Mercury.

Corresponds to 3rd House

Gemini moves out into the world and is on a mission to see it. The whole world, everything and all of it! In constant motion, Gemini is all about communication and information, networking and technology. Exploration, connection, writing, travelling, talking, singing, story-telling, quick wit, intelligence, teaching and speaking many languages, natural curiosity, appreciation, wonder and enthusiasm.

Of course seeing the whole world is an impossible mission and without stopping it can be difficult to see clearly in the confusion. Anyone absorbing that amount of information naturally needs processing time.

The shadows of Gemini are an over-stimulated psyche and nervous system, constant chatter, skewing facts to own ends, manipulation, overextension, exhaustion, over-thinking, loss or complete lack of direction, insomnia, comparing and measuring of acquisitions, shallowness and two-faced behaviour or lying due to regular changeability of mind.

Magically, works associated with Gemini are those of communication and appreciation for the outward world.

Cancer – The Crab

Awareness of feeling and the inner world.

22 June – 23 July

Cardinal Water – action through emotions and needs.

Archetypes – the mother, the healer, the invisible man/woman, inner child.

Symbol – the crab protecting its vulnerability with the shell.

Planetary Ruler – the Moon.

Corresponds to 4th House

Cancer is like the beginning of self-awareness and is very much like the inner child. Frequently overlooked and misunderstood in western society the inner child is often ignored or devalued. Only when the inner child is taken care of, loved and accepted and the emotional needs are being met can we form emotionally balanced, integrated beings as adults. Cancer has something precious to teach us and our society! The crab may often feel vulnerable and so finds protection inside the shell, yet finding a voice, finding self-expression and self-acceptance may require the uncomfortable shedding of old shells for new ones as growth occurs. Cancer has strong mothering instincts and is a natural healer full of compassion. It's all about feeling and sensitivity and as with all things finding balance and acceptance.

Themes for cancer are honouring emotional needs, allowing time to play, self-acceptance and acceptance of others, processing the unconscious as it arises, learning to keep appropriate boundaries, letting life and other people in, trusting life, integrating intense feelings, emotional balance, owning personal power, security and survival.

Shadows of Cancer are not overly self-sacrificing or losing oneself causing feelings of invisibility or insignificance or a loss of identity, extreme shyness resulting in hiding behind a mask possibly also resulting in self-loss or alienation from others, over defensiveness stopping growth and/or deepening relationships, being stuck in the self and self-absorbed, unawareness of others, loneliness.

Magically all these themes for personal development and deep inner healing seem the most profound. I think they can be applied more broadly too within our society and group dynamics. There's a lot of compassion and altruism to be found in Cancer.

Leo – the Lion
Awareness of expressing the self outwardly.

24 July – 23 August

Fixed Fire – sustained strength of will, consciously directed creation.

Archetypes – the king, the performer, the clown, the child (teenager).

Symbol – the lion roaring in self-expression.

Planetary Ruler – the Sun.

Corresponds to 5th House

Sustained strength of will, consciously directed creation. The inner child has become the adolescent lion roaring in the sunshine. He's full of life force and vitality and a newfound awareness to express himself and create! He is wilful and opinionated and charged. Oh my goodness he knows everything and he's brilliant and wants to shine like the sun. He's very endearing and positive. He says yes to life and to living and he wants to be involved in the creation process.

Leo's themes are found in expression, creativity and personality. Developing the ego in a healthy way empowers him as do opportunities of leadership and self-love brings him happiness and the ability to live in the present. He has presence and charisma and is playful, spontaneous, innocent, honest, generous, loyal and transparent. His love of performing finds many forms of expression in painting, storytelling, dancing, singing, painting and he loves to have an audience. The love and appreciation of others makes him happy and gives him the encouragement he needs.

232

The Shadow of Leo is that he may need too much applause or feel rejected if his performance is not well received. He can come across as overly proud or full of ego and as needing a lot of validation much like the child showing off.

Magically, works of creativity and creation and self-expression and most importantly self-love and appreciation.

Virgo – The Virgin

Awareness of growth and perfecting the self through higher service.

24 August – 22 September

Mutable Earth – transition through patience and self-discipline.

Archetypes – the servant, martyr, perfectionist, virgin.

Symbol – the Virgin symbolic of purity.

Planetary Ruler – the Mercury.

Corresponds to 6th House

The virgin's symbol is symbolic of purity because she wants nothing and is therefore set free. Her natural progression of growth from the lion of Leo is like a coming of age and it brings her to a point of adulthood where she wants personal transformation and sees that growth is found in working on herself and helping others. She has reached a new level of self-awareness and responsibility and is polishing herself, trying to perfect herself wanting to fulfil her highest potential. She is meticulous, honest, practical, efficient, precise, driven, trustworthy and conscientious. She likes things clean, clear, working and in order and she values simplicity and clarity.

Virgo's themes are those of service to others, service to a higher purpose or calling, self-development and perfection, transition and transformation through effort and the first conscious stage of initiation. Whilst she uses self-criticism as an incentive to improvement it is really important that it is equally balanced always by self-love. Magically her logical extensions are the same.

The shadows of Virgo are over analysing, being critical of herself and others, being overly controlling and judgemental, high stress levels and anxiety and conditions like OCD.

Libra – The Scales

Bringing awareness to relationships and growth through the Other.

23 September – 22 October

Cardinal Air – birth, the beginnings of awareness of the Other.

Archetypes – the peacemaker, lover, artist.

Symbol – the scales, coming into balance, harmony, equilibrium, justice.

Planetary Ruler – Venus

Corresponds to 7th House

Libra is the beginning of awareness of the Other. The scales are all about coming into balance and equality whether through equal partnership or through fairness and justice. Libra is powerful, strong and intelligent. She is the peacemaker, the counsellor, the mediator, representative of the law and promotes communications and co-operation. Essentially she has the ability to see both sides, accepting the validity of both without diminishing either truth and weighing them fairly and the understanding that even truth is objective and made of two halves as are all things. The Egyptian Goddess Ma'at embodies this principle and her feather of truth is balanced and weighed with the heart to determine *maa keru,* right or honourable speech, i.e. integrity.

Libra's work is found in forging deep connections in relationships which offer growth and in learning to maintain inner balance and conscious harmony.

Libra's shadows are indecisiveness, lacking commitment, holding no position or opinion, co-dependency or self-loss or denial by over immersion in the other.

Works of magic involving justice, harmony, the ability to have clear-headed and unbiased judgement and perception, works of peace both personally or on a larger scale.

Scorpio – The Scorpion

Being aware of death and meeting forces beyond our control, deep soul connections.

23 October – 22 November

Fixed Water – deep, strong, sustained emotional pressures and love.

Archetypes – the detective, sorcerer, hypnotist, shaman, therapist.

Symbol – the scorpion, can feel such intensity it can sting itself or others.

Planetary Ruler – Mars (Pluto in Higher Octave).

Corresponds to 8th House

Scorpio is the second water sign and deeply spiritual moving through the point of death and dying of the self in preparation for Sagittarius. On the calendar it makes sense that Samhain also falls at this time of year. Scorpio deals with forces beyond its control found through relationship and partnership with the Other in all areas of life. Evolution and transformation involves learning these forces and Scorpio feels their effects deeply as intense emotional pressure. Scorpio lives with such intensity that everything except what matters falls away and all that remains is authentic. There are no pretences or safety nets in the realm of Scorpio and despite feeling fear it is met with the courage to face death and the depths of the psyche, prioritising what's important. Magnetic, analytical, perceptive, psychic, sharp minded, intelligent, sensitive and instinctual. Despite the aspect of truth that has earned them a passionate and sexual reputation it is important to know that the intensity of emotion in their relationships and encounters and the merging of souls is in truth what is essential to the Scorpio. Sex can be medicine and there is healing, comfort and celebration to be found here. There are lessons in Scorpio around empowerment, power, vulnerability and nakedness, surrender and letting go.

The shadows of Scorpio are introspection, suspicion, continual analysis, being too deep, fear of loss and abandonment, moodiness, despair, replay, anxieties, suppression, obsession, brooding, over protectiveness and paranoia.

Magical workings of transformation and metamorphosis, deaths and endings, letting go, sexuality, deep emotional response and release, particularly past lives or trauma.

Sagittarius – The Archer
Becoming aware of seeking wisdom, the philosopher/guru.
23 November – 20 December
Mutable Fire – changing and adapting, expanding though stages and will.
Archetypes – the gypsy, student, philosopher.
Symbol – the archer, sending out arrows with intention.
Planetary Ruler – Jupiter
Corresponds to 9th House
Sagittarius has passed through the gates of death and made it and now he's on a search for the meaning of life. His arrows project outwards and he is intentionally searching and expanding his awareness through life's

experiences. Expansion may be physically in terms of travelling all over the world or from county to county or it might be through books and learning and reading about other places. It might be from gaining other perspectives through meeting other people and studying their work. Sagittarius is interested in learning about different cultures, places, natural law, customs, points of view and education. He wants to broaden his horizons and open his mind to higher realities. He is the seeker, on vision quest, who might become the philosopher or guru. He loves feeling free, being outdoors in the countryside, going on adventures, has established principles, is intuitive and knowing and has faith or belief in some way whether of a spiritual or more mundane nature.

The shadows of Sagittarius are over optimism, over extension and agreeing or committing to too much, feeling threatened if his beliefs are challenged or questioned, naivety, misplaced trust, blind faith.

Magical workings of shifting perspectives, studying, expansion of the mind, reaching higher realities and deeper understanding, seeking truth.

Capricorn – The Sea Goat
Becomes the elder.

22 December – 20 January

Cardinal Earth – implements the physical laws of structure, form and limitation.

Archetypes – the hermit, father, judge, elder, advisor.

Symbol – the Sea goat, master of both land and sea.

Planetary Ruler – Saturn

Corresponds to 10th House

Capricorn is the master of sea and land and when he focuses his will he is certain to achieve his aim. He has learned self-discipline and has a strong will. He's ambitious, patient and responsible. He has integrity and he is sensible, dutiful, reliable and secure in his deep foundations. There's something quite unshakeable in Capricorn, a steadfastness born of meeting responsibility with order and security. He often takes positions in society of worldly power because his intrinsic nature in life is in keeping and this gives him a sense of wholeness. That being said he needs a lot of time alone learning himself before he can mature into holding himself in this way. His approval has to be sought within himself and he views the approval of others as of secondary value or sees it just as confirmation. He may have learned to be detached in some ways from the needs of validation from others. His role is one of coming into fullness and the maturity of the elder in higher service of the law. In his positive roles he is the good father, the advisor to the king and the fair judge.

The shadow aspects of Capricorn are abuse of his power through calculation, dictatorship, manipulation or exploitation. He may be materialistic, distort anger, be a workaholic, power hungry or lacking strength in his integrity and seeking adulation. His self-control may tighten and constrain him too much forcing him to wear a false mask he thinks others may approve of and separating him from them bringing much loneliness and a sense of loss.

His lessons are self-approval, learning to be self-sufficient and not dependent on others, wearing his power and authority with integrity and justly, remembering to be tolerant of others and their beliefs about what is right or wrong.

Magical workings surrounding responsibility, higher service, law, integrity, judgement and the many lessons found through the solitude and journey of the hermit.

Aquarius – The Water Bearer

Beyond the personal, moving out reaching further.

21 January – 19 February

Fixed Air – strong, maturing clarity and perception moving out beyond the personal.

Archetypes – the genius, revolutionary, truthsayer, scientist, exile.

Symbol – the water bearer, making his offering of life and spiritual energy.

Planetary Ruler – Saturn (Uranus in higher octave)

Corresponds to 11th House

Aquarius is both high and deep touching the outer space of Uranus, the higher octave of Saturn and is looking forward and outward seeking growth. He is concerned with equality and individual freedom, seeking to share his knowledge and vision of equality and individuality. There is a newfound freedom as he moves from the known into the unknown and this liberation moves beyond the personal and attachment to the bigger picture and things of a global or cosmic scale. Aquarius wants to be in and speak his truth, he wants to be free to choose his own path and hold his own values. He is community orientated, intelligent, seeks inclusion for all and individuality for all and he understands that there is unity in diversity. There's a streak of genius in him and he can see things in ways others may not. He is innovative, assertive, humanitarian and at times eccentric. His learning ground is in balancing attachment and detachment and finding the middle ground, protecting his individuality from conforming in order to remain free and in integrity with himself despite feelings of being different or separate as a result.

His shadows are found in stubbornness, protecting things without purpose, arrogance, over detachment or losing himself in order to conform to others, feeling alienated or missing in some way.

Magical workings centred around community, both global and local, matters of freedom, moving beyond outdated modalities of behaviour or thought patterns and seeing new perspectives.

Pisces – The Fishes

Pisces – returning to spirit and oneness.

20 February – 20 March

Mutable Water – infinite change and potential.

Archetypes – the mystic, dreamer, poet.

Symbol –fishes, the ocean, primordial water of creation, symbol of life.

Planetary Ruler – Jupiter (Neptune in higher octave).

Corresponds to 12th House

Pisces is both the beginning and the end of the cycle leading to the spring equinox and Aries. He is infinite change, infinite potential, symbolic of life and he is consciousness and awareness. He is moving towards and returning to spirit and he understands we are one. Connecting with the infinite there is also a touch of the chaotic and formless unordered possibility and traditionally this sign is sometimes referred to as the house of self-undoing. Pisces observes consciousness and consciously, meditates and recognises that consciousness is the only true reality and that any adjustments need to be in the way of thinking. His ground is that found in religion and psychology. He is compassionate, empathic, helpful, gentle, understanding, instinctive and clairvoyant. Within the mind he finds inspiration, fascination, peace and wonder. He is illuminated with infinite love and creativity and he transcends himself, beyond ego and boundaries and is one with source.

The shadows of Pisces are found in the world of the illusory and of dreams and they present as the symptoms of disillusionment or as loss of direction or purpose. This lack can cause him to drift and powerful emotions and fear can erupt in him leaving him with feelings of shock and overwhelm. Pisces has a dream like quality and seeking relief from feeling too much may very easily turn to anything offering escapism hence the association with addictions and undoing. Of course in truth Pisces is just trying to find a coping mechanism. His balance is found in the evolving perfection of Virgo.

Magically works of being at oneness, becoming whole, completion, beginnings and endings, raising or higher consciousness, religious undertakings and psychological exploration and work.

The Houses of the Sun

It makes sense to look at the signs of the zodiac and the houses of the sun together because although the signs are large thirty degree areas of space lasting weeks at a time the houses lasting only hours echo them. For example the first house is known as the house of identity and echoes the themes of Aries in defining the self. Houses are like stages so if the first house is in Gemini then this is **where** the identity or self is defined, perhaps manifesting in the archetypes of the teacher, storyteller or journalist. Of equal importance magically if we are studying charts for timing is the suggestion that this is great timing for communication, studying and learning.

There are different systems for dividing the time represented by the twelve houses on paper but for simplicity an equal distribution is most commonly used. In truth the size and correct timings of the houses are worked out simply by calculating the duration of day and night and dividing each into six equal parts. At times near the equinoxes these house lengths are quite similar but at high summer or midwinter they are significantly variable due to the longer days and short nights or vice versa.

239

1st House (The Ascendant) – The House of Personality
Corresponding to Aries and Mars.

The establishment of personal identity. Internally I am, externally I appear. Our sense of direction and definition and decisiveness in life. Personality, appearance and expression of ourselves which best meets our inner needs. Our social identity.

2nd House – The House of Money
Corresponding to Taurus and to Venus.

Things of value and importance including money, possessions, talents, confidence, self-esteem, confidence, management of resources, skills, self-improvement and development. Worth.

3rd House – The House of Communication
Corresponding to Gemini and Mercury.

All forms of information gathering and sharing and clear unbiased perceptions. Research, speaking, teaching, writing, reading, listening and learning. Two-directional flow, comparing notes with other perceivers.

4th House – The House of the Home
Corresponding to Cancer and the Moon

Establishing roots in the form of a home, family and alignment to inner self through intuition and meeting of unconscious, emotional needs.

5th House – The House of Children
Corresponding to Leo and the Sun

This is the house of joy, pleasure, falling in love, romance, playfulness and creative self-expression. A healthy appreciation of the pleasures found in all areas of life from connections made with loved ones to a well-made loaf of bread.

6th House – The House of Servants
Corresponding to Virgo and Mercury

Fulfilment found through the perfecting of meaningful skills and their work. The skills are developed, applied and put into service and we are recognised and appreciated by others for our abilities.

7th House (The Descendant) – The House of Marriage
Corresponding to Libra and Venus

Partnerships and relationships where we meet the Other. Equality between partners, sustainable and enduring relationships, romantic relationships, empathy and understanding of another's point of view.

8th House – The House of Death
Corresponding to Scorpio and Mars (Pluto)

The cycles of sex and death are interwoven. They are the basics of life. The French call the orgasm *la petite mort* for a reason. The "la" can refer to any release, metaphysical, spiritual, transcendence or climax from expending "life force" as in orgasm. This life force literally generates the new life of the fertility cycle through reproduction. Losing the self, accepting death, merging with this uncontrollable force in this vulnerable process and being transformed and changed by it. Resurrection and belief in life after death expressed through the occult or an awareness of invisible dimensions and the immortality of spirit.

9th House – The House of Long Journeys Over Water
Corresponding to Sagittarius and Jupiter

To reach the realms of philosophy and religion one must cross the water, symbolic in every culture of the journey into spirit. This house is where ethics, philosophy and belief systems are changing, growing in understanding and expanding and there is a newfound awareness of natural law. Here too the potential to question and change behavioural patterns liberating the self and purging unwanted or non-serving patterns. Attention shifts to a sense of life purpose and any planets in the 9th House point areas of fulfilling growth.

10th House – The House of Career
Corresponding to Capricorn and Saturn

The tenth house or mid-heaven is the highest point in the chart and it is what is most obvious about us to other people, it's how we appear, what we symbolise and our functions in society. Career, reputation, how we are seen, what's expected of us, what duties and responsibilities we have in our social role. Developing aspects of our inner nature here allows us to fulfil our destiny and give a sense of personal satisfaction. Our role is secure in our individuality, an expression of us and unique to us.

11th House – The House of Friends
Corresponding to Aquarius and Saturn (Uranus)

The house of our hopes, our plans, our intentions, the focus of our own becoming and our wishes for the future. "Show me your friends and I will tell you who you are". Friends are our best mirror. In our friends, associates, groups from tribe or herd with stripes down to our spotted associations we see our reflections. The people we spend time with make our own aims seem more real and it is likely that we are surrounding ourselves with people who support our vision for ourselves and who appreciate our support and value us in return. When we choose consciously and with awareness people who are good for us and our purpose, we engage in furthering our development.

12th House – The House of Troubles
Corresponding to Pisces and Jupiter (Neptune)

Maybe we could affectionately call it the house of wisdom gained through experiences that challenge us!

Bringing light and focus to areas of unconsciousness, letting go of attachments, willingness to travel inwards to our depths, meditation, a sense of the presence of divinity, spiritual experiences, higher levels of awareness, exerting a degree of choice in our emotional responses. Understanding that only consciousness is eternal.

Empty Houses
Often there are houses in the chart that have no planets travelling through them. Whenever this occurs it is usual to talk to the owner of the house and refer to the ruling planet of that sign. For example if the third house were empty and in Gemini then refer to Mercury. If the third house were empty and in Aries then refer to Mars. We will look at the planets in the next chapter.

Exercises

Use an online resource to look at your birth chart. Many offer free interpretations and natal charts.

Spends some time sky watching and find at least three constellations in the night sky. Note their positions relative to the time of year.

Chapter Fourteen
The Planets

We are an extract of the starry heavens and the planets are mirrored within us in our constellated psyche the movements of which are felt deeply within the soul.

Anyone who did science at GCSE or O level has probably played with triangular prisms and light rays in the classroom and has seen how light can refract, bend or change in transmission depending upon the prism or filter. The zodiac acts much like heaven's wheel of light made up of twelve parts being shone like the light beam in the classroom through the prisms, which in this case are the filters of the planetary lenses. For the light of the zodiac signs to touch us they have to come through the channels of the planets. The planets then act like a filtration system to carry zodiacal powers, allowing them to reach us and connect with us on the deepest levels of our being. Like-wise for us to work with these higher cosmic powers we in turn need to work with and through these channels, and it is through developing our relationship to the planets that we may learn to call energies forth and to climb the lights upwards between worlds.

We have already seen how these filters change and react differently depending upon the sign they are in, like the artist mixing paints upon his palette. When we are reading a birth chart we look at which signs the planets are in to understand their context and how they are working. We never actually see a sign directly. There is always a bridge and this bridge is found in the elements, spirit and planetary correspondence. Including the two luminaries and the three "new" planets, Pluto, Neptune and Uranus, there are ten of these light streams of the rainbow transmitting to us from the cosmos. The ten in combination with the twelve signs and the twelve houses continuously making shifts and with so many variables create unique and unrepeatable combinations over vast expanses of time and space. Times, seasons and tides come and go and each revolving planet has varying cycles of time and varying angles of incidence to Earth over time and relative to one another. Each moment we are in is sacrosanct. The Great Artist and Creator create beauty moment by moment in a perfection of colour we feel through the soul.

Timing our workings for the pre-ordained moment wherever possible is key. To each event will have its time. Often our soul tells us and we know deep within us when we should do our work. Even then, when we know, it can be wise to double check and to confirm our intuition with relative fact and assess the necessary chart for favourable conditions or to be aware of any potential hiccups. There is a Jungian term, Absolute knowledge, which means the causal fore knowledge, relatively independent of time and space, possessed by the unconscious and apparent in constellated archetypes and in synchronicity. The implication is that the *constellated* Archetypes in the psyche are responsible for fore knowledge! As with all systems, whether philosophical or physical it makes no sense to look only at one piece without also looking at the whole. The planets then should be viewed holistically and although one alone might be the focal point of a working it is important that they are considered in union and in balance.

Deciding not to write about the various pentacles, symbols and sigils that are often the focal point of planetary magic and alchemy was deliberate. There are numerous books available that talk about these things in much detail for those that seek it. Instead it seems that the way forward is to develop a real and meaningful relationship with the planets and to get a feel for them. All other rituals, pentacles, signs or words are hollow and meaningless without a firm bedrock underfoot and an established connection, and when a good connection has been established some of these other things may at times be superfluous in any case. Better to focus upon learning about the physical attributes of a planet and gain metaphysical understanding. Gathering herbs, flowers, incenses, the right colours and stones corresponding to each and sitting with them in turn can be useful either in meditation or in prayer, whatever feels right, until a feel for them develops naturally. Incantations, spell work or anything can come later. At the end of the chapter the recognised and accepted table of planetary hours used almost across the board is given and an explanation as to how they are devised.

For now we will look at the planets in regards to magical workings and the potency of timing.

The planetary themes echo clearly the themes of their corresponding spheres upon the Tree of Life and can be studied and understood much more deeply when they are considered together. For example the qualities of Saturn are ever more apparent when we study Binah and those of Mercury when we study the sphere of Hod. Whilst our focus is upon the planets both planets and Sephiroth are regularly cross referenced in books and all the planetary correspondences given for plants by Culpepper and other botanists have been based upon the symbola system discussed previously.

THE PLANETS AND THEIR SYMBOLS

☉ Sun	☽ Moon	☿ Mercury
♀ Venus	♂ Mars	♃ Jupiter
♄ Saturn	♅ Uranus	♆ Neptune
♇ Pluto	⊕ Earth	

Space.

Corresponds to the sphere of Kether, The Crown upon the Kabbalistic Tree of Life .

Archetypes – the potter, creator, architect, an ancient bearded king seen in profile from the right.

Symbols – the flame, the Sah, the point in the circle, the crown, the swastica (in its pure form the four arms represent the primordial elements swirling around a point), the infinity symbol (lemniscate).

The root of the powers of Air. (The roots of Space, Breath, Sound.)

Tarot – The four Aces.

Colour – brilliant white.

From the point of creation flows forth spirit, life force. I always think of the dot in the middle of the circle where the compass left a mark or the three lines in sacred geometry at the beginning of creation. The first circle, the first square, the beginnings of the first pillar at the top. Here is the point of permanent light, pure consciousness and both Union with God and Separation in creation. In this process, the four elements are born, Earth, Fire, Water and Air represented by the Holy Living Creatures the Bull (Taurus), the Lion (Leo), the Eagle (Scorpio) and Man (Aquarius) i.e. the first four quarters and fixed signs of the Zodiac.

The Zodiac.

Corresponds to the sphere of Chokmah upon the Kabbalistic Tree of Life..

Archetypes – bearded male figure.

Symbols – the phallus, the cross, the standing stone, the tower, the straight line, the cloak (spirit incarnated in human form), inner robe inner light.

Element – the root of Fire.

Tarot – The four twos and the four Knights.

Colours – grey.

From the four elements and the first four signs come forth the rest. There is a massive kinetic force, impetus and expansion where the entire energy of the Universe pours forward manifesting through polarity with form in a fluid energy exchange between poles. It is disorganised, boundless, coursing and potent. Essentially it is yang, primordial maleness and vitality surging into the world and creating the sphere of fixed stars.

The Planetary names are given in English, Greek and Hebrew

Saturn, Kronos, Shabbathai.

Corresponds to the sphere of Binah upon the Kabbalistic Tree of Life.

Archetypes – Father Time, The Ancient, The Celestial Queen.

Symbols – scythe, keys, hourglass, compasses, cauldron.

Element – the root of Water.

Zodiacal Correspondence – Capricorn (10th House) and Aquarius (11th House).

Planetary Orbit – 29.457 years.

Average orbital speed – 9.69 km/s.

The triangle and the three-pointed star. The first number from one and two taking **form**. The north pole of the planet Saturn has a hexagonal cloud.

Tarot – The four threes (The Universe).

Colour – black.

Day – Saturday.

Saturn is named after the Roman God of Agriculture and its astrological symbol represents the God's sickle.

247

Having received the emanated influx of cosmic energy from the zodiacal signs Saturn is the first prism or filter the cosmic light must pass through. Primarily this filter may be considered to manifest here as Time and as the governing natural Laws of three-dimensional existence. Her themes then are forming through restriction, constrictions, limitations, concentration, crystallisation, external authority and time.

Saturn functions in us as development of self-discipline, self-respect and faith. Saturn offers us opportunities to grow through the restrictions, obstacles and limitations we find in life. Often this is embodied in an external authority or those in a role of judgement such as the parent, teacher, police officer or as circumstances over which we have no influence. We learn growth primarily through responsibility and the meeting of obligations here and also through the keenly felt consequences of not having done so. This is the ground of the equal and opposite reaction. It's also where we may meet and overcome blocks and sticky spots including any childhood or past life difficulties. Saturn is like the strict parent who gives us tough love when we haven't done our chores or homework until such time as we learn self-discipline and accept working out karma. Learning rules and laws and working with them, dealing with them and overcoming challenges allows us to step into our own authority and truth. It has to be said and understood that this is where some of our hardest lessons and tests are found. As a result of this influence we may find fulfilment, inspiration, stability, endurance, reverence and faith in life. In Hindu astrology Saturn is known as "Shani" and sits in judgement of all according to the good or bad deeds performed in life. Graduation from Saturn is hard won and will happen naturally when we reach a new level of understanding. This understanding is both realisation that we are responsible for creating our own reality through manifestation, focussed will and discipline and an acceptance of those things which are destiny and beyond our control.

The shadows of Saturn are coldness, depression, sadness, unresponsiveness, brooding and suppression of emotion and expression. Distortion can present as fear of authority, regular disagreements with authority, self-incrimination and blame, blocks and restrictions that hinder or an inability to relax or unfreeze. Suppression or constriction in the wrong ways can manifest as becoming authoritarian in the first house, or holding onto money too tightly in the second house etc.

Magically the themes of Saturn are in works of form, gaining Understanding, seeking the counsel of the wise one i.e. the primordial Mother presiding over the cauldron of time and birth in creation, responsibility, manifestation and faith. Affinity to the land, the depths of earth, age, knowledge, death, reincarnation, restrictions, protection, the passage of time and creativity.

Retrograde Planets

Regarding the movements of planets as observed from Earth and the strange things they seem to do with their stopping, starting, speeding up, slowing down, clustering together, spreading out in patterns and alignments, drawing close and bright, then fading into the distance and even moving backwards these things are of course all illusory in one sense. To the scientific astronomer there is sensible order to the planets with immutable universal laws but to the astrologer who studies them relative to us as perceived from Earth they behave in the most erratic manner! As discussed, retrograde motion is created by a planet the Earth is coming around and passing by (overtaking). The ways in which retrograde motion manifests is primarily individualisation whether that is by breaking free, rebelling, reflection, inward movement or breaking patterns pertaining to the sphere i.e. Mercury may think differently or Mars may act differently, Saturn may rebel against authority.

Jupiter, Zeus, Tzedeq.

Corresponds to the sphere of Chesed (Mercy) also known as Gedulah (Majesty, Glory) upon the Kabbalistic Tree of Life.

Functions – expansion and majestic leadership.

Archetypes – the Mighty Old King upon his throne, the Good Ruler, the Priest.

Symbols – Tetrahedron, Pyramid, the Royal Sceptre, the Staff, Oak Crown, Cup of Abundance, Cornucopia.

Element – Water.

Zodiacal Correspondence – Sagittarius (9th House) and Pisces (12th House).

Planetary Orbit – 11.86 years.

Four-pointed star corresponding to the number of the sphere and fours easily multiplying and expansive. Square building blocks of expansion.

Tarot – The four fours. (The Wheel Of Fortune.)

Colours – deep violet, blue, deep purple, deep azure flecked yellow.

Day – Thursday.

Jupiter is the Roman name after the God also sometimes called Jove. Jupiter is likened to his Greek counterpart Zeus and it is the symbolic representation of Zeus' lightning bolt which forms the astronomical symbol. The Babylonians considered this the God Marduk and used the approximate twelve-year orbit along the ecliptic to define the constellations of their zodiac. In Vedic astrology it is named after Brihaspati the Guru which means heavy one. In English Thursday comes from Thor's day whom is associated with Jupiter in Germanic mythology.

This planetary filter acts like gravitational outward push, predominantly as expansion! The functions of Jupiter are growth, evolution and stretching and this is how he shows up in us in our psychic counterpart. He is steadfast and life affirming, supporting all that is pure, natural and true and shedding light, sometimes uncomfortably, on all that is not. His domain is one conducive to good health and to prosperity and advancement. To achieve this though we must be willing to grow, to expand, to evolve. Thankfully the lessons here feel more supportive and Jupiter's sense of responsibility and concern are benevolent and compassionate. In the birth chart Jupiter signifies an area of luck, enthusiasm, optimism and where to seize opportunities. It is also where to bring awareness not to take such for granted or hold unrealistic expectations.

The shadows of Jupiter are found in over expansion, imbalance causing lack of growth, over indulging, unrealistic optimism and denial of negative realities, taking things for granted, over playing one's hand, holding pretences and foolishness.

Retrograde the expansion is individualised and turned inward so that inner growth can take place, finding individual truth and experiences of déjà-vu. It can also be procrastination and planning and re-planning without getting the job done!

Magically the themes of Jupiter are found in works of expansion, the affirmation of life, maintaining faith, lifting the spirits, law in the capacity of supporting all that is good and the metering out of justice. He is the image of the good king and experienced ruler. Also works for good fortune, luck, honour, abundance, gratitude, generosity, contentment and joy.

Mars – Ares, Madim.

Corresponds to the sphere of Geburah (Strength) upon the Kabbalistic Tree of Life.

Archetypes – the warrior, the protector, the champion.

Symbols – swords, lance, shield, scourge, helmet.

Element – Fire.

Zodiacal Correspondence – Aries (1st House) and Scorpio (8th House).

Planetary Orbit – 1.8808 Julian years or 686.971 days at an average speed of 24.077 km/s.

Pentacle, pentagram, five-pointed star. The place where elements combine with spirit and movement is added to matter.

Tarot card – The four fives (The Tower).

Colour – red.

Day – Tuesday.

Mars has two small irregularly shaped moons, Phobos and Deimos, and is itself named after Mars the Roman God of War.

Mars echoes Geburah's directed strength giving motion to matter as action! As such the functions of Mars can be found in the development, exertion and direction of will power and giving movement to desires and expression of needs. Mars has a direct approach and exerting will and movement in any direction in life is of course always subject to encountering opposing forces and opinions. Still the movement is necessary and so is the destructive force of challenge and opposition because it brings to our attention that which is to be defended, protected and encouraged and that which is to be broken down and removed, thereby allowing any wasted energy to be recycled into more beneficial or productive areas. In a way it acts like life's disinfectant getting rid of anything not serving through use of strength and will power and protecting all of value with a strong arm. Mars therefore provides us with opportunities to learn discernment and opportunities to find courage. It is also the area where we may focus upon the strength and fitness of the body, the sharpening of the mind, developing a sense of belonging to a group or supporting a cause, protecting the vulnerable, self-determination, assertiveness and staying power. Mars gives us the steam power to shape our lives and the enthusiasm and daring to seek adventure and opportunities to test our limits. This is also a very instinctual sphere, the will of I want and I desire. It's instinct, sex and sexuality, hunger, passion, spontaneity and impulsiveness.

The shadows of Mars are rage, selfishness, irritability, cruelty, sadism, bullying, aggression both outwardly and passively, dictatorship, blood lust in war, killer instinct, annihilation.

In the birth chart the position of Mars shows the area of life one needs to nurture in this way whether through awareness of areas in which to avoid conflict and strife or areas to develop assertiveness and self-empowerment.

Retrograde Mars might bring up issues around reliving the past (the backward motion of focus on ego), sexual energy turned inward and not flowing, neglect of the physical body. Individuality of action may manifest in innumerable ways!

Magical themes are works of power, developing courage, energy, initiative, generative force, practicality, facing conflict, strengthening and aligning will, judgement, decisions, purification, elevation and works of power.

Sun, Helios, Shemesh.

Corresponds to sphere of Tiphareth (beauty) upon the Kabbalistic Tree of Life.

Functions – universal harmony and judgement.

Archetypes – the Solar King, the Eternal Child.

Element – Air.

Symbols – the Rose Cross, Solar cross, Breastplate, Solar diadem, Depictions of the Sun Shining, Solar Cup symbolic of Ruach (the Spirit Breath of God), The Grail.

Zodiacal Correspondence – Leo (5th house).

Orbital Centre of the Solar System.

The Hexagon, hexagram and six-pointed star. Merkaba.
Tarot – The four sixes.
Colour – golden.
Day – Sunday.

The Sun is the star at the centre of our solar system and the power source of energy for all life on Earth. The life-giving warmth and light controls our climate and weather system and supports photosynthesis.

The Sun is the centre of the whole system both physically and spiritually. Here in this beating heart the union of all and power in balance is found. Here is the place where the heart is weighed in balance, where love and truth synonymously coexist.

The Sun is all about consciousness, creation and powering, through connection, the whole system. Wherever our Sun Sign falls in our chart this is where we have the potential to shine and this is what we radiate. The Sun functions in us as Ego, I am, identity, the roots of personality and personal power. It is in the domain of the Sun that we develop a healthy and functional self-image and learn to make choices and act on them. Here is our purpose, our goal and our deepest earthly expression of who we are. When we nurture this area in ourselves we care for our Spirit and our well being too. Sunlight do not forget brings warmth and life to all things and is a wonderful healer. Money can be found here too as an earthly exchange of expended energy through our area of work when we are fulfilling our purpose.

The Sun's shadows may be found in the distortion of Ego, warmth and light. Lacking purpose, timidity, lack of confidence, selfishness, delusions, pompousness, insensitivity, tyranny, inflexibility, vanity.

Magical themes are works of wealth, spiritual illumination, alignment with Spirit, good health, healing, abundance of all things, wealth, direction of energy, integration, sincerity, loyalty, good advice, leadership, organisation, psychic ability, peace, balance, harmony, vitality, growth.

Venus, Paphie, Nogah.
Corresponds to the sphere of Netzach (Victory) upon the Kabbalistic Tree of Life.
Archetypes – Flame of the Sea, the shining morning and evening star

253

depicted as birthed from the ocean in iconic artworks.

Element – Fire.

Symbols – the lamp, the girdle, rose, candlestick, mirror, necklace, seashells, pearls, sistrum, flaming torch, garland of flowers, cup, chalice.

Zodiacal Correspondence – Taurus (2nd house) and Libra (7th house).

Planetary Orbit – 224.7 days at an average speed of 35.02 k/s.

The Heptagon, heptagram and seven-pointed star.

Venus also has an association with the five pointed star due to the pattern made by the course of the planet.

Tarot – The four sevens (The Empress).

Colour – green.

Venus is the brightest object in the sky, other than the moon, and is bright enough to be seen even in daylight when the sky is clear.

Venus appears to overtake Earth every five hundred and eighty-four days i.e. goes retrograde and as it does so changes from the evening star visible after sunset to the morning star visible before sunrise. Venus was known both as the morning star and as the evening star to ancient civilisations and the Venus tablet of Ammisaduqa 1581 BCE shows that the Babylonians understood them to be the same object referred to as "bright queen of the sky". The Greeks called the two aspects, Phosphorus (light bringer) in the morning and Hesperus in the evening. The Romans called them, Lucifer and Vesper.

Although Venus' orbit of the Sun is two hundred and twenty-five days it takes Venus almost five hundred and eighty-four days to reappear in the same spot in the sky as observed from Earth. This is called the synodic cycle of Venus.

Primarily this filter, sometimes called the Green mystic ray is about loving relationship and love of Nature. Our relationship to the Earth and to Nature, our relationship to our self, learned in Taurus and our relationship to others learned in Libra, the two signs ruled by Venus. This is where we learn to develop supportive emotional bonds and sustainable relationships. We also learn emotional balance and equilibrium. Wherever Venus falls in our chart this is a good clue as to what we need in a partner and also as to where personal peace can be found.

Venus functions in us as love, inner values, physical beauty, attractive personality, courtesy, grace, vitality of nature and artistic ability expressed through music, dancing, poetry and the arts. She brings the gifts of inner serenity, peace, empathy, balance and harmony and the ability to form relationships.

The shadows of Venus are vanity, manipulation, lack of backbone, laziness and unbalanced sexuality.

Venus retrograde individuates as different ways of loving, difficulty expressing or receiving love, misunderstandings about love, measuring self-value in love received or lost, inability to move past previous hurts in love. Cures are found in art, beauty and things which nurture the heart.

The magical themes of Venus are all works of love and Earth and Nature magic, relationships, romance, fertility, marriage, beauty, kindness, artistic creativity, reconciliation, harmony, synthesis and passion.

Mercury, Hermes, Kokab

Corresponds to sphere of Hod (Splendour) upon the Kabbalistic Tree of Life.

Archetypes – the divine messenger, the hermit, a hermaphrodite.

Element – Air.

Symbols – quill, book, scrolls, names (words of power), versicles (mantras), apron (craftsman, maker).

Zodiacal Correspondence – Gemini (3rd house) and Virgo (6th house).

Planetary Orbit – 88 days at an average speed of 47.362k/s.

The Octagon, octagram, eight-pointed star.

Tarot – The four eights (The Magician).

Colours – orange.

Day – Wednesday.

Mercury is the smallest of the planets in our solar system and is the closest to the Sun with the fastest orbit of only eighty-eighty days, although it appears to take one hundred and sixteen days when observed from Earth. Every one hundred and sixteen days, or to be more precise 115.88 days, upon completion of the orbit we observe from Earth the backward motion of the retrograde cycle which lasts for around three weeks roughly three times a year. Because Mercury is an interior planet, (like Venus), meaning it orbits the Sun within the Earth's own orbit, it can appear in the sky in the morning or evening but not in the middle of the night. It is however harder to see than Venus because it is so close to the Sun. The planet Mercury is named after the Roman deity Mercury who was the messenger to the Gods.

Mercury is the scribe, the first of magician's, lord of the holy words and he is all about the transmission of divine information. Predominantly Mercury collects, forms and orders thoughts and ideas and translates them into outward communication. Wherever Mercury falls in our chart this is where our intellectual strengths and weaknesses can be seen, where our natural interests lie and is also indicative of how we communicate and come across. It is how we think, how we colour our perceptions and transfer information internally. Mercury functions in us as our left-brain thought processes and all of the analytical, logical, rational ways in which we navigate life. Well dignified it indicates clarity of perception and quick thinking. Traditionally Mercury is the messenger of the Gods and associated with the word both as the power of speech i.e. words of power, right speech i.e. truth and with the abilities of writing and reading to convey that word to others. Mercury is the student, the teacher, the scribe, the magician, the traveller.

Mercury's areas of shadow can be found in warped or biased thinking clouded by fear or by ego resulting in blinkered sight, a constantly noisy, whirring mind, hyperactivity, nervousness, worry, sketchiness, incessant talking and a changeability of mind that is so quick as to be unstable, at times appearing two faced, superficial and insincere. From these shadows comes the word mercurial meaning volatile, unpredictable and erratic.

When retrograde Mercury allows a natural time of reflection inwards, offers alternative ways of thinking and points of view, shifts in perception and a deepening of self-understanding and knowledge if the time is used this way. Trying to work outwards whilst Mercury is retrograde may cause frustration and strange results. It's not a great time for decisions but is good for thinking about possibilities. Retrograde motion may also affect communication, travel and other outward going activity. That being said it's a great time for re-establishing connections with friends, reorganising the house or the paperwork, realigning with nature, releasing the past, re-establishing order. You get the theme it's all the re's with the backwards motion of the natural movement. Because this happens approximately three times a year and is within Earth's inner field so to speak, so close to the Sun, it's one to be aware of and to work with wherever possible.

Magical themes are books, learning, initiation, linking spirit and matter, knowledge, communication, divination, discernment, science, psychic development, memory, prediction, harnessing natural forces, self-mastery in regards controlling, holding back and regulating ourselves and the direction of such forces.

Moon, Mene, Levanah.

Corresponds to the sphere of Yesod (Foundation) upon the Kabbalistic Tree of Life.

Archetypes – a beautiful naked man, very strong.

Element – Water.

Symbols – sandals (walking the circle, treading holy ground), perfumes (changing focus of consciousness).

Zodiacal Correspondence – Cancer (4th house).

Orbits the Earth every twenty-nine days.

Tarot – the four nines and the Moon/HPS.

Nonagon, enneagram, nine-pointed star.

Day – Monday.

Colours – violet or silver.

The Earth and Moon may be considered in some sense as etheric doubles of one another in that they are of one ether and shared composition in constant flux with one another. The Moon waxes and wanes growing light and dark with the Sun and the Earth moves through day and night growing light and dark with the Sun, both having cycles governing tides and phases for the same reason. The Moon orbits the Earth and her relationship with us is more intimate and more direct than those of other planetary spheres, except the Sun. Whilst the Moon is a luminary we must remember that her luminescence is always in fact caused by the reflections of the Sun. She is like a watery surface reflecting the sky above. She is also the receptacle of all the other planetary influx coming to Earth as it streams through her reflections. Both physically and on the Tree of Life the Moon is positioned between the Earth and the Sun and it is for this reason that she is so powerful and her effect so greatly felt particularly at times of natural alignment such as during an eclipse.

The sphere of water, cycles and reflections holds a thousand moving pictures at any one moment. It is beautiful and can be the pathway to higher consciousness offering us still deep waters as we align with the truth found in the solar sphere above. Without the alignment to the higher light however the water may also be full of illusion and the hidden things of humanity's unconscious.

The position of the Moon functions to establish emotional development, sensitivity, responsiveness and feelings. This is where psychic abilities and intuition can be consciously developed. Thoth is the Egyptian God of the Moon and also of Mercury which is interesting not solely because of the dual nature of both of these spheres and their position in relation to one another but also because He is the "first of magicians" and the Moon must be considered first and foremost as magical. Here too is transformation and sexuality in cycle.

In the birth chart the Moon is primarily the focal point of our emotional needs. Anyone with a Moon sign in Libra likely has emotional needs likely centred around balance, balancing feelings, harmony and maintaining peace. A Virgo Moon sign may be indicative of needing order and routine to feel settled and secure and function well in the other areas of life. To feel happier and more fulfilled in life look to nurture and brighten your Moon sign by listening to its needs and also to the needs of your Sun sign which is where you shine and what your Moon reflects!

The shadows of the Moon are found in the subconscious and in the unconscious surfacing, in chaotic, irrational or illogical thoughts and in an inability to accept or see reality, instead living as a dreamer drifting in and out of fantasy, out of touch with the rest of the world. Dysfunction and imbalance of the Moon affects emotional stability and contributes to depression and feelings of overwhelm.

Regarding the Moon's Nodes, sometimes referred to as the dragon's head and tail they are two opposed points on the diameter of the Moon thought by many astrologers to symbolise the direction of the individual's evolutionary journey. The South node is said to represent the past and the influence of karma, our ancestors and their impact on us, previous incarnations, habits learned, instinctive automatic behaviours, security and familiarity. The North node is said to represent the future, the lessons yet to learn, growth, challenging experiences, the way forward, habits broken, the unknown and unfamiliar.

All works of magic concern the Moon. However primary themes are found in domestic matters, the sea, transformation, change, reproduction, childbirth, psychic matters, removing illusion or delusion, prophetic dreams, clairvoyance, peace, healing, sleep, fertility, women, visions, divination, love and feelings.

Earth.

Corresponds to the sphere of Malkuth (the Kingdom) upon the Kabbalistic Tree of Life.

Functions – purification and grounding.

Archetypes – a young woman crowned and veiled. (She represents nature and spiritual forces hidden from outer form.)

Element – Earth.

Symbols – sphinx, the altar (as above so below), the equal armed cross (four elements balanced), the magic circle, crystal.

Earth's orbit around the Sun is 365 ¼ days.

Tarot – the four tens and the four Princesses.

Two interlocking pentagrams or two pentacles forming a ten-pointed star, i.e. two life forms joining together to manifest in the physical world.

Colours – earthy colours: citrine, olive, russet and black.

Mother Earth, Terra Firma, Pachamama, the inferior Mother, the fertility Goddess, the God of the hunt and the trees. Here is the final result and the birth into existence in the four elements and four conditions in which energy exists solid, liquid, gaseous and electrical. Her main functions as the last filter are those of purification and grounding. All that passes through her now passes quite literally through the Salt of the Earth and appropriately the stone corresponding to Malkuth is rock crystal i.e. salt. Upon the altar the salt is in the North representing Earth. Psychically and physically it is important to ground ourselves and magically our works are only effective when the energies are grounded in order to manifest and take physical form or action.

The "New" Planets

The three invisible "new" planets are generally thought of as the higher octaves of the first three planets in the solar system i.e. Uranus as the higher octave of Mercury, Neptune as the higher octave of Venus and Pluto as the higher octave of Mars. These planets are considered to represent possibilities and transcendent qualities attainable only through work on the self by aligning will and conscious choice. There is a further school of thought held by some that these higher octaves may then rule certain astrological signs of the zodiac. However whilst it might be possible to consider Pluto in regard to ruling a higher octave of Scorpio because it is ruled by Mars, it may be illogical to ascribe Uranus as the ruler of Aquarius when Aquarius is traditionally ruled by Saturn and not Mercury. Likewise it is illogical to ascribe Neptune to rule Pisces when Pisces is traditionally ruled by Jupiter not by Venus. Therefore they might be considered as higher octaves of planets but not as sign rulers in any way, rather as evolutionary potentials that may be fulfilled by considering them individually for their merits in combination with any planets transiting through them.

One theory suggests man has only discovered these "new planets" in the moment that was appropriate for the age and therefore the stage of humanity's evolution at the time. The discovery of Uranus in 1781, and subsequently the others found afterwards as a result of this initial discovery, coincided with an era of revolution in the Western world socially, politically and industrially. Not surprisingly Uranus functions as overcoming the confines and boundaries of cultural and social conditioning.

Uranus
Higher Octave of Mercury.

Planetary Orbit – 84.016846 years an average speed of 6.80 km/s.

Discovered with a telescope in 1781 by Sir William Herschel, Uranus traverses the zodiac every eighty-four years and takes seven years to go through each sign. Unlike all the other planets, Uranus is tilted completely on its side with a magnetic field that moves like a corkscrew as the planet rotates! This is caused by the combination of a magnetic field fifty times stronger than that of Earth with 60° tilt to the rotation axis. Uranus also has a ring system made of billions of tiny pebbles and these rings appear vertical to us. For about a quarter of the Uranian year the Sun shines directly over each pole, leaving the other half of the planet in cold, frigid darkness. The planet's beautiful blue-green colour is caused by the absorption of red light by methane in the atmosphere.

The word most associated with Uranus is Humanitarianism which is achieved through its functions. At a personal level Uranus functions as the development of individuality and the capacity to question authority in order to do what is right for oneself. Its function in a broader sense is to overcome and revolutionise thinking regarding cultural and social conditioning in order to benefit all. As the higher octave of Mercury, Uranus is eccentric, extreme, unpredictable and lightning fast. It questions everything, positively argues with authority, brings about revolutions, and ends them as quickly. It governs electricity and science, but also astrology and paranormal activities. It is brilliant, a genius, crazy at times, inventive and out there! It can be volatile, nervous and highly strung, and shows where we are apt to find sudden insights. Uranus shows where we express the greatest innovations. Without it we would not reach for the higher planes of being or more specifically the higher planes of thought and mind. Uranus is radical thought and opens up our minds and our thought patterns, changing how we see and navigate life and showing us a bigger picture beyond our personal experience. It brings awakening!

Uranus' areas of shadow are in unreliability and irresponsible behaviours and decisions, sometimes bordering on lunacy. There is a fine line between genius and crazy. Selfishness, lack of sensitivity or respect for the traditions or beliefs of others and intolerance. Hyperactivity and burn out can lead to mental trauma and disorders of the nervous system.

Uranus is retrograde for five months at a time and the outward transcendence can be turned inwards positively as Genius bringing awakening within and aiding the overcoming of personal conditioning or negatively in such a way as to inhibit individuality and avoid or suppress anything controversial.

Uranus has no Kabbalistic correspondence on the tree of life but some connect it to Ain Soph Aur, the veil of Infinite Light, and some to Chokmah, the force and action of the Father and Zodiacal energy. My own thought is that as the higher octave of Mercury its clear functions are as thought and higher learning, its logical position is Hod. It has no traditional Tarot correspondence, but some connect it to the air card of the Fool, the starting of a new journey symbolising the awakening. Often people who are themselves on a conscious journey after some kind of awakening in life say that they feel they are starting again, relearning everything from the beginning and shifting their perceptions as they repeat their footsteps with new found understanding and open eyes. I quite like the image of the fool having completed the first journey, resting, understanding and starting out again to improve himself and the welfare of others. Equally to consider the higher implications of the Magician seems appropriate. Uranus rules no chakra but can be likened to the etheric body, the part of us that shows vitality and connects the body with the spiritual aura. The symbol is two crescents framing a cross above a circle. This indicates matter formed from both spirit and emotion.

The magical themes of Uranus are those of humanitarianism, global consciousness, welfare, overcoming conditioning and limitations, new ways of thinking and doing things, asking for inspiration and insight.

Neptune
Higher Octave of Venus.

Planetary Orbit – 164.8 years at an average speed of 5.43 km/s.

Neptune is named after the Roman God of the Sea and its astronomical symbol is a stylised version of His trident.

Neptune was discovered in 1846 by John Galle as a result of mathematical prediction of gravitational perturbations rather than by observation. The mid 1800s was an era of a new romantic movement the influence of which was expressed in art and music and felt throughout society in cultural developments such as the abolition of slavery in the United Kingdom, women's rights and an increase in social awareness. Spirituality was also changing and there was an increase in mystical organisations and a thirst for knowledge.

Neptune represents the higher octave of Venus and functions as transcendental planes of love, compassion and harmony. As the second planet beyond the border of the visible, Neptune gives us the chance to step out beyond ourselves and our self-interest and experience true altruism. Here is the ocean, the river, the waters that separate the physical and spiritual worlds depicted in all cultures as necessary to cross over to the "other side". It is this crossing over that is associated with Neptune and the journey over water. Love when it has transcended the personal level found in the other person is concerned with love of the other as a concept and focuses upon communion with Spirit, God, Goddess and the welfare of others and society as a whole. It opens up new channels deep within the psyche which can access a great sea of visions. These visions may only be trusted when we are open hearted and aligned with truth as they may otherwise be illusionary or seek to trick. It is worth knowing that when illusion does trick us this is just a way of elongating the journey so that we may discover the truth.

Wherever Neptune falls in our chart this is a good clue as to where we are likely to either need a reality check due to confusing thoughts or imaginings or where we should trust our intuition more and listen to our deeper self. The position of Neptune is also the pathway to consciousness, personal possibilities, peace with life as a whole, seeing our place in the whole and it's uniqueness, compassion, feelings of unity, oneness, wholeness, inspiration, extrasensory perceptions and artistic talents. It shows where we may be of greatest spiritual service, where we move with the flow of Spirit.

The shadows of Neptune are as with other shadows mostly imbalance or misunderstanding and they are in danger of showing up as complete loss of self, areas where we are most confused, glossing over gritty parts of life in favour of easier ones, daydreaming, confusion, drifting, delusions, escapism, addictions, avoidance, self deception and deception of others, dishonesty, psychic disturbances.

Neptune retrograde turns compassion and harmony inward with a loving but high and deep gaze correcting misunderstandings about love, sorting out truth from fiction and re-evaluating. It's often felt as a wake up call!

Magical themes of Neptune are all works of altruism, love on a global scale, love as works for social awareness and improvement, channelling, miracles, healing and empathic connection with all of humanity. Neptune has no Kabbalistic correspondence, but some connect it to Ain Soph, the Veil of Infinity, and some to Kether, white sphere of total union with Deity, merging of all parts, and the Crown. My own thoughts are that as the higher octave of

Venus with the emphasis upon Love and Nature albeit the nature of humanity it belongs to the sphere of Netzach at a heightened pitch or frequency. It has no traditional tarot correspondence but some consider the water card of the Hanged Man, self-sacrifice and giving up the former life for greater understanding. Neptune rules no Chakra, but has connection to the aura and astral body. Appropriate stones, plants or animals are those of the Ocean and or large bodies of water, or those associated with Venus.

Pluto
Higher Octave of Mars.

Planetary Orbit – 247.68 years at an average speed of 4.7 km/s.

Discovered in 1930 Pluto initially classed as a planet nowadays has minor planet designation as a dwarf planet.

The 1930s experimented with surrealism in art, with abstract acid jazz music, with new philosophies, with radical writing and essentially with new ways of being and self-expression. The world was recovering and shell-shocked from the First World War and people wanted to redefine themselves. Pluto as the higher octave of Mars echoes this theme. Where Mars is the ego, the self, and self-definition so too is Pluto but it is concerned not with the individual so much as with the collective. Pluto is said to rule the underworld and its job is to expose all that is hidden beneath the surface. It functions as the strength and power of the collective and is connected with group identity needs, feelings, hopes and fears. Like Mars (Geburah) there is a breaking down destructive force which removes harm by exposing it thereby protecting the good. Pluto is the riches of the Earth and of knowledge. It is gossip, it is secrecy and it is power wielded in the shadows. With Pluto comes understanding of death and rebirth.

In the birth chart Pluto shows us where we can find our destiny and significance in life, where we have something which can benefit the world in some way. It can also be where we must be most mindful of our behaviour and its consequences. It takes us to our depths and forces us to look at our shadows so that we can do our healing and transforming work. We all have things in the closet we'd rather not look at! Refusal to look, however, may mean that the lesson and opportunity are repeated and presented as crisis so that we have to go there.

The higher we climb the longer and deeper the shadows may fall! The shadows of Pluto echo those of Mars. Rage, violence, selfishness, dogmatism, rigidity, cruelty, sadism, bullying, aggression both outwardly and passively, dictatorship, blood lust in war, killer instinct and annihilation.

Retrograde Pluto may bring rude awakenings, fear of dis-empowerment, or a hesitancy to speak out or be seen. The retrograde period can be used to deal with subconscious stuff we ignore and to clean things up.

Pluto has no Kabbalistic correspondence, though some connect it to Ain, the veil of Nothingness, and some connect it to Daath; the hidden sphere of Knowledge. Again my own thought is perhaps that the logical correspondence is to Geburah as the sphere of Mars. It too has no traditional tarot correspondence, but some connect it to the judgement card. The symbol is a monograph of the first two letters. Plants, stones, animals and colours corresponding either to Mars or sacred to deities associated with the underworld.

The Traditional Planetary Hours

The Egyptian and later Helenistic *symbola* system of planetary hours are the ones we still use today and these planetary hours are assigned by rotating the seven planets in order throughout the hours of day and night, starting with the correct hour for each day at sunrise.

The length of the planetary "hours" varies depending on the time of year because it is calculated by dividing the hours of light and dark between sunrise and sunset. For example, if it is a Sunday at the beginning of May, sunrise is 04.33 a.m. and sunset is 19.23 p.m. Then the duration of daylight is 14 hrs 50 min and the duration of night is 9 hrs 10 min. These durations are then divisible by twelve to work out the length of each planetary hour. The hours of the day are then seventy-four minutes long and the hours of the night are forty-six minutes long in our example.

Naturally in the winter the hours of night are longer and the hours of day shorter. Because we have chosen a Sunday the first hour starting at 04.33 a.m. should be assigned to the Sun, the other hours then following in rotation throughout the day and night until the next dawn when the system resets. On Monday morning when the Sun rose at 04.31 a.m. the first hour would be assigned to the Moon.

Each morning starts with the hour corresponding to the day and descends in rotation through the day. The order of the rotating planets is Saturn, Jupiter, Mars, Sun, Venus, Mercury, Moon. This echoes the order of the spheres upon the Kabbalistic tree of life Binah, Chesed, Geburh, Tipheret, Netzach, Hod, Yesod.

Sunrise/Sunset	Sunday	Monday	Tuesday	Wednesday	Thursday	Friday	Saturday
1	Sun	Moon	Mars	Mercury	Jupiter	Venus	Saturn
2	Venus	Saturn	Sun	Moon	Mars	Mercury	Jupiter
3	Mercury	Jupiter	Venus	Saturn	Sun	Moon	Mars
4	Moon	Mars	Mercury	Jupiter	Venus	Saturn	Sun
5	Saturn	Sun	Moon	Mars	Mercury	Jupiter	Venus
6	Jupiter	Venus	Saturn	Sun	Moon	Mars	Mercury
7	Mars	Mercury	Jupiter	Venus	Saturn	Sun	Moon
8	Sun	Moon	Mars	Mercury	Jupiter	Venus	Saturn
9	Venus	Saturn	Sun	Moon	Mars	Mercury	Jupiter
10	Mercury	Jupiter	Venus	Saturn	Sun	Moon	Mars
11	Moon	Mars	Mercury	Jupiter	Venus	Saturn	Sun
12	Saturn	Sun	Moon	Mars	Mercury	Jupiter	Venus

Working with all seven planets in balance with the Sun in centre of a six-pointed star of interlocking heaven and Earth, Sunday and the Sun is the natural choice seeking to climb the ladder of lights seeking self-illumination and the divine light that shines in darkness.

Exercises

1. Look for planets in the night sky. The five brightest planets are Venus, Mars, Mercury, Jupiter and Saturn and they can regularly be seen by the naked eye. They are visible for most of the year, except for intervals when they are too close to the Sun to observe. Venus for example is visible as the morning or evening star most of the year except for a few days when she dips below the horizon before rising again.

2. Find the position of the Moon in your birth chart. Do the same for your other close family members especially children. This is the key to understanding where our natural emotional needs are as the Moon governs water, emotions and feelings. Someone with the Moon in Virgo may need things to be ordered and on time at home in order to feel secure and happy and to function well for example.

Part Three
Practical Magic

Part Three: practical magic looks at the more involved action and doing aspects of magic. It also considers forms of physical, emotional and psychic self-protection, the different types of casting sacred space and ways of connecting with spirit. There are development tools for writing and designing prayers, ceremonies, rituals and spells specific to the individual with examples given of some in various contexts and instructions as to how to construct complementary aspects into one whole using a number of cultural and spiritual pathways.

Chapter Fifteen
Physical and Emotional Self-protection and Well Being

"What matters is how quickly you do what your soul directs."

Rumi

Good magic is safe magic. At least primarily for all things have risks. That is to say that it seems sensible to think things through well, do them with light and love and to take the necessary precautions to ensure well-being and safety as much as is possible. This is part of good judgement or essential discernment. It's taking care of ourselves. Looking at all the physical practical things we can do to protect ourselves helps us to create a healthy happy space for ourselves. This principle begins as most things do in the way we live our physical lives. There is no point in looking to spiritual, psychic or magical protection until we have taken care of the basic practicalities of our emotional and psychological well-being and assessed who and what we are choosing to share our lives with. Are we making ourselves happy? Do we shine? Are we living well? Are we aligned with Love?

We are creations of Love and there is no stronger force. Love is powerful, we are powerful and love is all. When we remember this we are able to stand in our light and be our authentic selves.

It is true that we live in a world of duality, as it is intended to be in this three-dimensional reality between the poles of the cosmic pillars of creation. This is the world of yin-yang, of positive and negative, dark and light, good and evil, right and wrong. This duality allows us to learn, feel and experience emotions and lessons that develop our soul's expansion. It also teaches us to learn how to work with, clear and protect against negative forces. Part of our growth could include learning how to be in the presence of difficult relationships and harsh circumstances and somehow to hold ourselves in okayness and not okayness. Part of our growth may be learning how to remove ourselves from harsh circumstances and disentangle from drama filled or damaging relationships and to understand that our first duty of care is to look after ourselves and our children. That everything else is secondary to that. Deciding which circumstances are which comes down to discernment.

Even though we live in this world of duality the most important thing to remember is not to go into a place of fear and fearful energy because there are things to protect from. Instead protection should come from a place of love, self-worth and confidence to assert necessary boundaries.

Some people, such as empaths and intuitives, are highly sensitive to their spiritual and physical environment. As a person's psychic awareness increases it is likely that their sensitivity may also increase in response. This is a necessary and in fact healthy and beneficial ability, as the extra sensory perceptions become faster and have greater capacity. All animals have this ability in fact as do babies, it is only lost to us through desensitisation. Everyone has a degree of sensitivity and awareness and anyone can be affected positively or negatively by the people around them and with whom they choose to engage either through influence or absorption. Everyone has had an experience where people around them or the environment they are in has had a direct part in cheering them up or bringing them down. A sensitive and feeling nature is part of our power and not a sign of weakness though it may be misconstrued to be by some. It takes great strength to feel everything intensely and still choose to feel. It takes great courage to feel everything deeply and to trust intuition based upon those feelings. Feelings are there to be felt and to tell us something. Listening to them is part of good judgement.

All solid matter is, as we know, vibrating energy. Vibrational frequencies, energy and resonance of all visible matter make up our known world. We experience this in human form continually and this is the basis of healing modalities of numerous civilisations in myriad ways. Different examples can be found in Ayurvedic medicine, Chinese medicine, Bach flower essences and all vibrational medicine and reiki. Everything is energy from our thought patterns and dreams to our brainwaves, the physical earth under our feet and the air in our lungs, including all other waveforms such as gamma waves. This includes extra sensory perceptions and what may we have come to know as paranormal activity.

Our minds act as transmitters and receivers of vibrational energy. By training our minds to interpret and become aware of outside vibrational stimulus we can help expand our knowledge and understanding of the world. We do this by receiving inbound energy frequencies as well as sending outbound energy frequencies. In addition to this when one person thinks of a thought or image this can be transmitted to another person, internalised and reordered by their mind into a similar thought or image. We've all had that experience where we think of something and one of our loved ones says the exact thing we were thinking of a few minutes later. This ability to send and share thought forms and images by mind is known as telepathy. Telepathy can also extend from our own plane of existence, and transcend into other dimensions allowing us to connect and communicate through vibration with Spirit. Our own energy affects those around us. We all know if we're sad we can accidentally make the dog feel sad too! Therefore it seems important to consciously put good out into the world where possible because harmful energies affect others and draw similar ones towards them. (See the chapter 8, Seven Universal Principles.)

There is a clear distinction here between harmful energies and those emotions such as sadness which may be mislabelled as negative. All emotions are here to tell us something helpful and to be felt and experienced and they are not negative as such. Harmful energies or forces are specifically those things of a low frequency that are damaging or toxic. Positive and negative, yin and yang, masculine and feminine, all expressions of natural force can be either beneficial or harmful dependent upon whether they are in balance, healthy and harmonious. Imbalance is the usual cause of shadow. Forces working in opposition to good orderly direction or with the sole purpose of pulling another off course are those that are harmful and toxic.

One of the most important things when it comes to learning both emotional and psychic self-protection is developing the ability to recognise and distinguish between different energies and thought forms and between what is real and/or imagined. As in life learning what is good, bad, genuine or false is necessary and comes down to good judgement. The blessing though is that with a little practice this need not take a long time to learn or be difficult because when we pay attention to our divine guidance and listen to our body's reactions we will receive loud and clear feelings and information that we can choose to act upon. In this chapter we will look at the ways in which we can receive this divine guidance, the ways in which we may detect different energies in our lives, how we might become more aware of them and the steps we can take to do something positive to effect good changes.

Whilst it is true that we may seek to become non-judgemental of others on one hand it is also true that we do still have a very real need to make judgements for our own well-being on the other. Part of life is making healthy choices and using good discernment and magically speaking this is particularly important when it comes to deciding what work to do and also who to work with.

The Astral

The Astral realms contain the thought forms of all other beings on the planet and all spirit beings passing through, influencing or communicating with those on the planet. Effectively this is an electromagnetic astral soup with billions of thought forms and spirits. For the psychic the ability to distinguish between what is genuine and what is imaginary, what is benevolent and what is unsafe and the knowledge to shield ourselves, particularly if we are of a sensitive nature is valuable. Firstly we can listen to our divine guidance. Secondly and just as importantly we can learn to develop and help ourselves and take positive action by working on our abilities of good judgement and protecting ourselves by increasing the beneficial and removing the harmful. The first step that can facilitate this process is identifying the causes of good and harm or positive and negative in terms of how we choose to live.

If the astral is predominantly thought forms we need to pay attention to which thought forms we are connecting with in order to navigate well. People who don't watch frightening movies or play violent video games for example have far fewer nasty images stored in the mind and are less likely to attract similar energies. They are therefore much more likely to be able to distinguish should they see an image of something genuine. However, for someone who watches horror movies regularly it would likely be much harder to differentiate between a lower frequency form or an imagined nasty from a film. This is not to say that cathartic release cannot be found in loud music or sensationalist films. It's just a matter of how consciously we are using those things and in what way. Again it's about judgement. Can we rock out loudly at the top of our voice? Well yes it can probably do us good. But should we do it when we know it's bringing us down or making us angry, may not be advisable. If every thought form and image makes up the astral soup it pays to be aware of who and what we let into our homes and keep company with. It makes for a lot less filtering.

Shadow

Just as the purpose of God/Goddess is towards good orderly direction in our lives, helping us to fulfil our life purpose and move towards happiness, the purpose of lower frequency things is simply to cause disorder and move away from good orderly direction, wobbling us off course out of fear because of the light we are bringing to the planet. Evil primarily tries to work through us and other people by trying to get in, either through influences around us or absorption of things around us therefore we need to clear these forces away. They are the opposite of divine guidance and are best not connected with or engaged with in any way for the main motivation is to sway us off our path, distract us from our purpose, corrupt and pull us downward, effecting negative change.

In spiritual truth of course all power comes from God/Goddess. We are hugely powerful beings because we have a part of God/Goddess within us, it is inherent, eternal and we are connected to heaven. It is not really possible for us to lose this power and even when we give it away temporarily it is illusionary in that it still belongs to us to take back. Our job then is to reclaim any power we've inadvertently given away temporarily, keep our focus and not give our time or energy to lower things because we need that time and energy for ourselves for good use and fulfilling our life purpose.

We all have light and dark and shades of grey and every conceivable colour of the rainbow within us and the potential to choose of our free will which parts we will encourage, work on, develop, heal, bring into balance and so on. It is important that we recognise our own shadows because otherwise we cannot be real with ourselves, we may slip into victim mentality and self-delusion or project them onto others. To progress or grow we must acknowledge these parts and lovingly correct, accept, nurture as appropriate. Our emotions are just energy in motion, like the weather passing through us. Ignorance is not bliss and running and ignoring our shadow will not lighten it.

Instead let us lay claim to these parts of ourselves and open up the internal dialogue of energies, because when we no longer shrink away from the depths of ourselves we can choose to bring in love and gain deeper understanding.

The shadow is also that part we that know as the Ego. The ego is not all bad and in many ways tries to protect us. However, it may do this too effectively and can become out of balance. The imbalanced ego works through the mind by running fearful thoughts and comparisons that give the feelings and illusion of separation, convincing us that we are separate from God/Goddess or somehow inferior or superior to others. In other words it creates divisions. In reality it is in direct opposition with our soul truth which is that we are One, we are Love and we are connected. Buddhist belief recognises this predisposition towards altruism and gentleness as something with which we are born and that other more harmful behaviours are developed later and come solely from the mind. Fundamentally then the work to be done is working with the axis of the love fear poles and cultivating the one that is beneficial to us in all circumstances. We must learn to love what makes us happy and balanced.

Healthy loving people are generally happier and seldom plagued by dark forces because there is nothing of interest for them to be attracted to or feed on. They are also significantly less vulnerable to their influence. This is particularly important for those who work magic because ultimately the natural forces that we work with are powerful emanations of God/Goddess and we will not be able to hold and direct them safely if we are not in balance, grounded and well protected. Certainly the more advanced the types of work being undertaken by the practitioner the greater the need for protection and the more necessary to take precaution in preparation as a preventative measure. It is also true that there are certain types of magic that are dangerous without being done in higher service or with a spiritual and/or religious lifeline. Perhaps then our best bet is to aim for happiness of the real variety rather than fleeting pleasures in life and it is towards being happy that we must orientate ourselves. To do that we need to look to our relationships firstly with God/Goddess, with Nature and how we interact with the world around us, with our relationship to ourselves and with our relationships with others.

Relationships with Others

Our relationships with other people are our main connections in the world, and to the world whether that is with our family members, friends or partners. The people we spend time with affect us emotionally and energetically and influence our experiences in life. We feel their influence and we may take on or share characteristics with the people we spend the most time with. Others form our reflections, our comfort and support systems. They are our equals, our peers, our source of shared interests and commonality, our sounding boards and confidantes. Having good people around us really does make all the difference in the world and people with good friendship groups and supportive families are generally happier in life and have better health. With our focus upon happiness and well-being then it is important we choose our friends wisely, that we nurture our friendships and relationships with those we love and want to spend time with and that we also do any necessary weeding or pruning where any of our relationships are imbalanced or in need of redressing or releasing.

If a relationship is making us unhappy or pulling us off our path and distracting us from our purpose or draining us so that we have less energy for our purpose, our well-being or to spend time with people who make us really happy or doing things that make us really happy it is worth reviewing it. When we hold onto people that are no longer good for us we can sometimes inadvertently harm ourselves by putting up with behaviours that aren't good for us. Something to consider is that those people who are givers in life must be the ones who set the limits and appropriate boundaries for themselves because those people who are takers in life rarely will.

Warning Signs

These questions are intended for identifying persistent and repetitive negative patterns and behaviours and to help us recognise our true feelings in order that we can then make positive changes and establish better boundaries.

Am I relaxed with this person and do I feel safe?
Is there any anxiety or tightness in my body?
Do I look forward to seeing them or am I apprehensive?

Can I express my opinions honestly or do I sensor myself?
Do I often feel drained, ill or exhausted when this person visits or leaves?
Do I feel respected and valued by this person?
Are they thoughtful towards me and my personal space or home?
Do I feel overpowered, overshadowed or undermined with them?
Do they respect my privacy or do they push my boundaries?
Do I sometimes feel like I want to avoid them or leave?
Do I feel sad or worried when they are around?
Am I feeling bored or like I'm wasting time when I'm with them?
Do I feel frustrated or angry with them or with myself? If so why?
Is this person always having some kind of drama?
Do they gossip, lie or skew the truth about me or others?
Do I feel put upon, unloaded on or talked over?
Do they say or imply hurtful things or are there unspoken undercurrents?
Do they behave the same in private as they do in public and vice versa?

Even when the mind is confused the soul knows and will tell us truthfully.

The most important questions:
Is this an equal and two directional relationship?
Do I feel good when I am with this person and after they leave?
Am I happy when I am with them?
Do they bring me closer to living my life purpose or away from it?
Do I like myself when I'm with them?
Is love the foundation of this friendship?

Positive Change

Once we've looked at what's going on with our relationships we can make better-informed decisions about what to do. In the case of family members or people we genuinely love and want to keep in our lives this might mean looking for solutions, doing some damage limitation and effecting positive changes. With others it may be that after consideration we need to do some pruning. Letting someone go from our lives does not have to be traumatic on either part and we can do this kindly and lovingly whilst remaining in our power. It may be that we gradually drift apart naturally or that we have a definitive moment and honest discussion about why we are moving on. We have the right to choose how we spend the limited time and energy we have on Earth and who we spend them with.

Often when we tolerate behaviours from others that are not good for us it is because we want the other person to still like or love us and we are afraid of losing their love if we complain. We therefore put up with all sorts of things that make us unhappy and are not good for us. It could also be that we want to avoid confrontation and we don't want to tell this person to stop or change their behaviour. Of course when we do this the reality is that we are not being real or genuine with them because we are lying to them in a way rather than being honest about our feelings. Consequently that person may not know how their behaviour makes us feel and they may not know us as a person either because we haven't given them the chance to get to know our true nature. In addition to that by allowing bad behaviour towards us we don't do the other person any favours in the long run because by being complicit with it we enable and encourage the behaviour and stop any possibility of growth or responsibility on their part. An example of this is the person we make excuses for. Those excuses only enable the behaviour and on some level rob the other person of a chance to develop. It's far more loving to tell someone we are not prepared to put up with any more of x or y or z because it's kinder to ourselves and them. They may not have been aware of their behaviour. Or if they are it becomes apparent that it is deliberate and moving on becomes a much simpler decision.

The flip side of this is recognising that a lot of these behaviours are caused for the same reason. The person who is controlling or manipulative or attention seeking almost certainly wants to be liked and loved too. These behaviours are just insecurities that are presenting this way. With regards our own negative behaviours too which we touched on when discussing owning our shadow, this is true also. We all have egos, we all have fear and we are not robots so we probably have some behaviours we could do with working on and they are probably being driven out of a fear that we will not be liked or loved unless we are better than, slimmer than, sweeter than, stronger than etc.

Once we see that all these dysfunctional behaviours are being driven out of a fear of losing or obtaining love it's far easier to see the situation compassionately. That being said whilst we can view the other and ourselves with compassion our job is to work towards well-being and happiness by learning to honour our emotional and physical needs. By extension we may perhaps also teach the people we are in relationship with, or they may teach us, the way to do the same.

Tips for Establishing Boundaries

It is possible to be powerful and honest and to stand in our truth in a loving way that is assertive without being aggressive or unkind in any way. Being "nice" is not the same thing as being loving. When we stand in our truth and establish good boundaries we respect ourselves because we honour our true feelings and we respect the other person because we consider them worth the time and effort to be real and genuine with them. We also show them that it is safe for them to stand in their truth too.

Energy in our relationships needs to be a two-directional, equal or nearly equal exchange and in balance to remain healthy. How much time and energy are we giving to that person? Are we giving them too much or more than we really want to? If so can we cut back a little and work out what would be better for us such as making it clear in advance that we need to leave by three. By doing this we have set the boundaries of the time parameters in advance. We leave feeling happy to have seen our friend and not tired out or put upon. Sometimes saying "No" or "I'm busy, I'm tired, I don't know", or Can I have time to think about that?" is a good thing and saves us from perpetually giving our time and energy away. I had "I'll have to think about that and get back to you" taped above my telephone for a year once!

Everyone has needs and no one should have to feel that they owe anyone else an explanation for this. Justifying ourselves makes us feel accountable to another when we are not and reduces our feelings of security and authority. It's okay to say, "Thank you but no thank you, that doesn't work for me", or a simple "No", without explaining why. All animals and children do this instinctively all the time without thinking about it. They are honest and haven't learned false politeness at their own expense as a result of conditioning. Perhaps as adults we may phrase things differently than we would have done but we are as entitled as we were as children to say no and not to have to feel bad about it. If the tables were turned and we were the one who were doing the asking would we want the other person to say yes even when we knew they really didn't want to?

Good communication is the key to most healthy relationships. Communicating our experience can be worth the risk even if it's scary and we are afraid of the outcome because it is the only way that we are likely to effect positive change. Expressing ourselves is the only way the other person can understand us or get to know us. Doing nothing is the same as saying everything is fine exactly the way it is! If we don't say anything or change anything when we're unhappy there's a good chance we'll leave in the end anyway. If having this conversation feels daunting writing notes beforehand can help or we could write a letter. By being courageous and saying something we open up new possibilities and dynamics. Even small changes can be the catalysts to effect big changes. If we are ever in a relationship where we feel so scared we are unable to express ourselves we need to seriously question whether this is one we want to remain in. At other times in life a little distance and breathing room from the friendship or relationship might help to gain perspective. Things can look a lot clearer from a distance or after some time to recharge and recover.

Sometimes there might be times where we do speak up and say something, even perhaps repeatedly and the other person doesn't change their behaviour. At this point we must do what is necessary to take care of ourselves even if that means moving away from them. Even if the other person does not like what we have to say at least we will know we have done what is necessary to love and take care of ourselves. This in turn creates feelings of self-worth and security. By establishing clear boundaries we protect and respect ourselves and we show that we consider the other person worth taking the risk of being honest with them even if they don't like it. The people we do have in our lives will know that they are there because we feel loved and respected by them and we in turn value them and love and respect them too.

Like the tree in the forest, each person we are connected to is connected through their own root systems and myriad of leaves to hundreds of others. Occasionally and certainly in a psychic sense it is worth having an awareness of who and what we are connecting with and in turn what they are connecting with. This discernment is just a part of making good healthy judgements and decisions for our own well-being. Yet whilst choosing what is good for us we need also to be tolerant of others and their viewpoints and compassionate in our view of others and so these two must be weighed and balanced and tempered. The Temperance card of the tarot comes to mind.

Steps to Help Clean, Clear and De-Clutter

Our well-being and happiness requires us to take the steps necessary to look after ourselves whether that is through going to the dentist, paying the bills, getting a massage, reorganising our diaries so that we have more relaxation time or consciously developing healthy good friendships.

Learning to tune into our bodies and our mind allows us to feel our true feelings and sensations which are an accurate barometer and are there for a reason. When we give ourselves permission and time to pay attention to them and to honour them rather than dismiss them it will always pay off. If there is a tightness or discomfort in the body it is also there for a reason. Effectively the body is a highly sensitive vibrational instrument in tune to the energies around us.

Resentment is one of the primary causes of emotional and physical discomfort. When it's directed at ourselves it may show up as guilt or when it's directed at another it could show up as frustration, anger or sadness. Releasing resentments can also be thought of as practising compassion and forgiveness. Forgiveness allows us to see ourselves and others in a compassionate light and to let go of holding on to blame. Blame for making the choices we have made where it didn't turn out as we had hoped, blame directed at others for not being or doing what we had hoped and blame directed at life for circumstances we couldn't control. Forgiveness and compassion eases and releases these hurts. Forgiving someone or something doesn't mean that the behaviour or action is now acceptable; it just means that we don't need to hold onto it. We can see it is not our business what someone else says or does. We can now see that we were doing the best we could at the time with the knowledge we had. We shift our thoughts to love and love lets go.

De-cluttering the mind could be thought of as changing worries and anxieties into prayers. Instead of worrying which is low energy and aligns us with problems, we can choose to ask for guidance and assistance and align ourselves with solutions. Counting the blessings and the good things in life also helps because it creates an upwards-positive flow of thought which is more likely to bring solutions. Other times when we don't know how to stop the worrying or anxieties it may be that allowing our emotions and acknowledging the worry or anxiety is the way to go. Seeing ourselves in a compassionate light as someone who is doing their best and loving ourselves despite feeling a certain way or worrying, can have a strange effect of dissolving and melting away the worry or at the least supporting ourselves better and more kindly. Some things in life that are hard help us gain strength and understanding even if it might not feel like it at the time. This is often true of the healer, the shaman, the priestess, the initiate. Knowing this on any level can help. Knowing too that all things come to pass.

Physically de-cluttering! Remove any unnecessary clutter. If it hasn't been used for ages and no longer serves a purpose then sell it, recycle it, give it to someone who will appreciate it. Physical clutter attracts psychic clutter and a clean ordered house with plenty of light and fresh air will always have a better flow of clean energy. Messy spaces can get stagnant and attract unwelcome things. It doesn't need to be immaculate but taking the time to open the windows once a day and air the house and give it a good clean even once a week will keep those energies moving and bright! The Chinese have a whole system called Feng Shui based upon the principles designed to maximise and balance energetic flow and movement. Cleaning really does work on many levels too and it is common that many people find their state of mind shifting as they clean or in some cases that they feel the urge to clean when they shift their mindset!

Consciously avoiding dark games or oracles that are likely to connect with dark forces such as ouija boards. Ouija boards are one particularly dangerous way of connecting with spirits because they operate by indiscriminate summoning, so not only by demanding a presence but by doing so randomly with no filter and no care who or what they connect with in a mindless snatching or pulling. This act leaves an open doorway that the person using the thing may not know how to close. There are also certain oracle and tarot decks which work in a similar way and it is good to choose with discernment a safe and light deck from someone you trust. These boards are often marketed as games with no explanation as to how they operate. Even those practitioners who are experienced may well encounter problems with the ouija board or with dark decks of cards should they go wrong, often followed by long drawn out conversations about how to close doorways that have been opened or seeking out another to help. The person they approach then has to do a clear up operation or put themselves at risk. Dark cards decks are ones that specifically give frightening or negative messages and guidance and that connect with low frequencies. Far better to take preventative action and avoid such things, keeping a clear space.

There are other safer ways of communing with spirit, for example, using light card decks filled with positive and safe imagery and guidance or by spiritual invitation in a held secure space. For some this may involve looking for a reputable medium or clairvoyant. Others may have this ability naturally themselves already and others may choose to learn and develop the skill and undertake the study required to hold a sacred space and discern which messages to accept, by invitation and who to speak with. Whilst there are no set methods for learning to do this there are good practices of conduct and safety that can assist the practitioner. The fine tuning of the virtual radio dial and differentiating between spirits through what can only be described as their pitch of frequency is something which is learned over a prolonged period of time and not something which can be imparted in a book though there are things to look for. All beings and spirits have an individual harmonic resonance which we can come to recognise. The basic and obvious things, however, are the use of self-protection, a further held sacred space opened for the duration and later closed and most importantly that these things and any communication made should be done with respect and love. These same things are key when it comes to other magical workings and ritual. Whilst communicating with spirit and reading cards is part of the spiritual things such as physical card decks are tangible energy with which we connect and choose to have in our homes or not. Keep a clean and clear loving space.

Other things to be aware and make conscious decisions about are as we have already touched upon: music, imagery and media. Loud and discordant music with aggressive lyrics can increase fear, anger and anxiety. This is particularly true if the music is also coupled with dark imagery. Effectively these are the building blocks of ritual, music, words and images. Is it a ritual with which you want to connect? If not avoid it in favour of harmonious, fun, peaceful, upbeat, happy and positive music, with imagery that you like and which makes you feel good, and with people you want to be like and have around you. The exception is when such things are being used for cathartic release in a conscious way. Connections through other forms of media can also increase fear. People regularly watching horror movies, or watching violent or graphic news reports, or videos about terrorism, war or natural disasters can experience very real fear, terror and discomfort. Depression is higher in people who choose to regularly engage with these media. Clean, clear and de-clutter! The upside is that people who consciously work with higher frequency beings where the primary focus is love are likely to attract more of the same there too. Chances are these same people invest their time in positive pursuits and watch and listen to harmonic and uplifting or profound media that is likely to affect their spiritual, mental and physical health positively.

People who spend a lot of time watching recorded paranormal activity and shows about ghost hunting, especially where there is a lot of fear are more likely to draw these things towards themselves than those who do not. The ways in which these things can and do travel and connect with other people are not limited to physical doors or pathways. The doorways of the mind are sufficient as are pathways of transmission such as electrical current or WiFi.

Stop comparing and consider avoiding spending time with anyone who compares you to them or to others. Comparison is the tool of the ego and separation and gives rise to low frequency feelings of envy, greed and reduced empathy. It always divides and never brings happiness because there will always be one up or one down and it's not nice to be either. We all know someone with a superiority complex and we have all thought of ourselves as better in some way that someone else. Likewise we have all met someone who is constantly self-berating and we have all felt less than someone else. Neither is positive or useful and comparison is the root of almost all division between people. It divides families and nations and we don't need it. We are all created equal and unique and there can be no comparison.

Addictive behaviours are something we can detox from. Most of us have experienced addiction in some way or another whether it is as overeating, overdosing on caffeine or alcohol or anything else. Drugs, alcohol, smoking, gambling, pornography, overspending, overworking, keeping ourselves so busy we never sit still, or high stimulants such as sugar and caffeine can all be addictive. Nearly all addictive behaviours are the result of a desire to self-medicate feelings that are uncomfortable, overwhelming, painful or inconvenient to us in some way. Of course the truth is we need to feel those feelings and work through them and then the addictions will ease. So perhaps this small section should say instead be kind to yourself, be gentle with yourself, ask for support if you need it and give yourself permission and time to feel however you feel without censorship. When we do that the addictions may ease off.

Chemicals and pesticides that hurt us or the Earth. If it's poison we shouldn't eat it, or drink it, or spray it. It seems almost ridiculous to type. It seems beyond obvious and yet we do in our thousands every day. If it's poisonous we don't need to flush it into the water system or put it on Mother Earth. We can choose organic food, we can grow our own or buy from a farm shop or if money is difficult buy when reduced. GMOs and pesticides are optional; it is our choice if we wish to consume them. We can choose eco-friendly cleaning products and holistic bath and skin care products. Or we can make our own cleaning products and use baking soda, coconut oil, lemon juice, vinegar and essential oils like our grandmothers before us. We can choose to only use utilities from renewable energy companies. We can choose to buy organic meat from farms and buy a little less of it. Animals who have lived in distress their whole lives have that energy in their bodies not to mention all of the antibiotics they are fed because of the disease spreading conditions they are kept in. We can choose not to support their mass production. We can choose not to eat meat at all. When we don't think about our choices we support the current systems. The more we spend our money on ethical products the more notice big business takes. Over time this can effect positive changes. Everything we take in has a frequency and an energy that affects our life force and our energetic signature. We can reduce wherever possible the things we use or buy that are harmful.

Pollution in the home can extend to anything with an electromagnetic field such as any electrical items we have on standby or running in the background, WiFi signals and background noise. We can help this by simply turning them off at the wall when we go to bed or are not using them or by using crystals and other ways of purifying our space. These electromagnetic signals are often felt by sensitive people as are the effects of fluorescent lighting and computer screens. By reducing our home pollution we can give ourselves a cleaner space, deeper relaxation without high-pitched electrical noises in the background and better sleep patterns.

Any media that is demeaning or disrespectful is likely to lower frequency. Examples are those that are sexist and derogatory towards women, racist, discriminatory, inciting hatred or feelings of disrespect. Luckily it's as simple as "click" and we can choose to watch something uplifting, educational, funny or worthwhile in some way that is almost certainly going to make us happier.

Is there anything else in our personal space, our homes and our lives that we need to let go of? Do we need to clean the kitchen cupboards or burn paperwork from ten years ago?

We've started with the physical and the practical things in life first. This includes honouring our body. If spirit is within us and within all living things then our body is our temple because it carries our soul and our consciousness through life. Certainly, although temples, churches and other sacred sites can be beautiful and a positive place to come together, the true temple is within. The body is the point of connection for all of our parts, our soul, spirit, intellect, emotions and physical feelings and we need to treat it with respect, kindness and love which includes being kind to ourselves in how we view ourselves and our bodies. Not everyone is made in the likeness of Adonis or Venus. It's worth remembering the Goddess figures around the world are made in many slim and voluptuously curved shapes and sizes. Positive change effects positive change so it's always worth doing something to help, even a small movement in the right direction can gradually cause huge shifts to occur.

Are we doing what makes us happy? Are we being kind to ourselves?

At this point we have physically done everything possible on a practical earthly level to encourage light forces in our lives. These might also include the obvious things we can do to relax and recharge ourselves, such as time spent painting or reading, have a relaxing bath, cuddling the cat or the dog, walking in nature, stretching, exercising, writing our thoughts and feelings in a diary, meditating, singing or doing some other kind of artistic or creative hobby that we love. When we shine we are happy, we bring light to the world and we inspire others to do the same.

Assuming all these things are checked and in good balance and order and that we are aware of any areas we are currently working on, we may now look to other aspects of psychic protection.

Exercise – Observation of others.

This one can be quite fun though it must be used respectfully. Take yourself out to a cafe or somewhere for lunch or out for a walk and whist you're there observe the people around you. It is important to do so in a way that is psychically considerate and not intrusive in any way. Watching other people can be a great way to see the three aspects and parts of the whole. When we look at someone and wonder what were they like as a child and visualise them we can so often see the inner child still present. Likewise when we look at someone and wonder about their highest self and soul their divinity can become apparent to us. I have heard of this same approach being used to visualise others as angels. The expression Namaste feels appropriate which is an ancient Sanskrit greeting still in everyday use in India and in Nepal Himalaya. Translated roughly, it means, "I bow to the God within you", or "The Spirit within me salutes the Spirit in you" – a knowing that we are all made from the same One Divine Consciousness. It can feel so much easier and more natural to be compassionate and understanding towards others when we can see them in this way. It can also allow us to see the parts of ourselves in the same compassionate, kind and honourable way.

Chapter Sixteen
Practical Psychic Self-protection

Love is our Greatest Shield.

    Pray for protection, then act upon the guidance.

My temptation throughout this book is not to include harmful or evil forces at all for my attention would rather be focussed elsewhere, but they are included out of necessity because it is only in bringing light to the ways in which such things operate that they can be understood, avoided or protected from. It is through the silence of fear and lack of clear information that they primarily operate. Why would anyone avoid something without understanding thoroughly why. We explain to our children not to touch something hot because it will burn them. When we understand how something works we have a better basis from which to make a conscious and informed choice.

    Our focus then is to work with ascending light beings of love and truth and in so doing we remain in the bandwidth of love and are encoded by it in a way over the course of time. In any moment call for God/Goddess, Angels, benevolent guardians or spirit guides or goodness from any divine source and ask for help. They will be there!

    Just as with making good discernments in the practical areas of life it is common sense to take sensible precautions psychically speaking too. In the same way as we would put on the seatbelt before driving the car, there are some basic ABCs of psychic self-protection. Protection is the first of the purpose of the magic circle traditionally cast prior to any magical working.

    As we consider psychic self-protection our focus remains firmly upon Love.

The Nature of Duality

Three-dimensional life on Earth is one of duality and the spirit world as experienced from Earth is as a result also one of duality. In the higher planes and heaven we are One, at the highest vibration of perfect love and light but on Earth we are in contact with many different forces of nature and spiritual forms. In almost every culture various forms and depictions of evil exist upon the earthly plane. Earth is the cosmic filter through which all must pass and sits at the foot of the tree. From here we experience duality and it is only when we raise ourselves up higher on the planes that we may escape the pains of the lower ones and be at One. Our focus then is partly on how to raise our vibration and avoid contact with low frequencies and partly on casting light on these lower frequency things so that we can understand how they operate and protect ourselves.

The spirit world is a complete reflection of life on Earth and in addition reflects other parts of the cosmos and includes some beings at higher or lower vibrational frequencies. The One Divine source that is God/Goddess is the highest loving frequency there is. Any Gods and Goddesses called with loving intention or representative of beneficial forces are also at this high frequency of spirit. Those we call Angels operate at a very high frequency too as the messengers of God. Angels, although they were not necessarily recognised by the older European pagan religions, do appear throughout many other cultures and religions throughout the world. Over time they have been incorporated by some following neo-pagan paths in much the same way that early Anglo-Saxon and Celtic Christianity blended and merged with the older religions. Various other higher frequency beings include certain types of fairies, wights (landvaettir) who are guardians of specific places they reside, nature spirits, elementals and other loving, light beings such as spirit guides. There are seven gradations of the planes reaching from Earth to heaven. The heavens are also said to have seven planes and these are divided or multiplied by further gradations of seven.

There are also lower frequency planes stretching below the cosmic filter of Earth in the shadow of the tree and these are the realms of lower frequency entities or unstable forces. There are some examples of Gods and Goddesses or religious practices that are aligned with harmful or lower frequency energies. Generally to identify them look at whether they are primarily concerned with promoting good and acting with love or causing harm and promoting fear. There are also many natural forces personified as Gods that may act for good or for harm depending upon their own priority or depending upon the intention of the initiate working magic. For example a God representing death can be called in a loving way to help transition and to safely carry a soul over at the end of a life or can be called to help with letting go of a situation in life at the end of a relationship. These are beneficial causes. The same natural forces could be called by someone working in a harmful way towards damaging or selfish ends. In these cases it comes down to intention. That same God may be willing to support a ritual that in some way benefits the land or may actively work against one that does not.

There is a clear difference between harmful forces and necessary destructive forces. The much needed destroying aspect of Geburah acts as a necessary disinfectant breaking down and removing anything toxic and can be employed in the removal of harm. This healthful breaking down destructive aspect can be seen in numerous aspects of the crone Goddess and in most deities associated with Death. Death and destruction is a necessary and healthy part of life without which there could be no cycles or rhythms and all would stagnate.

Higher Frequency Forces

We have already discussed how differences in frequency are determined often by levels of spiritual awakening and being. People often describe higher frequency beings as having a brighter aura and resonance. Generally those who are more spiritually awakened work at a higher frequency than those who are just beginning their journey or awakening. Buddhists call this process seeking enlightenment. This is the soul journey. Just as souls pass from life to life and are recycled through death and birth until such time as enlightenment or union is achieved energy can never be destroyed exactly just recycled by God/Goddess and transformed. Learning to raise our frequency lifts and allows us access to higher realms with more evolved entities.

Higher frequency beings such as angels or other light and good forces come down into manifestation to help into the physical world though the process of the Tree of Life. We all do in a way, however the tree can also in some ways be seen as an existential map or ladder leading back to and from God/Goddess. There are also masters and yogis and spiritual teachers who are of a higher vibrational level who choose to dematerialise into human form in order to incarnate and help on Earth.

When we are working in our truth and in a place of Love we are always protected by God/Goddess, and when we follow our divine guidance it is inevitable that good will be the outcome. We are also protected by the Divine Law as anything outside of it is operating in a different band width or frequency. It is important to know that as we get stronger and our frequency increases, the brighter we become and consequently the more visible we are to everything that we come into contact with. This is another reason to consider what we are connecting with and how and to make good choices where possible. Whilst that high frequency loving energy protects us and we certainly don't want to go into fear about anything it is true to say that it becomes increasingly important to take precautions for protection from lower forces that would like us not to bring in so much light! Taking these precautions also makes it easier for heavenly and good forces to help and support us because it's much easier when we're working with them!

Lower Frequency Forces

Lower frequency forces, entities or beings can come up from the shadow of the Tree of Life or from outside its existence either to learn lessons seeking genuine reconciliation and development or to do harm in some way. Lower frequency energies are specifically those aligned with fear and harm. These should be avoided wherever possible and not communicated with. There are also less harmful things operating at low frequency which are commonly caused by a serious or long term imbalance or damage but these should still be treated with caution.

All things in creation within the universe are made by Divinity from One source. The decision taken then to remain in separation from Divinity also brings universal exclusion and separation. The illusion of separation then is only ever about choosing not to be One with the Divine source or to return to Love. Lower frequency or dark forces who choose separation effectively no longer have a place in the universal whole which is One and are therefore outside of it somehow and this is what we may understand as various concepts of the word hell, the depictions and theosophical concepts of which vary across culture but remain essentially centred around separation from divinity.

These realms are those we may understand to be the gradations of the shadow of the Tree of Life. Ultimately it is worth remembering that both duality and time only exists here and that to God/Goddess both are irrelevant. If and when the end of days come all things created go back to God/Goddess and back to Source and become One for there was never really anything else in existence anyway. Love is the Law and Love is all.

Any system of magic which is clearly operating without love may be considered to be outside of this law and any form of magic that comes from a place of fear or distress should be avoided as the consequences may cause more of the same, for like attracts like and the pursuing of such paths particularly over prolonged periods of time may be detrimental to the well-being of the practitioner, physically, emotionally and psychically.

Be clear about making informed choices based upon understanding and clear out, remove or avoid anything which might be harmful. Books which suggest deliberate calling and working with demonic or lower frequency spirits are an example of this. So too are those whose primary instruction is to encourage service only to one's self and belief in one's self only at the expense or denial of all that is divine in any form. These works may appeal directly to the ego and disguise their true nature under the guise of a measured argument. There are hundreds of books some of which are quite famous and widely available that suggest the practitioner connect with lower forces or denounce God/Goddess or the sacred in nature in favour of self. To the inexperienced, young or naive they might seem sensationalist or thrilling.

Lower frequency forces and entities can be dangerous in more ways than one and ignorance is not bliss in this regard in that it affords little protection. The fact is that a deliberate choice has been made and the act done knowingly which affords the practitioner less help in the event that it should go wrong and as with other such things may have karmic implications later.

These things work against good orderly direction and against love. Knowingly working dark magic or walking these pathways through choice can and does often cause damage to the worker psychologically or spiritually. It causes damage to the soul by disconnecting from Spirit or God/Goddess. It causes damage to the psyche as over prolonged periods of time this way of thinking takes hold and becomes embedded and fixated in self-interest and self-service. It causes damage to the body as many who are functioning in this embodiment of negativity draw like towards them, like attracts like, feelings manifest into physical health as any homoeopathist will tell you.

Identifying Signs of Possible Lower Frequency Energies

The most common sign of lower frequency energies is sudden depression that comes out of the blue or for no apparent reason when time has been taken to listen to our feelings, there is no obvious cause and we are not suffering from clinical depression. Likewise with feelings of anger or rage that are unfounded and out of character.

Thoughts and feelings that cause distress, discomfort, unease, worry or other unpleasant reactions. To be clear this is not including any issues which we have avoided working on or that we know to affect us anyway. It is important to differentiate. This is one of the reasons for doing our own shadow work because without having done so we cannot recognise what is our own stuff and what is coming from elsewhere, or if an outside cause is affecting an inner one.

Negative or frightening images in dreams or imagination that come out of nowhere or start fearful chains of thought that we would not usually have. (Far easier to identify and eliminate if we generally avoid TV with excessive nasty imagery.)

Extreme tiredness without any logical explanation where there is no physical or emotional health condition.

Resistance to meeting normal needs and taking care of oneself such as not sleeping when tired or eating when hungry.

Harmful behaviours that are against self-love, such as over spending to the extent that rent or other important needs cannot be met. Especially if it is out of character.

Sore throats, raised temperature and other symptoms that tell you your immune system is fighting something off when there is no other cause of illness. This does not apply if it is usual, everyone is different. With all physical or psychological illness always seek a medical opinion or support before eliminating it.

Electrical items, especially internet connections and mobile telephones that either do random things or connect you with things you have not chosen of your own free will to engage with particularly if they are of an unpleasant nature.

Electrical items that are faulty and temperamental which are not normally. When there are more than one or two items and you have checked mercury isn't retrograde. This can be a sign of possible spirit activity but not necessarily dangerous.

The dog barks at something you can't see or the cat hisses and seems on edge at something.

You feel uncomfortable, uneasy or frightened suddenly and with no logical explanation. Often combined with the feeling you'd like to leave a place or get out of the room or the house.

Things that physically move such as doors opening or the light shade swinging. Sometimes this is called poltergeist activity.

Items that move and disappear regularly (only applicable provided your home is in order and you know where you left them!). For example a figurine is always on the left of your windowsill and now it's on the right or somewhere else. You have checked with family or anyone who has been to visit that it was not them and/or this happens regularly. This could include continual losing of things or finding things that have moved and are not where you left them. Pay particular attention if this is an item from your altar or a magical item that feels like it may have been tampered with.

Some low frequency spirits are accompanied by unpleasant odours such as sulphur or gas. Check there is no physical gas leak. Other spirits may also be accompanied by smells but are not necessarily low frequency or harmful in any way.

Infestations of insects in your home which are unusual and frequent where you have made sure there is nothing attracting them. Try to deal with the problem humanely but remove it.

Accidents or unpleasant happenings if and when there is more than one of them, they are unusual in some way, or accompanied by uneasy or heavy feelings.

Nightmares and bad dreams where you have been battling and fighting or where something dark threatens you or hurts you in some way. You have taken care to consider first and eliminate honestly any current cause of distress or hidden meaning. These dreams feel different and can give the same sensation as astral travel. The person then wakes feeling exhausted as though they have not slept or are more tired than when they went to bed. This is often accompanied by a woozy feeling like a head full of water. Everyone experiences this differently but once you know your own reactions it's easier to identify. These are symptoms of psychic attack or battle.

Always wash the bedding, air out the room and have a warm salt bath if you can to clear the space so you don't sleep in the same energy again.

Physical pains that come out of the blue and are not accompanied by any medical or physical explanation. If they persist always go to the doctor to check! These may or may not be accompanied by the thought of a person who is upset or angry towards us on some level or by an image of something else unpleasant. It is worth remembering that a lot of psychic mud-slinging happens between people at a sub-conscious level and if this is just from someone who's upset it can probably be easily resolved and protected from. More serious pains or things from lower frequency beings are more serious but can also be protected from.

Anything or anyone declaring "holy war" or committing atrocities in the name of God is acting from a place of fear and low frequency and untruth. God/Goddess are Love and it is peace which is holy.

The possibilities are endless and often vary from person to person so ultimately it's up to each of us to recognise what is normal for us and in our home and to make note of patterns. Experiencing a combination of these on the same day, or in a short amount of time especially if they are not regular occurrences can help us see what is happening. It becomes clearer as we learn to tune-in our awareness.

Our job then is to align with Love and with healthful good forces that promote well-being and raise our vibration.

Identifying Signs of High Frequency Energies

High frequency energies aligned with love present in many ways too and it is equally important if not more important to notice them. This is how we tune in to our guidance and align with supportive and good orderly forces.

Sudden or increased feelings of safety, security and love often accompanied by peacefulness, serenity, laughter, and connectedness.

Having positive thoughts, being able to see the big picture, dreaming big, having good visions and the belief and support to act upon them.

Engaging in joyful and healthy behaviours aligned with love, self-respect, care and compassion for ourselves and others.

Electrical items and technology that somehow instantly connects us with exactly who and what we need to help us on our path. For example a workshop or an invitation to the very thing we were thinking of that pops up in our news feed.

Content relaxed animals that display signs of love and feelings of security.

Finding things easily and without problem when we ask.

Manifesting things easily when we ask, from car parking spaces to other opportunities.

Synchronicities that come out of the blue!

Pleasant smells and odours such as incense, flowers or other plants when there is no other obvious source of the smell.

Silver sparkles or light sparkles in the air surrounding us or someone else. (When there is no other source of optical illusion.) This looks different anyway and there is no mistaking the two. Sparkles are usually a sign of a loving spirit or angels.

Butterflies, beetles, ladybirds, bees or other insects accompanied by warm feelings or a sense of blessing.

Having seemingly good luck and a sense of knowing all will work out.

Sleeping well and soundly and having good dreams and visionary dreams and messages.

Recurring number sequences imparting a meaning (see the chapter on number and sacred geometry).

Visible signs, sometimes literally physical signs that appear and give direction when we need them. Just ask for them.

The feeling we are being helped, guided and supported even and especially at difficult times.

There are many more and these also vary from person to person. The more we pay attention the clearer they become.

Align with the natural flows and cycles

The collective beliefs of many people or the will of many people may create a finite quantity of a thing. Examples of this might be that an old prayer that has been spoken many times before is likely to hold resonance and effect more than a new unuttered prayer by the collective quantity of times it has been spoken and the intentions of all who have ever uttered its words. It is the spiritual difference between addition and multiplication resulting in amplification.

When there is war on earth it is likely a reflection of the consciousness of a great number of people and a symptom of those societies engaged in it. It may also therefore have a finite quantity at the time, hence although it may be stoppable in one area it may likely arise in another for the quantity has not changed. Better then to speak with prayers of peace than attempt to work against its opposite. This is a strong example but a more common version of the same would be to promote peace and good relations within a family or a relationship than to try and fight conflict being there in the first place. By doing this we are acting as the cause of change rather than fighting the effect of what has passed. Aligning and working in harmony with the natural rhythms and cycles and energetic momentums harnesses the forces.

Check List

Before assuming a psychic cause check:

1. Have we taken care of our physical and emotional well-being?
2. Have we eliminated other physical causes?
3. Have we eliminated other natural cycles as the cause i.e. planetary influences?

There are many ways to clear and dispel lower energies from our minds, bodies, energy fields and homes. No one and nothing has the right to hook in to, tamper with or affect our energy and we have the right to command that they leave us alone. The reverse is also true, even if it is unintentional.

In most cases all of the following may be used as preventative measures to help and to align with good forces and to keep a clear strong and vibrant space. There are however times where they may be needed to clear, remove or protect from lower forces.

Practical Forms of Protection

Shielding

Shielding is the equivalent of using an umbrella when it's raining. We cannot control the weather but we can shield ourselves from the worst of it. By first connecting with the earth to remain grounded and then connecting with heaven to align with light forces we can pull in huge amounts of prana or chi using the same energy bubble technique we learned to cast around ourselves. We can do this at the same time as setting the clear intention that this is to act as our shield.

We can then choose to add layers to our shield in the form of the elements, earth, air, fire and water. We do this by visualising additional layers to the force field one at a time. At the same time we draw in more powerful light energy and set the intention. For example:

Drawing light in with the in breath, shield activated.

Drawing light in with the in breath, a circle of salt or crystal visualised with the intention of Earth and purification.

Drawing light in with the in breath, a circle of sage smoke surrounding us with the intention of Air and clearing.

Drawing light in with the in breath, a circle of violet flames surrounding us with the intention of Fire burning away all that is lower frequency than it.

Drawing light in with the in breath, a cascade of bright white water encircles us washing away anything that is not high frequency.

Wearing a pentacle can help with this simple process as it connects with the four elements and spirit. Those pentacles with a circle around them offer the stability of them being enclosed, those with a circle in the centre offer some stability but are stronger. It's advisable to progress from one to another having learnt to contain and stabilise the elements within first. The open pentacle with no circle offers direct connection to the elements and is the strongest but offers no stability so the user must be sure of their own. The pentacle is useful both for drawing in these forces and for projecting them outwards and is therefore invaluable in this kind of shielding.

After practising this technique and learning to sustain it over a period of time, say an hour, it can be extended to remain in place throughout the day or during a specific situation where it is needed.

More Advanced Shielding (Three-Fold Law)

Once the shielding technique has become second nature it is possible to add a further dimension to it that can best be described as a mirror effect. This can be done in the same way through the breath and pranic inflow combined with clear intention and placement on the out breath. Once this mirror effect is in place around the bubble it can have two effects. Firstly it is a kind of cloaking and secondly it bounces back anything that comes towards it. Now if what comes toward it is at a high enough frequency to match that with which you put it in place i.e. love, it will pass though and all is well. If what comes towards it is harmful or low frequency it will bounce back.

It is worth adding here that returning something nasty that is sent or aiming for you intentionally or not is not attacking in any way it is just self-protection. The chances are that in that split second we may not know exactly what hit us or what the intention was. We may just feel something like a physical pain or a flashing thought or image. Sometimes it takes a few minutes to process, attune to it and work it out. In the actual moment all we are doing is shielding and effectively returning to sender or returning to its source anything harmful.

Very much like a rubber ball hitting the wall in a squash court, the harder it hits the wall the harder and faster it bounces back. It may in a way amplify because this is sometimes what happens. Shielding and returning anything sent towards us acts in the same way. On other occasions it may hit the wall slower or from a different angle and therefore have a different effect but it is fair to say that on occasion the speed and strength can amplify and/or gather momentum. Throughout many new age pagan writings there is this concept of three-fold or sometimes ten-fold law being applicable in the case of self-defence. It is possible that if a person is well shielded whatever is sent back may well return to the sender three-fold.

Set a Strong and Clear Intention

Placing both hands over the heart speak the intention out loud. Writing it on a piece of paper and burning it will also amplify the strength of it. When burning it connect with God/Goddess or directly with Nature because this is the source of our strength. Our voice is a powerful instrument because sound creates waves and moves out into the space. Examples:

'I bless, purify and consecrate this item to protect me and my loved ones.'

'I invoke and call upon the divine to shield us from all harm.'

'I cast out all that is outside of God/Goddess, in perfect love, in perfect trust.'

'I trust in the strength of the Great Mother to hold us and to keep us safe.'

'I call forth healing and blessings.'

Blessed Water and Salt

We can bless the water we are using by asking God/Goddess to bless the water either by praying over it or by making a request. We can do the same with salt, incense and flame. Any words that make the intention clear in a respectful way are fine. This combining of salt and water usually takes place in the chalice and is combined with the athame by drawing an invoking pentagram representing the elements and spirit in the water and three clockwise circles. Invoking means calling those forces inwards, into the chalice of salt water.

When we draw the invoking pentagram the first downward stroke comes towards us. In contrast when the banishing pentagram used to protect or ward away is drawn with the energy of the first stroke going away from us. (See diagram).

Invoking   **Banishing**

Water collected from a holy place, a holy well or stream of some kind perhaps dedicated to a Goddess or Saint is also very special.

Salt comes from the Earth and Mother Earth herself, the kingdom of Malkuth is the cosmic purifier and filter of all things.

Any combination of water and salt is a powerful one when used in full understanding.

Asking for Blessing

A wiccan request to the God/Goddess may be for example:

'By the power of the Goddess and the God may this water be cleansed, a blessing be upon this salt, may their power drive out all harm and allow in only good. So mote it be.' (Or Amen which translates as so be it).

These words can of course be changed with any that feel appropriate to you.

This water and salt can now be considered as cleansed and blessed and this means it can be used to cleanse, bless and consecrate other items not limited to but including ourselves, our house or vehicle, our keys, any item of jewellery or protective amulet. It can also be added to other water. The God/Goddess and Blessing is not diluted but infinite and therefore adding a drop to other water will only make more blessed water. Great for salt baths to recharge and release or to add to the steam cleaner when cleansing the house!

Praying for Blessing

Depending on the path followed the initiate may prefer to pray over the item or to God/Goddess. A Hebrew candle blessing for example might involve a traditional prayer that must be said in the correct way to light the candles just before the sun sets on Friday. The Shabbat is Saturday and they must be lit the sunset of the evening before. The blessing for the Shabbat candles is:

Hebrew Transliteration:
Barukh atah Adonai, Eloheinu, melekh ha'olamasher kidishanu
b'mitz'votav v'tzivanu
l'had'lik neir shel Shabbat. (Amein)

English Translation:
Blessed are you, Lord, our God, sovereign of the universe
Who has sanctified us with His commandments and commanded us
to light the lights of Shabbat. (Amen)

This prayer can be used to bless these candles to shine God's light in order that anything outside of God's light will be raised to match this high vibration of love and any lower frequency energy will be burnt away and lifted. Anything else unpleasant will probably choose to leave.

It is possible to reflect and shine this candlelight into any shadows or intensify it upon any areas that feel particularly heavy through the use of a simple mirror.

Visualisation

Visualisation techniques through meditation and intention are a good way of employing thought forms aligned with high frequencies to protect us. A golden pyramid signifying the protection of the Egyptian Gods could be visualised over us as a form of protection that shields us and raises us to the frequency of the Gods' protection.

Mirrors

Many older sources of magic refer to mirrors as doorways and as such it is worth considering closing the doorways at night simply by covering them. Other people choose to bless their mirrors and other reflective surfaces like windows with blessed water. Mirrors are also traditionally used for the purpose of scrying (a form of vision seeking) and perhaps this is one reason this notion has come about. There are also many forms of simple but effective mirror magic.

Praying to God/Goddess or using our own strength and harnessing power directly for the purpose are not mutually exclusive and are similar in many ways. It is possible to do both or for either to be suitable in any number of ways.

Consecration

Any item can be consecrated if it is used or given over to service of God/Goddess or to a higher cause or use. Consecration is a word given to special or sacred items that are blessed specifically for such a reason. Such an item can be passed through a sacred flame or submerged in blessed water followed by words appropriate for example:

'Hail to the Gods, I ask for your blessing upon this blade that it be forever in your service. I will use this blade only to gather herbs and natural things of goodness and I shall use these things only to do good and to heal.'

Simple Prayers

Prayers do not have to be elaborate or complicated. Some prayers particularly older ones may choose to use flowery language or detailed imagery and some people prefer this however a simple prayer is just as strong and just as effective. Although words can call God/Goddess closer to us or more accurately bring us closer to them it is ultimately the intention of those words that hold us there.

'Dear God/Goddess please clear away any energies within me or around me or my children that are not of your love or light. Dear God/Goddess please clear away any forces from our home that are not of your light. In perfect love and in perfect trust, Amen.'

Our Children

Our children are given to us by heaven and they are under our protection, it is therefore appropriate that we pray for them and act on their behalf. Once they get old enough to know what they're doing and choose for themselves they may want to join in and make it a joint effort.

Praying for Other People

Praying for those we love, for the world, for situations can always help the situation. Whilst it is not generally acceptable to work magic for someone without their knowledge (there are a few exceptions to this but not many) it is completely acceptable to pray for them. This is because our prayers go to God/Goddess and they know what they're doing. They also know if what we pray is in alignment with the soul of the other person or not which means we cannot accidentally violate their free will in any way. Be aware that the other soul may know better and not be open to receiving your prayers. A good way of wording prayers can be: "please help with this situation in the best possible way for all". Or alternatively: "if this prayer is not needed please send it to where it can do the most good". In this way we never interfere with the person's free will so unless another person has specifically said please do not pray for me, pray away, you might just help them or someone else. The more people praying for the world and for peace the better for the more light will be given to the situation.

If everyone stopped fighting, especially over religion and how to pray, and engaged in saying prayer instead in whatever way they wanted, the whole world would be at peace and in light!

Sound

Sound births creation in so many stories from so many cultures. Sound calls things into being. It is often said that to know the name of a thing is to know its essence. Sound vibrates through the universe at different pitches and corresponds with sacred geometrical shapes which are effectually the building blocks of creation found within every living organism and spiral. When we speak or sing or chant with the conscious thought of intention we may co create and call forth within our lives.

Sound can be used to clear a space and raise the vibrations in a space and to restore harmony. It is especially effective if two or more people sing together creating strong resonance arches and intervals of pitch. Singing bowls and gongs are especially useful as are drums. With drumming it is important that the focus of the person drumming remains upon the task at hand as the drum may not only break up existing energies but call in those to which we connect. In the sweat lodges the drum is used as the heartbeat of the lodge to call Great Spirit.

Sound in Prayer

Singing or speaking mantras and prayers that have been used for thousands of years by others before us can be a very effective way of praying because the prayer has the strength of thousands of years and millions of people, in other words it is cumulative. It is also possible when we say a prayer often enough that it becomes inherent in us as if it is in perpetual cycle.

An example of this is that many Catholics speak the Hail Mary also known as Ave Maria, which is a Catholic prayer of intercession to the mother of the Christ, many times with a rosary. The prayer says:

> *Hail Mary, full of grace, the Lord is with thee;*
> *Blessed art thou amongst women,*
> *and blessed is the fruit of thy womb, Jesus.*
> *Holy Mary, Mother of God,*
> *pray for us sinners,*
> *now and at the hour of death. Amen*

Intercession is a type of prayer that asks for a Saint or in this case the Madonna Mary to pray for us on our behalf, the idea being that the Saints are unlimited and eternal and that the prayer may therefore be perpetual. There are other versions of the Ave Maria in Latin and Greek and other languages because it has been spoken all over the world and for such a long time.

There are other prayers and mantras with very specific purposes too. For example this is the Gayatri Mantra which is a devotional Hindu chant calling upon God to protect, energise, purify all and align us with the right path:

Hindu Transliteration:
Aum Bhur Bhuvah Swah
Tat Savitur Varenyam
Bhargo Devasya Dhimani
Dhiyo Yo Nah Prachodayat

English Translation:
Oh God, the Protector, the basis of all life, Who is self-existent, Who is free from all pains and Whose contact frees the soul from all troubles, Who pervades the Universe and sustains all, the Creator and Energizer of the whole Universe, the Giver of happiness, Who is worthy of acceptance, the most excellent, Who is Pure and the Purifier of all, let us embrace that very God, so that He may direct our mental faculties in the right direction.

Lighting Candles

Bless the candles first either by stating the intention clearly or through prayer or both so that they are more effective and will remove anything that is not at their frequency. One candle may be enough for something simple, or one for each room with the intention that the flame burns away lower energies if clearing or blessing the house. White ones are easy to find and burn bright clear light suitable for most purposes. Let them burn all the way down without interruption; this may take about four hours for tea lights and five or six for dinner candles. Plan accordingly and start at sunset if sleep is needed at a reasonable hour!

Smudging and Smoke

The burning of white sage, cedar and other herbs like rosemary and lavender is an effective way to clear a space. Herb bundles called smudge sticks are easy enough to buy in new age shops or online or even better it is pretty simple to make your own with dried herbs from the garden. Once lit smudge sticks burn slowly, the smoke can then be consciously directed by hand or with the use of a feather around the body (paying attention to head, feet, hands, heart and back of the heart as well as chakras).

After smudging oneself and taking the necessary precautions against dropping hot embers, use the power of intention and go around the entire room (or the whole house) with the smudge stick still smouldering, making sure to get into all the corners and under furniture. Open windows for the smell and to encourage the lower energies to leave the space as commanded either mentally or with voice. Pay special attention to certain areas such as openings air vents that are easily missed and to the bathroom which is where our waste goes. Remember to include electronics, inside wardrobes, handbags, wallets and other items that could be easily overlooked.

Smoke from incense resins like frankincense have also been used traditionally for thousands of years. Medicinally frankincense is antiseptic, disinfectant and astringent so its use for clearing and cleaning is founded on a logical extension of its attributes.

Burning of sacred wood and or herbs is also a common way of blessing and cleansing whether that is with rosemary for Archangel Michael or with a holy fire made of the nine sacred Celtic woods for the God Bel. The nine woods are willow, hazel, alder, birch, ash, yew, elm, oak and hawthorn.

There is scientific research supporting the use of traditional medicinal herbs such as burning white sage for fighting infection and clearing space.

Jewellery

Certain items of jewellery can serve as useful protection as can the use of crystals. Jewellery can be strong when it has a deeper significance to us. Christians all over the world wear the cross, Jews wear the Star of David also known as the seal of Solomon or six-pointed star, many pagans and Wiccans wear the pentacle or five pointed star, Buddhists wear the Om or aum symbol. The power of the piece of jewellery is not in the metal so much as it is in the meaning and symbology of the forces it represents. One of the meanings often given to the Om is the sound of the earth and of the universe, the sacred sound of creation itself. Wearing a piece of jewellery with this symbol is therefore a way to connect with that and to work in harmony with it. Regularly clean, bless, cleanse and recharge jewellery items either by putting them in full midday sun or full moonlight after washing in salt water.

Amulets and Talismans

An amulet is an object whose most important characteristic is the power ascribed to it to protect its owner from danger or harm. An amulet differs to a talisman in that it has natural magical properties whereas a talisman must be charged with magical powers by its creator in other words in must be made. It is this act of making that gives the talisman its magical powers. This usually requires using the right metal, stones and symbols for the purpose and working with the correct planetary forces for its creation at set times or during planetary transits. The talisman is generally made for a specific purpose whereas an amulet can be used for any number of purposes.

Crystals

Crystals both as items of jewellery to be worn and as items to keep in the house or use for specific purposes can be very effective at protecting us from lower energies. There are some like obsidian or black onyx that can absorb these lower energies so that we don't and there are others like amethyst that can be charged to repel them and shield us. Crystals need regular clearing, cleaning and recharging. Only give a crystal one job to do at a time and try not to put ones you've used in with ones that are clean and charged. This way you have a clean and clear supply ready when you need them. Crystals are fantastic for healing and have many healing properties.

Card Decks

We have already considered choosing which card decks we use wisely. It is also worth remembering to cleanse and clear card decks regularly through prayer or smudging or both. It is also inadvisable to lend and or share card decks with friends. The only people who should touch them are those we read for at the time because we are responsible for all contacts through those cards. No one should touch our card decks or anything on our altar without first asking express permission to do so. It is considered very bad manners in pagan circles to move or touch things on someone else's altar. Many other people may not know this though. Non-pagan friends who come round could easily move items or pick up card decks so it's worth being vigilant and keeping cards wrapped up in cloth. This also applies to other magical or sacred tools and items.

Angels

Angels appear in numerous religions throughout the world sometimes by the same name or a very similar one. They are very easy to work with and will communicate with us with clear and easy guidance. They are non-denominational and omnipresent and like God/Goddess they are infinite. This means they have the time to be with us simultaneously to anyone else calling them. They are happy to help us when we ask but it is very important that we do because like God/Goddess they will not interfere with our free will. We can simply ask for help at any time with anything. Asking for their protection can wrap us in their wings, shield us from harm and surround us with light.

Ascended Masters and other Benevolent Forces

Ascended masters and other benevolent spirits and forces can be called upon and give us good guidance, protection and support. Like all relationships it takes time to develop these friendships and good discernment and judgement to know for sure who we are talking to and communicating with. These relationships can last for lifetimes and may be people we have shared previous incarnations with, spiritual guides or highly evolved spirits serving a specific purpose with whom we can converse and learn from. They can watch over us and provide practical guidance and support.

Nature Spirits and Guardians

Nature spirits and guardians of land and specific places can also help and support us provided that we are working in alignment with them. Note that asking a nature spirit for access to working with an area of land or a specific element or place is bad form if we are not aspiring to common values for the good of the Earth. For this reason it is usual that dryads (tree spirits) and other elementals and faery often only choose to reveal themselves to those who are in alignment with their cause. Always be honourable in dealing with these magical earthy beings for their reputation for trickery is not without cause though usually only enacted upon those who disrespect them or the Earth. Note that not all of these folk choose to be friendly with humans.

Spending time with Nature

Perhaps this should be the most important thing on the list. Nature is our true nature, nature is the expression of God/Goddess, the Earth is our mother. Any time that our personal energy or home space feel low frequency the first thing to do is to get some fresh air, look at the sky, connect with the Earth, lift our arms to the sun or to the moon and connect.

Spending time with the trees can really help too. Trees are amazing because they ground us literally to the earth when we connect with them, through their root systems. They are also able to use the same process that they use for photosynthesis to help us release any negative or lower frequency emotions and recycle them into harmless energy. If we're sad they can help us release and feel better and if we're tired they can revive us. Always take the time to properly connect with the trees first. Find the right one and ask for their help. Wait for the answer and if there is a no feeling listen to that and find another tree where there is a yes feeling. Be respectful and say thank you when it's time to go. Hugging a tree is a very real thing to do.

Cutting Cords

Each thought, person and place that we connect with is an energetic link. Most of these are good but sometimes they can affect us in unhelpful ways. The

Cutting of these cords can be as simple as requesting that forces of good, God/Goddess or the angels do it for us. Archangel Michael is particularly good at this as he is a protector and carries his sword and shield to defend us from harm. Just ask him.

Alternatively it is possible to cut them symbolically and energetically one at a time by cutting or burning through a thread in a candle whilst holding a very clear intention. Each thread may only represent one connection.

It is also possible to do this energetically by passing (very carefully!) a blessed knife or sword over the energetic points of the body i.e. the terminals (over the head and under one foot at a time), over the palms of the hands, the front of the body's chakras and the back of the body's chakras. This should only be done by someone skilled in energy work such as practitioner of alternative medicine or reiki or an experienced initiate.

It is common to feel a shudder, shiver, or other sensation as these cords are removed. Also be aware they will only be removed whilst we keep them that way. If we then invite the person or thing immediately back into our lives whether knowingly or at some level the process may need to be repeated.

Exercise

Write a Clearing and Protection Prayer or adapt or use this one:

I call upon omnipresent goodness or God/Goddess.

I (insert your name), do not give my permission for anything outside of goodness or God/Goddess to influence me or to enter my body, mind, spirit, soul or energy field for any reason other than love.

I ask for Divine assistance and protection from any lower energies that may intend me harm or harm me in any way and I command them to leave me, my home and my life now.

This is my intention and the expression of my free will in accordance with the Law.

In perfect love, in perfect trust, in perfect light. Amen/So mote it be.

Chapter Seventeen
The Altar and Working Tools

Mother I feel you under my feet, mother I feel your heart beat.
Chant, source unknown.

The Earth is always the most sacred of altars and we are held by her, our lives playing out within the tapestry of the creation.

In different cultures and traditions the altar is designed differently and has different things upon it. Here we will look at some of the more usual designs in Western paths and traditions. The most important thing about the altar is that it is highly personal and unique. Any three altars with the same or similar objects upon them can feel entirely different. Magical items more so than any others take on the resonance of the person to whom they belong.

Having an altar can give us a physical focal point and have an anchoring and grounding effect spiritually and psychically. It can also be a great source of comfort and support and a solid reassuring space that is permanently held just for us and our connection with the divine source. The purpose of the altar is not just to create a sacred space but to acknowledge and bring our focus into that which is already sacred. Each thing we place there should be of significance and purpose. These items are not physically different from others rather it is the intention with which we put them there that differentiates them. The cumulative effect of such sacred items is often one of amplification. That is to say that when we put together items of magical or spiritual significance with intention they can create something which is stronger and more powerful as a whole than the addition of the parts would be separately.

The first thing to consider is where we want our altar to be. Ideally we don't want it to be in a place where other people will touch or move our things without express permission for them to do so. Such a space is sacred and it's advisable not to mix up other people's energy and connections with our things or in any way that could affect our work. Ideally it should either be somewhere where it will be untouched. Alternatively and more likely it could be somewhere that we can make sure to always be observant and aware of it. In this case it might be advisable wherever possible to only invite people in who will understand and respect such a thing or who it feels comfortable to explain it to if needs be. If that is not possible perhaps somewhere it can be disguised or hidden? Or in full view and just keep a very careful watch upon it and accept that extra cleaning and care is required in order to do so. This may mean dealing with the occasionally raised eyebrow, inconvenient question or odd enquiry from whoever has come to read the gas meter!

Once a space has been chosen perhaps designate a specific item whether it is a piece of furniture or a large slab of stone or wood. Choose whatever feels right. It's worth noting here that an altar can be laid anywhere and upon any patch of earth. Another alternative is to store your magical items carefully and just lay them out onto an altar of some kind or onto the earth as and when you feel to. In fact Earth is always the first altar and the hearth. We are specifically looking at something more permanent here as a way to bring our spirituality into our home and life. Practical spirituality is functional and for many new age practitioners or old way initiates the kitchen holds the contents of the altar or the physical hearth of the fire. Whatever feels most appropriate to living conditions and to who we are. The first step is always a clean space that feels right.

The direction that the altar faces is always a personal choice. Traditionally the Egyptians faced the Tuat in the West. The temple of Solomon faced the East and the rising Sun as do most Christian cemeteries. Many modern esoteric books on Wicca suggest facing North and it is traditional here as the direction of Earth and the mother. There are other things that can be taken into consideration such as the direction of any place of great significance, or where in the house gets the most light throughout the day. Also where is it of most value? Some people like to have it in their bedroom where they have quiet to reflect on it, others in the room where they spend the most time and others in their kitchen where they can prepare herbs and other things they regularly work with.

It is important that each thing there is there by design with a purpose and intention and that its use is fully understood. It is usual for any and all working tools or things of significance to be purified and consecrated before use. This may be done simply by the elements with incense, a candle, salt and water and any words of blessing or prayer that feel appropriate. You might also want to charge them by imbuing them with light either by putting them out in the full moon or at the height of the midday sun.

Traditionally if you are facing the altar those things with female attributes are on your left and those things with male attributes are on your right if they have no other designation.

Earth

The earth element is usually described as female hence the downward facing triangle that is often given as her depiction. She is the Mother and gives birth to all life, she nourishes life, she sustains us, she supports and grounds and holds us. Her recesses and caves and soil are her womb and her cornucopia our sustenance. She holds all and in her layers of rocks and salts she purifies all. Our physical bodies, our flesh, our blood, our bones are from her and a part of her in birth and when we die we return to her. From her we have our practical earthly abilities, skills and functions. Upon the altar she is the chalice, the womb which holds the waters of life, she is the cauldron of death and rebirth, she is the salt of purification and any stones, fossils and crystals we place there.

Air

The air is described as male primarily and the sky as father. He brings breath to all life and he carries the sound of creation and indeed he scatters the seeds of creation. He fills our lungs and gives us voice and communication. He blows away the cobwebs of our mind as he blows the leaves. He caresses all and watches over all. Upon the altar he is the athame, the sword, the incense and feathers.

Fire

The fire element is also usually seen as male as the physical embodiment of the Sun. On earth his warmth and light brings life through photosynthesis and the alchemy of fire itself purifies and burns and changes wood for example into heat. Within us he physically brings melatonin (which aids good sleep) and serotonin (which makes us happy). He is our Spirit breath, inner fire, passion, creativity and drive. Upon the altar he is the wand and the candle, bringer of light.

Water

Water is attributed to the feminine. She is the sea and the rivers, streams, lakes and rain. She is the primordial source of creation from which the mound of earth rises in various creation stories. She is life source and she cleanses and washes away and replenishes us. We drink from her and she renews us continuously. She rules the emotions and it is within the deep wells of our water that we express tears of sadness or joy. Water is held within the earth and upon the altar water fills and is held within the chalice. Shells or anything else connected to the sea are sometimes placed here too.

Here in the centre where the four elements meet is the tree and the point of spirit where all connect to one another and the rest of creation.

Athame

The athame is a double-edged knife or dagger that is used specifically for magical purposes and traditionally represents the masculine principles. It often has a black handle and is made of steel but this is not a necessity and it is of far more importance that it feels right for purpose. It can be used for directing energy when casting a circle or space and cutting energetic cords. It is not usual for the athame to be used to cut anything physically, however, this is a matter of personal choice. It could for example be used to mark symbols upon candles or similar tasks where the penetration of the masculine element such as the marking or infusing another object with potency could be useful and increase the strength of the object being marked i.e. the candles.

There are two schools of thought regarding its position upon the altar as in some traditions it is associated with air and the wand with fire and in other traditions it is associated with fire and the wand with air. It is possible that both are true and possibly interchangeable provided you are clear in intention as to how you are using it and why. Most usually however and corresponding with its suit in the tarot the athame represents Air and is the suit of Swords. The action of the athame is associated with *Ruach Elohim* which is the spirit breath. When used in conjunction with the chalice of wine or water, which represents the female principles and the moon, the athame can be thought of as the spirit breath moving on or through the water. Note here that spirit breath whilst air is also a fundamentally male principle and in this way could also be considered as fire or spirit light in a way, which we may also see in the union with the chalice, the two being Sun and Moon, Fire and Water, within the symbolism of the Great Rite of creation. It makes as much sense to see fire in the water as the alchemy of the primordial elements and the rainbow.

If designated to the element of fire, within wicca and neo-paganism, the usual position of the athame would be in the South. More commonly if designated to Air, its position is in the East.

The purpose of the athame dagger is to divide, cut and inscribe.

Wand

The wand is a personal choice and although there are some who use crystal wands they are more commonly made of wood taken from a tree of our choosing or sometimes a combination of both wood and crystal. In the tarot wands are the suit of fire. Ideally take a wand from the tree in winter when the tree is dormant so as to enhance growth effectively through coppicing on a small scale rather than to harm it by sapping life literally in the summer months. Many people choose the tree for its properties according to their belief system. For those of the Nordic traditions ash might be desirable as it represents the world tree. For those following an Egyptian path the sycamore or acacia wood might be suggested as both are seen as sacred; or for the Celtic path perhaps any type of wood within the Ogham according to its attributes. It may feel appropriate to have more than one wand in order that each has different purpose. As with wood the choosing of any crystal should be made for its attributes and our compatibility with it. It may also feel right to decorate it in some way or mark it with a symbol of some kind if there is one of significance we regularly work with.

As with the athame there are two schools of thought as to whether it is

317

associated with air or with fire and again it is possible that they are interchangeable and both able to direct the male principle forces when done with clear intention. To consider the wand with Air we can envisage how a tree grows and how its branches move in the breeze. There is a subtlety of movement like breath moving through it. When considering the crystal tip or a particularly warm feeling wood we can see that Sunshine flows through and it literally carries light and the creative surge and impetus of male expansive growth and potency. It too can be used to cast a circle or sacred space and is generally warmer in feel than the athame and has a different kind of strength. If designated to the element of air it should be positioned in the East. It is however more usual to be designated to fire and positioned in the South. Many consider the energy and potency of fire to be within the wood.

The purpose of the wand is to point, direct or indicate.

Both the athame and the wand are used to direct the Masculine Principle energy of the Divine Source and the point of connection or contact for that source is the practitioner. As in the earlier exercise of drawing in prana or life force into the body which meets in the heart and then projecting it around the body in a "bubble", this same energy is now channelled through us directed with the wand or athame in our work or casting of sacred space.

Chalice

The chalice is a deep cup, glass or goblet which holds water. The choosing of it is a personal thing and there are numerous choices. Blue glass the colour of water, cut crystal that encourages light, earthenware or any with an appropriate symbol or something of meaning and significance. There are many chalices available in new age shops and online suited to any number of paths. The Cups or Chalices suit are attributed to water in the tarot and associated with love.

The chalice is in essence the female principle and always contains Water (life force). It is representative of the Goddess and the womb of creation. It is worth pointing out that these primordial waters of female principle and creation are held within the womb of Mother Earth and that as such there is a correlation between these two for is it the womb of Earth that is doing the holding or the Water and life force of primordial creation that is being held which it represents. In truth perhaps both despite its designation to Water and they are interconnected as are the masculine principles. Beyond that in invocation and when drawing down the moon or Goddess the invoking pentacle is often drawn in the water. Whilst many see the pentacle as the earthly embodiment of all five elements it is also the symbol for Earth. The chalice of water is traditionally positioned in the West.

The purpose of the chalice cup is to contain.

Water and Earth are often directed together because it is common to mix and bless salt and water. Salt is added to the water and they are mixed together and directed by athame, wand, fingertips or feather depending upon the practitioner. We connect with Divine Source in the same way as before as we do this but in the case of Water or Earth it is the Feminine Principle which we channel through us.

Pentacle (or Disc)

The pentacle (or disc) is representative of Earth and also of the earthly embodiment of all five points and elements in creation, the fifth being spirit, the pathway and connection point of which is found when these other four are in conjunction on the earthly plane. Whilst it is possible to buy metal pentacles to place upon the altar and many people choose to wear them made from silver, for the altar it may be preferable to make one possibly from wood or clay or something you have taken from the earth. Indeed with all these things personally made tools have the love, effort and intention you create them with imbued within them. In the Tarot the suit of pentacles correlate to Earth and are associated with practical matters.

Though the pentacle itself is orientated to Earth it is often drawn into the water representing all five points in invocation and these two female principles of Earth and Water are intrinsically linked in the same way that the rivers, seas and underground waters flow in, through and on our planet. Earth and the pentacle are traditionally positioned in the North.

The purpose of the pentacle disc is to layout information and represents personal design of workings and wisdom.

*As a side note for anyone considering buying a pentacle as an item of magical jewellery the difference between those that are contained within a circle or those that are an open five points is worth consideration. The five-pointed star when contained in the circle affords more protection as the circle represents the magical circle and the containment and harnessing of the elements within. This helps both with direction and protection. It is also possible to buy pentacles which are an open five-pointed star containing a smaller circle within the centre. This smaller circle has a stabilising effect whilst still allowing the strength of the open elements. The open five-pointed star with no circle is literally "open" to the elements. As such it is stronger but not as easily managed and is better suited to those of more experience, as being open to these forces denotes a need to be entirely sure in our personal capabilities to hold our space and protection at all times. Further to that should a pentacle have a stone in its centre or other symbols of any kind it might be wise to look up any magical properties, attributes or meanings in order to choose the one that is most beneficial. Always buy these things from somewhere that feels good and right. If there's any hesitation or doubt it's better to be patient and wait for the right one to present itself.

These first four items of the altar have been given deliberately in this order for they are the essential tools and correspondents of the elements. The following list is now in no particular order though each is important in its own right.

The Sword

The sword has the same attributes and capabilities as the athame and like the athame can direct the Masculine Principles. It is particularly useful in large circles and outdoors where the energy directed must encompass a greater area. Most commonly it is associated with Air and with the Swords suit of the tarot however like its smaller counterpart the athame it can also be used to channel spiritual Fire in that alchemy of uniting the male and female principles with water in the cauldron or in its natural state. The word also has a protecting force and associations both to Archangel Michael and to other protective deities and archetypes. Whilst its technical position might be one of the East it is usually impractical to have it upon the altar but it is invaluable in front of it, guarding and protecting its contents. The sword represents courage earned.

The Staff (or Rod)

The Staff is often overlooked in its significance and confused by many as a larger version of the wand and this it is not so, for its workings and use are entirely different. It is of the male principle and can direct potent male energy but the way in which we use it is different because rather than channelling the energy up and out as we do with the wand, with the staff we channel the energy down and deep into the Earth and primordial waters. This creates the same spiritual alchemy we see with the athame and chalice combined on a greater scale in direct contact with the Earth and bypassing all symbolic altars altogether, in the union of masculine and feminine principles and therefore Creation. In its highest potential all five elements come together in this alchemical formula. The energy can be directed both through the earth and water or travel back up the staff to be projected outwards directing both male and female energies combined outwards. It can also be used for Earth magic projected inwards and for tapping into old earth knowledge and memory and for grounding oneself strongly. The staff is therefore the most powerful tool but there is a warning here too because it is only in skilled hands that this force can be held and directed. Thankfully each practitioner can only carry through him or herself the amount of power they are able to, for we are all in effect like copper wires carrying electrical and magical current. Without sufficient current carrying capability, depending on the thickness of the wire, attempts to work in this way may be ineffectual until learned over time. That being said there are some who are able to bring in and channel more than they are able to ground and advice to anyone inexperienced would be to proceed with caution, and then to start by only using the staff to connect to one predetermined element at a time until it is second nature and established. If at any point in the learning process there is a feeling of being ungrounded, disorientated, spinney or tingly it would be wise to sit with a tree and ground or get hands and feet on the earth and then rest for a while.

The staff or rod represents will.

The Robe

Many people choose some kind of Robe for working that they keep specifically for that purpose. Fabric (and our hair in fact) is very good at picking up and holding onto energy within the weave. Therefore when we are entering a sacred space to work we shower or bath first head to toe, followed by dressing in a robe which we keep clean and only for this purpose and quite often then smudge ourselves as well when it is for ritual. The reason for that is that in being as clean as possible and free of anything unneeded we enter the space at the highest and clearest we can possibly be and do not bring anything unwanted with us. Be intuitive about what feels right and study the attributes of colours before choosing a robe.

Candles

It is usual to have two candles to represent the Feminine and Masculine principles whether that be reflected as God and Goddess, the two pillars, pantheon or directly connected with nature. Of these the feminine is on the left and the masculine is on the right as we are facing the altar and it is usual to light the feminine first and then the masculine.

There is often one further candle which has a sole purpose of representing fire or the sun and this is most commonly placed in the South (nearest us if facing North).

Another variation of this instead of the candle representing sun and fire is that there is one candle in the centre which has been passed through both feminine and masculine flames of the other two and represents the alchemical combination of both in creation (or the central pillar) if you are working with the Kabbalah or Egyptian magic.

It is likely that for each of these candles a specific colour may have been chosen to reflect the nature of its purpose. If ever in any doubt plain white is usually a good option.

The Cauldron

The Cauldron can be associated with Cerwidden and other womb-like

Goddesses and with the cauldron of rebirth and the divine feminine. Like the cave deep within the earth or the recesses of crevices and cracks in the land that lead deep within the cauldron is both earth like in its holding capacity and powers of renewal and birth. Like the chalice it can hold water too but in larger quantity and yet its essence although feminine is not of water for it will happily hold fire, that male sacred seed of creation or air as a vessel for incense burning and offerings made. In truth then like the pentacle of earth it can hold and accommodate all the elements within it and its own orientation is earth. Depending on the size of the cauldron it may well not be practical for this to sit upon the altar but if it does it should be on the left-hand side because of its feminine nature.

We have always had a few simple rules about the use of the cauldron. These are recounted from my own personal experience. Rule number one is to always wash it three times before using it for any spell work even if you think it already looks clean. Residual energy can and does build up with any magical item but due to its holding capacity the cauldron is particularly susceptible to this and it is usually within it that spells are cast and offerings are burnt. Mixing workings and trace energies up with new ones is ill advised! Rule number two: remember to keep the lid on it. Once it has built up its own energy (and it will with use over time) it can have a powerful effect even when not in use so it's advisable to keep it closed. Rule number three is not to let the cat sit in said cauldron! Animals are so often drawn to magical items and in fact often help. One of my cats will climb into my altar cupboard and knock out for me various herbs that I need instinctively which is quite something to watch. I don't ask how but I observe that she does! Helpful as she is though I don't want her fur in my spell work or to be weaving her in or involving her DNA effectively with what I am doing. Rule four is do not eat things out of the cauldron. Yes I was reminded of this twice years ago, once for cooking jacket potatoes in a fire and once for scrubbing it out for mulled wine making! As I was reminded at the time eating traces of a spell, even if it be of your own making, may have consequences and allowing other people to eat something that may be connected with your working a definite mistake.

Offerings

Any offerings or anything for burning mentioned here as it directly follows the cauldron i.e. wood or branches, hand written spells or prayers, offerings of any description (poetry, incense, crystals, cake etc.) or prayers. These may not have a place on the altar per se but could be prepared on a charger plate or somewhere ready for this purpose.

Wine

Wine is usually an offering and logically follows the ones listed before. It is the fruit of the vine and therefore of both the God and the Goddess and Masculine and Feminine principles. It could be placed in the West with the Water or with the charger plate of other offerings. Though we may sip it in communion with the Divine either the first or the last of the wine is traditionally given back in thanks and poured onto the earth or into the cauldron after any burning.

Incense

Different resins and plants used in incense making have different effects upon the senses and so it is worth taking time to study these and choose something appropriate to the work you are doing. Homemade hand-grained incense made from high-grade ingredients will always be far better than anything we can buy pre-rolled. Not to mention the beautiful billowing white smoke and uplifting experience. For this something made of stone or cast iron is needed, like a small cauldron for burning charcoal discs on safely in order to burn the incense. That being said we live in an age of smoke alarms and for every day purposes convenience is a factor. Perhaps look for some boxes of good quality pre-rolled temple incense or buy a few for different purposes and see what works best. This beautiful scent is carried on Air to our senses and is therefore traditionally in the East as well as the incense holder itself and any any feathers used to carry or direct the smoke for smudging, blessing or casting sacred space.

*Feathers although they are attributed to the air may also be used to "flick" or direct water in blessing or consecration.

Smudge Sticks

Originally Native American, these have very fast been adopted as an essential item for cleansing, clearing and blessing. Often and most commonly made of white sage but also sometimes pine, sweet grass or copal these are dried herbs which have been bundled and wrapped tightly in cotton string for the express purpose of burning slowly. They can be a little tricky to light initially and it is gentle and continuous movement through the air that keeps them burning. Ideally when using these the eyes of the practitioner need to be trained enough by now to see auric fields and the energy they are moving, clearing or cleaning with the smoke. (Refer to the auric field exercise where we started with fingertips.) If this is not the case it may still be of use if the practitioner is sensitive enough to feel it and know where to direct the smoke, for how long and in what way. Pay special attention to above the head, the heart chakra both front and back of the body and to the palms and soles of the feet. These are also especially useful for cleaning tarot cards or other oracle decks as they can get a bit "sticky" with use. If there are herbs growing in the garden try making some smudge sticks and adding useful variations of herbs that will help with the purpose. As with incense these are attributed to Air and therefore the East of the altar if and when they are in use. Keeping them in a drawer or somewhere dark may keep them fresh for longer. It also saves from cluttering the altar itself which should be clean and clear save for essentials.

Salt

Salt is the great purifier and protector taken from the earth and represents earth on the altar. It is therefore kept in the North. It is usually blessed and mixed with the water which is charged to keep out negative forces and "allow in only good". We can see clearly that its magical properties of cleansing and purification echo its physical properties. Mankind has used salt to wash wounds, clean infection, preserve food, maintain health and hydration and in all manner of things requiring any form of cleaning throughout the ages. This is often the way of it: that the magical attributes of a thing are the logical extensions and expressions of its practical earthly uses and are firmly grounded in proveable fact. If you are able to find raw or natural salt the quality of it is usually better than that which has been bleached or overly processed but the latter will still loyally serve its purpose where the other is not available. In every fairy tale or story told where there is some evil force to be warded off or protected against salt is the redeemer and these tales, though they are stories, are based on old and common knowledge. So that it acts as a protective barrier when put there with the right intention.

Statues or Figures

Statues or figures of Deities or Archetypes or items that symbolise them – these may also be something you choose to keep on the altar. The positioning of these is to the left if feminine in essence and to the right if masculine in essence. There may be some exceptions to this.

The Besom

The Besom or broom is a traditionally made broom of twigs tied together with a wooden handle. Its twigs are often made from broom wood (an evergreen genista shrub native to Europe) or heather though not exclusively. If planning to make our own ideally we should try to coppice the wood for the handle in the winter if possible, when the tree is sleeping and won't be harmed and then pick a suitable shrub like "brush" of twigs. If choosing something like heather, including lavender or anything with antiseptic or protective, cleaning or banishing properties is all the better. The besom or broom is used for sweeping the circle or sacred space prior to working. This is usually done three times and it is as much an energetic clearing as a physical one. It can be used also within the home for clearing and is versatile like most altar tools to whatever purpose you need it for. It can be used to clear doorways and sweeping out the house before a house blessing. It sweeps and moves things physically and energetically through the air and therefore can be attributed to air. Whilst it does not strictly belong with the altar it is an essential and useful tool and it makes sense to keep it with our other magical items where it will be safe and untouched.

The Book of Shadows

This may be thought of as a book of both shadows and as illuminations, insight, knowledge and revelations of which shadow is only one part. This is just its common name. Strictly speaking this is not an altar tool but it needs to be kept somewhere safe and is the most sacred item of any practitioner containing everything and all that has been experienced. It therefore makes sense to keep it in or with the altar, as this space is sacred and untouched by anyone else.

No matter how experienced we are or where we are on our journey, the one thing that never changes is change itself and so we are all learning. This book is essentially a blank journal where we can write our experiences, dreams, drawings, diagrams or visions, information on plants and formulae and anything else that seems noteworthy. I have often found mine to be an invaluable source of information years after writing. Sometimes something found later or a piece of information channelled may seem to have no immediate purpose at the time and three months or seven years later it clicks into place. In that moment I am so glad that I wrote it down! Likewise old workings or rituals, lesser-known spell ingredients and their uses, healing properties of crystals. This book holds it all and is as unique to us as our fingerprints. As a precautionary measure as with all magical items it is worth blessing this book and in addition possibly wrapping or securing it in blessed cotton or cord. Many practices also recommend that you have a pen specifically for your work and also offer various methods of preparation of it, not just for use within shadows but for magical workings and undertakings. Another option is to keep pens specifically for this purpose, not to worry and use whatever feels right or to try out making home made ink.

Other

Other things that might be welcomed or wanted upon the altar for their attributes or magical properties or healing abilities, most importantly things that have personal significance, represent us in some way and/or have hidden deeper meanings or secrets known only to us.

The Bell is used in traditional Wicca as a tool for calling in spirit through sound.

The Sistrum is used in Egyptian magic by the Priestess to worship and call the Gods.

The Mirror has many uses in many different cultures. Its most common use is for sight and visions but it also has associations with self-protection and reflecting things away from the user.

Stones, crystals or fossils, shells, leaves, flowers, crops or plants you have collected.

A Horn – Sometimes used to blow and call in each of the four winds or directions.

Animal totems or images i.e. butterfly for transformation.

Symbols of protection such as Thor's hammer or the eye of Horus, dependent upon path. Do not mix up symbols and cultures as this may produce unstable energy.

Planetary symbols.

Angel cards or an oracle deck associated with the culture you are working in.

One Clear System

Most of the things covered on this list are found and could be used with most pathways of most cultures. This is deliberate so that it is applicable to all orientations and choices. That being said it is inadvisable to mix these cultures up together in a magical working space as it has the potential to make for messy and unpredictable magic. Decide for your working which culture you are working in and why and then use the appropriate symbols and correspondences and working tools. If you regularly work with more than one path it may well be worth your while to keep two sets of the things you need. In some traditions such as Kabbalah it is acceptable to use the same magical items across various different cultures, the reason being that it is still grounded in the foundation of one unchanging magical system and even then there is strict guidance about being clear with which deities or archetypes you are working and why. Some Norse and Celtic traditions are close enough in nature that there may be a sharing of tools for the purpose though the two systems should never be mixed up. If you intend working with Egyptian magic particularly it is unalike from any other and needs its own set of working tools for it does not lend well to being mixed up with other cultures and its magic feels so different in essence to anything else that it should be honoured as such.

It makes no sense to mix up two completely different cultures anyway. They would have been speaking different languages at different points in time and place with different cultural normalities and moralities and widely varying types of religious practice and magic. Even two similar Archetypal figures from two cultures both representing the same natural forces in Nature can manifest and work entirely differently to one another. The more precisely we work the more respectful we are to the sources we work with and the greater the likelihood of favourable outcomes.

Exercise

Choose or make a chalice to represent the divine feminine principle or Goddess.

Choose or make an athame to represent the divine masculine principle or God.

Take them to a source of natural water and bless them.

Chapter Eighteen
Holding and Casting Sacred Space

Your heart is your temple and a sacred space.

Sacred, consecrated and held space is found in most religions and spiritual practices. It's a human necessity. As with all things the nature of this varies depending upon culture. Some natural places in the landscape are considered holy and other man-made permanent sites such as temples are also considered holy as are some semi-permanent structures such as sweat lodge. Here however we are primarily concerned with the holding and casting of personal sacred space as an individual or for a group or circle of like-minded individuals. As with other aspects of practical magic it helps enormously if we can work with one clear system at a time. By learning one system well, others will make sense later and will be in relation to the first. Examples are given within this chapter of some of the various means and types of sacred space and how they are cast. These are only suggestions to illustrate and explain the process and there are many other variations to be found elsewhere.

In some customs the ground or room or place must be blessed in some way first before any sacred space can be considered. In Aboriginal tradition eucalyptus leaves are routinely burnt in each new place and a leather coat carved with ancestral knowledge and blessings, which holds the collective memories of the tribe, may be brought with members of the tribe when moving. In numerous Native American traditions sage, sweet grass and copal are used for smudging and clearing the space prior to any ceremony. The grounds and graveyards of Christian churches are consecrated ground that has been effectively given back to God. Within the church itself a censor of incense is used throughout the congregation and this custom dates back to the burning of incense in the temple of Solomon in Jerusalem and quite probably to the Egyptians before that who made the finest kyphi incense and routinely burnt it in the temples. These are all forms of smudging. Most modern day circles are swept with a besom prior to working and smudged with herbs or incense.

Casting a circle or sacred space is not always necessary for every ceremony or ritual. There are plenty of ceremonies such as sabbats where a coming together of people is easier and just as effective without casting and holding sacred space. In fact if there is no other purpose or specific working to be done a circle or held space is probably not needed. Also there are many cultures that did not traditionally use circles or cast space in the first place. This may have been because it was not the custom or more commonly because there was a permanent temple or site that was always in use and it was therefore unnecessary.

Most of us are unable to hold a permanent temple and so casting a circle or space can be thought of as the creating of a personal and mobile temple of sorts. The circle or cast space is also a protective shield and boundary. This boundary is one that the practitioner has cast with intention by connecting with spirit and drawing in and harnessing prana or chi and then directing it outwards by means of hand, finger, wand or athame. It is in a way the same principle as the one we developed as shielding in the chapter on self-protection in that it is a pulling in of divine energy followed by a reforming and using of that energy in a protective and loving way. This circular boundary when set with clear intention will protect those within it from all harm and lower frequencies, which gives a clear safe space in which to work without outside interference. It also means that the only forces that are connected with are those specifically invited for the purposes of doing good and compatible to the purpose of any working. Within the circle energy can be contained, raised and directed. The circle, like the temple, is the sacred space between the worlds and stands between the physical earthly expanses and the heavens. The circle is eternal without beginning without end, both the boundary and the pathway.

Whilst most esoteric descriptions discuss the casting of a circle, the circle is of course in truth three-dimensional and therefore actually a sphere. It is also true that it is just as practical to cast a rectangle or a cube in place of a temple if it is more in keeping with the custom with which one is working. In both cases the sphere and the cube are cast using the four cardinal points and the central axis aligned with heaven and earth and with the central point of God/Goddess. Both square and circle are One. (See the diagram of the first sphere and first cube in the chapter sacred geometry.)

The four cardinal points are typically addressed as the four winds, four directions, four elements, four elemental spirits, four watchtowers, four colours or four pillars. These four cardinal points are usually called through speech and invitation or invocation. In some examples a horn may be blown or a chant may be sung. In other neo-pagan systems they are verbally called as the four directions and ascribed symbols to be traced in the air or on the earth. An example of this may be seen in runic circles which are a neo-pagan reconstruction used to serve the purpose of sacred space in which to work Germanic magic. The eight quarters and cross quarters of a runic circle may be warded by specific runes with protective qualities or associations with deities.

In some magical systems the four directions or quarters are called and the two additional points of above and below are called too. For example calling six points in an angelic circle may include calling upon archangels Metatron and Sandalphon as well as the archangels Raphael, Michael, Gabriel and Uriel. In other four directional systems the pillars or winds are considered to bridge the expanses from earth to heaven anyway and act as both quarters and axis. Both are entirely good systems and work well.

A central pillar, point of balance, internal spirit or divinity is also sometimes called or acknowledged visibly as a seventh point. This can be seen in the colours of the sweat lodge prayer flags. Black in the west, red in the south, yellow in the east and white in the north representing the four directions. Green on the Earth representing the Earth, blue above representing the sky and purple at the centre.

FOUR EXAMPLES OF SACRED SPACE

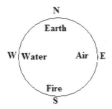

Circle with four
directions and elements
The circle is in truth
a sphere.

Rectangular temple space
with four directions and
elements. The rectangle is
in truth a cube.

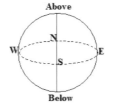

Sphere with the four
cardinal directions and
visible central axis above
and below.

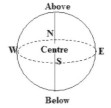

Sphere with the four
cardinal directions and
the visible central axis.
Above, below and center.

If the altar is facing north as most Wiccan and modern pagan books in this country suggest, the east will be the right hand side of the altar, south behind, the west to the left and the north in front. These are deliberately noted in a *deosil* (clockwise) direction as this is the usual direction in which to cast a circle here in the British Isles and Europe. The reason for this is that we go in the same direction as the sun and work in harmony with it rather than going against it. In the northern hemisphere this means clockwise. The sun rises in the east moves south and then sets in the west.

Generally speaking most magical circles and altars require two candles on the altar to represent the male and female creative forces, Lord and Lady or God/Goddess and four further candles to mark the four cardinal directions. These candles should be new or if they are larger ones should be kept specifically for this purpose. The four candles for the four quarters are lit and each is accompanied by the invitation or invocation said to the respective wind, deity, pillar or element. The two candles representing the masculine and feminine principles or God/Goddess are also lit, the feminine first then the masculine, accompanying their invitation or invocation also. Some simple examples of invocation or invitation are included in the chapter on Composing Rituals and Spells.

Circles are usually cast in this order:

The space is ritually swept with a besom to clear out any old energies. Sometimes it is also smudged. Some traditions carry out banishing rituals such as the banishing pentagram.

The God/Goddess candles are lit upon the altar.

It is usual for a blessing to be said over a chalice of water and salt which is stirred with an athame. The invoking pentagram is sometimes drawn upon the water's surface symbolic of invoking spirit into the water. This combines the chalice (womb of the feminine) containing the elements of water and earth/salt with the athame (phalic masculine) potent male principle of air and fire.

The circle is walked three times.

First with the blessed water which is sprinkled around the intended perimeter of the circle.

Second the incense is lit and carried around the perimeter of the circle.

Third the masculine spiritual energy is directed by the initiate casting with a wand or athame. This spiritual fire or air is masculine potency and life force, prana, chi or *ruach elohim* spirit breath in large quantities which is being channelled, harnessed and directed by the person through the wand or athame to cast a boundary.

Alternatives to the wand or the athame are the candle symbolically carried around the boundary representing spiritual fire or casting by use of finger or hand alone. The effect is the same if the intention is clear.

It is at this point that the four-quarter candles are lit and the four directions are called in turn. In most cases the logical place to start is in the east moving clockwise with the rising and setting sun. There are exceptions, however where it may make more sense to start elsewhere. For example if working with Egyptian culture it might be preferable to start in the west as this is the direction of the *Duat*, the Egyptian underworld and land of the dead through which one must travel and pass judgement in order to reach heaven and the realms of the Gods. Examples are given later of different ways of calling the four quarters or directions.

Once the four directions, pillars or deities have been called, the invocation or spoken invitation is made to the God and Goddess for although their candles have been lit upon the altar they have not yet been formally invited or thanked. Once they have been welcomed and all seems well the circle is cast.

It is here within this sacred beautiful and held space that any ceremony or ritual can be held and any magic worked. There is time to pray, to sing, perhaps to dance, to think or ask for guidance. In the event having cast a circle that something has been forgotten it is better not to "cut a doorway" as some might suggest. Unless it's a real emergency do not break the circle that that was created with so much care. In most cases we can ask for an item outside a circle to be blessed for its intended purpose because magic has far reaching effects and will take effect the moment the energy is released. Whatever has been forgotten can then be done afterwards, slightly delayed and yet still safely included without having broken the circle. In the event of a real emergency where there is no choice but to break it, pray in the instant it is happening because the divine are capable of holding infinitely. The work can then be resumed or restarted at a later date and another circle cast.

When the working is done, the ceremony has taken place, the offerings or prayers have been made and time has been taken the circle must be properly and safely closed down. This is the same process in reverse order.

The God and Goddess are thanked in turn and their candles extinguished.

The four quarters (directions, elements, Archangels, winds or watchtowers) are then also thanked in turn and their quarter candles extinguished.

This is usually done widdershins (anti-clockwise) in the northern hemisphere thereby un-casting the circle. Provided that all have been thanked and bid farewell and the candles extinguished the circle has been closed down regardless of which way. Still it is always best to be thorough. The circle now un-cast the full potency of the energy built up is released to take effect and instigate the manifestation process.

Any offerings should be taken outside and given to the earth if working indoors. If working outdoors care should be taken to leave only offerings and to make sure the earth is left clean and respectfully. If working outdoors jam jars are very useful to stop candles from going out. They are useful indoors too if we have pets or children and need to take care with open flames.

Working with Others

Working with others can be a wonderful thing but there are many factors to consider first. For example coming together in an un-cast space or at a relaxed gathering to celebrate a sabbat is entirely different to working as part of a circle, coven or group. When it comes to actively working magic with other people and casting sacred space together consideration must be given to the other people in the group. Both consideration towards them as other people sharing the journey and consideration of them as to whether we should share the journey and the rightness of working together for all concerned. Working in groups takes far more patience, a willingness to cooperate with and understand others and a degree of tolerance for our differences.

Dependent upon the level of involvement of the group and the level or type of work being done, the implications of working together vary and have greater or lesser consequence. Generally speaking if in a large group the gathering is a casual or celebratory one and the more the merrier is the usual way of things. In smaller groups more important work can be done for example earth healing concentrating on a specific area or personal works of physical, emotional and psychological healing. In any group no matter the size it is really important to have confidence in the person who is casting and holding the circle or space and faith that this person is decent and together, knows what they are doing and is capable of holding the people present. It is also important to be in harmony with the people within the group.

We are spiritual beings in physical bodies and when we stand within a sacred space we bring with us who and what we are both physically and spiritually. Whilst the space itself is held and the forces coming in are those invited, it is worth remembering that when we leave if we have formed any psychic attachment with other members of the group we may be affected by any and all other forces with which they mediate. Because the work within a circle or group requires the energy and effort of all who take part, it also involves taking on and mixing with the energy of others. Usually this is completely fine and if anything affords us opportunity to grow but it is still sensible to consider if we want to connect in this way with everyone in the group. The overall pitch or light frequency of the group too is made up of a combination of the frequencies or vibrations of all of the people in the group. It is therefore really important that everyone is in harmony particularly in soul harmony. Some souls coming together in this way have karmic connections or work to do. The overall frequency must adjust to accommodate not just the highest but the lowest pitch. Loving beings even when they have an unhappy day or time are always considerably higher frequency than unloving beings.

A group of course can do far more than an individual and is far more powerful because they can raise considerably more energy. However, one may argue that if working with the divine a true request alone may still be as effective because God/Goddess is all powerful and may bring about the same result in a different way. It may be the difference between dial-up and broadband but ultimately a clear line is the essential part! A solitary initiate like the single dial-up line working clearly will be as effective if not more effective than the group broadband line if there is interference or unclear signals within the group. However a group with a clear connection aligned with love is a wonderful thing.

Two or three people working together can also be extremely strong because it is likely that they hold similar values and are working from the same principles and are therefore in harmony with one another. In addition to this energetically speaking harmonising frequencies tend to amplify one another and open portals of manifestation. All forces and contacts are concentrated within ritual particularly in group workings.

Sometimes circumstances in life change and people change and grow in different directions and when this happens it is usual for it to have an effect both in friendships and in working groups and circles. What is good now may not be right later and that's okay. The important thing is honest communication and being true to oneself. If something no longer works within a group it is completely fine to say so and if necessary to leave if it is something that cannot be resolved or worked through. People develop at different rates and speeds spiritually speaking and it might be that a divergence of pathways comes. If and when this happens even if we are saddened with the situation it helps if we can let that person go in a loving way and move on healthfully. Cutting cords may be appropriate in a magical and psychic sense in order to end the working arrangement cleanly and separate any further workings. This protects us and them from being tangled with each other's future workings which we may know nothing about. This can be a sensible precaution even if the two people have remained friends in every other sense. This same principle can be applied to other relationships when necessary and cords can be cut lovingly with the intention of keeping the good memories and moving on cleanly. It can be especially helpful where healing work has been done. It can also be useful with finding closure.

This principle of ending any workings cleanly is one that can be extended not just in cord cutting but in energetic clearing of spaces generally. If we provide a physical space such as a room, building, structure or garden to someone or to a group for magical purposes, although the group or person in question should have properly closed down their working that space still technically belongs to us and therefore we are responsible for making sure it is properly cleared. As a facilitator offering space there is a responsibility to close any doorways if necessary and clear the space regularly. This is particularly important if the space is used for many different purposes. What a jumble that could be otherwise! There are even circumstances where we may have a karmic accountability for allowing use of the said space in a certain way or facilitating something unethical in the event we were aware of it.

When we hold space for others we are responsible for holding them and anything they bring with them into that space. It is therefore important to be sure we can safely hold them and that we want to provide this service. If we don't like something they are bringing perhaps we shouldn't be holding space for them. Ultimately as the one holding or casting the space there is a duty of care to anyone who comes to us and to anyone they are responsible for in turn. Because it is so important that the people who work with us can trust and rely upon us, this trust cannot be broken and there are circumstances where there may still be a duty of care to people, places or groups we have provided space to before, in so much as making them aware if there is something they need to know about for their well-being. It is reasonable to expect the same level of responsibility and care from another in turn should we choose to go to them to hold sacred space. We should remember though that even the oracle, the high priest or priestess, the shaman or medicine woman are still human and have their own lives and own stuff going on too.

White magic is aligned with the law of love and as such we work within this law. If and when we do make mistakes whether we are the medicine woman, priestess, practitioner or new initiate they are usually our teachers and bring us life lessons. Usually our mistakes and our lessons are proportional to our development and we somehow grow and benefit from them even though we may not always feel that way at the time. We are allowed to fail sometimes and acknowledging failure is part of our learning. We are not expected to get everything right. It's part of our humanness that we don't.

And sometimes there are things that happen in life that are not our mistakes or our lessons. Some things in life just are and we do not have control over them except as to how we cope with them or recover from not coping

338

with them. Bad things can happen to good people. Sometimes in life something awful happens and we can't do anything about it other than to somehow survive the experience. In these moments when we have stood in the fire and all else has burned away we are transformed and loss and grief changes us. When they hit the only thing we can do is to somehow survive them and learn to sit with and bear the sadness or suffering that arises in us without somehow trying to make it go away or change it or deny it in some way. Saying that all things are for a reason somehow seems to diminish and not acknowledge them fully. Can we support another through what seems unendurable? Can we learn to love or trust again? Can we recover and heal and cope again? Can we be altered by the experience and rise from the ashes even when we have lost greatly? Can we find love even in the darkest hours? Can we find love and compassion for ourselves and for the world?

An Example of a Formal Request to Observe and Hold the Circle Boundaries
This example may be used for any similar purpose.

Beltane Gathering in a Stone Circle

'For the duration of the ceremony over the next hour please could everyone here present respect and observe the boundaries of the sacred circle which should not be broken. The reason we ask this is that the circle acts as a protective boundary of the sacred space for all within its casting and will contain the energy we raise within it so that we can direct it to our purpose. It is important that if you begin within the circle you please remain so and avoid breaking it. That includes animals and children so if the grown-ups could keep an eye on them it would be very much appreciated. You can see around the circle that there are eight people just inside the red cord, they are the circle guardians. The red cord is the boundary and is not to be crossed please. (We had used red cord around the stones as well as a visible and clear reminder because some of the people attending may not have been to a ceremony before.) If you do not wish to remain in the circle you are welcome to observe from the outside but you may not enter once we have begun. Thank you.'
After the announcement a horn was blown to the four directions.

In addition to this formal announcement, prior to this ceremony a further precaution had been taken and a larger psychic "safety net" put in place through prayer and crystals at cardinal points of the land just in case one was needed.

Examples of Circle Casting

Please note that although throughout the rest of the book the terms initiate or practitioner have been chosen, within this chapter the abbreviated terms for priest (PR), priestess (PS), high priest (HP) and high priestess (HPS) have been used and left in place with the examples of casting space so that the reader can see who is doing what and gain an insight and understanding of how things may be divided within working groups. These terms may also be useful when reading other esoteric material. Where applicable throughout this chapter the key wording is given in speech marks and the group or congregational response given in brackets in italics.

1. Welsh Celtic Circle for a Sabbat. (Calling upon Arianrhod and Beli.)

Spoken primarily in English because it was the first language of most of the congregation. Cast in a large outdoor stone circle. The Goddess and God candles and incense lit upon the altar by HP and HPS.

HPS: 'By the power of the Goddess and the God may this water be cleansed of any negative influences. A blessing be upon this salt may its power drive out all ill and allow in only good.'

Stir three times then invoking pentacle in the goblet.

Consecrates self and others with the water then cast the circle deosil.

Because it was a large circle three people cast it together one following the other.

PS casts first with blessed salt water.

PR following with flaming torch of fire.

HPS last casting with sword.

Two singers leading a chant to call upon the elements whist the circle is being cast. (*The earth, the air, the fire, the water, returns, returns, returns, returns…*)

HPS: 'By Air, By Fire, By Water, By Earth and By Spirit may this circle be bound and purified. We cast this circle as protection from all forces that may intend harm. We charge this circle to draw in only the most perfect, powerful, correct and harmonious forces and energies which are aligned with love and are compatible to our purpose here today and to preserve and contain the power raised within. We cast this circle as a sacred space between the worlds, a place of perfect love and perfect trust. So mote it be.'

Calling the Quarters (PR)

Alaw (East) 'Ye Lords of the watchtowers of the East, ye Lords of Air, we do respectfully call upon you to witness these our rites and to protect this our circle and we do bid thee hail and welcome.' (*Hail and welcome.*)

Tan (South) 'Ye Lords of the watchtowers of the South, ye Lords of Fire, we do respectfully call upon you to witness these our rites and to protect this our circle and we do bid thee hail and welcome.' (*Hail and welcome.*)

Dwr (West) 'Ye Lords of the watchtowers of the West, ye Lords of Water, we do respectfully call upon you to witness these our rites and to protect this our circle and we do bid thee hail and welcome.' (*Hail and welcome.*)

Gweryd (North) 'Ye Lords of the watchtowers of the North, ye Lords of Earth, we do respectfully call upon you to witness these our rites and to protect this our circle and we do bid thee hail and welcome.' (Hail and welcome.)

'In a circle formed of spirit, of song, of love, we stand. We stand on the sacred ground that is the altar of the Earth. We stand under a hallowed sky. We stand together as one.'

HP
'Yma ni anrhydeddu y duwies a duw.'
'Here we honour the Goddess and the God.'
Read in both Welsh and English.
Offerings made.

2. Angelic Circle for Raising Healing Energy

341

Casting the circle

Sweep once deosil with the besom. Light the male and female Divine candles and the incense on the altar.

Take the athame to the goblet. 'By the power of Elohim, the male and female God force, may this water be cleansed of any negative influences.'

'A blessing be upon this salt may its power drive out all ill and allow in only good.'

Consecrate self and others with the water then cast the circle deosil, once with the water, then the same with the incense, then the same with the wand.

'By water, Earth, fire, air and spirit may this circle be bound and purified. We cast this circle as protection from all forces that may intend harm. We charge this circle to draw in only the most perfect, powerful, correct and harmonious forces and energies which are compatible to our purpose here today and to preserve and contain the power raised within. We cast this circle as a sacred space between the worlds, a place of perfect love and perfect trust. So mote it be.' *(So Mote it Be.)*

Calling the quarters:

'Arch Angel Raphael, heavenly Lord of the East and of Air, we do respectfully call upon you to witness these our rites and to protect this our circle and we do bid thee hail and welcome.' *(Hail and Welcome.)*

'Arch Angel Michael, heavenly Lord of the South and of Fire, we do respectfully call upon you to witness these our rites and to protect this our circle and we do bid thee hail and welcome.' *(Hail and Welcome.)*

'Arch Angel Gabriel, heavenly Lord of the West and of Water, we do respectfully call upon you to witness these our rites and to protect this our circle and we do bid thee hail and welcome.' *(Hail and Welcome.)*

"Arch Angel Uriel, heavenly Lord of the North and of Earth, we do respectfully call upon you to witness these our rites and to protect this our circle and we do bid thee hail and welcome.' *(Hail and Welcome.)*

"We call to you Archangels to come to us and to protect us and this circle of light. We pray for your help and guidance with our spiritual working and undertaking.

In perfect love, in perfect trust, in perfect light, Amen.' *(Amen.)*

3. The Kabbalistic Cross has become widely used and is frequently included in esoteric writings. It is therefore given here as a form of protection which can be used either in conjunction with casting an Angelic circle as above or independently as a form of protection. It is given with invocations for God and the Archangels. No altar or tools are needed to perform this.

The Kabbalistic Cross aligns the practitioner with God through intention, physical movement and prayer. The lines are most commonly recognised as that of the Lord's Prayer.

Touching the forehead say Ateh (unto thee)
Touching the breast say Malkuth (the Kingdom)
Touching the right shoulder ve-Geburah (and the Power)
Touching the left shoulder ve-Gedulah (and the Glory)
Clasping hands together on heart, say le-olahm, Amen (to the ages, Amen).

In addition to the kabbalistic cross the names of God can be called as an invocation to call spirit forth and connect with the Divine. They should be called with vibration in the voice and with love. They are:
Facing East, Yod-Heh-Vau-Heh
Facing South, Adonai
Facing West, Eheieh
Facing North, Agla.

The Invocation of the Archangels
The Archangels may be called upon in a similar way.
Facing East, extend the arms outwards to make a cross of the whole body and say:
Before me Raphael, Behind me Gabriel, On my right hand Michael, On my left hand Uriel.

Repeat the "Kabbalistic Cross" at the start.

4. A Greek Circle or sacred space such as a Temple Space

This is also suitable to adapt for a Roman Circle or sacred space as the Romans adopted many of the Greek religious practices.

Traditionally the four Winds are called:

Boreas (Septentrio in Latin) God of the North wind and the bringer of winter.

Eurus (Subsolanus in Latin) God of the East wind and not associated with any of the seasons.

Notus (Auster in Latin) God of the South wind and bringer of late summer storms and autumn.

Zephyrus (Favonius in Latin) God of the west wind and bringer of light and summer breezes.

The four elements are called:

Hudor (water), Gaia (Earth), Heile (Sun's warmth), Aer (air).

Invocation of Gods

The Greeks worshipped many Gods and Goddesses and religious beliefs varied across regions, however many people worshipped the same twelve Olympian Gods. There are twelve Olympian Gods (listed below) as well as other creative deities and Pan who is Nature personified.

Uranus or Ouranos meaning sky or heaven is the primal Greek God personifying Father Sky. His Roman equivalent is Caelus.

Gaia meaning land or earth is the primal Greek Mother goddess personifying Mother Earth. Her Roman equivalent is Terra.

From their union come all of the heavenly Gods, Titans and Olympians.

In a working it is important to be clear about who we are calling and why. For example we may wish to call upon Hestia (Latin name Vesta) for help with a family situation or something at home for example.

The names of the gods may be incanted either after casting the circle or sacred space or at the eight quarters and cross quarters of the circle.

With some research and study the Greek circle and Gods could be called in Greek or the Roman Gods could be called in Latin.

The following list of the twelve Olympians give both Greek and Roman names. While the number was fixed at twelve, there was considerable variation as to which deities were included. These are the most common:

Greek	Roman	God/Goddess Of...
Zeus	Jupiter	King of the gods; god of the sky, lightning, thunder, law, order, justice.
Hera	Juno	Queen of the gods and the goddess of marriage and family.
Poseidon	Neptune	God of the seas, earthquakes, and tidal wave
Demeter	Ceres	Goddess of fertility, agriculture, nature, and the seasons.
Athena	Minerva	Goddess of wisdom, reason, literacy, handicrafts, science and defence.
Apollo	Apollo	God of light, prophecy, inspiration, music, arts, medicine and healing.
Artemis	Diana	Goddess of the hunt, virginity, archery, the moon, and all animals.
Ares	Mars	God of war, violence, and destruction.
Aphrodite	Venus	Goddess of love, beauty, and desire.
Hephaestus	Vulcan	Master blacksmith and craftsman, God of fire and the forge.
Hermes	Mercury	Messenger of the Gods, God of communication.
Hestia	Vesta	Goddess of the hearth, domesticity and the family.
Or		
Dionysus	Bacchus	God of wine, celebrations, and ecstasy.

5. Egyptian Temple Casting

Light the Goddess and God candles. HP and HPS

'By the power of the God and the Goddess may this water be cleansed of any negative influences. Blessed be this salt may its power drive out all ill and allow in only good.' (stir with athame) Consecration of the perimeter and those within it, followed by incense and fire/candle.

'By water, earth, air, fire and spirit may our temple be bound and purified.'

'We ask that our temple be blessed for our purpose here today supported by the four pillars of Shu as is right and proper.'

'We cast this sacred space as protection from all forces that may intend harm. We charge this sacred space to draw in only the most perfect, powerful, correct and harmonious forces and energies that are compatible to our purpose and to preserve and contain the power raised within. We cast this sacred space as a place between the worlds of perfect love and perfect trust. So mote it be.' *(So mote it be.)*

Calling the Quarters/Pillars of Shu

The four pillars of Shu are the four sons of Horus the Sun God and chief protective deity and are said to be the four pillars that set the bounds to the celestial expanses.

PR or PS
Begin facing West in the direction of the Duat.
Facing West: 'We do call on Quebsennuf, bringer of libation and refreshment, the falcon headed son of Horus to witness these our rites and to protect this pillar of Shu. *Ahh Neterw.* 'Hail the Gods. *(Ahh Neterw.)*
Facing North: 'We do call on Hapi, great runner and navigator of the stars, Baboon headed son of Horus to witness these our rites and to protect this pillar of Shu Ahh Neterw.' *(Ahh Neterw.)*
Facing East: 'We do call on Tuamutef, worshipper of Isis, Jackal headed son of Horus to witness these our rites and to protect this pillar of Shu. Ahh Neterw.' *(Ahh Neterw.)*
Facing South: 'We do call on Amset, the Man who revives, son of Horus to witness these our rites and to protect this pillar of Shu. Ahh Neterw.' *(Ahh Neterw.)*

Calling the Gods – These are simple examples by all means change or elaborate them or adapt them for other Gods.
'We do respectfully call upon the great mother Isis, for she is all that has been, that is or that shall be. We ask Goddess that you witness these our rites and protect this our temple.'
'We do respectfully call upon the great Osiris, Lord of Life. We ask God that you witness these our rites and protect this our temple.'
'We do call upon you Thoth, God of wisdom and knowledge. Inventor of

the arts and of hieroglyphs. Lord of the Holy Words and first of magicians.'

'We do call upon thee Ma'at, Goddess of justice and Divine Order who are the true balance and the weigher of hearts.'

'We do call upon thee Nepthys Goddess of Surprises, Sisters and Midwives.'

'We do call upon thee Bast, Goddess of Protection and of Cats who traverses the stars of the heavens.'

'We do call upon thee Anubis, Jackal formed God who sets the bounds to the celestial expanses.'

'Ahh Neterw.' Hail to the Gods. *(Ahh Neterw.)*

'We do respectfully call upon you to bear witness to these our rites and to protect this our temple. In perfect love, in perfect trust, in perfect light.'

Whilst the introductions have been written and said in English it is possible that you may want to write a prayer or spell in Egyptian such as a sacred utterance to be said with one of the examples of knot magic. In this instance there are many good resources now where ancient papyrus scrolls and manuscripts are available to read online or in book format and it is entirely possible these days to find something suitable and to copy it. In copying hieroglyphic text there is a lot to be learnt. Just as we copied words at school when we first learned to write it is our way of understanding quickest in the doing and emulating of a thing. When writing the hieroglyphs their pictorial shapes and symbolisms are more significant than that of later written forms and there is a different sort of connection with the text as a result. Hieroglyphs also make beautiful works of art.

Exercise

Try casting and holding sacred space for prayer or to connect with God/Goddess and reflect. Keep it simple and not too long. When you are ready give thanks and close down the space properly.

Write about your experience.

Chapter Nineteen
Sacred Sound and Holy Words

Music connects people with each other and with themselves bridging boundaries and reaching the heart mind and leading towards healing as a result.

There is a common belief amongst many cultures that to know the name of a thing is to the know the essence of the thing itself and that by extension knowing the name gives the means to connect with, influence or have governance over the thing. The significance of words and the power they hold is at the heart of every prayer, spell, song and incantation.

Sound and in particular the harmonics of the voice are the expression and vocalisation of sacred geometry and creation itself. The voice has breath, intention and life force behind it and speaking aloud, singing aloud or even whispering sacred or holy words has great power. Bringing those words to paper or to stone in a written language formulates a record for posterity, perhaps for thousands of years, to pass down the ages or to be given to others for the purpose of sharing information. There has been research into the effects of singing upon social bonding suggesting that singing in groups of people may promote faster cohesion between people who were previously unknown to one another, and help create positive social relationships through willingness to coordinate and harmonise with one another in order to enhance positive effect. In other words singing connects people, brings them together and breaks down social barriers. It is also a sacred geometrical expression of creation that can align us with love. The voice rising up from the heart and down from the crown and meeting in the akasha of the throat reverberates across the abyss in beautiful waves of sound. The best forms of magic and of medicine may be found through singing and music and in every culture and religion there are traditional chants and songs.

Words are the vessels of expression and intention, they can influence nations;

they can change history; they carry the stories of our ancestors; they carry our story to the next generations. They have the power to harm and to heal; there are those that are unthoughtful and those that are kind and they affect others around us. We align ourselves with their vibrations and frequencies. We are affected both by the words of others around us and also by our own words, very quickly manifesting in our lives the thoughts and images we attach to them. We all know that choosing good words can make the difference to what sort of day, week, month or even life we are having.

A Brief History of The Language and Religion of the British Isles

Because the emergence of language lies so far back in human prehistory we don't really have any direct historical knowledge of how speech came about. There are a number of theories from gestural development, to language developed from the calls of our ancestors, to an inherent ability which is not an adaptation but part of human culture as a whole. Most of the world's languages are known to be related to others because of patterns of similarities shown between linguistic family trees and the human genetic tree. The common ancestor of most modern day languages is rarely known and more rarely still in existence, however it is possible to make reconstructed Proto languages based upon a common root or stem. For example Proto-Indo European dating from the early to late Neolithic period 4000–7500 BC is the linguistic forerunner of all Indo European languages including most of the current languages spoken throughout Europe and parts of Asia. On a family tree it is the parent language of Germanic, Slavic, Hellenic, Italic and Celtic for example. The earliest forms of Indo European written language appear in the Anatolian languages and Mycenaean Greek in the Bronze Age.

Proto-Uralic, is a language originally spoken circa 7000–2000 BC in the area of the Ural mountains running through Russia from the Arctic ocean to Kazakhstan. It is the parent language of Uralic and Samoyedic, which in turn gave rise to all of the Slavic languages i.e. Finnish, Latvian, Estonian Russian, Siberian, Hungarian and Baltic.

Proto-Dravidian is the parent language of all the Dravidian languages spoken in South India including Tamil, Malayalam, Kannada and Telugu.

The Proto-Afro Asiatic language family descends into Berber, Chadic,

349

Cushitic, Omotic, Egyptian and the Semitic languages (Hebrew, Aramaic and Arabic). Semitic languages are amongst the earliest found in written form with some Akkadian texts written from around 3500 BC in an adapted form of Sumerian cuneiform script. The Egyptians of course also had ancient writing in the form of the hieroglyphs dating back to at least 3000 BC.

There are in addition to these linguistic families some languages known as isolates which appear to have developed independently or quite possibly where the common ancestral line is too antiquated to trace and/or the language too far diversified for recognition. There is a concept of a Proto-Human language presupposing a shared origin of all human beings and monogenesis of all natural languages. Though this as yet cannot be proven and remains hypothesis.

In Qurta, Upper Egypt, a thousand kilometres south of Luxor, there is evidence high up in cliffs of signs of ancient life. The recent discovery has been made of a gallery of rock carvings dating from around 17000 BC of hippopotamuses and aurochs, a type of wild cattle which was the ancestor of the domestic cow. The aurochs were the main diet and sustenance of the Palaeolithic people living here and hunting in this area. These carvings may have been made to influence hunting or out of reverence for the mighty beasts that ensured survival. Both suggestions are forms of magic in a way, purely speculative though they may be.

The Egyptian Goddess Hathor appears as one of the earliest forms of cow or bull worship that we know of, although these ancient carvings may well be her forerunner. Hathor was the Goddess of motherhood, love, joy and beauty who would sustain the soul in the afterlife. Over thousands of years bull worship in Egypt developed into the cult of the Apis bull who upon dying became one with Osiris, "Serapis", as did the pharaoh. In the absence of a pharaoh in unsettled or turbulent times the significance and importance of the Apis bull was increased massively as a living breathing connection with the Gods to be prayed to.

It is in Abydos in Upper Egypt that the first signs of hieroglyphic Egyptian writing have been found. Abydos was the first Royal burial ground and here dating from circa 3250 BC, bone and ivory tags or labels the size of postage stamps have been found. These ivory tags are pierced with a small hole in order to hang them from various items to be traded. Each tag is depicted with animals, birds or plants symbolising their regions of production. By marking them a system was introduced in order to collect taxes or duties from the geographical area of their production. These depictions vocalised are essentially the origins of the hieroglyphic writing system. Hieroglyphs mean "sacred carvings". The secret of the Egyptian hieroglyphs had been lost to us until in 1822 AD the Rosetta Stone dating from 196 BC, representing every aspect of life was translated into common language by deciphering Greek, demotic script and hieroglyphic script which were written alongside one another.

The linguistic history of the British Isles mirrors the religious and cultural journey of the land wave by wave through series of invaders and settlers. There have been fossilized human footprints dating from eight hundred thousand years ago found on a beach in Happisburgh, Norfolk, that belonged to early humans pre dating *HomoSapiens*. The oldest anatomically modern human bones discovered to date in the British Isles are around thirty-three thousand years old and belong to "the red lady of Paviland" who was misnamed upon first discovery and is actually male. These people were hunters and there is evidence that they lived following the migratory route of the animals as these bones were discovered buried with the head of a mammoth suggesting a shared and intertwined existence. The only cave art found in England so far dates to around fourteen thousand years ago and is in a cave near Sheffield. It depicts an ibis, a type of water bird which was also sacred in Egypt.

It is only in the later example of Cheddar man, dating to 7150 BC, that we see the first complete skeleton of a man who would have been one of the first re-colonisers of this land after the last ice age. In that time period during and after the last ice age the landmass of the British Isles was still connected to continental Europe. Only as the ice melted did the land gradually give way to sea. The last such land prior to Britain becoming an island was called Doggerland and this too gradually flooded as a result of rising sea levels around 6500 BC.

As the open tundra gave way to the first wild woods of birch and alder the Palaeolithic (stone age) inhabitants of the British Isles in pre-history were hunter gatherers until the Neolithic period (later stone age) when they adopted agriculture and became farmers quite possibly as a result of coming into contact with other people from continental Europe who had already done this. As a result of farming there was great deforestation of the landscape, development of society and an increase in the production of skilled tools.

We do not know a great deal about religious beliefs of the Palaeolithic, early Stone Age people but we do have evidence found in North Yorkshire dating to 8000 BC of a red deer skull antler headdress designed to be worn with the hide or full pelt of the animal suggesting a magical, spiritual and ritualistic use. Quite possibly this headdress was worn for the person wearing it to *become* the stag or *transform* into a hybrid metamorphosis of stag and man. This has great similarity to shamanistic practices still performed throughout the world and in remote tribes and the act itself is deep within the human psyche as something which has been part of our existence for thousands of years. There is a reverence, an acknowledgement of the spirit of the animal and of the spirit of nature. There is a sense of kinship and belonging between man and animal that is inherent and ageless.

The later Neolithic Stone Age period brought with it the construction of many monuments, huge circular stone temples, megalithic sacred sites and chambered tombs in the landscape. The Ness of Brodgar site in Orkney dates from circa 3500 BC before even the first pyramids and has been described as a Neolithic cathedral or palace. There are massive stone walls with foundations, decorated stone slabs and evidence of housing. The decorations of stone slabs may also be seen as a precursor to writing for these spirals and shapes had meaning and significance to the people that inscribed them. This was not a primitive people, this was an intelligent, organised community working together to farm the land and build monuments and cathedral like temples clearly aligned to the four directions with a sound understanding of the solar year and stars.

The language spoken by these Neolithic people of the British Isles is lost to us now as we do not know the words for the only carvings written. The earliest language spoken here which can be studied is Proto Indo European (PIE) and this is reconstructed from the languages descended from it. The first languages spoken on the British Isles of which there is evidence were those spoken by the Insular Celts prior to the Roman invasion in the Iron Age. The Insular Celtic languages had two divisions and were Brittonic in Great Britain, spoken by the Britons and the Picts, and Goidelic in Ireland, spoken by the

Goidels (Gaels). Goidelic has become the Gaelic languages of Ireland, Scotland and Manx. The Celts had many different tribes ruled by kings or chiefs and there was often fighting amongst tribes. For defence they built hill forts with earthen banks and wooden walls. They walked the green roads and ancient ridgeways. They lived in round houses with thatched roofs and were primarily farmers who travelled by horse, chariot or boat. Some Celts crossed the sea to Gaul (modern day France) to trade with the Roman Empire who ruled there.

In 55 BC Julius Caesar first invaded Britain from Gaul. He didn't stay but returned the next year with more soldiers and captured a hill fort. However, he decided Britain wasn't worth a long battle and returned to Rome. It was a hundred years later that Emperor Claudius sent an army of four legions to invade Britain and this time Rome succeeded and conquered the southern half of the country making it a part of the Roman Empire. The Romans built straight roads stretching for miles across the country such as the Fosse Way cutting through Cirencester and intercepting several other older and established trade routes. They brought technological feats of engineering such as viaducts and underground heating. They also brought with them the Roman language and writing and a number of other influences such as Greek philosophy, Graeco-Romano works of art and spices from all over the world as a result of such huge and diverse rule and trade.

Rome was a vast multicultural, intellectual melting pot of new ideas and opened Britain up to the world at large. At this time Rome was still practising her polytheistic religion and there was a merging of Roman and Brittonic Celtic culture and spirituality. There is certainly some evidence that the Romans identified the names of the local deities with those of their own deities as was their custom and at Bath Spa, Sulis who is a Celtic deity once worshipped at the thermal spring, was worshipped as Sulis-Minerva by the Romano-British. Many Celts allied with the Romans in return for peace and in order to keep their kingdoms, agreeing to Roman laws and taxes. Many people may well have been glad of the new innovations coming into the country, the opportunity for upward social development and increased trade. There is evidence that upon the departure of the Romans that the people here felt abandoned by them and vulnerable to invasion and war both from competing tribes and from external influence.

From around 280 AD onwards the Romans had to guard against Saxon pirates from Germany raiding the shores of Britain and in the north they had to be constantly vigilant of the Picts overcoming Hadrian's Wall. These raids continued and escalated with the Picts, Irish and Saxons eventually joining forces. Although this combined effort was unsuccessful on their part, in 406 AD the last Romans left Britain anyway as a result of an unstable political situation at home with adversaries vying to be the next Emperor of Rome and an unstable physical position in other parts of the Empire as barbarian tribes repeatedly attacked in Northern Europe and Rome recalled her soldiers and resources there as reinforcements. There are reports four years later of the Romano-British requesting help from Rome and quite clearly not receiving the help asked for. Rome had left Britain and was not returning.

Over the course of several hundred years the migration of the Germanic peoples coming from Scandinavia and Germany had moved west in waves. It is one of these waves of Germanic people who were moving west who were described by the Roman historian Tacitus in *Germania* written in 98 AD and by Julius Caesar when they stopped them in Gaul. It was another later group of Germanic tribes moving east and south in waves that descended in time into the Franks, Alemmani, Saxons and Frisians as a result of intermarriage and it was some of these people who had been raiding the shorelines of Britain even during Roman occupation. Now in the fifth century AD, after the Romans had withdrawn the Angles, Saxons and Jutes arrived and invaded the British Isles.

There has been wide speculation that there was an enormous influx of violent invasions, however a more recent school of thought favours a series of smaller waves of invasions. These smaller invasions combined may attest to a large total number of invaders, some coming forcibly resulting in battle and others more peaceably settling and intermarrying with the local people which resulted in a primarily Anglo-Saxon population over a number of generations. The Anglo-Saxons ruled over the south and east creating the new kingdoms of the early Middle Ages and we see their language in the existing names of Essex, Wessex, Sussex and Mercia as well as prevalent throughout our own current English language.

The Anglo-Saxons brought with them their polytheistic religion which shared some similarities with the Celtic polytheistic and animistic nature based religion and the already partially Romanised Celtic deities merged, amalgamated and were compared to the Norse deities. Similarities or reflections can be seen in Berkano or Berkana the Birch Goddess also seen in the B-rune letters of both the Anglo-Saxon futhorc and the Celtic Ogham alphabets. Both the Celtic Ogham and the Icelandic and Norwegian Futharks, which are the pre-cursors to the Anglo-Saxon futhorc alphabet, survive from our ancestors and can be studied and practised as alphabets, both for reading the heritage left to us from those who went before in order to better understand their customs, faith and lives, and for writing and formulating prayers or spells or songs which are authentic to the culture with which we are working. It may be noted here that although these alphabets existed the primary source of written material at this time is either in Greek or Latin across Europe and primarily Latin within the British Isles.

Although Christianity had existed in the years of Roman rules in Britain it had not yet found acceptance even with Rome and had almost entirely left these shores with the Romans when they left save for a few scarce places where it survived on the Western shores. Amongst the people in these places was Saint Columba (543–615 AD) a missionary who brought Christianity from Britain to Ireland and then to Scotland establishing a number of monasteries the most famous of which is upon Iona. This Celtic Christianity then returned to Britain and there was a merging of Anglo-Saxon, Celtic and Roman Christianity coinciding with the mission of Saint Augustine who was sent by the Pope to King Ethelbert of Kent in a meeting that established a strong alliance between Roman Christianity and Kingship. Prior to this, sovereignty or kingship was considered to be given by the deities and guardians of the land. This is the case at Tara in Ireland where the High Kings were sworn upon the Kingstone and was also the case at Scone in Perth in Scotland where traditionally kings were sworn upon the stone of destiny said to have also come from Tara. As such early kingship was seen as sacred and a king is made so because he marries the sovereignty of the Goddess, the earth, and lives according to and in harmony with all that is right and honourable to the land and people he represents.

The Anglo-Saxons gradually converted to Christianity. Whilst for some this was genuine, for others it has been suggested it may have been a necessity in order to continue to trade with Roman Christian countries who would not deal with heathens.

Vikings landed in longships in 787 AD in Southern Britain which had been settled by the Anglo-Saxons, they fought the local people and then left. However it heralded further struggles and in 871 AD the Vikings invaded Lindisfarne monastery heralding a series of relentless attacks, plundering the unfortified and wealthy churches and monasteries and forcing the unarmed monks to escape if they could. The Vikings were Scandinavian raiding parties from Denmark, Norway and Sweden and the word Viking itself comes from the old Norse meaning a pirate raid. Some came to fight and steal, others came for land that could offer a better quality of life and agricultural climate and settled as farmers, craftsmen or traders.

Norwegian Vikings or "Norse" made settlements in the North of Scotland and on the Orkney and Shetland islands. They also settled on the Isle of Man. Although they raided Wales few settled there. Primarily they settled in Northern Scotland and in Eastern England. From circa 900 AD until 1400 AD Vikings ruled the North of Scotland, the Orkney and Shetland Isles and the Hebrides and in Ireland they founded the city of Dublin. Around 1000 AD they sailed to North America and settled for a short time. Viking traders could be found as far as Constantinople, Iceland, Greenland, Russia and Spain and it was Danish Vikings who founded Normandy (Land of the North Men), which they were given as part of a peace treaty by King Charles III of France. Whilst the Norsemen who settled in Normandy adopted French customs, culture and the Christian religion over time, the Vikings throughout the rest of Europe still followed the old ways and worshipped the old Germanic Gods.

Alfred, who later came to be known as Alfred the Great (849-899AD), the Anglo-Saxon Christian King of Wessex, gradually managed to recapture the land from the Viking invaders, securing a victory at the battle of Eddington and successfully defending his kingdom from conquest. Alfred was the first Saxon king to style himself as the King of the Anglo-Saxons thereby unifying the kingdoms of southern Britain in the formation of England. Alfred went about improving education and the legal system, rebuilding and repairing, reorganising military infrastructure and generally increasing the quality of life of the people in his kingdom. Alfred himself a devout Christian ensured that Christianity flourished again throughout the country. In the tenth century lords began providing small chapels on their land where local people could use the services of a priest. This sowed the seeds of the parish system that is in place today.

Alfred's son Edward succeeded him and won control of the north part of England, the Danelaw. His grandson Athelstan gained power as far north as Scotland. The most powerful Anglo-Saxon king was Edgar, who held sway even with Welsh and Scottish rulers. His court was held in Winchester. It was during his reign that Anglo-Saxon England reached its peak. In 1016 under the rule of Ethelred the Unready England was to fall to Danish rule and Cnut (Canute) became king of England. Cnut ruled also in Denmark and in Norway and consequently he left much of the running of government to his noblemen or earls. When Cnut died in 1035 his two sons succeeded him in turn. Upon their deaths however whilst there was rivalry for his succession in Denmark English kingship was briefly restored to the Anglo-Saxon line and in 1042 Edward, son of Ethelred the Unready, became king. Edward had spent much of his youth in Normandy prior to becoming king because his mother came from there. He was very religious and was called "Edward the Confessor" because he so often confessed his sins. On 5th January 1066, Edward died and the next day the Anglo-Saxon Witan elected Harold Godwin, Earl of Essex and Edward's brother-in-law to succeed him. This was not a decision that was well received in Normandy by Duke William who refuted the vote of the Witan and claimed that he had been promised the crown of England. In addition, he had three years previously tricked Harold into swearing to support his claim to the English throne thus strengthening his claim. William prepared to invade and we see first the battle at Stamford Bridge and then the culmination of this invasion in the Battle of Hastings and the ultimate Norman conquest of England.

Throughout these tumultuous years the British Isles saw Anglo-Saxon polytheism and Anglo-Saxon Christianity, Roman polytheism and Roman Christianity and Celtic polytheism and Celtic Christianity. These have been entwined, merged, developed and then interspersed with Viking Norse religion and stories. The languages and linguistic heritage of the people here is a rich tapestry already woven and now the French Normans come. It is following the Norman conquest of Britain that the power of the church really took over. William the Conqueror implemented building on a massive scale, building monasteries and stone churches and establishing castles across England in a grand and powerful gesture that made it unmistakeably clear that the Normans now ruled and were here to stay. Almost twenty years after establishing his kingship in 1085 William implemented the Domesday Survey and all of England was recorded and accounted for so that he knew what was within his kingdom and could tax it accordingly. The Domesday Book was, in effect, the first national census. William ruled simultaneously in both England and parts of France. Although we think of the Normans as being French they were initially the Viking invaders who were offered a peace settlement of land in the north of France.

The Norman dynasty was the first French rulership in England and presided until 1154 when the Angevins the first of the Plantagenets came to power. The Plantagenets were a huge powerful family not just in England but throughout Europe who owned vast lands in Anjou and Aquitaine in France. They were the richest family in Europe and ruled England and half of France. This dynasty is normally subdivided into three parts: the Angevins (1154-1216); the Plantagenets (1216-1399); and the Houses of Lancaster and York (1399-1485) who are usually separated from the other Plantagenets because they are considered the first truly English rather than French Kings. Altogether the House of Plantagenets ruled for three hundred and thirty-one years. This long period of time established French as the courtly language and firmly cemented the Roman Catholic religion throughout England bringing with it centres of monastic learning and literacy, beautiful Latin books and a flourishing also of French literature.

During the French rule of the Middle Ages there were also new influences from the East and from Jerusalem as a result of the Crusades where men waged war upon one another in the Holy Land and throughout the Middle East under the guise of God's will, both sides claiming God or Allah as theirs by whichever name. Holy and war are two words that never belong together though they have been bandied about for as long as there has been organised religion. Both sides proclaim God is on their side and neither considers they are acting against love, against life and against the good or God/Goddess entirely. All war is an abomination of life and all that is sacred.

In understanding our cultural history we gain insight and context for the origins of words and of the cultures that they come from revealing further significance. For this reason the etymology of words can help understand the essence of the thing itself and connect us with the entirety of the meaning.

Words and Sound in World Myths and Religions

All human societies, including our own, tell stories of how the world began. These stories are infinitely variable but tend to include some recurring basic themes. Creation by the splitting of a cosmic egg, creation by bringing order from chaos, creation from the inhumed parts of another primordial being, creation from primeval abyss as an expanse of infinite waters or space, creation by emergence where progenitors pass through a series of worlds and metamorphoses until reaching the present one and creation brought about by the thought, word, dream or physical body of a divine being.

Many of these myths begin with earth, or with the emergence of the earth from primordial space or water. In some of them Gods, Goddesses, humans and animals emerge from the earth like plants. In others the process begins when a creature, such as a bird or amphibian, dives into a primordial sea or ocean and brings up a small piece of earth from which the universe develops. Myths of these kinds are common among Native Americans and aboriginal Australians who refer to the place or time before the moment of creation as "the dream time". In other types of creation myths there is an originator deity who creates life through sound and word and in others still, such as the Egyptian myths, there are various more complex stories in different places, ages or kingdoms whereby a first deity creates other God forms and from amongst these Gods comes another who creates within the world and other beings by means of sound or speech. Ptah the Egyptian creator God is described as thinking the world and speaking the world into existence.

Across almost all religions and cultures words are not just important but sacred. The search for the origin of language has a long history rooted in mythology and though we have looked at the physical practical emergence of our current language in this country we must also look to the religious or spiritual mythology. Most mythologies do not credit humans with the invention of language but speak of a divine language that pre-dates human speech. These divine or mystical languages were used to communicate amongst deities or with spirits, nature or animals.

In Hinduism Vāc is the Goddess of speech, or speech personified. As Brahman's "sacred utterance", she has a cosmological role as the Mother of the Vedas. Brahaman is a Vedic word conceptualised in Hinduism as the creative principle which lies realised in the whole of creation. In the Rig Veda it is written that "As far as Brahman extends so far does Vāc", meaning that wherever there is Brahman there is Vāc, and wherever there is Vāc there is Brahman. In other words speech or word may be seen as an expression of Brahman or divine creation in reality. Brahman itself originally meant the formulation of the sacred utterance of truth or words of power, by the inspired poet, who as one capable of such formulation was known as *Bramana*. Brahman may be seen as the eternal word or truth in manifestation. The *Prasna Upanishad* (a Sanskrit text from the fourth Veda) tells us that "by meditating upon Aum the wise man attains Brahman".

The Aum or Om symbol signifies Brahman, (the conceptualised Divinity, ultimate reality and entirety of the universe) and Atman (the soul or inner self). It is often written at the beginning and end of sacred texts and chapters in the Vedas. Aum is also part of a further reaching iconography in Buddhism and Jainism as well as Hinduism and has spiritual meaning in all Indian dharmas although the meaning alters dependent upon varying traditions. Aum or Om is most often defined as the sound of creation, the cosmic sound, the primal creative vibration, a mystical syllable or utterance, an affirmation or a melodic or harmonic confirmation that gives momentum, energy or life force to a hymn.

The sounds Om, Ah and Hum are often chanted together in a common Buddhist mantra. The three sounds are Sanskrit seed syllables, three words implying trinity. In Buddhism the most usually found trinity is that of Kaya (body), Vak (sound or speech) and Citta (mind or spirit) see mind, body spirit discussed in the chapter on the self. Om Ah Hum reflects the perfect state of being of each of these three bodies.

Om is the primal vibration or harmonics of the universe out of which comes all of creation and to which all things will return at the end of the cosmic cycle. Om is the first manifestation of Shiva-Shakti (male and female creative life force) as conscious sound and the quintessence of the universe. In the microcosm it relates to Kaya, the body, both the physical human body and the reality of the material world of the individual and corresponds to the crown chakra.

Ah symbolises divine spirit and relates to Citta, the individual spirit and corresponds to the throat chakra.

Hum is the root vibration, reflecting on a tiny scale the enormity of the universal Om within the human heart and relates to Vak, the sound or life energy of the body known as prana. It corresponds to the heart chakra. The mantra said together connects the primal, universal, infinite vibration into one's heart, being and awareness.

In the Christian Bible the sacred words come from the Hebrew written before. The word Amen means "so be it" and effectively brings the words said before it in prayer into being. In Neo-Paganism a rough equivalence is "so mote it be". Both are phrases intending to bring something into being just as the symbolic Om is written at the end of chapter so too is Amen.

Examples of creation from sound are in the Christian bible both in Genesis and John.

"In the beginning God created the heaven and the Earth. And the Earth was without form, and void' and darkness was upon the face of the deep. And the Spirit (breath) moved upon the face of the waters". (Genesis 1:2).

"In the beginning was the Word, and the Word was with God, and the Word was God. The same was in the beginning with God. All things were made by him". (John 1:1-3).

The Jewish Torah consists of two parts: The Written Torah, and the Oral Torah. The written Torah is made up of twenty-four books, including the five books of Moses and the prophetic writings e.g. Psalms and Proverbs, etc. The Five books of Moses are Genesis, Exodus, Leviticus, Numbers and Deuteronomy. These five books are also known by many names and are referred to as the Bible meaning book in Greek, the Chumash meaning fifth in Hebrew, the Pentateuch meaning five scrolls, or the Torah which is Hebrew for instructions.

The Jewish Torah has a second part which are the oral traditional teachings that explain the written part. These oral instructions were out of necessity later written down and compiled into the Mishnah (teachings concerning ethics, law and worship), which were combined with the Gemara a large volume of rabbinic discussions discussing them that together form the "Talmud". The Oral Torah also includes the works of Kabbalah, a tradition of mystical secrets of the metaphysical universe received by Moses at Mount Sinai. It was first published as "The Zohar".

The Torah is also called the Tawrah or Tawrat in Arabic and is integral to Islam as are a number of other shared major narratives recounted in the Jewish and Christian scriptures. Muslims believe the Tawrah to be a holy book given to God by Musa (Moses). The Tawrah is not the entirety of the Tanakh (Old Testament) as it is given as instructions but is frequently referred to within the Quran which is the central religious text of Islam. Within the Greek and Hebrew words and origins of these writings we find spiritual and religious language and shared ground for three or more of the major religions and their numerous expressions and denominations.

Music is used throughout the world particularly in song, to chant or to pray and connect with the divine. Through music people express thoughts and emotions, often communicating the inexpressible and freeing the mind from boundaries enabling emotional healing and sensitivity, imagery and deeper insight and understanding of life.

Common musical spiritual themes across the world vary and include praise, worship, celebration, penitence and mourning. Most Christian worship involves singing accompanied by instruments and the Bible has many references to music. The Christian Psalms are songs of praise to God and were first sung in the East as "verse and response" led by Levite leaders specifically assigned to singing or playing music in the temples and monasteries. Hymns followed psalms, adapting melodies of early chants. The Catholic Church developed the "Canticle" where passages of the Bible were sung at specified times in worship and these are still part of the Roman Catholic liturgy today. The first chants were associated with Pope Gregory and are known as "Gregorian" chants. Traditionally the Christian call to prayer is the sound of the church bells ringing and in villages and towns throughout the British Isles and the rest of the Christian world this is still the case.

The earliest music used in Jewish synagogues was based on a system used in the Temple in Jerusalem consisting of twelve instruments and a choir of twelve male singers, twelve being a sacred number in the Jewish faith. Today within the traditional synagogue the majority of the service is chanted or sung out loud, and the Torah reading is also chanted. The Jewish calendar is lunar and the holy days are therefore also lunar. Please see the chapter on the Moon. In ancient Israel a shofar, a bent horn of a ram or another kosher animal, was used to announce the New Moon (Rosh Chodesh) and call the people together.

The "Adhan" is the Islamic call to prayer, recited by the "muezzin" from a minaret, which is a traditional part of a mosque, five times a day. Islamic worship incorporates "music" into worship and the call utilises tonal variation and rhythm in the human voice unalike from the western scale. Recitation of the Quran recognises the words as those of the first recited word of Allah, sounded with perfection and beauty. Muslims believe that life itself is the Divine expression of melody and harmony by Allah. In the beginning there was nothing until Allah spoke and commanded that all things should come into existence.

The holy book of Sikhism, the Guru Granth Sahib, contains hymns that praise God, reveal his nature and give guidance on how to live a good life. Each hymn has its own traditional tune. The singing is called kirtan, call and response chanting of mantras and Bajan, devotional song.

In Hinduism worship at home, Puja, is as important as worship in the temple and although people come together to worship in the temple there is no strong tradition of congregational rite or ceremony. Worship may be through words, music, dance or silence. An important element of Hindu worship is Bhajari, which means adoration and indicates worship with love. This often refers to devotional singing or the hymns themselves. In the Hindu tradition, the world was created by Shiva (and Shakti), whose aspects include Lord of the Dance, therefore dance often forms part of the worship in a temple, along with music and songs of praise.

In faiths all over the world dance and music plays an integral part of ceremony. In shamanic rites people dance and sing things into being. They dance to influence the weather, they sing to raise energy, they influence the hunt, they gain wisdom from the animals and from spirit. In Wicca and many neo-pagan paths it is usual to chant and sing during ceremonies to raise the energy, or in devotion to the Earth, or to bring together and connect the hearts of the people who have gathered together. It is the most ancient and natural thing. Song runs through us like water runs through the earth and sound expresses spirit.

What of our Celtic ancestors in antiquity? What were the chants and songs and words of the Palaeolithic Stone Age man dancing barefoot, wearing the red deer headdress? Did our ancestors dance and sing to their ancestors before them with the drumbeats echoing through the earth beneath their feet. Are we still in touch with all that flows through our blood, through our souls, through our lives? Our time lines stretch back into the past. We carry the responsibility to our descendants; we carry them forwards into their future. We will come to them as elder spirits when they call with their feet upon the earth and their prayers in the fire as we do now.

Some things are inherent; they are part of our genetic makeup, part of our essence. Gazing upwards at the beauty of manmade monument to heaven or feet firmly planted upon the ground and gazing upwards directly into Father Sky, our words are carried. They rise up with our songs and our prayers and our hopes. We carry our words as yet unformed with us in our consciousness and in our hearts waiting for their moment of utterance, their moment of channelling and flowing forth in streams of creation.

Blessings

Blessings are used in many spiritual practices to bless people, the land, their homes, their families, places of worship, sacred sites, events, rites of passage like marriage and personal items with a religious, spiritual or protective function or significance such as an amulet, a token, or an item of jewellery.

The Oxford dictionary defines blessing as: God's protection and favour; A prayer asking for divine favour and protection; grace said before or after a meal; A beneficial thing for which one is grateful; sanction or support.

Merriam Webster's dictionary defines blessing as: help and approval from God; something that helps you or brings happiness; the act or words of one that blesses; a thing conducive to happiness or welfare; grace said at a meal.

To bless another person is to wish good for them and bestow upon them that wish or intention. Blessing comes from a place of love and through a connection with and to a good orderly direction, love, God/Goddess. To bless a house, a sacred item or life event is an extension of this principle and is to ask from a place of love for Divine protection, favour, help or sanctity upon the intended person, date or item.

Blessings are used throughout our lives in prayer and worship, in giving thanks for food and at ceremonies such as weddings, feasts and festivals. There are traditional blessings that are appropriate to the time of year in all cultures. For example Beltane celebrated by the Celts was a time of blessing the cattle and livestock by driving them between the two Bel fires sacred to the God of Light in order for blessings of good health upon them and for increased fertility and wealth. The harvest festivals around the world are thanksgiving festivals that also bless the earth and the produce of the harvest in anticipation of the next cycle. Samhain or all hallows marks the time of remembrance with the dead and is also a time to pray for blessings from or for deceased loved ones.

To invoke or pray to a deity for the blessing of a specific item is also common throughout the world such as the calling upon Thor in order to ask for his blessing upon a symbolic amulet of his hammer Mjolnir, thus affording the wearer of the amulet his protection.

Healing or the laying on of hands, as it is sometimes referred to, can also be seen as a form of blessing where one person is helped, healed or comforted as a result of the intention of love and connection with God/Goddess via another, the person giving the blessing or healing. This is usually done in parallel with aligning with and channelling prana or chi from the unlimited divine source.

Many ancient blessings are still in use today.

"The Lord bless you and keep you. The Lord make His face to shine upon you And be gracious to you. The Lord lift up His countenance upon you And give you peace". This blessing is also used in the Jewish tradition.

The Hebrew for "blessing" is berachot or baruch and there are thousands of Jewish blessings which are short prayers uttered directly to God to give thanks for daily comforts or blessings received by God in a mutual appreciation.

A Gaelic Blessing, *Slainte mhor agus a h-uile beannachd duibh,* meaning good health and every good blessing to you!

Exercise

Write a blessing for your family, home or something else specific.

Chapter Twenty
Composing Rituals and Spells

Rhyming is often used to bind,
Coherent ideas together in lines,
For prayers and spells and incantations,
Watching stars and counting lunations,
Just remember that more importantly,
is intention and love and good orderly... direction.

The writing of rituals and spells varies greatly depending upon the type of work to be undertaken. Some examples of spells are very simple actions based upon folklore or superstition. For instance the folklore of fourteenth century Europe saw shoes often hidden inside chimneys or other parts of a house which were open to outside influences. This was done for protection from harmful spirits by means of confusing or tricking them. It is thought shoes were chosen because a shoe is perhaps the only item of clothing that retains the shape and essence of a person. We have all heard the expression to walk a mile in someone else's shoes. Other common customs are the tying of rowan crosses with red ribbon for protection, the hanging of dried rosemary for purification or blessing and the beating of the walls of a house with birch, hawthorn or another sacred wood in order to drive out anything unwelcome.

A spell is usually defined as a verbal formula or set of words either spoken or unspoken which are considered to evoke magical effect or magical force. The idea of sacred words, utterances or words of power is as we have already discovered inherent in almost every culture. The word "spell" can have fearful or negative connotations in the same way that some other magical words do. In truth of course as with all magic it comes down to intention. Are these words to heal and to do good or words to harm? Are they words to help and cure and support? There are many practitioners of white magic who prefer to refer to their magic as magical working or undertaking or ritual and who avoid the word yet it is the correct word and there is no reason to avoid it. Instead let us illuminate the concept and surround it with so much clarity and light that it is understood the word itself does not depict "what kind" of spell, what kind of magic. Intention and clarity!

Some spells are as simple as lighting a single unmarked candle with an intention and here the line between prayer and spell is almost indistinguishable. Prayer is a vital component in many spells and it is important to remember that the folkloric customs and components of any spell we find from any culture do not come from a place without religion but rather are a product of the culture and religion from which they developed. They may therefore well have been performed alongside prayer to the appropriate deity or personification of natural force. There are examples in Britain of astrological symbols combined with Saints names for instance, after the coming of Christianity, but whilst it was still common practice to continue with pagan customs. Various other symbols too have been engraved onto wooden beams and sometimes drawn into plasterwork on ceilings. The most common of these is the "daisywheel", a circle with petals within it which appears on and within buildings throughout Britain. It appears to have been a general protection against ill fortune or a good luck symbol. Many examples of daisywheels look just like the flower of life design which would explain their association with good and with light patterns!

Spells and rituals work by combining and bringing together harmonising forces through the synthesis of words, sound and ingredients with other factors such as timing. Alchemy is found here in the understanding of how to connect and harmonise with the frequencies of plants, planets and God/Goddess. When we harness all and work in a good orderly direction with the natural flow we have everything in our favour. Words and sound play a massive part in many spells and rituals and it is for this reason that we have considered the linguistic and spiritual heritage of our words before attempting to compose spells. Words are also hugely powerful and it is for this reason that we have spent a considerable time looking at how energetic connections work and the ethical implications of magic. By this stage of development the practitioner should have a good understanding of the function and significance of each aspect of a working when choosing the timing, ingredients and words. There is a checklist at the end of the chapter on ritual which might be helpful.

The written and spoken word have the ability to amplify one another strengthening the intention behind them and therefore writing as well as speaking the words of a spell or prayer increases their effect. Whilst it is true that the ultimate and essential part of any magic is to act from a place of love and to set a clear intention it is also a good idea to word things appropriately. There are many examples of people getting exactly what they asked for through carelessness of wording! Therefore let us start with magical safety nets that are the equivalent of fastening the seatbelt.

As a standard rule of thumb to add on or into any spell or magical working there are safety nets that may be employed. Here are three examples. They may of course be adapted to suit your needs.

1. May this manifest in the best possible way bringing only good and harming none.

2. Please allow for any human error and make any necessary divine adjustments for me.

3. May this come about in the highest possible form of perfect love and perfect light. (All else outside of that will fall away.)

In addition to these we can ask God/Goddess, either out loud or in thought, to look into our heart and mind and see our intention and a perfect solution for us. Sometimes we ask for something that is not in our highest good by mistake but generally unless there is something useful that we need to learn from that experience. These safety nets will only allow us to attract that which is genuinely beneficial to us.

Whilst some prayers are ancient and have gathered great potency and momentum from their repetition across the ages this is not necessarily true where rituals and spells are concerned. Neo-pagan paths are primarily based upon reconstructions of the past and/or a particular culture. Such reconstructions can only be formed from the evidence available through archaeology, mythology, folklore and of course written records. However as with all literary sources and archaeological records they are subject to massively variable interpretations from person to person. I would therefore encourage the reader to seek out material that is as close to the source as possible and read it for themselves. The closer to the original source, the clearer and more authentic the spiritual water and true representation.

Spells then may be best sought out from archaeological records of authentic examples to draw from or are better written oneself because they are personal and may be more authentic if they have not been altered by generations of interpretations. There are of course common customs that can be used such as knot magic and candle magic but if the wording and intention are one's own it is often clearer and stronger. Whilst there are many spell books readily available it is always a good idea to consider any ethical implications of the magic before working it and to study how the spell works and why. Check that it is in keeping with the cultural path you wish to work with and then adapt the spell to suit your own purposes.

Colours

Please see the chapter on the planets to check planetary correspondences including further information on colours, days, hours, plants and stones or crystals. Also please be aware that the categorising of plants is variable and that the most important thing is a logical reasoning. For example lunaria is often used in money spells or kept for prosperity and yet is associated with the moon not the sun. There is often also found an association based upon colour as much as association upon the properties of a plant and as such sacred blue lotus may be used for lunar or water based magic, and yet in its highest form is in truth aligned with source, Kether and the divine opener of ways. To understand the magical capabilities of a plant just look at the plant's physical properties and homeopathic use. Regarding crystals these are primarily categorised by colour. In works of magic the colour of a crystal or stone is chosen to correlate to the intention and planet. In works of healing the colour of the crystal or stone is usually chosen to correspond to the chakra colours of the body. Either is appropriate.

Clear/White	Always	Universe	All sacred to purpose
Yellow	Sunday	Sun	Frankincense, amber, grapefruit, cinnamon
Violet	Monday	Moon	Myrrh, lotus, lily, mugwort, lavender, rosemary
Red	Tuesday	Mars	Myrrh, ginger, cardamom, cloves
Orange	Wednesday	Mercury	Sandalwood, lemongrass, orange blossom
Blue	Thursday	Jupiter	Copal, hyssop, juniper
Green	Friday	Venus	Rose
Black	Saturday	Saturn	Mullein, olive, cypress

Rainbow Magic

Rainbows have always been considered magical and to see one is considered a blessing. There are various examples of magic involving rainbows from around the world such as the Germanic custom to utter prayers and wishes to the rainbow to be taken to the Gods via the rainbow bridge. Rainbows have also been associated with purification and consecration of anything touched by a rainbow. Rainbow water, i.e. water that has reflected the rainbow, may be collected and used for any special magical purpose. Sunshine water, rain that falls whilst the sun shines may also be considered as rainbow water as it imbues the two qualities together as can rain that falls whilst the rainbow is in the sky. Rainbow water may be collected for multi-purpose magical uses as it contains the full colour spectrum. Keep it as a potent addition for spells especially those for peace or hope, salt baths, herbal teas, blessings or water used for artistic and creative works.

Knot Magic

Knot magic is a very simple and practical way of setting a clear intention and is found repeatedly in neo-pagan and Wiccan spells. Use a cord of a colour appropriate to the intention, preferably of natural fibres clearly visualise upon a need or intention. Take the cord and when the intention is firmly established and you feel focussed upon it tie a firm knot in the cord. Then pull the ends of the cord until they are taut. The power isn't inside the knot rather it is released in order to bring the intention to manifestation. The knotted cord is a physical representation and should be kept safely until the magic has taken effect. It may then be burnt or buried with thanks or an offering such as incense.

The same may be done to remove or cast out a thing in reverse. Think of the problem or situation and meditate upon it then firmly tie the knot. Do not forget to do this in a loving way even if feeling upset because we want a peaceful solution here without harm. When ready burn the cord and release it to God/Goddess or Mother Nature and ask them to remove the problem or situation. Again give thanks and burn some incense. Be open to receiving divining solutions out of the blue!

Knot magic can be used for healing and for protection. It can also be used to manifest wishes and there are examples of knot magic which involve tying herbs and plants into the cord as part of the spell.

In Ancient Egypt the amuletic function of knots was a part of life found in religion, magic, mythology and medicine. Different types of knotting were used for different purposes and the most usual of these was linear overhand knotting of one strand or cord although there are other examples of multiple cords. Theoretical explanations for different types of knots and their functions include both polar effects, positive and negative, caused by knotting or un-knotting.

Knotting – holding good in, supporting, containing good, including, connecting, uniting and protecting.

Unknotting – blocking evil out, restraining, removing power, removing harm, releasing blockages, freeing connections, restoring power.

There are many examples of knot magic written in papyrus and the most usual of these is a cord of seven linear knots on a long string worn for protection likened to that which Isis gave to Horus. In these papyruses are frequently instructions for the timing of the knots i.e. one in the morning and one at night until seven have been knotted. These instructions are often to be completed alongside sacred words, utterances or prayers that should be said whilst making the knots or said over the knots daily until they take effect.

Simple Egyptian Amulet

Take a natural cord and pray each evening for seven consecutive nights whilst adding a knot. Wear this amuletic-knotted cord as a protective bracelet. Make an offering of incense by burning a simple incense stick each evening. Traditionally these prayers would have been said to the Goddess Isis. However only pray in whatever way feels right. The knot magic could be done with prayers said to beneficial and loving cosmic force for example.

Isis is the Egyptian mother Goddess and wife of Osiris. She is a Goddess associated with protection, magic and healing. She takes her name from the Greek form of an Egyptian word for "throne". She became one of the most important deities of ancient Egypt and was later worshipped throughout the Roman Empire.

This is very likely also where the concept of cutting cords originated from the idea being that we form cords and attachments in life to other people and situations. If another person is not good for us we can energetically "cut" these cords and this is usually done by cutting or burning, a physical cord symbolising this energetic connection. This can also be done without a physical cord by those who are used to working with energetic connections and able to sever the connection by hand, by magical implement or by asking for divine assistance.

Candle Magic

Candle magic is another very simple form of natural magic, which requires very little other than a new white candle or one of an appropriate colour and a clear intention. Some people like to make their own candles or seek out special candles for a specific purpose. Candles can be used positively for attracting and calling in and negatively for removing and casting out. Always check the moon phase first so that you can work in harmony with natural flow. Freeing oneself from financial worry when the moon is waning makes more sense than trying to attract incoming abundance, which should be done when the moon is waxing.

Candles may be anointed with essential oils to enhance their purpose. Avoid chemically synthetic oils as they have no magical properties. Magical properties are extensions of the physical curative, beneficial and medicinal properties which come directly from the plants which the essential oils have been distilled from. For example a yellow solar candle lit with the intention of attracting blessings and abundance may be anointed with frankincense, prior to lighting it, which is sacred to the Sun and both physically and spiritually uplifting.

Candles may also be carved with names and symbols. For example a pure white candle anointed with lavender (known as cure all in folklore) may be lit for healing and, in order to help the process and make a direct connection with the person, their name may be carved upon it.

Always ask for the person's blessing first or add a worded safety net such as, "I send healing to... in perfect love and perfect trust that it will do only good and shall only be received if their highest self so wishes".

This gives the highest self or soul of the other person the opportunity to refuse it if it is not welcome or not in their highest interest or plan to accept. A further instruction to send the healing to the earth or to another who wants and needs it could be added too, in the event that it is not needed where originally intended i.e. an earthing or recycling.

The same may be said of any form of magic involving another person. Either ask their express permission or word a safety net in such a way that the magic will simply return to the earth, or to the universal whole, or back to you should it not be needed.

Symbols may also be carved upon a candle. In both of the examples given a six-pointed star made of two interlocking triangles would be appropriate. This symbol is used to signify the Sun and makes it perfect for our yellow solar candle (above). This symbol is also used to restore balance and bring things into harmony, which makes it suitable for healing and our white healing candle (above). This symbol is also known as the Star of David or Seal of Solomon and is the symbol of the Jewish faith. It may therefore also be used in any appropriate Kabbalistic context.

When Does a Spell become a Ritual?

A spell can become a ritual either because it is something that is ritually done, for example a prayer said every night before sleeping or at the point where it has developed into something that is more intricate and requires more mediating and harmonising of combining factors. This may be done because of the importance or the significance of the purpose and some people consider this to be the distinction between high magic or ceremonial magic and low magic and folkloric beliefs. The two are not necessarily quite so clear-cut and as with most things there can be overlap, merging and blending of factors. The word "ceremony" is usually used to indicate a more embellished and intricate weaving of individual factors used in natural magic, however advanced spell work, any intricate magical working, rituals, rites and ceremonies share their common components and it is a matter of personal choice as to how one sees them. Below are laid out the key components in composing a ceremony, ritual or more complex or important spell or magical undertaking.

Composing Rituals, Ceremonies and Magical Workings

Preparation time

Different types of workings need varying lengths of preparation time and this might be anything from three hours to three moons. The preparation time is not just the time needed to compose the working but also factors in thinking time. Over the course of three moons it is amazing how much can change and how many new insights we can gain. We may also need to wait for the optimal timing for something specific for example the summer solstice. The preparation time is for setting the intention and deciding the what, why, when, where and who of the working. A good way to start is to remember to write down a "safety net", which can be added to the final working before embarking on the other details. In this way even the preparation time is more secure. All things have a vibrational frequency even as we write and think upon them.

Safety

Safety always comes first and it is important to consider whether the forces or culture we are working with require us to seek any other form of protection in keeping with the customary beliefs attached to it. For example wearing an amulet of Thor's hammer makes sense if working with Germanic culture just as wearing a solar cross makes sense if working with Celtic culture. Be cautious without being fearful and always work only from a place of love. If it doesn't feel loving look for an alternative way or another kind of magic.

Intention

Set a very clear intention. Write it down and spend time considering it. Look at any ethical implications and spend time imagining a wonderful outcome. Try to remain open minded though as to how things may come about because often there's something better than we could have imagined or a reason why things have to happen in a certain way. Be open to divinely ordered solutions!

Clarify which forces of nature you wish to connect with specifically or which deities God/Goddess you intend to call and the forces they represent or are associated with. Consider your wording to harness or connect with those forces. Consider your wording if you are calling upon a deity and be respectful. Do you want to describe them or a particular aspect of them in the way that you address them?

Invocations

This calling or addressing of a deity or spirit for assistance or guidance is often referred to as an invocation, meaning that the deity is invoked either as a channel through the person calling them or more usually in spirit mind communication with the person calling them. Invocations have been written for thousands of years and examples of them can be found across the world. Some have very flowery language and others a more practical approach. In choosing or writing an invocation use language which feels comfortable. It's important to be clear about whom we are calling and to perhaps elaborate upon that by expressing their attributes and/or physical appearance. Hymns, poems and prayers from the original culture are also often used as invocations.

Examples of Invocations

These are examples of Celtic invocations to the Goddess Don and God Beli Mawr and to the Goddess Arianrhod and the God Derg Corra. These invocations were used at large open ceremonies in Wales for sabbats. They are primarily in English because it was for an English-speaking congregation of people. In the first example several Goddess and God names are called. This is not a mixing of systems and is because these specific Goddesses are the lands of Wales, England, Scotland and Ireland personified and the Gods are the father Gods corresponding to each.

'Great Mother Don of the earth, of Light and of mankind. She who is known to us by many names: Don, Danu, Dana, Danann, Anu, Anann. Great Goddess, who gives fertility to the land, who controls the elements, who flows and gives us the water of life and the harvest in abundance. Come to us now in this our sacred circle as we call upon you to honour our celebration with your divine presence and to be with us here and now. Great Mother. We do bid thee Hail and Welcome.' *(Hail and welcome.)*

'Great Father Beli Mawr, shining one who is father of both Gods and men. He who is known as Bilé, sacred tree, Daghdha, the good God, "Ollathair", that is "father of all". He who brings light and healing and who presides over death's pathway to the divine waters of rebirth in the otherworld. Come unto us this sacred day when all the world is sleeping and must soon awake. Honour us with your presence here and now in this our circle as we mark and celebrate the turning of the wheel. Great Father, We do bid thee Hail and Welcome.'

'Yma ni anrhydeddu y duwies a duw.' ('Here we honour the Goddess and the God.')

'Arianrhod Mother Moon of the starry skies. Goddess of the Silver Wheel that descends into the Sea. Benevolent silver sky-lady, come down from your pale white chariot in the heavens. Goddess of reincarnation and the journey of our souls. Eternal ruler of Caer Arianrhod, the circumpolar stars, to which we withdraw between incarnations. Shape shifting Owl Goddess come unto us and through your great Owl-eyes, see even into our subconscious minds, hearts and souls. Guide us with your strength and purpose through the night and always. Place your wings of comfort and healing over we who seek you and honour these our sacred rites with your blessings. We do bid thee Hail and

Welcome.'

'Derg Corra, Father of the Earth and trees and the turning seasons of the Sun. Great God, Green Man of the wild woods and the hallowed land we walk upon. We ask that you hear our call and come to us with love. Shepherd of our hearts lead us from darkness unto day, guide us with your light reaching even into our souls and minds now and always. We ask you be with us this eve and honour these our sacred rites with your blessings. We do bid thee Hail and Welcome.'

'Yma ni anrhydeddu y duwies a duw.' ('Here we honour the Goddess and the God.')

In these first two invocations to Don and to Beli Mawr different names of associated deities are called alongside one another, which is a neo-pagan construct recognising that the same forces or concepts were deified and worshipped throughout the British Isles in different forms. This must be done carefully so that only harmonising choices of name are used and are not muddled.

In the next two invocations this is not so and the invocations are directed solely to Arianrhod and Derg Corra with some description of their personification and the natural forces they represent.

Tradition

Have a look for any associated cultural traditions, prayers, or similar spells. Perhaps there is one that would be appropriate to use in its entirety or one that may inspire writing an adaptation for the purpose.

If it is possible it is good to use the correct language. For example a prayer or chant might be most emotive sung in Gaelic to Brigid, the Irish Goddess of poetry, at Imbolc to ask for blessings upon the land and for good health. That being said as in the cases above if the congregation or circle gathered do not understand Gaelic then it's better to use the language understood by all so that the intentions of the group are focussed. Another alternative is to read one language followed by the translation.

If working in English it is important to understand the linguistic heritage of the language with the cultures that came before it. This is why we looked at the origins of language and religious influence in the British Isles. Through this understanding a living breathing connection with the past is made with our speech. This is one of the reasons for understanding the linguistic and cultural heritage of our country. Connections can also be made genetically through our bloodlines with our ancestors and in almost all cultures the ancestors, grandparents and elders are honoured. Further connections can be made through past life incarnations for those who are able to recall and retrieve past life information in this way and are able to maintain a tangible connection.

It may also be that in some instances a combination of spoken English and another written language copied or learned solely for the purpose of a prayer or component of a magical working may also be used. In these cases a prayer that has been written down may be activated and initiated by fire. As part of the ceremony or working the written prayer or spell may be burnt with incense, offerings or blessings either as well as speech or instead of speech. The combination of both is always amplified.

Words and Language

Apart from a clear intention our choice of words is the most important part of any ceremony or working. Each word we speak or write or think has a frequency as well as a meaning and a heritage. When words are combined to form a sentence or sacred utterance they can carry great potency if they have been chosen and brought together consciously and with full intent. It therefore makes sense to choose them well.

In terms of written language, other than English, those most relevant to the British Isles are Hebrew, Greek, Latin, and the Celtic Ogham and Germanic Futhark alphabets. Hebrew and Greek are relevant because of the origins of the Christian Bible which is based upon the Torah and manuscripts both in Greek and Hebrew. Without recognising this connection all the gnosis which accompanies the Bible may not be fully understood. The Bible in the form we would recognise was first written and spoken in Latin until William Tyndale translated it into English from the original Hebrew and Greek texts. This was not appreciated by those in power at the time and was rewritten and re-branded as the King James Bible soon after.

Christianity was first brought here by the Romans and for many years the prevalent written language was Latin. The Celtic Ogham and Elder Futhark are relevant because although they did not come into being until around the same time as Roman occupation they are authentic to the cultures from which they derive and are based upon the original language. Much of what we know about these runic alphabets is from reconstructed Proto-Germanic and Proto-Celtic language and they are the oldest forms of non-Latin writing native to the British Isles.

Timing

We have already covered timing and understanding the natural seasons extensively so this can be kept simple. Choose an appropriate date, perhaps one of the blots or sabbaths or a holy day that suits the purpose. Then consult a lunar calendar to check the moon phases and choose either the correct moon phase or adapt to the best way of working with a specific working moon phase in order to use a preferred date. Additionally consider any other planetary influences. Perhaps read an astrological forecast for the date in consideration or study a natal chart. Or alternatively work with planetary hours and time it to support the purpose. Remember to account for any daylight saving hours.

Correspondences

Correspondences are the key to bringing forces together harmoniously and choosing correct alignments of moon phases, timing, words, traditions and plants and other ingredients is the best way to strengthen the connections and amplify the working. Choose the ingredients carefully to support their purpose, from buying the right-coloured candles and finding the right-coloured stones to hand picking plants from the garden or seeking out specialist ingredients such as raw resinous incenses. Where possible choose plants that are native or relevant to the place or culture the working is based in e.g. frankincense (Egyptian), rosemary (Mediterranean), heather (Celtic). Choose plants for their physical and magical properties.

Offerings and Other Contributions

Is there an opportunity here to have a reading or poetry? If working in a group can the other members contribute here by reading about the Sabbat or the purpose of the ceremony in more depth or by bringing and sharing other prayers or songs?

Are there offerings to be made either as a group, such as wine and cakes, or have other people brought individual offerings, artwork, feathers?

Is there anything symbolic to be burnt in the ceremony such as a Yule log, a corn dolly, or prayers written on paper by the members of the circle?

Is there anything to be passed around or to keep for posterity such as a stone or a keepsake of some kind?

Is there oil to anoint one another or a moment to hug the person standing next to us or to connect more within the group?

What about singing or dancing together to raise the energy? Is this intended as a fun and light hearted ritual? Add any movement, music, songs, chants or spontaneous sound that feels right. Music is sacred geometry in expression and the highest human expression possible particularly through song and the voice.

Prepare a sacred space and/or altar in which to hold the ceremony or working.

Prepare a clean, clear and beautiful sacred space and altar or place to work that is suitable for the working. See the chapters on holding sacred space and the altar. Sometimes this altar may be upon the earth or be a clearing in the woods also.

Watch the moon and wait for manifestation! Most workings take effect in one moon, three moons or nine moons depending on their potency, depth, significance and other possible contributory factors.

In the event of making a mistake or not having enough time to plan anything elaborate, lighting a candle to pray is often the quickest and easiest way to ask for assistance.

Examples of Blessings, Spells and Prayers

Hindu Blessing on a House. (Translated into English.)

From the eastern direction I summon a blessing to the glory of the House. Praise to the Gods, the praiseworthy, forever and ever! From the southern direction, the western direction, from the northern direction, from the depths below, the heights above, I summon a blessing to the glory of this House. Praise to the Gods, the praiseworthy, for ever and ever. (Artharva Veda 1X, 3.)

Scottish Gaelic House Blessing *(Beannachd Taighe)*
A Dhé, beannaich an taigh,
Bho stéidh gu stàidh,
Bho chrann gu fraigh,
Bho cheann gu saidh,
Bho dhronn gu traigh,
Bho sgonn gu sgaith,
Eadar bhonn agus bhràigh, Bhonn agus bhràigh.

English Translation
God, bless this house,
From foundation to stairs,
From beam to side wall,
From roof to upright beam,
From ridge to basement,
From floor-joist to roof-truss,
Between foundation and attic,
Foundation and attic.

House Blessing

To bless and cleanse a house water, salt, incense (preferably white sage) and a bag of plain white tea light candles will be needed. A mirror is also useful!

Start with a physically clean house free from clutter and turn off electrics especially WiFi and mobile phones as these are direct connections into the space. It is the equivalent of closing the doors. Start at night whilst it is dark either after the sun sets or at midnight.

1. First say prayers over all of the items intended for use. Pray in whatever way is natural and feels right whether that is to good cosmic order and love or to God/Goddess. Ask for the items to be blessed for their purpose.

2. Engrave white tea lights with a holy or sacred symbol and light one in each room of the home. If possible arrange the candles around the house in a geometric shape. A six-pointed star for example to restore balance. By placing the candles in this way sacred geometry made of light will fill the house and raise the frequency of all else into alignment. The number of candles can be increased to make other light patterns. Prayers appropriate to the culture may also be said over the candles at the point of marking them.

3. Whilst the candles are burning sprinkle all the rooms with blessed salt water paying particular attention to any shadowy places or anywhere that feels stuck or heavy.

4. Then carry the incense around the house and smudge the rooms in the same way.

5. Then carry a further candle symbolising both male and female cosmic principles combined and use a mirror to reflect the light into any hidden places previously not reached.

6. Wait for the candles to burn out around the house obviously paying close attention to them and regularly checking each room. Never blow out spell candles, always wait for them to do their work. Candles are of course a fire hazard so they must be placed in safe places perhaps on plates or in glass jam jars and on non-flammable surfaces away from anything that could catch.

7. Wait for the light of dawn before opening the house to fresh air and new light. Greet the dawn by burning incense and giving thanks.

N.B. If the candles were lit after sunset and burnt out late at night either go to sleep until dawn or read or draw or something until dawn but still wait for first light before opening the house as the intention is to greet the new light of dawn with a clear house.

This house blessing not only removes and banishes anything of a low frequency but also draws in the harmonious and good leaving you with a clear and bright safe space. It can also be used to consecrate a sacred space such as a temple.

Egyptian Incense for a House Blessing

Can be used for offerings and for other compatible purposes.

Mullein leaf – for purification, protection, cleansing and the banishing of harmful influences.

White sandalwood – for protection, healing and clearing. Helps to manifest intent and increase concentration and energy flow.

Frankincense – for successful ventures, consecration, purification and aligning self-will with the divine.

Myrrh – for spiritual opening, meditation and for high vibration that will enhance, strengthen and amplify all other ingredients and the working.

Rose – for love, friendship, domestic peace, happiness, emotional healing and lasting relationships.

Amber – for divine universal balance, mental clarity, protection from harm, transforming negative into positive energy.

Wherever possible look for ethical suppliers of plants and incense or pick and grow the most helpful herbs and plants.

Abundance Blessing

Great Mother of the Earth, Great Father of the skies.
We ask for your divine blessings to be bestowed upon us.
May we be entrusted with your land and may it be rich and fertile and our crops grow well.
May our families and our children be blessed with good health, happiness, abundance and love for one another.
May our minds, bodies and spirits be healthy and strong.
May our plans and projects be inspired and successful.
May our homes be warm, secure and safe, giving us sanctuary.
May our animals and pets be healthy and happy and may their young grow strong.
May our hearts be open to receiving your divine guidance in order that we might work towards our true life calling and fulfil our true potential.

May our strength and courage to do so be unfailing and overcome all obstacles.

May we be helped and lifted by you and open to receiving your help and guidance and support.

May our eyes be open to see truth and to see the joy and beauty of life.

May our minds be open to receiving wisdom and knowledge.

May we learn to exercise patience and to act with loving kindness towards others and ourselves.

May we live together peacefully and in harmony with one another and with the land.

May love and light be with us and be reflected in our daily lives.

We are your children now and always and we thank you with our whole hearts.

Love Spell

To be worked upon a waxing moon.

Take one pink candle and engrave it with the words "I am love".

Anoint the candle with rose oil.

Take a piece of rose quartz or rose quartz jewellery and anoint it with the rose oil too.

Light the candle at sunset and repeat the words "I am love" seven times.

Do not specify or think of any one person whilst doing this rather think of a soulmate and be open to the universe bringing you the right person in the right way.

I am Love will open the heart chakra to a loving vibration.

I am Love will align us with loving thoughts and images.

I am Love will support loving forces to bring and attract love to us.

I am Love will call out to the soulmate or person who can love us back.

I am Love will melt any distrust we have around love and replace it with trust.

I am Love will prepare us so that we are ready for the love we are attracting.

I am Love will bring love into our own hearts and fill us up so that we already feel it.

Give it a little time and remember that love is worth waiting for. There may be other factors to consider like the other person's free will and divine timing but be assured love's on its way. Love works in many ways so remember to try to be open minded as to the how part, that's in heaven's hands. Don't be surprised if ways of preparing for love appear out of the blue or invitations to new places or groups start popping up!

If the rose quartz is an item of jewellery it can be worn as a daily reminder of I am Love.

Calling for Justice

When it comes to asking for justice it can be tempting to take matters into our own hands particularly where feelings are hurt or tempers are up. However, we do not see the whole picture and have no idea what will happen in another person's life or what karmic lessons they will learn when. In the event that we feel the need to act the simplest way to ask for justice is to pray to good cosmic forces or God/Goddess for it.

Whilst praying, light a plain white candle anointed with sage oil and engraved with the name of the other person or thing and the name of ourselves and the word "justice". Upon lighting the candle give all worries to God/Goddess and trust that this will be taken care of. Sometimes we may get to see this played out but often we do not and it is up to us to trust that heaven is taking care of it.

Only ask for justice where one is sure of integrity as it can and will always fall on both sides of the scales!

Exercise

Write and perform a house blessing for your home.

Chapter Twenty-One
Divination

The blueprint of the soul in the birth chart shows that some things are predestined or fated and others are governed by our choices and will. To see the future is to see one possibility unfolding and to predict it giving us time to prepare for the new or make adjustments to our course.

Divination is the practice of seeking the knowledge of the divine about the future or the unknown. It is synonymous with prophecy, prediction, fortune telling, soothsaying and augury. The word divination comes from the Latin *divinatio*, (*divinare*) meaning to foresee, to predict or to be inspired by a God and it is related to the word *divinus*, meaning divine through its etymology *deus*, God.

Generally speaking there are two types of divination, the first is augury, divination by means of reading and interpreting earthly signs or omens, sometimes thought of as the lower form of divination. The second is inspirational, divination caused by direct communication with or inspiration by the Gods, enabling the diviner to see or channel as an oracle, sometimes referred to as higher divination. Underlying all methods of divination there is the belief that spiritual beings, whether Gods or spirits, possess knowledge or an overview and can help and guide us as to our best course of action and advise us of information otherwise unknown. There is of course a great deal of crossover to be found between the types of divination and they need not be separate. The observance of the stars and planets for example can be thought of as charting the heavens or even in many cultures as observing the movements of the physical Gods themselves as the planets and stars were often personified with theophoric names. The physical movements of those stars and planets may as a result be interpreted as divinely imparted signs.

Whilst divination of outward signs was the Roman preference, an inward looking divination due to the inspiration of the Gods was the Greek preference and it was this kind of inspirational divination that we associate with the Greek oracles and also with prophets who receive and pass on a message from deity. Chrysippus, a Greek philosopher who died in Athens in 207 BC defines divination as "a power in man which foresees and explains those signs which the Gods throw in his way". Of course in either case the divine can bring guidance and communication to the seeker and both types of divination can work and are valid ways of seeking information or guidance. We all use our natural abilities and gifts as best we can and some people have strengths in different areas. Certainly the ancient Babylonians, Egyptians, Greeks and Romans believed that not only oracles but also omens of all kinds are given to men by the Gods and express the minds of these Gods. This belief in signs gave rise to many superstitions found readily throughout all cultures that were once founded upon relevant religious belief systems.

Primarily most forms of readily available divination that can be easily taught are of course augury, the reading of signs and omens. There are many books available on folklore, omens and superstition. One could also consider some books on dream interpretation in this category to some degree, as they tend to draw upon unconscious or archetypal images and meaning. Divine inspiration is not something that can be taught or instructed upon through the pages of a book and is generally received only at the choosing and invitation of the Gods. However the Gods may be asked for assistance through prayer or by the simple lighting of a candle with the intention of making connection in order to receiving messages or signs through physical observances or inner feeling. Examples of inspirational divination that are more common include inspirational dreams, visions found in states of altered consciousness and unsolicited spontaneous knowledge or inner knowing brought about by an epiphany of some kind.

Among the ancient Babylonians, Egyptians, Greeks and Romans the priest, priestess or oracle generally stood in the service of the state and was officially consulted before wars and other great enterprises were undertaken. There were also priests and priestesses in some of these cultures who specialised just in divination or astronomy for example or in the reading of physical omens. There were, however, certain types of diviners who were forbidden from working magical arts such as divination. It is probable that this is visible magical discernment at work and that what we see in these examples is the state or the priests, priestesses or advisers of the state disallowing certain types of hostile divination. Here we see the differentiation of the time to light or dark magic. These unwelcome forms of divination may have worked through lower types of magic, dangerous or unstable spirits or Gods, or other things threatening to the good of the state or against good order. These attributes and definitions would of course alter depending upon time and culture.

As with all other subjects in this book the focus is primarily upon the most commonly used forms of magic and esoteric study in Western society. The focus of this chapter is therefore mainly to outline the Tarot, the Germanic runes and the Celtic Ogham.

Whilst at first glance the Tarot, the Germanic runes and the Celtic Ogham have no obvious correlation beyond divination they have been chosen specifically because of their widespread popularity and because of their cultural, religious and spiritual significance and connections with western religious beliefs. Whilst all three have been presented in the context of divination they are therefore of equal significance as spiritual tools for self-guidance, meditation and for spiritual development, and for obtaining a deepened understanding of the cultural and religious paths from which they originate. Most of these divination practices have developed over time as an inherent part of a specific path and heritage and are groundless and certainly less effective without an understanding of their holistic origin and surrounding teachings. It is common that many forms of divination correspond astrologically with stars, planets, signs and various other forces of nature and that they therefore have relevant mythologies and inherent lessons and teachings associated with them.

Whatever the form of divination being used by the practitioner, its function is primarily to connect with cosmic forces, earth energies and/or Archetypal forms in order to receive wisdom. Card decks and runes are useful tools that make direct communication easier and allow guidance for the seeker. Some clairvoyants will of course also gain other insights and the cards may be unnecessary or simply a convenient guide. For those who are learning or developing clairvoyance the cards or runes alone are still sufficiently useful to be able to offer a valuable and insightful overview.

As with all natural forces and Archetypes it is important to be respectful and this includes how we treat our cards. It is essential to clean them regularly with incense smoke or prayer preferably before and after each reading and to keep them within their correct decks and not muddled up with other cards and energies. Many people also recommend not letting anyone else touch them unless it is because they are being read for. It is sensible to have a clean cloth that can wrap the cards and also to use as a tablecloth for card spreads solely for that purpose. Lighting a candle and praying or making connection before working with the cards can be helpful and bring illumination and over-lighting to the reading. Many packs of tarot and oracle decks have books that come with them with suggested card layouts and these are useful to begin with. Over time the reader may be encouraged to devise their own reading layouts and questions. Drawing it out on paper first can be helpful to get a clear outline and think through the purpose.

A deck of cards is only as safe and as light as the mind and the hands that created the deck and the mind and hands of the person holding and reading the deck. Therefore the most important thing is to pick a bright, light deck of cards that feels good and reliable. If it doesn't feel right or the images aren't right for you choose another. It's so important to feel happy with the energy of the deck and that they represent the forces you wish to connect with. The same can be said of runes, oracles and any other item used for scrying such as a crystal ball. Scrying is the art of reading or perceiving images or information through the means of looking into a crystal ball, mirror, water, reflective surface, smoke or fire. Crystal balls take extra cleaning, need to be wrapped when not in use so as to keep them clean, as they pick up so much and must be chosen with great love and care to find the right one.

The single most important thing as with all things is of course to proceed with love and to always read from a place of love. Cards are sensitive and fearful or unstable thoughts can affect the reading. Many would say that the cards are only channelling one's higher self and wisdom and what is likely already known on some level. It is therefore important to be in a balanced frame of mind because otherwise how might the truth be discerned. Others consider the cards are a channel for God/Goddess and a way of asking directly for guidance. In this case it is equally important to be in a balanced state of mind and acting from a place of love, in order to be a clear channel and receive the messages as intended without affecting either the cards chosen or the interpretation of them in any undue way. My own opinion is that both are true and that one is not exclusive of the other as God/Goddess are omnipresent and within as well as without. In either case what matters is a clear mind and a loving point of connection. Where there is love there is truth.

Whilst it is true that within the tarot deck there are a small number of cards that may seem daunting or scary my own experience is that when they are viewed with love they are not necessarily so and are there either to acknowledge suffering we have been through, to aid us in understanding harder parts of our lives, to guide us through difficult times and/or in some cases to let us know that this is a possibility and that we may either need to prepare ourselves for something or change our path in order to attract a different outcome. The same can be said regarding the interpretation of some of the Germanic runes, as well as a reminder that they originate from a different time and a culture much hardier than our own.

None of these things are negative in themselves but rather are an acknowledgement that life has ups and downs and that the human condition is subject to going through times of sadness, challenges of life and of growth, as well as the times of happiness. It is of course possible to consider difficult things with tact and consideration and it would be unrealistic and ultimately not helpful to skim or shirk facing anything difficult with the cards. There is in truth no need to be fearful of any of the harder cards because they are in fact only here to help us, to empower us and to ease our way with guidance. The same may be said of the interpretation of cards.

Some people read some cards "reversed" if it presents upside down in a read, other people may just feel which way the card is intended. For example the temperance card, which is about nurturing and balance, may be an indication of qualities inherent in a person or those advisable to handling a situation, or it may be an indication of qualities lacking in a person or in the handling of a situation. This depends upon its context. The context of a card is made up of the surrounding cards which combined give an overview of the situation, whether the card is the right way up and any thoughts or feelings that come up in relation to the card. Querent is the word for a person who is enquiring i.e. being read for.

There is a great deal to be said about choosing a deck wisely and seeking one that feels loving, light, supportive and safe. May your readings be blessed and guided by love.

The Tarot

The origins of the tarot have been a subject of much controversy. However, there is evidence to suggest that the first playing cards may have originated in China, then spread to India, Persia and into Egypt before reaching Europe through both the Italian and the Iberian peninsulas in the second half of the 14th century. In the *Llibre de Concordances*, a Catalan rhyme dictionary compiled by the poet Jaume March in 1371 Catalonia, the cards are referred to as *naip* defined as "playing cards". In 1376 Florence a game called "naibbe" was forbidden in a decree, with the implication that the game had only recently been introduced there. This word *naip* probably comes from the Arabic *na'ib* (deputy, viceroy, governor) who is a court figure in the Arabic Mamluk deck. Giovanni di Juzzo da Covelluzzo, a 15th century chronicler, related that in 1379 a game of cards was introduced into Viterbo in Italy and that the rules of this game were said to be something similar to Bridge. The oldest tarot decks still preserved in museums today date from the time of the Italian Renaissance. The English word tarot is a French derivation of the Italian *tarocchi,* originally *trionfi*, meaning "trumps" or "triumphs".

Antoine Court de Gebelin was a French archaeologist who wrote a book called *Le Monde Primitif* in 1773-1782. He suggests that the tarot preserved the wisdom of the Book of Thoth, the legendary book of the greater Egyptian mysteries. This book included a description of how to lay out and read the cards as they would have been used by the ancient Egyptian priests though how this theory was supported is unclear. In 1785 another book, *Maniere de se recreer avec le jeu de cartes nomees Tarots* (*How to Entertain Yourself with the Deck of Cards Called Tarot*) was published by Etteilla. Etteilla provided explanations as to the meanings of the cards and suggestion as to how to lay them out and read them for divination. Etteilla believed the tarot to be Egyptian in origin and said that he had studied the tarot and learned the art from an Italian who shared the secrets of his folk tradition to him. The Italian who taught him may well have used the cards for both divination and magical purposes and this could have contributed to the spread of their use and popularity. Many suggest the cards originated with the Romany people. This may be the result of a fictitious writing about their being brought to Europe by gypsy travellers or based on truth. The Romany, or Gypsies, were originally from India, not Egypt, and did not arrive in Europe until the 15th century, one hundred years after the tarot appeared. However, the cards did travel from India, to Egypt and then into Europe on the same route as the Romany. It is possible that there is a slight discrepancy in the time line or that the earliest versions of the cards were not immediately widespread or well documented.

The seventy-eight cards are made up of two different types, the Major Arcana, (from the word *arcane* meaning secret, or hidden), of which there are twenty-two and the Minor Arcana, of which there are fifty-six.

The tarot eventually became associated with the Holy Kabbalah, particularly the Kabbalistic Tree of Life. There is disagreement about when and how these two constructs of metaphysical thought came together with theories ranging from biblical times to the 19th century, perhaps as a result of a suggestion of shared ancient Egyptian origins pre-dating either individually. However, by the nineteenth century, the two modalities were clearly used together and in 1856, Eliphas Levi published the first book to associate the twenty-two cards of the Major Arcana with the twenty-two letters of the Hebrew alphabet, and the four suits of the Minor Arcana with the four-letter name of God. Further similar variations by others followed soon after.

The Kabbalistic Tree of Life (see chapter ten) is itself a diagram of the organising principles found in the structure of creation and the dynamics of the relationship between God/Divinity and creation. This symbolic illustration of the working structure of the universe and our place in it may be considered effectively a map for the journeying soul, as a means of progressing through the twenty-two initiatory paths of existence known as The Fool's Journey and symbolised in the major arcana cards of the tarot. These twenty-two pathways further correspond to the letters of the Hebrew alphabet and therefore to sound in creation. The Fool's Journey encounters the actual or virtual reality of all the diverse forms of experience available to the human race, different states of consciousness and subjective experiences arising from internal conditions of the individual psyche while travelling the various paths. The story of the Fool's Journey makes them memorable and easy to relate to for the reader. Therefore the initiate who has knowledge of the Tree of Life understands and better sees the cards of the tarot and the guidance offered is both physical and existential.

The tarot offers a physical, tangible seventy-eight card version of the Tree of Life to the reader where parallels may be drawn between the tree and the cards. Please see the Tree of Life chapter for the correspondences of all the individual cards.

The Germanic Runes

Recent genetic analysis suggests that over fifty percent and up to one hundred percent of the current native population residing in England are of Anglo-Saxon descent. The Angles and Saxons in turn are of ancient Germanic descent, a Northern European people also sometimes referred to as Teutonic or Gothic, with a shared linguistic group which later diversified from Proto-Germanic during the pre-Roman Iron Age. The initial Germanic settlement of Britain by Angles and Saxons is thought to be during the 5th century when the Romans withdrew. However, Germanic influence may have already been felt as a secondary influence of trade. The existence and similarities of the Germanic runic alphabets with the Celtic Ogham runic alphabet of between the first and fourth centuries AD would certainly support a crossover of ideas and developing cultures throughout Europe and the British Isles. The current genetic evidence supports that the pre-Angle Frisians have an identical DNA structure to the one we still see today in England which means this can only be as a result of genetic heritage. A large number of people from the British Isles then are directly descended from Anglo-Saxon Germanic genes and it makes perfect sense that there is a recent resurgence of interest in our Germanic cultural and spiritual heritage. This is not true of Welsh people, however, who are descended from different DNA and are of Celtic origin although there is obviously marriage and blending of the two.

Prior to Christianity the religious beliefs of both the invading Roman empire and the Insular Celts of the British Isles were polytheistic, so too were the beliefs of the Germanic settlers. Germanic polytheistic paganism took varying forms across Northern Europe depending upon area and local influence. However, the best-documented version may be found in the 10th and 11th century Norse religion. There is also some information from Anglo-Saxon and continental Germanic sources, a smaller amount found in Roman documentation and some traceable through pre-Christian folklore.

These Germanic Angle and Saxon settlers brought with them to our shores their religious customs and beliefs and Norse Mythology in the form of stories known as the Sagas. The primary written sources of Norse Mythology are the *Prose Edda*, composed in the 13th century by Snorri Sturluson, and the *Poetic Edda*, a collection of poems from earlier traditional material anonymously compiled in the 13th century. The bulk of this earlier material are versions of much older oral traditions that were compiled and written in manuscripts in Iceland by the first settlers there. There are thousands of these stories that make up the saga corpus dating from the migration period legends onwards to the family histories of the Icelandic people written in runic script. These sagas were the stories of Gods and of men. They were poetic, naturalistic expansive narratives written in prose about heroes, money, love, affairs, marriages, blood feuds, revenge, sex, death, shamans and nature spirits. They presented deities and supernatural beings as actual or magical beings and as founders of dynasties and races of physical people as forefathers.

Runic inscriptions are found on objects such as jewellery and on stone monuments and amulets. There is also evidence of significant or spiritual objects such as Thor's hammer being used as amulets and found amongst burials.

The Elder Futhark is the oldest form of these runic alphabets and therefore the origin of all later runic alphabets to develop from it. It dates from the migration period and was a secret only known to a literate elite; around three hundred and fifty inscriptions survive. Pre-dating the runic alphabet's development were pre-runic symbols, or hällristningar, which have been found in various Bronze Age rock carvings, primarily in Sweden. Some of these symbols are included and are easily identifiable in the later alphabets, while others may depict ideas which have since been enshrined in the names of the runes. Although the exact meanings of these hällristningar may not be clear it is thought they served a magical or prophetic function and as such they are the magical foundation upon which the later developments of the alphabet were built.

In a literary capacity the shapes of the Elder Futhark runes are thought to originate from an older Italic script, possibly Latin, or one of a number of now extinct Etruscan or Raetic alphabets, or even a combination of these. Its possible source of invention is attributed to someone of Germanic origin coming into contact with Roman culture perhaps through trade or invasion. The Elder Futhark was used by Germanic tribes from as early as the 2nd century up until the late 8th century when the script was simplified and predominantly replaced by the Younger Futhark within Scandanavia and simultaneously expanded upon by the Frisians and Anglo-Saxons developing into the Anglo-Saxon futhorc.

Inscriptions of the Elder Futhark are found dating from around 150 AD onwards in Scandinavia, South East Europe, Germany, the Netherlands and England. Whilst the Scandinavian Younger Futhark and the Anglo-Saxon futhorc were in use during the Middle Ages the knowledge of the Elder Futhark itself was forgotten until it was deciphered by Budge, a Norwegian scholar in 1865. The Elder Futhark is so named "elder" because it is the older alphabet and "futhark" after the first phonetic sounds of the first six runes, just like the Greek word alphabet is named after *alpha* and *beta* the first two letters of the Greek alphabet. The Elder Futhark alphabet consists of twenty-four runes in total, which are usually arranged in three lines of eight runes called an *ætt*. The rune names come from the vocabulary of daily life, nature and mythology.

Whilst the Elder Futhark is in the first instance an alphabet, the runes each symbolise these natural forces, daily, life, mythology and associated religious beliefs. It makes logical sense that they were also used for the purposes of divination each rune being representative and embodiment of the forces they depicted. Runes for divination are usually carved upon wooden staves.

The diagram shows the Elder Futhark runes with their common Germanic transliterations and meanings.

The Elder Futhark Runes

ᚠ	ᚢ	ᚦ	ᚨ	ᚱ	ᚲ	ᚷ	ᚹ
Fehu cattle/ wealth	Ūruz wild ox/ aurochs	Þurisaz giant	Ansuz God/ Aesir	Raidō Ride/ Journey	Kaunan/Kenaz Ulcer/ Torch	Gebô Gift	Wunjô Joy/ Glory

ᚺ	ᚾ	ᛁ	ᛃ	ᛇ	ᛈ	ᛉ	ᛋ
Haglaz hail	Naudiz need	Isaz ice	Jera year/ harvest	Eiwaz yew	Perþ pear tree dice/luck	Algiz elk/ protection	Sōwilō sun

ᛏ	ᛒ	ᛖ	ᛗ	ᛚ	ᛜ	ᛞ	ᛟ
Tiwaz The God Tyr	Berkanan Birch	Ehwaz horse	Mannaz man	Laguz water/ lake	Ingwaz The God Ing	Dagaz day	Opila heritage/ inheritance

The Younger Futhark descends from the Elder and is found throughout Scandinavia on thousands of Runestones. It gradually replaced the Elder Futhark and stabilised around 800 AD, at the beginning of the Viking age. It was the alphabet in main use in Norway, Sweden and Denmark throughout the Viking age but was largely replaced by Latin by around 1200 AD as a result of Christian conversion. The Younger Futhark became known in Europe as the "alphabet of the Norsemen" and is referred to as the "Ogham of the Scandinavians" *ogam lochlannach* in the Book of Ballymote.

The Anglo-Saxon Futhorc

Old English or Anglo-Saxon was first written with a version of this Germanic runic alphabet collectively called the Futhorc between the 5th and 11th centuries.

There are three poems known as the Rune Poems which have preserved lists of the letters of the runic alphabets with an explanatory poetic stanza for each. The first is Anglo-Saxon, the second Old Norwegian and the third and oldest poem is in Old Icelandic. Similarities can be drawn between languages derived from common cultural roots and cognate languages in order to uncover the most likely authentic customs, older ways of thought, original ideas and expressions of those cultures. The Rune Poems are a good example of this and it is widely accepted that combined they form a cultural precedent.

Although the exact date by which the twenty-four-rune Elder Futhark alphabet was complete is unconfirmed it was probably by the end of the 4th century and some of the runes almost certainly predate that. This is especially so of those used magically such as Tiwaz and Ansuz which were used for the symbolism and invocation of the Gods. Magical staves or sigils (symbols) called Galdrastafur were also used in Iceland in a similar way to the Tiwaz and Ansuz runes, to ward off evil, to protect the wearer or to influence or bring luck in some way.

Tacitus gives a detailed account in Germania 98 AD of the Germanic people's divination and means of reading omens: "They attach the highest importance to the taking of auspices and casting lots. Their usual procedure with the lot is simple. They cut off a branch from a nut-bearing tree and slice it into strips these they mark with different signs and throw them at random onto a white cloth. Then the state's priest, if it is an official consultation, or the father of the family, in a private one, offers prayer to the gods and looking up towards heaven picks up three strips, one at a time, and, according to which sign they have previously been marked with, makes his interpretation. If the lots forbid an undertaking, there is no deliberation that day about the matter in question. If they allow it, further confirmation is required by taking auspices".

There are also examples of inscriptions that have been interpreted as magical chants and charm words such as *Alu* found upon numerous Iron Age artefacts in Central and Northern Europe found individually or with other words as part of a formula. Whilst the translation of Alu remains ambiguous it may mean, amulet or temple. There are also a number of Viking rings that have been found bearing magical inscriptions. Folklore and superstition are interwoven with magic and the Old Norse poem *Sigrdrífumál* from the *Poetic Edda* is full of runic magic and talks of ale charmed with "gladness runes", victory runes, spells for healing, spells to help in childbirth, to protect ships, and for protection and quick wit. In the last century new forms of runic magic have developed in Germanic neo-paganism, predominantly based on an amalgamation of historical information and traditional uses with more modern day mysticism and practices. One example of this is in circle casting where appropriate runes have been used as representatives of the four directions.

The Ogham Alphabet, Tree Lore and Celtic Mythology

The Ogham is both an alphabet and a learning tool which was developed to communicate in old Irish. Scholars, as is usual, debate both its origin and date. There are a number of theories. Firstly, that it was developed as a way of communicating secret information that could not be understood by the Romans around the 4th century at the time of invasion and occupation. Secondly, that it developed organically as a practical way of communicating messages in the native language rather than translating it into Latin for ease of passing and writing messages and that it was devised by the early Christians also around the 4th century. Thirdly, that it was devised either by the druids or ovates of the native population as a common alphabet and was based upon either the Latin or Greek alphabets or quite possibly upon Germanic Runes with which it has great similarities and with which some of the etymology of the rune names share cognate linguistic roots.

Whichever version of events is the true one it was passed down through generations as a way of recording and teaching knowledge and spiritual wisdom. Though its flowering was in the 6th century there is evidence that it is older from early inscriptions and some consider it may date back to the 1st century BC. Others say it is older still. Sadly most Ogham script was destroyed by the Romans in their campaigns here when many monasteries were ransacked. Luckily some remained protected and hidden and there are some three hundred and sixty plus standing stones that have survived in Ireland, Wales, Southern England, the Isle of Man and Scotland.

In Robert Graves' book about poetic myth *The White Goddess*, he supports the druidic theory of origin and even suggests a way in which the alphabet could have been used in simple sign language, using the fingertips and joints of one hand. He attempts within this work to solve and piece together the riddles and meanings given by the early bards, in one of the earliest written manuscripts to speak of the "Beith, Luis, Nion" Ogham trees. The manuscript is *LLyfr Taliesin – The Book of Taliesin*. Taliesin was a renowned bard and early Brytonnic poet in the 14th century. His work is thought to have been written down within this collection of Welsh poems that were said to have been verbally passed down from the bards of the 10th century. The manuscript still survives in the National Library of Wales. The poem is called "Câd Goddeu" – The Battle of the Trees. Inspirited by the magician Gwydion to fight against Arawn the god of the underworld, each tree in the poem represents one of the twenty letters of the Ogham alphabet amongst poetic allegory, myth and legend.

Much of what we know today comes from a beautifully illuminated 14th century manuscript called "Leabhar Bhaile an Mhóta" – the Book of Ballymote. The manuscript contains a discourse on the construction and use of the Ogham alphabet and shows many forms of the script, including the Beth, Luis, Nion Ogham in the form of a wheel, known as "Fionn's Window". It also includes a little known set of Ogham symbols called the "The Sacred Branch" which were thought to have been used in magic. The "Word Oghams" from the Book of Ballymote, were compiled with other manuscripts from earlier texts and oral records called The Yellow Book of Lechan and the "Trefochul" from The Book of Leinster. These were used in the mediaeval schools of classical poetry and only much more recently collected together, transcribed and published by George Calder at the University of Glasgow as *Auraicept na n-éces,* which translates as "The handbook of the learned" or the Scholar's Primer. According to this book the origins of the Ogham were devised by Ogma, the Sun faced archetypal father figure and Sun God.

There are some variations of Ogham script in different areas and times though they are similar. Likewise although the diagram gives the words in Irish Gaelic they can of course be translated and used in Scottish Gaelic and Welsh. In the north of Scotland there remain non-deciphered inscriptions written in the Pictish Ogham of Argyll. The *Book of Ballymotte* lists some number of the Ogham alphabets and even includes the Younger Futhark as a Viking version of the same that stems from the Elder Futhark (see above). The Book of Ballymote is in the Library of The Royal Irish Academy, Dublin.

The letters of the tree alphabet were generally cut into branches or lathes of wood to form strokes coming off a central line and it is said that messengers would often deliver written information that was carved into walking staffs using this alphabet. The symbols were also painted or carved into pieces of wood and cast for divination.

The Ogham was developed as a phonetically arranged alphabet of four groups (aicme) of five letters and an additional group of five called the Forfeda which were added at a later date and consist of sounds that were considered to be missing from the original twenty.

The Ogham or Beth-Luis-Nuin is made up of:
B group letters (labials) – B L F S N
H group letters (dentals/aspirants) – H T D C Q
M group letters (gutterals) – M G Ng Ss R
A group letters (vowels) – A O U E I
The forfeda (additional) sounds – CH OI UI IO AE

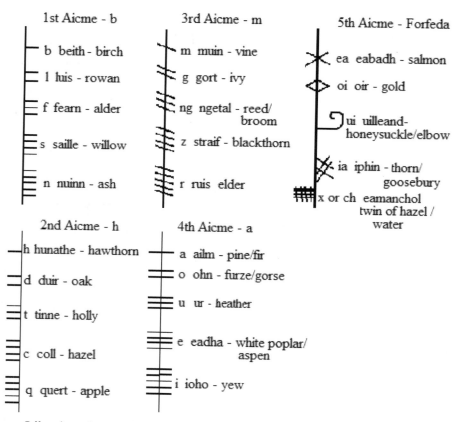

Like the other runic alphabets the Ogham can be used for divination and each rune represents the natural forces and properties of the tree or things in nature that it represents. It may also have by association relation to archetypes and relevant mythologies.

Within the confines of one chapter it is not possible to give these systems in their entirety. These are subjects for further books and as with the other chapters of this book they are offered only as a beginning and introduction to the subject so that the reader has a basis to seek out other information. At this point the initiate should be able to pick up most other esoteric books and have a foundation from which to ground the knowledge and an understanding to build upon.

Note: there are some circumstances where previously made soul contracts cannot be broken. Call these the mitigating circumstances of spirit if you like. This is usually because there is some purpose being served even if the purpose is reaching deeper understanding as a result of the consequences of a previous action. In every moment we have choice and we can choose to take a new path and release things that are no longer serving our highest potential. In the moment of initiation there is a convergence of spirit with the individual soul of the person choosing to be initiated.

Initiation Ceremony

This has been kept simple but may be adapted or elaborated upon.

Standing in the height of the midday sun on a Sunday.

Call upon the Goddess and the God, or a specific deity aligned with love, or upon high frequency loving cosmic forces of good order. (Adapt the wording below as appropriate.)

Cast a sacred circle or space.

Make an offering of frankincense and let the resin burn on charcoal disks and billow white smoke.

a) Collect in advance a large vessel of water and charge the water by putting it out in the sun and moon to imbue their power.

Ask for the water to be blessed.

The vessel needs to be large enough to submerge your head and face for a moment. (Take care to do this safely.)

Do this three times.

Then anoint your body with the blessed water.

Then stand within the water vessel.

Or

b) Alternatively if you prefer not to cast a sacred space and to work directly with nature choose a place where there is a natural source of water where you can fully submerge yourself for a moment. Do this safely and maybe have a close friend with you just in case, who can also bear witness to your initiation. Call God/Goddess and ask them to hold you whilst you do this and for the ceremony. Ask for the stream or water source to be blessed.

Standing in water and the sunlight, connect with love and allow the elements to rise and meet in your heart chakra.

Visualise a rainbow of light being created through you and in you of which you are part and aligned with love.

Then speak your intention and your promise. Remember this is between you and God/Goddess or between you and nature or cosmos.

Oath of Initiation

I call upon omnipresent divine good/God/Goddess.

I (insert your name), align myself with Love and with Truth and with all that is good and sacred.

I cast out all that is not Love and allow in only good.

I cut all cords and I break all soul contracts, vows and agreements that I have made knowingly or unknowingly in this life or any other in existence that are not serving my highest purpose or are not in alignment with love and light. I break them in all directions throughout all of time and space and at a soul level and every level of my being and I ask to be released from any karma that is related.

I ask that Love fills me and my life and illuminates my path forward in order that I live my highest purpose.

I ask for your help and guidance to do this and I put my trust in you.

I ask that you protect me and my loved ones now and always as I walk this path.

I devote myself to the Love and Light of good/God/Goddess.

I devote myself to working within the law of Love and Truth.

I devote myself to the process of my spiritual progression as I take this step.

This is my choice both physically and at a soul level.

This is my intention and the expression of my free will in accordance with the Law.

This is my Initiation and my oath.

So mote it be/Amen.

When the initiation is complete change into new clothes or robes which you have chosen for the occasion.

By whatever path you take may the ground beneath your feet support you and give you firmer footing. By whatever route you choose may the light shine on you and guide you steadily. By whatever way you design may the pattern be eternally revealed to you.

With love and in great gratitude for the sharing of the journey.

Bibliography

A History of Ancient Britain – Age of Ice, (2016). [TV programme] 2: BBC.

Academia.edu. (2016). *Entangled, Connected or Protected? The Power of Knots and Knotting in Ancient Egypt*. [online] Available at: http://www.academia.edu/866612/Entangled_Connected_or_Protected_The_Power_of_Knots_and_Knotting_in_Ancient_Egypt [Accessed 17 Apr. 2016].

Ancientscripts.com. (2016). *Ancient Scripts: Futhark*. [online] Available at: http://ancientscripts.com/futhark.html [Accessed 17 Apr. 2016].

Antl-Weiser, Walpurga. *"The anthropomorphic figurines from Willendorf" (PDF)*. *Niederösterreichischen Landesmuseum*. Retrieved 14/04/2016 http://www.zobodat.at/pdf/WM_19_0019-0030.pdf

Bede, and Wallis, F. (1999). *Bede, The Reckoning of Time*. (*De Temporum Ratione*). Liverpool: Liverpool University Press.

Billet, F. (1858). *Traité d'Optique Physique*. Paris: Mallet-Bachelier.

Britannia.com. (2016). *Anglo-Saxon Chronicle*. [online] Available at: http://www.britannia.com/history/docs/asintro2.html [Accessed 17 Apr. 2016].

Bruton, J. and Seal, M. (2008). *Hedgerow Medicine*. Ludlow: Merlin Unwin.

Bryson, B. (2003). *A Short History of Nearly Everything*. New York: Broadway Books.

Budge, W.E.A. (1971). *Egyptian magic*. New York: Dover Publications.

Budge, W.E.A. (1973). *Osiris and the Egyptian Resurrection*. New York: Dover Publications.

Calder, G., Isidore, and Virgilius Maro, (1917). *Auraicept na n-éces*. Edinburgh: John Grant.

Cameron, J. *The Artist's Way: A Spiritual Path to Higher Creativity.* Tarcher Perigee.

Carmichael, A. Carmina Gadelica vol. i (1900 edition) T and A Constable, Edinburgh p. 147 available at https://archive.org/details/carminagadelicah03carm [Accessed 6 Apr. 2017].

Chakrabarti, V. (1998). *Indian Architectural Theory*. Richmond, Surrey: Curzon.

Cicero.44 BC, *De Officiis* Book 1. Published by Loeb Classical Library 1913.

Classics.mit.edu. (2016). *The Internet Classics Archive | The Gallic Wars by Julius Caesar.* [online] Available at: http://classics.mit.edu/Caesar/gallic.html [Accessed 16 Apr. 2016].

Collins Latin dictionary plus grammar. (1997). [Glasgow]: HarperCollins.

Connolly, E. (1995). *Tarot*. London: Thorsons.

Culpeper, N. (1992). *Culpeper's Complete Herbal and English Physician.* Leicester, UK: Magna.

Dalai Lama XIV, The Dalai Lama: *A Policy of Kindness: An Anthology of Writings By and About the Dalai Lama*

Da Vinci, L. (1478-1519), *Codex Atlanticus, fol.459r.*

Davies, T. (2016). *Divination in the International Standard Bible Encyclopedia..* [online] International Standard Bible Encyclopedia Online. Available at: http://www.internationalstandardbible.com/D/divination.html [Accessed 17 Apr. 2016].

Denning, M. and Phillips, O. (2011). *Planetary Magick*. Woodbury, Minn.: Llewellyn Publications.

Elliott, R. (1981). *Runes, An Introduction*. Westport, Conn.: Greenwood Press.

Ellis, P. (1998). *The Ancient World of the Celts*. London: Constable.

Emick, J. (2009). *The Everything Celtic Wisdom Book*. Avon, Mass.: Adams Media.

Encyclopaedia Britannica. (2016). *Bo tree | tree*. [online] Available at: http://www.britannica.com/plant/Bo-tree [Accessed 16 Apr. 2016].

Encyclopaedia of World Religions. (1975). London: Octopus.

Etymonline.com. (2016). *Online Etymology Dictionary*. [online] Available at: http://www.etymonline.com/ [Accessed 14 Apr. 2016].

Fagan, B. and Beck, C. (1996). *The Oxford Companion to Archaeology*. New York: Oxford University Press.

Fibonacci, L. and Sigler, L. (2002). *Fibonacci's Liber Abaci*. New York: Springer.

Finn, J. (2015). *https://www.wooster.edu/news/releases/2015/february/stars-lindner/*. [online]
Physicists Discover that for Certain Stars 'the Beat Goes on'. Available at:
https://www.wooster.edu/news/releases/2015/february/stars-lindner/ [Accessed 16 Apr. 2016].

Forrest, S. (1988). *The Inner Sky*. San Diego, CA: ACS Publications.

Fortune, D. (2000). *The Mystical Qabalah*. York Beach, ME: Samuel Weiser.

Fortune, D. (2000). *The Training & Work of An Initiate*. York Beach, Me.: S. Weiser.

Frazer, J. (1994). *The Golden Bough*. London: Chancellor Press.

Freke, T. and Gandy, P. (1999). *The Hermetica*. New York: J.P. Tarcher/Putnam.

Gove, P. and Merriam- Webster. (2000). *Webster's Third New International Dictionary of the English Language Unabridged*. Springfield: Merriam-Webster.

Graham-Campbell, J. (1980). *The Viking World*. New Haven: Ticknor & Fields.

Graham, W. (2010). *Islamic and Comparative Religious Studies*. Farnham, Surrey: Ashgate.

Graves, R. (1966). *The White Goddess*. New York: Farrar, Straus and Giroux.

Gray, H., Pick, T. and Howden, R. (1977). *Anatomy, Descriptive and Surgical*. New York: Bounty Books.

Greenler, R. (1980). *Rainbows, Halos, and Glories*. Cambridge: Cambridge University Press.

Greg C Grace, (2003), *The Art of Creative Drawing, Symbols, Shapes and Geometry*

Hall, J. (2003). *The Crystal Bible*. Old Alresford: Godsfield.

Harrison, J., Coppendale, J. and Head, H. (2002). *Early Britain, 500,000 BC-AD 1154*. London: Kingfisher.

Hippisley-Cox, R. (1908). *The Green Roads of England*. Oxford: J. Parker and Co.

Horizon – Aftershock: The Hunt for Gravitational Waves, (2015). [TV programme] 4: BBC.

Horizon – Cosmic Dawn: The Real Moment of Creation, (2015). [TV programme] 4: BBC.

Horizon – Secrets of The Solar System, (2015). [TV programme] 4: BBC.

Hornby, A., Cowie, A. and Lewis, J. (1974). *Oxford Advanced Learner's Dictionary of Current English*. London: Oxford University Press.

How the Celts Saved Britain – A New Civilisation, (2016). [TV programme] 4: BBC.

How the Celts Saved Britain – Salvation, (2016). [TV programme] 4: BBC.

Immortal Egypt – The Road to the Pyramids, (2016). [TV programme] 2: BBC.

Jenny, H. (2001). *Cymatics*. Newmarket, NH: MACROmedia.

Jewishencyclopedia.com. (2016). *JewishEncyclopedia.com*. [online] Available at: http://www.jewishencyclopedia.com/ [Accessed 16 Apr. 2016].

Jung, C. and De Laszlo, V. (1959). *The Basic Writings of C.G. Jung*. New York: Modern Library.

Kaplan, A. (1997). *Sefer Yetzirah*. York Beach, Me.: S. Weiser.

Katie, B. and Mitchell, S. (2002). *Loving what is*. New York: Harmony Books.

Knight, G. (1979). *A History of White Magic*. New York: S. Weiser.

Kroonen, G. (2010). *Etymological Dictionary of Proto-Germanic*. Leiden: Brill.

Lee, R. and Fraser, A. (2001). *The Rainbow Bridge*. University Park, Pa.: Pennsylvania State University Press.

Lescher, T. (n.d.). *Astrology 101*.

Lewis, E. (1993). *Welsh Dictionary*. Lincolnwood, Ill.: NTC Pub. Group.

Mallory, J. and Adams, D. (1997). *Encyclopaedia of Indo-European Culture*. London: Fitzroy Dearborn.

Mallory, J. and Adams, D. (2006). *The Oxford Introduction to Proto Indo European and the Proto Indo European World*. New York: Oxford University Press.

Melchizedek D, (1999) *The Ancient Secret of the Flower of Life: v. 1*.

Mercado, J. (2016). *People and Trees: Intimately Connected Through the Ages*. [online] Available at: http://www.pachamama.org/blog/people-and-trees-intimately-connected-through-the-ages [Accessed 16 Apr. 2016].

Merkaba Article
http://www.patinkas.co.uk/Merkaba_Feature_Article/merkaba_feature_article.html [accessed 1 March 2017]

Michell, J. and Brown, A. (2009). *How The World is Made*. Rochester, Vt.: Inner Traditions.

Moskowitz, C. (2016). *Strange Stars Pulsate According to the "Golden Ratio"*. [online] Scientific American. Available at: http://www.scientificamerican.com/article/strange-stars-pulsate-according-to-the-golden-ratio/ [Accessed 16 Apr. 2016].

Murray, L., Murray, C. and Card, V. (n.d.). *Celtic Tree Oracle*.

New World Encyclopedia contributors, 'Metatron', *New World Encyclopedia*, , 21 October 2014, 15:51 UTC,
<http://www.newworldencyclopedia.org/p/index.php?title=Metatron&oldid=984938 > [accessed 1 March 2017]

Newscientist.com. (2016). *Short Sharp Science: First ever image of fourth-order rainbow*. [online] Available at: https://www.newscientist.com/blogs/shortsharpscience/2011/10/third-and-fourth-order-rainbow.html [Accessed 14 Apr. 2016].

Newsome, E. (2001). *Trees of Paradise and Pillars of the World*. Austin: University of Texas Press.

Newton, I., Clarke, S., Bousquet, M. and Dibner, B. (1740). *Optice, Sive, De Reflexionibus, Refractionibus, Inflexionibus & Coloribus Lucis, Libri Tres*. Lausannae: Sumpt. M.M. Bousquet & Sociorum.

Niranjanananda Saraswati, (2009). *Prana and Pranayama*. Munger, Bihar, India: Yoga Publication Trust.

Oakes, L. (2001). *Sacred Sites of Ancient Egypt*. London: Lorenz.

Olmsted, G. (2001). *A Definitive Reconstructed Text of the Coligny Calendar*. Washington, D.C.: Institute for the Study of Man.

Pagans and Pilgrims: Britain's Holiest Places – Trees and Mountains, (2016). [TV programme] Four: BBC.

Parker, J. and Parker, D. (2001). *Parkers' Astrology*. New York: DK Pub.

Parker, R. (1950). *The Calendars of Ancient Egypt*. Chicago: University of Chicago Press.

Patterson, R. (n.d.). Moon *Magic*.

Newworldencyclopedia.org. (2016). *Rainbow – New World Encyclopedia*. [online] Available at: http://www.newworldencyclopedia.org/entry/Rainbow [Accessed 14 Apr. 2016].

Rawles, B. (1997) *Sacred Geometry Design Sourcebook: Universal*

Dimensional Patterns. Nevada City, CA: Elysian Pub., p. 15.

Regardie, I., Monnastre, C. and Weschcke, C. Internet Archive. (2017). Israel Regardie - The Golden Dawn - Vol 1 - 1937 : Israel Regardie : Free Download & Streaming : Internet Archive. [online] Available at:
https://archive.org/details/IsraelRegardie-thegoldenDawn-vol1-1937 [Accessed 6 Apr. 2017].

Roberts, G. *Jesus 888; The Myth Behind the Man* p244-245 Troubador Publishing (2011)

Roberts, P. (2002). *Empire of the Soul: Some Journeys In India*. Chichester: Summersdale.

Rockefeller, J. (2016). *The Complete Guide to Chakras and Auras: With a Special Focus on the Third Eye*.

Roychowdhury, A. (2016). *Culture Articles – Find Culture Related Articles on Articlesbase.com*. [online] Articlesbase.com. Available at: http://www.articlesbase.com/culture-articles/vedic-civilization-the-progenitor-of-egyptian-civilization-1043661.html [Accessed 14 Apr. 2016].

Rumi. *The Essential Rumi*

Snorri Sturluson, and Young, J. (1964). *The prose Edda of Snorri Sturluson*. Berkeley: University of California Press.

Stache-Rose, V. *German Indologists: Biographies of Scholars in Indian Studies Writing in German,* p 15-16. (1990)

Stern, S. (2016). *The Babylonian Calendar at Elephantine: Zeitschrift für Papyrologie und Epigraphik 130 (2000) 159–171* © *Dr. Rudolf Habelt GmbH*. [online] http://www.uni-koeln.de. Available at: http://www.uni-koeln.de/phil-fak/ifa/zpe/downloads/2000/130pdf/130159.pdf [Accessed 16 Apr. 2016].

Svensson, H. (1995). *The Runes*. New York: Barnes & Noble Books.

Optica.machorro.net. (2016). *The Amateur Scientist*. [online] Available at: http://optica.machorro.net/Optica/SciAm/Rainbow/1977-07-body.html [Accessed 14 Apr. 2016].

How to Create and Observe a Dozen Rainbows in a Single Drop of Water *by Jearl Walker July, 1977*

Tacitus. *Germania (98 A.D.)*

The Holy Bible. (1673). Cambridge [England]: Printed by John Hayes .

The Kyballion. (1908). Chicago: Yogi publication Society.

The World of Playing Cards. (2016). *Early references*. [online] Available at: http://www.wopc.co.uk/history/earlyrefs [Accessed 17 Apr. 2016].

Tisserand, R. (1977). *The Art of Aromatherapy*. New York: Inner Traditions International.

Tyndalehouse.com. (2016). *Egyptian Royal Genealogy: Ptolemaic Chronology - - Babylonian calendar*. [online] Available at: http://www.tyndalehouse.com/egypt/ptolemies/chron/babylonian/chron_bab_cal_fr.h tm [Accessed 16 Apr. 2016].

Waldman, G. (2002). *Introduction to Light*. Mineola, N.Y.: Dover Publications.

Walter, M. (2004). *Shamanism*. Santa Barbara, Calif.: ABC-Clio.

Weisstein, Eric W. (2002) *CRC Concise Encyclopedia of Mathematics, Second Edition Hardcover*

Weisstein, Eric W. "Flower of Life." From *MathWorld*--A Wolfram Web Resource. http://mathworld.wolfram.com/FlowerofLife.html (accessed on 01/03/2017)

Wescott, tr W.W. *Sepher Yetzirah Or The Book Of Creation* (1887)

Williams, T. (1996). *The Complete Illustrated Guide to Chinese Medicine.* Shaftesbury, Dorset: Element.

Wolfram, S. (2002) *A New Kind of Science.* Champaign, IL: Wolfram Media, p. 43 and 873.